Death Sentence

ALSO BY JERRY BLEDSOE

Bitter Blood

Blood Games

Before He Wakes

JERRY BLEDSOE

Death Sentence

The True Story of Velma Barfield's Life, Crimes and Execution

A DUTTON BOOK

DUTTON
Published by the Penguin Group
Penguin Putnam Inc., 375 Hudson Street, New York, New York 10014, U.S.A.
Penguin Books Ltd, 27 Wrights Lane, London W8 5TZ, England
Penguin Books Australia Ltd, Ringwood, Victoria, Australia
Penguin Books Canada Ltd, 10 Alcorn Avenue, Toronto, Ontario, Canada M4V 3B2
Penguin Books (N.Z.) Ltd, 182–190 Wairau Road, Auckland 10, New Zealand

Penguin Books Ltd, Registered Offices:
Harmondsworth, Middlesex, England

First published by Dutton, an imprint of Dutton NAL,
a member of Penguin Putnam Inc.

First Printing, October, 1998
10 9 8 7 6 5 4 3 2 1

 REGISTERED TRADEMARK—MARCA REGISTRADA

LIBRARY OF CONGRESS CATALOGING-IN-PUBLICATION DATA

Bledsoe, Jerry.
 Death sentence : the true story of Velma Barfield's life, crimes
and execution / Jerry Bledsoe.
 ISBN 0-525-94255-6   p.   cm.
  1. Barfield, Velma, 1932–1984.   2. Women murderers—United States—
Biography.   3. Murder—United States—Case studies.   I. Barfield, Velma,
1932–1984.   II. Title.
 HV6248.B26B56   1998
 364.15'23'092—dc21
 [b]   98-25730
                                                         CIP

Printed in the United States of America
Set in Sabon
Designed by Julian Hamer

This book is printed on acid-free paper.

CONTENTS

AUTHOR'S NOTE

Some names in this book have been changed for privacy's sake. They are indicated with an asterisk upon first usage.

PROLOGUE

I ONLY MEANT TO MAKE HIM SICK

To millions of travelers passing through on Interstate 95, the primary New York–to–Florida highway, Robeson County, North Carolina, seems to be little more than piney woods, marshes and endless fields of corn, tobacco and soybeans. They have no reason to know that they are passing through one of the most unusual counties in America.

For nearly two centuries Robeson's population has been about evenly divided between blacks, whites and Lumbee Indians. Until the 1960s, doctors' offices, and train and bus stations in the county had three separate waiting rooms, designated by race, and movie theaters had three different seating areas. Long-simmering racial tensions and high rates of poverty and unemployment gave Robeson an unwanted distinction. It was one of the most violent counties in America.

Until 1974 the county's murder rate was among the highest per capita in the country year after year. Nobody seemed to know what to do about it until a lanky Robeson County native named Joe Freeman Britt became the county prosecutor.

Britt was offended by lawlessness, especially murder, and he was certain that the people of his county were fed up with it as well. He mounted an offensive against murderers that came to be known as "Britt's Blitz." In a twenty-three-month period he won death sentences for more people than resided on the death rows of two-thirds of the states that embraced capital punishment.

At six feet six inches tall, Britt was a man of imposing presence and immense fervor. Many viewed him as an avenging angel, and he sometimes literally played out the role, swooping from the heavens onto crime scenes in his own helicopter.

By 1978, as he entered the final year of his first full term in office, Britt had won twenty-two death sentences and sent twenty-one murderers to death row without losing a case. And the *Guinness Book of World Records* proclaimed him the world's deadliest prosecutor.

To many, Britt was a hero. One of his admirers and staunch supporters was a young family man in Lumberton, Ronnie Burke, who had lived his entire life in Robeson County. Ronnie firmly believed that a person who with forethought maliciously killed another should pay with his, or her, own life. But he couldn't have conceived that Britt soon would put his beliefs to a test almost beyond endurance.

Ronnie was married with a three-year-old son, struggling to hold a full-time job while carrying a complete load of college courses. In just two months he was to receive a degree in business from Pembroke State University. He was twenty-six, and although he was a good student who consistently got high grades, getting through college hadn't been easy. Yet he was determined to become the first on either side of his family to earn a four-year degree.

Monday, March 13, started off sunny and breezy, the air holding the balmy promise of spring. Yellow bells and jonquils were in bloom, and fruit trees were already blossoming. Ronnie had crammed all of his classes into the morning hours so he could work afternoons. After finishing his last class, he hurried to his car, a gray, Navy-surplus Dodge Dart station wagon, to drive the fifteen miles from Pembroke to Robeson Technical Institute in Lumberton. Ronnie had started college at Pembroke only to drop out after his first year. Later he enrolled at Robeson Tech to study business and had been valedictorian of his class before returning to Pembroke for the final year of his education. Now he worked at Robeson Tech in the student financial aid office.

As he drove to the campus, a collection of modern brown brick buildings in a greensward alongside Interstate 95, Ronnie was looking forward to the day when he wouldn't have to be rushing to class by seven each morning, when he wouldn't have to study until after midnight each night, when he could get more than a few hours' sleep at a time. He could picture himself in cap and gown, striding across the stage to receive his diploma. His mother, he knew, would be in the audience. It was she, after all, who had always stressed the importance of education, who had always pushed him to study hard and make something of himself.

Ronnie had only been at work a short time when the telephone rang about two. "I'm a friend of your mother's," said a woman who didn't identify herself. "I've heard she's going to be arrested today. I thought you ought to know."

Startled, Ronnie asked, "Are you sure?"

"Yes, they're going to charge her with Stuart's death."

"How do you know?"

"I know somebody who works in the sheriff's department."

Despite his shock, Ronnie hadn't been without warning that something like this could happen. Now he realized that he shouldn't have been so quick to dismiss what his mother had told him two days earlier.

He had been visiting his in-laws Saturday morning when his mother called, nervous and upset. The police had come the evening before and asked her to go downtown with them, she told him. The first thing that popped into Ronnie's mind was that she had been writing bad checks again. She was dependent on prescription drugs and, when they ran out, she had to have them whether she had money or not.

"What did they want?" he asked, though he thought he knew.

"They wanted to talk about Stuart," she said, surprising him "They said he was poisoned. They seemed to think I had something to do with it."

Her words stunned Ronnie. Poisoned? Stuart Taylor, the man his mother had planned to marry in May, had been dead for five weeks. He had been a neighbor of Ronnie's boss, the president of Robeson Tech.

Ronnie was all too aware that his mother had problems—lots of them—but it was inconceivable that she could deliberately harm somebody. Not Velma Barfield. She made her living caring for others. She had been at Stuart's side throughout his sickness, had tended him lovingly and had been lauded by his children for it. Clearly, this had to be some kind of misunderstanding.

"Just calm down," he told her. "I'll be home in a little while. Come on over and we'll talk about it then."

Ronnie lived in a duplex apartment owned by one of his professors off a country road near Lumberton. He took his mother for a walk along that road—Snake Road, it was called, because of the way it wound through the flat countryside. She told him a police officer had stirred her from sleep late Friday afternoon—she worked at a nursing home from eleven at night until seven in the morning and slept during the day. He had told her that he needed her to come downtown to the sheriff's department to talk about some checks.

It was true, she acknowledged, she had recently written checks without enough money in the bank to cover them. She didn't know what else to do. She had to have her medicine and she thought she could get the money to the bank in time. Ronnie shook his head at these familiar excuses. But then, she said, the officers had changed direction, telling her that they knew Stuart had been poisoned—they mentioned arsenic.

"I believe they think I had something to do with it," she said. Clearly, she was offended that anybody could imagine such a thing.

"Well, you didn't, did you?" Ronnie asked jokingly.

She stopped, turned to him and said, "Son, you know I couldn't do something like that."

"I know that," he said, putting his arm around her. They walked back to his apartment arm in arm.

"Do you think I ought to get a lawyer?" she asked, as she was about to leave.

No, Ronnie told her, there was no point to it. She'd probably heard the last about that. Surely, the police would see that she had nothing to do with any poisoning, and hiring a lawyer would just be an unnecessary expense she couldn't afford. A bigger concern, he thought, was how she'd get the money to pay off the bad checks she'd written, but he didn't bring that up.

"Don't worry about it," he said. "Everything will be fine."

He genuinely believed that, too. But he couldn't stop thinking about what his mother had told him, and to settle his mind, he called Stuart Taylor's daughter, Alice Storms, to find out what was going on. She seemed cool, reluctant to talk, but she confirmed that an autopsy had revealed that her father had been poisoned. Surely, it must have been from chemicals he'd been using on the farm, Ronnie suggested.

"There is no known use for arsenic on a farm," he would recall Alice telling him icily.

Still, he knew his mother, knew it was impossible that she could have had any part in poisoning somebody, and he pushed the matter out of his mind until the stunning call Monday afternoon.

*   *   *

After hanging up, Ronnie sat staring at the phone as the implications of what he had heard sank in. His concern was not that his mother could have committed murder—he knew that couldn't be so—but what effect such an accusation could have on her. He knew how fragile she was. He was all too aware of what depression and the drugs her doctors had so willingly prescribed had done to her since his father's death nine years earlier. His first thought was that he had to straighten this out quickly to prevent his mother from falling into despair and perhaps trying once again to kill herself.

Ronnie informed his supervisor that he needed to attend to family problems and drove downtown to the courthouse. His anger grew with each mile, and by the time he got to the Robeson County Sheriff's Department he was ready for a confrontation. He identified himself and asked to speak with the officer who had interviewed his mother.

Wilbur Lovett soon appeared and invited Ronnie into his office. Lovett had spent nearly thirty years with the Lumberton Police Department, had risen to the office of chief before a political falling out had cost him his job. Sheriff Malcolm McLeod had hired him as a detective a couple of years earlier. When Ronnie demanded to know why Lovett was harassing his mother, Lovett replied that nobody was harassing her; she'd only been questioned.

"I heard you are going to arrest her today," Ronnie said heatedly. "Is that so?"

"We don't have any plans to arrest her," Lovett responded. "We do consider her a suspect."

That was crazy, Ronnie told him, his anger flaring. She wasn't capable of such a thing. They didn't know her the way he did. Her "nerves" were bad; she'd been hospitalized because of it many times; she was dependent on prescription medicines; several times she'd attempted suicide.

"You're going to push her over the edge," he railed at the detective. "This is going to do it. And you'll be responsible!"

"This is a homicide investigation," Lovett told him calmly, "and we have to follow it wherever it takes us."

Ronnie took a few moments to compose himself.

"Do you really think that she's a suspect?" he asked, still incredulous.

"Yes, I do."

"Why?"

"I can't tell you that."

"So you can offer me no proof?"

"That's right. That's all I can tell you."

Ronnie was still angry when he left the courthouse. He wasn't sure what to do, but he knew that he had to protect his mother. It was a responsibility he'd borne for longer than he cared to remember. He was always having to extricate her from the fixes she got into, always trying to save her from herself.

The situation obviously was far more serious than he had at first imagined. If the police were about to arrest her—and he was fairly sure that they were—he needed to be there to break the news, to stop her if she attempted to hurt herself.

For several weeks his mother had been living with an elderly woman she had met at the Pentecostal Holiness church where she was a Sunday school teacher and volunteer office worker. Mamie Warwick gave her a room in exchange for companionship and minor household duties.

Ronnie drove to the small white house in northeast Lumberton and found his mother asleep, her room dark, the curtains drawn. She stirred when he shook her shoulder, her puffy eyes slowly focusing on his face. Even in the dim light she looked pallid and worn, aged beyond her years.

"Ronnie . . ." she said. "What are you doing here?"

"I need to talk to you."

She sat up groggily, modestly pulling the covers to her chest. Ronnie could tell that she had drugged herself to sleep. "You seem upset," she said.

"I am," he replied. He sat on the foot of the bed, facing away from her. "I'm upset with the police. I got a call today at work that they're going to arrest you for Stuart's death."

"Arrest me? They didn't say anything about arresting me. Do they still think I had something to do with that?"

"Yes, they do. I just left the sheriff's department. The detective told me they do."

"I told you I couldn't do something like that. You believe that, don't you?"

How many times had she asked him to "believe" something?

"I'm beginning not to know what to believe," Ronnie found himself saying, causing his mother to burst into tears.

"I know you're not capable of killing anybody," he added quickly, turning toward her. "I'm just afraid for you. I'm afraid it might make you try to do something to yourself."

He could think of nothing else to say. He had no idea how to deal with this. He sat silent and dejected, staring at the wall while his mother cried. When she spoke again, it was in a near whisper: "I only meant to make him sick."

Ronnie couldn't have been more shocked if he'd been stuck with a cattle prod. This was the person who had loved and nurtured him, who had taught him right from wrong, who had made certain he'd grown up in church. She had been the touchstone and guiding force of his life, and in those few incredible words, she was admitting the unimaginable.

"I didn't know what to do," he would recall many years later. "I felt so hopeless. I'd never felt more hopeless."

Instinctively, he knew that his life would never be the same, but his first thought was for his mother's safety. If he left her alone, he was certain she would kill herself. Whatever he did, he would have to take her with him. She would have to be watched constantly.

"I think you should get dressed," he told her, although at that moment he still had no idea what he planned to do.

Obediently, his mother climbed from bed, wobbly on her feet, and started for the bathroom. But when Ronnie saw her reach inside her nightgown and remove something, he sprang up and grabbed her arm just as she got to the door. In her right hand she was tightly clutching a wad of tissue.

"Give it to me," he said firmly.

"No, Ronnie," she cried.

He had to pry the tissue from her hand. Inside was an assortment of pills and capsules—more than two dozen, he would later count.

"You were going to do what I thought you might do, weren't you?" he said angrily.

"No, no," she protested, still crying. "I took them to work like this. I've got to have 'em, Ronnie. You know that."

"I'll keep them," he said with finality. "You go on and get dressed."

"Why do you want me to get dressed?" she asked, almost in a whimper.

Only when he spoke the words did Ronnie realize what his intention actually was:

"We've got to go talk to the police and work this out," he said.

Deep down, he had known from the moment he heard those damning words that he had no choice but to turn his mother over to the authorities. She, after all, had always taught him to do the right thing.

Alf Parnell had known Velma Barfield for most of his life. He had been a year behind her in school, and they had attended the same church. Later, after each married and had families, they had been for several years next-door neighbors in Parkton, the tiny farm town north of Lumberton where Ronnie and his younger sister, Pam,* had grown up. For nearly twenty years a Robeson County sheriff's deputy, Parnell had been one of the detectives who questioned Velma three days earlier. He was waiting when Ronnie, a stricken look on his face, led his distraught mother into the sheriff's department. Ronnie had called and left a message for Wilbur Lovett that they were coming, but Lovett was out running down a lead in the Stuart Taylor case, and Parnell had gotten the message.

Ronnie was relieved to see a friendly face. He had warm feelings for Parnell, whose twin sons had been his childhood playmates. "Alf," he said. "I think Mama has something she needs to tell you."

"Is that right, Velma?" Parnell said. "Is there something you want to talk to us about?"

She was crying—she had cried all the way to the sheriff's department—but she nodded.

"Well, y'all come on back," Parnell said, leading them to Wilbur Lovett's office, where, after his mother had entered, Ronnie pulled Parnell aside and showed him the pills he had taken from her, told him that he was certain she had intended to take them all and kill herself.

After they had seated themselves in the office, Velma was crying so hard that not even Ronnie could quiet her. It took a couple of minutes for her to compose herself enough to talk.

"Velma," Parnell advised her, "you know that the rights that were read to you on Friday still apply. Do you understand that?"

She said that she did.

There was a knock at the door, and Wilbur Lovett, who had been summoned by Parnell, hurried in and took a seat.

"Now, Velma," Parnell said, "what was it that you wanted to tell us?"

Again she began sobbing. "I didn't mean to kill him," she said. "I only meant to make him sick."

Ronnie interrupted. "Does she need a lawyer?"

"That's up to her," Lovett replied.

"Mama, do you want a lawyer?"

Later, Ronnie would recall that at this point Lovett intervened, saying, "She's already told us this much. It would be easier on her if she just went ahead and made a statement." Lovett, however, would deny that.

"No, I don't want a lawyer," Velma assured her son.

"Are you sure?"

She nodded. She seemed to want to get this off her conscience.

Ronnie left so the officers could continue their interview. He needed to call his sister. He knew this would be devastating to her, and he wanted to be the one to break the news. Pam had a young daughter and also lived in Lumberton. Her husband, Kirby Jarrett,* answered.

"Kirby, there are some problems developing down here at the courthouse that Pam ought to know about," Ronnie told him. "Our mother's in trouble again." He didn't want to talk about it over the phone. "Just tell her I need her down here," he said. "I'm at the sheriff's department."

Pam and Kirby arrived a short time later, Pam looking frightened. "What's going on?" she asked.

"She's confessing to poisoning Stuart Taylor," Ronnie said. "That's first-degree murder."

Pam broke down, becoming almost hysterical. She demanded to see her mother, and the detectives took a break to allow her to visit. Later, Pam would only remember holding her mother while both cried, her mother saying over and over, "I'll never get to see my grandbabies again."

Lovett, meanwhile, went upstairs to meet with the district attorney, who had been alerted that a confession was underway. He wanted to make certain that everything was done exactly right.

As Lovett left, Parnell took Ronnie aside and explained that Velma would be charged with Stuart's death and held in jail. The interviewing and paperwork would take several hours. Ronnie and Pam might as well go home; they could do nothing here. He would call them later in the evening. He promised to call Velma's doctor to get whatever medicines she needed. To calm Ronnie's fears, he assured him that a close watch would be kept on his mother through the night.

Ronnie and Pam agreed that they would meet at her apartment later to await Parnell's call, and Ronnie left to tell his wife, Joanna,* what had happened. As he drove home, trying to grapple with the events of the past few hours, he was struck by a sudden, chilling thought: the man Wilbur Lovett had gone upstairs to confer with was none other than Joe Freeman Britt. That was when the real consequences of his actions hit him, and the irony was overwhelming. He had spent years struggling to save his mother only to turn her over to somebody who would, if his record held true, send her to the gas chamber.

Only then did he realize that he should have insisted that his mother have a lawyer before he allowed her to talk with the detectives.

It was almost ten before Alf Parnell called Pam's apartment and asked to speak with Ronnie.

Ronnie and Pam had spent much of the evening calling relatives. Their mother had a large, close family. Her sisters, Arlene and Faye, had just arrived after a three-hour drive from Charleston.

"Ronnie, I hate to tell you this," Parnell said, "but it's worse than we thought."

Worse? Ronnie thought. *What could be worse?*

"There are other people," Parnell told him.

"Other people?" Ronnie said. "What do you mean?"

"Other people she's killed."

Ronnie's pulse jumped. His stomach knotted. His brain didn't want to register what he had just heard.

"Alf," he responded, "you've got to know how unbelievable this is for me."

"It's the same for me," Parnell replied. "But she's told us this, and we're going to be looking into it."

When Ronnie hung up and turned to give the others the news, he looked pale and dazed.

"Y'all are not going to believe this," he said, the words coming slowly. "She's confessed to killing three other people."

"Who?" cried Faye.

Ronnie named two elderly people his mother had assisted as a live-in caregiver. Then he paused, as if unable to go on. He had to force out the next two words:

"... And Grandmother."

Her own mother.

Faye screamed and bolted for the door, running out into the rain that evening had brought, still screaming. Pam collapsed in her husband's arms, sobbing. Arlene stood rooted.

"What is wrong with her?" Arlene pleaded. "What is *wrong* with her?"

Many people soon would be asking that question. With time even Velma Barfield herself. For after her bitter encounter with Joe Freeman Britt had sent her to death row, she would begin an examination of her life that would lead her to repentance and would cause many people to believe in her redemption. And as she fought for her life in a society torn about the death penalty, she would draw more attention to the morality of capital punishment than any other murderer to that point, her case raising issues that still were being debated two decades later. But she could not foresee that in her despair and dejection as Alf Parnell drove her the two blocks to the Robeson County jail this night. Nor could her son foresee that the death sentence his mother would receive would turn into a life sentence for him.

PART I

Escaping South River

CHAPTER 1

A sense of desolation is inescapable in the flat, sandy farm lands that border the South River, which separates the east-ern North Carolina counties of Cumberland and Sampson. The river itself is narrow, black and forbidding, often without definable banks, wandering aimlessly through cypress-studded swamps. Even in the lushness of summer, with crops at their peaks and marshlands and woods in rampant tangle, an impression of emptiness prevails.

Bullards have lived on this land for generations. John Bullard raised cotton and tobacco on the Sampson County side of the river until he swapped farms early in this century with Frank Autry, who lived on the Cumberland side. In the deal Bullard ended up with more than two hundred acres and a small house into which he moved his wife Isabelle and their burgeoning family. Here they would finish rearing their nine children, losing a daughter, Sophia Velma, to fever at the age of three, and a son, Joe Tyson, to blood poisoning at fourteen. A daughter, Annie Belle, also would precede her parents in death, a victim of the flu epidemic that swept through the country in the winter of 1918–19, dead at twenty-six.

In 1926, ten years before his own death, John Bullard began dividing his land to parcel it out to his surviving children. The house and about forty acres surrounding it would go to his youngest child, Murphy, who was expected to remain at home to look after his aging parents and crippled sister.

Murphy was a gregarious young man, boisterous and volatile, but eminently likable. Lillie McMillan likely would have been drawn to him even if she hadn't lived in a place where choices were few, for she was his opposite.

Friends described Lillie as smart, sweet and docile. Tall and thin, with short, dark hair framing her thin, pretty face, she was from a Presbyterian clan who lived only a few miles from the Baptist Bullards. Like Murphy, she was the youngest in her family. Her mother had died when she was twelve, her father when she was fifteen. She had been left to live with her married siblings, staying first with one, then another, each for only a while. She hated that period of her life and carried deep resentments about it.

For a while she had lived with her brother Jim, thirteen years older. Jim was married to Murphy's sister, Mary Void, and they lived within sight of the Bullard homeplace in an abandoned frame schoolhouse that had been converted into a home. That was how Lillie had come to know Murphy. She was fifteen months older than he.

Neither family expected their wedding. Lillie slipped out of a window of her sister Nellie's house to run away with Murphy to South Carolina, where they married on July 27, 1929, two days before her nineteenth birthday. They returned to live with his parents.

The house into which Lillie moved with her new husband was neither as big nor as nice as some in which she had lived. It sat alongside a sandy lane by a swampy area through which a small creek—the Little Branch, local people called it—flowed into a pond a quarter of a mile away. The pond provided energy for a neighbor's grist mill, cotton gin, and country store, the commercial heart of the community. It was lined with young cypress trees and had a brooding aura of mystery about it. The black water actually was clear, and where the pond was deepest its bottom was sandy white. On hot summer evenings, boys slipped away to skinny-dip in the dark water and to dangle earthworms and caterpillars around cypress knees in hopes of catching sunfish.

The Bullard house was small and plain, built of heart pine, the unpainted boards brittle and gray with age. Lichens and moss grew on the gray cypress shingles of the roof, which leaked in heavy rains, calling for a marshaling of pots and jars. The main part of the house had but four rooms, three bedrooms and a living room. The kitchen was attached to the back of the house and could be reached only by going out the back door and passing along a narrow, L-shaped porch.

The heat inside the house could be insufferable in summer, and the front porch, shaded by chinaberry trees and a big magnolia, offered the only escape. It was worst in the kitchen, where Isabelle Bullard cooked on a wood range. No screens covered the windows or doors, and any time the weather was warm the house swarmed with flies and mosquitoes. In cold weather, a brick fireplace in the living room provided the only heat in the main part of the house. Winter winds whistled through the bare walls, and after all had gone to bed and the fire had died, the only warmth came from nestling deep under hand-made quilts.

The house had no modern conveniences, not even electricity. (Power lines would not reach the area until after World War II.) A shallow, hand-dug well, from which buckets of cool water were raised by a counterbalance, was just outside the kitchen behind the house. Milk and butter were suspended in buckets inside the well to keep them from spoiling in hot weather. Galvanized tubs for bathing and washing clothes hung from nails on the kitchen wall. There wasn't even an outhouse. Relief was taken in the woods in daylight, in crockery containers at night.

Despite the drawbacks of the Bullard place, Lillie didn't mind. After years of being shunted from house to house, she was satisfied to have a home where she felt wanted. It didn't matter that she had to share it with Murphy's parents and his older sister, Susan Ella, who remained at home because her right arm and leg had been shriveled by polio as a child and her marriage to a much older man had lasted only briefly.

Lillie adjusted quickly to these circumstances and soon began a family of her own.

People who lived near the river had to go to Fayetteville, fifteen miles away, to see a doctor, often a two-hour trip, even in a T-Model Ford, over muddy, rutted roads. Most chose home remedies except for the most serious illnesses and injuries. For many years babies in the area had been delivered by the midwife—the granny woman, she was called—but she had grown too old and feeble to continue her work by the time Lillie Bullard's first child arrived. A son, named Olive, his father's middle name, was delivered by Murphy's mother and sister, Mary Void, with the help of neighbor women, on December 2, 1930.

Lillie longed for a daughter next, and her wish was granted. The child was born on October 29, 1932, delivered at the home of Lillie's brother Jim, arriving just two days before Murphy's twenty-first birthday. Her parents named her Margie Velma. They would call her Velma.

The Great Depression had little effect on people in the South River area early on—they could always grow enough to eat—but after the price of cotton collapsed, life grew harder. Murphy found it impossible to provide for his new family, his aging parents, and his crippled sister on the money he made from the meager crops of cotton and tobacco he grew. He went to work for Clarence Bunch, logging for his sawmill, and he moved his wife and two children into a tiny house that Bunch provided near Bethany Church of God a few miles away. It was there that Lillie would give birth to her third child, another son, John Samuel, on April 28, 1935.

All across the South, men were leaving farms to take factory jobs in cities and towns, and Murphy soon was one of them. Not long after his second son was born, he heard from an uncle that the textile mills in Fayetteville were hiring. John Henry Faircloth, who had been married to Murphy's dead aunt, Annie Belle, already worked at one of the plants. He recruited young men from the area to work there as well, offering them transportation in his T-Model Ford and charging each a small fare. Murphy rode to town with him one day and was hired to learn to fix looms on the second shift, four until midnight, at Puritan Weaving Company.

His father's health was failing by then, and Murphy moved his wife and children back into his parents' house and devoted himself to bringing in enough money to take care of his family.

Murphy believed in doing a full day's work for a day's pay, even if the work was hard and the pay low—a lesson he would preach to his children. He went to work well or sick, never was late, never missed a day, stayed overtime if something needed doing, worked a second shift, sixteen hours straight, if his bosses asked. To advance himself, he would go in four hours early and work for free to learn new jobs. He got home at one or so each night, slept for a few hours, and was up at dawn to farm until he had to return to the mill. The steady pay made life a little easier, but Murphy never seemed to get ahead.

His deep need to impress people was one of the factors that caused him problems in handling money. "He bought what he wanted instead of what he needed," a relative would say years later. "His pocketbook was always too small for his operation, if you know what I mean."

On February 5, 1936, Murphy's father died at age seventy-four, followed eleven months later by his grieving mother, also seventy-four (Velma was four when her grandmother died and later had no memory of either grandparent). Eight months later, Lillie gave birth to a third son, Jesse. Over the next decade, five more children would follow: Jimmy in 1939, Arlene in 1941, Tyrone in 1944, and finally twins, Ray and Faye, in 1947.

Outside his family, Murphy was known as an amiable man, eager to please, a good friend and neighbor, willing to do whatever he could to help anybody. If somebody in the community fell ill and couldn't get in his crops, Murphy was the first to offer aid. If somebody needed the loan of a piece of farm equipment, it was theirs.

His family, however, knew a different person, a man beset by dark furies, sudden rages, and uncontrolled violence.

At home, Murphy would not suffer frustration. He would explode over the slightest thing: a tool out of place, a car that wouldn't start, an egg not fried exactly to his liking. He would smash a fist into a wall, kick in a fender, fling a plate of food across the room.

Sometimes his reactions were more violent. An avid quail hunter, he always had bird dogs, pointers and setters, and he was determined to train every one to perfection. A dog that balked, or disobeyed, or did not respond fast enough was quick to feel his wrath. Several family members would recall seeing him kick, stomp and beat dogs nearly to death, leaving them with blood running from their noses, mouths and ears. A son would recall him beating a mule with a chain until the mule's back was covered with bloodied knots.

Hot-tempered, his family called it. Nobody knew what might set him off, and everybody edged gingerly about him out of fear of provoking an outburst. But no matter how careful they were, they could not avoid his storms of anger.

On the farm, things happened that often were beyond the control of anybody. Dogs would kill the chickens; snakes would get the eggs; mules would kick out of their stalls and maraud through the corn or tobacco fields; pigs would get out of their pens and root up young crops. When such things happened, the whole family lived in fear of Murphy coming home. They knew that he would erupt—and somebody would pay in pain.

Oftentimes, Lillie would scurry about frantically trying to make things right before he got home. When the damage couldn't be disguised, she often took blame for it herself, even if the children had been responsible, hoping to spare them. But the gambit rarely paid off. Murphy still would line up all the children and whip them one by one with a leather strap.

Neighbors and others often remarked how well-behaved and obedient Murphy's children were, but only the children and their mother knew how they came to be that way. "There was Murphy's law, and that was it," a grandchild would say years later. "Do what I say, do it now, and don't talk back."

A child who did not move quickly enough would pay the consequences. A child who did not perform an assigned task to Murphy's expectations—and he was meticulously exacting about how everything was to be done—would have to do it over again after a session with the strap.

Back talk—"smart mouthin'," Murphy called it—would set him off quicker than anything. His younger children learned that lesson quickly by example and rarely uttered a word of protest. But Olive and Velma never quite acquiesced, despite hard experience. They stubbornly persisted in talking back, even if they had to mutter their defiance beneath their breath.

Olive paid the greater price for this. His father would sometimes hit him with his fist, or pick up whatever was handy, a tobacco stick or a hoe handle, and beat him with it. Years later, Velma would recall several instances in which her father was so out of control that she thought he might actually kill Olive, beating him on one occasion until blood flowed from the wounds across his back and shoulders. Murphy was a burly man, standing nearly six feet tall and weighing more than two hundred pounds, and if Olive tried to defend himself or, worse, fight back, his father only became more infuriated, prolonging the ordeal.

Although Velma "smart-mouthed" her father as much as Olive, she never received more than a session with the strap. This led to conflict between brother and sister. Olive thought that his daddy favored Velma, while she thought that her mother cared more for Olive. They sometimes argued about it to the point of fighting.

Velma resented her mother for this, resented her, too, for her meekness, for not intervening when her children were being abused. Every beating left her as angry at her mother as her father.

But her mother had her own problems. Murphy was intensely jealous, accusing Lillie of looking at other men, although she rarely ventured farther from home than her brother's house just up the road. "He was so jealous of her he didn't want her to even hardly speak to another man," Velma would recall years later. By then she thought that her father's jealousy had its roots in his own unfaithfulness. "I saw things as a child that makes me believe this," she said. "I would have never said anything, though, because I was afraid."

Velma slept in her parents' room, and many nights after her father got home from work she was awakened by his yelling at her mother, cursing and threatening. Sometimes it was her mother's cries that startled her from sleep. Velma would never recall seeing her father beat her mother, but many times, she later would say, she saw him twist her mother's arm behind her back, or push back her fingers until she screamed in pain. And many more times she saw her crying and trembling in fear of him.

Murphy didn't drink regularly, but he did like to go out now and then to buy moonshine (made in abundance in nearby swamps) and carouse with his old buddies, and these events sometimes turned into binges. When he came home drunk, his tirades were even worse. Velma would remember one occasion when she heard her mother screaming and ran out to the kitchen to find her drunken father holding a revolver to her mother's stomach, threatening to kill her.

It would be many years, long after her father had found religion, given up drinking, taken control of his temper and become a doting grandfather, before Velma would ever get up nerve to ask her mother why she hadn't left him.

"Where would I have gone?" her mother asked.

It would be many years beyond that before Velma could look back on her early years and see beyond the misery. Then she would sum up her childhood in just four words: "I was always afraid."

CHAPTER 2

For as long as Velma could remember, she dreamed of escape. Escape from the desolate countryside that bound her. From the crowded and jumbled house that embarrassed her. From endless chores that drained her. From the violent father she loathed, the docile mother she resented. Especially from the tension and anger, the frustration and bitterness, that brewed constantly within her, even as a little girl.

She found her first escape in the fall of 1939, as she turned seven. She started the first grade at South River School, a single-story brick building, about four miles from her house.

Velma loved school in the beginning, found it such relief from home that she wished it lasted longer each day and went on all year without break. She was a good student, too. Teachers, however, would note that she was given to boisterousness and occasional angry outbursts when she was offended or when things didn't go her way. But school did not offer refuge from Velma's steadily growing feelings of insecurity and inferiority. If anything, it accentuated them.

At school she encountered children from families more well off than hers. Some regularly got new shoes and wore bright, pretty clothes from department stores in Fayetteville. Velma could not suppress her envy. She got new shoes when school started—sturdy, clunky shoes, never anything pretty—and they had to last until school began anew the next year. Her mother made her clothes and she thought them shabby and shameful.

All students had to bring midday meals to school. Some brought sandwiches made on sliced bread bought at the grocery store— "light bread," country people called it, and it was considered a luxury. These children often had store-bought cookies and other treats. Velma's meal sack usually contained a biscuit, or a hunk of cornbread with a slice of fried side meat or sausage in it. Other students sometimes made fun of her meals and she began slipping off to the woods to eat alone.

A small store across the street from the school was a constant lure to students with its displays of candies and other goodies, but few could afford its enticements. Velma saw the store as a means of paying back her tormentors. She began stealing coins from the pockets of her daddy's overalls and used them to buy candy at the store, making certain to eat it in front of those who made fun of her.

Velma's success at petty theft gave her bolder ambitions. When an old man who lived on the other side of the river reported that $80 had been stolen from his tiny cabin, Velma, who had been visiting relatives nearby, was discovered with part of the money. She claimed the old man had asked her to keep it for him, but a session with her daddy's strap caused her to recant, apparently ending her budding career as a thief, for no more such incidents were ever reported.

By the second grade, Velma began complaining of headaches and stomachaches, both to keep from having to go to school and to relieve her of chores. She loved the attention that her ailments brought, but when the increasing frequency of her complaints convinced her father that she was malingering, prompting him to order that she go to school and do her chores sick or not, the number of complaints diminished drastically.

Even though school had its drawbacks, it still offered one great advantage in Velma's eyes: welcome relief from her father. She left for school soon after he got up, didn't return until he'd gone to work. By the time he got home, she was in bed. Still, Velma walked the quarter mile home from the spot where the bus dropped her off each day filled with dread because she abhorred the chores that awaited her.

All the Bullard children were assigned specific chores from the time they were old enough to perform them. In the beginning, Velma's were sweeping the sandy yard, which was kept free of all growth, feeding the chickens and bringing in wood for the kitchen range. But her duties increased as she grew older.

All the children had to work on the farm. As soon as the boys were old enough, they were taught to handle the mules, to plow and set rows. Velma had to work in the fields, too, planting, hoeing, and harvesting. Murphy grew less than an acre of tobacco, but to Velma it seemed much more. The plants were as tall as her head, and she had to pick worms from them and snap off the pungent blossoms when they flowered. She had to strip the huge, sticky leaves from the stalks—priming, this was called—and tie them to sticks so that they could be hung in her Uncle Jim's tobacco barn and cured with wood fires. Late in summer, Murphy hauled the crop to the markets in Fairmont and Dunn.

After the tobacco was in, the cotton harvest began. Murphy grew six acres of cotton. Velma hated picking it, but she was good at it. Her speed was motivated by two factors: she wanted it to be over with, and Murphy never let Velma and Olive start school until the cotton had been picked. School began in September, but it sometimes was November before Velma and her brother got to classes.

Murphy also tried to make extra money by growing corn, cucumbers, butter beans and field peas, which he sold to grocery stores in Fayetteville. But it was the children who got the extra work of weeding, picking and grading.

Velma was the only girl in the family for more than nine years—she would be grown before Arlene was old enough to take on chores—and as she grew older, her household responsibilities grew with her. She had to tend the younger children, help with the housecleaning, the washing, ironing and mending. She had to milk the cow and churn the butter, assist with the cooking and wash the dishes.

Lillie suffered incapacitating headaches that sometimes put her to bed for days, leaving all the household responsibilities to Velma, keeping her out of school.

While Velma begrudged her chores, she performed ably and with minimal protest—to do otherwise would provoke her father. But from an early age, she was convinced that the only reason her parents wanted her was to work. "I felt like I was just a slave," she would say years later.

Despite her unhappiness, Velma still had joyful times.

Murphy loved baseball and, on warm Sunday afternoons, he sometimes organized baseball games in a nearby field. At such times he seemed like another person to Velma, fun instead of fearsome. The games often went on until dark. Velma played shortstop, the only girl on the field, and she loved it.

On some hot summer Sundays, Murphy would take the children on outings to the nearby mill pond, where he had taught all of them to swim at early ages by tossing them into the deep water and letting them make for shore on their own.

On other Sundays, Velma found refuge at the home of an aunt and uncle, her father's eldest brother, Alex, and his wife Betsy, who lived a few miles away, across the river in Sampson County. Aunt Betsy was a woman of such good cheer that Velma wanted to grow up to be just like her. She was always teasing and telling stories, and she disdained distress and worry—"All it'll get you is a bad headache," she'd say, and Velma need only look at her mother to see that. Velma could not help but laugh around Aunt Betsy and Uncle Alex, and she always dreaded having to return to her own house, where the atmosphere was so different.

By the time Velma was ten, her father was calling her "Sugar" and "Honey." Now and then he would take her into his lap, hug her, even tease her good-naturedly. At those moments Velma realized how deeply she craved his affection. She loved the feelings of closeness, warmth and security it stirred in her.

About this time her father gave her the happiest moment of her childhood. She went with him to Fayetteville one Saturday. While he was off on business, she browsed along the sidewalk, looking in store windows. At a department store, she spotted a mannequin wearing the most beautiful dress she'd ever seen. The fabric was adorned with pink flowers. A wide ruffle hid the hem. She couldn't allow herself even to dream of owning anything so gorgeous. Still, she wanted her father to see it, and when he returned, she dragged him to the window. To her amazement, he marched into the store, checked the price, took out his wallet, and counted the money for it.

She would never forget the thrill of anticipation as she took the dress to show her mother. But like so much that she allowed herself to look forward to in life, it was a letdown. "That ruffle is going to be awfully hard to iron," was all her mother had to say.

But Velma refused to allow anything to stifle her joy. The pride and the power she got from wearing that dress was the greatest she'd ever known, and she would treasure the memory by making pink her favorite color.

Murphy was only thirty when World War II started. Most of the younger men around the countryside, and many of Murphy's age and older, went off to military service. But he stayed behind, working at the mill. Too many children were dependent on him.

In 1945, Murphy sold his farm to Albert Pope and bought the adjoining land, eighty acres, that his brothers, Huey and Jesse Martin had received from their father. Jesse Martin had built a small white house near the old homeplace, and Murphy moved his family into the more modern quarters. He was tired of mill work, and with eighty acres and crop prices climbing he thought that he could make farming pay. He increased his acreage of tobacco and cotton and began hauling his vegetables to the farmers' market in Raleigh. But two seasons was all it took to prove that he couldn't provide for his family by farming, and late in 1946 he went back to the mill.

Early the next year, Murphy quit Puritan Weaving and took a job at another textile plant in Red Springs, thirty miles south of Fayetteville, making his daily drive back and forth to work more than ninety miles. A coworker told him about a house for rent just north of Parkton, sixteen miles south of Fayetteville, and Murphy moved his family there after school was out that spring.

Once a tenant house on a large farm, this house was more primitive than the one his family had lived in for the past two years. Although Velma had dreamed of leaving South River, she now felt uprooted. She had grown up surrounded by family, giving her security and people to turn to in times of need, but here she knew no one, had no place to go. She had longed to live in a town with stores filled with wondrous goods, cafes to eat in, and lots of activities available. But all she got was Parkton, a sleepy little farm town, where nothing seemed to happen and there was nothing at all to do. Even that was a couple of miles away from this tiny, ugly, tin-roofed house where she quickly came to feel herself a prisoner.

Before the move, Olive had dropped out of school to work full-time on the farm. Now he went to work at the mill with his father. That fall Velma started the ninth grade at Parkton Public School, two months before she turned fifteen. Her grades had been falling for a couple of years, and they would get no better as she struggled to fit in and make new friends.

She soon discovered an activity, though, that brought her both pleasure and attention: basketball. She was good at it. Parkton had a girls' basketball team, and the coach saw her playing and encouraged her to try out. To her surprise she made the team. But she had to stay after school to practice, and before the season was well under way, her mother, who had just given birth to the twins, Ray and Faye, insisted that she drop out because she needed her at home. Velma's disappointment and the deepened drudgery she faced only strengthened her resentment of her mother.

But she soon developed another interest. Thomas Burke, the son of the Bullards' next-door neighbors, lived just a quarter mile away in a white house with French doors and a big front porch. The house was much nicer than the Bullards'. It was set far back from the road behind two long rows of pecan trees.

A year ahead of Velma in school, Thomas was tall and lean with shiny black hair, jug ears, and an impish grin. He wasn't the best-looking boy Velma had ever taken note of, but he was the first to pay attention to her. Velma was surprised. She had thought she never would be able to interest any boy. Although others thought her pretty, she felt unattractive, aware only of her defects.

In the fourth grade, she had run head-on into a boy on the playground at school and was briefly knocked unconscious. A big contusion grew on her forehead. In time it receded but not completely, leaving her with a small, permanent knot about which she was extremely sensitive (playmates who dared call her "Knothead" never did it but once). She never could quite devise a hairstyle to hide the hardly noticeable disfigurement adequately.

Velma thought her teeth were ugly, too. She had a gap that she thought far too wide between the two in front. And her legs were far too short in her mind—she stood only five feet three—and she worried that they were bowed. She also felt overweight and fretted about it constantly.

Thomas, who towered over her, seemed unaware of any flaws, however. She enjoyed his easygoing ways, and she loved that he made her laugh.

Murphy noticed his daughter's new interest and quickly developed a strong dislike for Thomas. He didn't want him hanging around.

Murphy had ruled that Velma could not date until she was sixteen, and she dared not question his edict. But when her sixteenth birthday came, he still wouldn't allow it. Thomas was persistent, however, and Velma pleaded with her mother to intervene. Eventually, her father conceded, but with reluctance—and firm restrictions.

Their first dates were to church and school events, usually double dates. Later, Thomas would come for her in his daddy's car, and they would go to Fayetteville to a movie or to hang out at the Skyview, a drive-in restaurant with a radio station studio that broadcast popular music.

But Velma's good times were lessened by constant worry about not getting home on time. She couldn't stay out past ten. One minute late and her father would be riding the roads searching for her. And when she did get home, not only did she have to face a tirade, her restrictions would be long and severe.

In the fall of 1949, soon after Velma had started the eleventh grade, tension over her dating and household responsibilities grew so great that as she departed for school one morning she left a note saying that she had had all she could take; she was leaving and would not be back. She made a point that it was not because of the extra duties that came with caring for Ray and Faye, who were just eighteen months old. She dropped by the classroom of her brother John to tell him what she had done. She would be staying with Olive's fiancée, she said, until she could figure out a way to make it on her own.

Lillie found the note that morning. Murphy had returned to Puritan Weaving once again by this time. He worked third shift and slept during the day. Lillie didn't wake him to tell him about the note. She knew what his reaction would be.

Enraged, Murphy took Lillie into town to search for Velma. They found her quickly. Lillie was almost as upset as Murphy. She couldn't understand how Velma could do such a thing. Cursing and threatening, Murphy told Velma to get into the car and she obeyed. Her father had not whipped her in some time and, surprisingly, he didn't when they got home. Instead, Lillie took the strap to her. Afterward, Velma was restricted for a month and told that she was not to see Thomas again.

Thomas was a senior that fall. Velma saw him at school and now and then she managed to slip off with friends and meet him surreptitiously. Only he gave her life any promise.

Thomas' sense of humor was what had originally attracted

Velma to him, but it was his tenderness that came to impress her more, a quality she'd rarely known. She never realized how deeply she needed tenderness until she met him. And when she couldn't see him she found herself longing for him.

By her seventeenth birthday, Murphy gave in and allowed Thomas to come back around. On a Saturday night not long afterward, Thomas drove Velma to Fayetteville to see a movie. On the way home, he told her that he had a solution to their problem: they should get married. He had mentioned that before, but this time he was in earnest.

She couldn't get married, she told him. Her father would never allow it.

They could run away, he suggested, go to South Carolina, where it was possible to marry without a waiting period or parental consent. Her father might get mad but couldn't do anything about it. She would legally be his wife, and Murphy would just have to accept it.

But Thomas didn't know her father the way Velma did, had never witnessed his full fury. She didn't know what he might do if she dared such a thing. She couldn't risk it.

Still, Velma was tempted, and the more she thought about it in coming days, the more her resistance wavered. On Thursday night, December 1, 1949, Velma told her parents that she had to attend a school function. A friend picked her up and delivered her to Thomas, who was waiting nearby in his daddy's car. They drove to Dillon, just across the state line, and were married at the home of a justice of the peace. Velma was so nervous that she would remember few details later. Her fear only grew as they drove back home.

Thomas wanted to tell her parents. Velma resisted. Her daddy was planning to move the family back to the farm at South River at the beginning of the year, she said, and she wanted to wait until then. Thomas wanted to do it now, tonight, get it behind them. Velma said no. She didn't want Thomas to see the inevitable explosion. She was scared of what her daddy might do to him. Tomorrow, she promised. He reluctantly dropped her off in front of her house in time to meet her curfew.

At school the next day, Velma had to confess to Thomas that she still hadn't gotten up nerve enough to tell. She would do it that afternoon. And she did. But she told only her mother, hoping she might get her to break the news.

Her mother was not surprised, but she wasn't about to tell Murphy. "You'll have to do that yourself," she said.

Velma couldn't muster her courage before her father left for work, and she spent the night in dread, getting little sleep. On Saturday morning when her father got home, Velma was waiting nervously in the front room. She had something to tell him, she said, and blurted, "Thomas and I got married Thursday night."

The eruption was even worse than Velma had imagined. "All hell broke loose," Velma's brother John recalled years later. He would not have it, Murphy raged. She was going right now to get it annulled! He would not allow her to live one minute with Thomas Burke. He knew that boy was no good, had known it all along. He never should have allowed him to come around in the first place.

Velma huddled on the couch crying as he knocked over a table, picked up a chair and hurled it across the room, then stormed into the kitchen in search of Lillie. It was her fault, he yelled. Why hadn't she told him about it? Why hadn't she done something to stop it?

As Velma begged her daddy to stop, he ordered her and Lillie to get ready and get in the car. Then he went in search of Olive, who was now working second shift at a different mill from his father and was still in bed. Murphy told him to get up, get the car started. By the time Olive got dressed, his father was blaming him, following him into the yard, yelling. He was part of the plot, his father accused. He'd known it all along and conspired with Velma.

Olive denied it. But his father would not hear it. "Don't lie to me, boy!" he yelled.

Lillie told John to look after the other children while they were gone, and they all assembled in trepidation on the front porch to watch as Lillie and Velma climbed into the backseat of Murphy's white '47 Ford. Murphy got into the passenger seat, Olive at the wheel. But before Olive could back out of the driveway, John saw his father yell something at Olive, who snapped back. Suddenly, Murphy lunged across the seat at his son. The car jerked to a halt and Olive leaped out.

"You've hit me the last damn time!" he screamed.

Murphy jumped from the car just as Olive bolted, running hard for the woods across the road. Murphy took off in pursuit, the two disappearing into the pines.

Lillie and Velma scurried back to the house. A few minutes later, Murphy emerged from the woods, struggling for breath. He got into the car and roared off down the road. At first Velma and Lillie thought he'd gone off in search of Olive. But when he didn't come back within a few minutes, Velma began to worry. Had he gone instead to find Thomas and kill him?

Not for several hours did Murphy return. The house was silent in dread. He had been drinking. He ordered Lillie to pack his clothes. He was leaving. Nobody in this family cared anything about him, he said. It didn't matter what he thought or what he wanted for them, they always went against him.

While Lillie went dutifully about packing her husband's clothes, he sat in his favorite chair with a look of despair. Then he put his head in his hands and began to cry.

In all her life Velma had seen a tear in her father's eye only once, when his brother Hucy had died two years earlier. Now he sat weeping openly. When he regained control, he got up, went to Olive's room and fell asleep on his bed.

Velma packed her clothes and her few other belongings while her father slept. That evening Thomas came for her in his daddy's car, and she moved into his parents' house with him. She had escaped at last, but somehow it didn't give her the pleasure she had dreamed it would.

CHAPTER 3

Both Thomas and Velma dropped out of school after their marriage. Thomas got a job at a cotton mill in Red Springs. Murphy took his family back to South River early in the new year, as planned. He had rented his farm when he had left it two and a half years earlier, and the tenants were not due to leave until late spring, so he could not return to his own house. The old home-place was standing empty, however, and Albert Pope allowed Murphy to move back into it rent-free. By the time the tenants had deserted the small white house on Murphy's farm, Olive had married, and he moved into the house with his new wife, Lucille. Thomas didn't like working at the mill, and Olive and Lucille invited him and Velma to move in with them. They went early that summer.

Thomas took temporary work at different farms, for a while picking butter beans. Soon he found a job in Fayetteville, driving a delivery truck for the Double Cola Bottling Company. Velma took a job, too, at a drugstore soda fountain in Fayetteville, but Thomas didn't want her working and she quit after a few weeks.

That summer Murphy left Puritan Weaving once again, taking a better-paying job at a new mill that had opened in Raeford, once again giving him a round-trip drive of nearly ninety miles. One morning, late that summer, he went to sleep at the wheel of his '48 Buick on his way home. The car hit the guardrail of the bridge over the South River. A board from the rail pierced the windshield, grazed Murphy's head and exited through the roof of the car, which went off the bridge and smashed into the trees. Murphy was bruised and bloodied, but he had escaped death by less than an inch, and it had a sobering effect, making him realize, for one thing, that he couldn't continue to live at South River.

He needed to be closer to his job, and by the end of the year, he had sold his farm and moved his family back to Robeson County, into a big white farmhouse he rented only a half mile from the house in which they once had lived near Parkton.

Thomas and Velma had preceded them. They moved into the small house where her family had lived earlier, just down the road from Thomas' parents. Soon Velma was pregnant, and on December 15, 1951, she gave birth to a son at Cape Fear Valley Hospital in Fayetteville. She had turned nineteen a month and a half earlier. The child was named Ronald Thomas.

The moment she first held her baby was unlike any other in Velma's life. "I was thrilled beyond words," she later wrote. "I cried I was so happy. Now, bless his heart, he was ugly, but I thought he was the prettiest baby I had ever seen. I checked him over and over and over from head to toe. He was so precious. I guess I was looking for any little blemish that maybe didn't look right. He didn't have any hair, and I would just rub lightly over his little bald head."

Velma could not hold Ronnie enough. She cooed to him, spoke to him in baby talk. He laughed, and his dark eyes connected with hers as nothing ever had.

Within a year of Ronnie's birth, Velma was pregnant again. By then a new soft-drink bottling plant had opened in Parkton, and Thomas gave up his job with Double Cola to sell Dr Pepper. On September 3, 1953, Velma gave birth to a daughter, Pamela Marie.*

Velma was adamant that her children would not have a childhood like hers. They would be loved. Nobody would scream at them or beat them. They would be treated with respect. They would have things that she never had. She also wanted her children to grow up with religion. From infancy she took them to the Baptist church where she was now a member with Thomas. The family rarely missed a service, and nobody doubted her devoutness.

From the time Ronnie was old enough to talk, Velma read to him. She bought children's books by the score. And when Pam grew old enough, she read to the two of them together.

"Some of the best times I had with them was when they wanted me to read to them," she later recalled. She read every book so many times that Ronnie and Pam knew them by heart. Still, they begged her to read more.

"Sometimes when I would be reading to them, I would intentionally mess up, rearrange the words, and believe you me, they had memorized all these stories so that when I would start messing up, they would stop me. I loved seeing the expression on their faces as I read to them."

This was the early fifties. Although attitudes were soon to change, in the South at that time men were expected to work and bring home the living. Women stayed home, cooked, kept house, tended the children. That was fine with Velma. She didn't want to be apart from Ronnie and Pam even for short periods.

Velma never had been to North Carolina's mountains, nor had her parents. Thomas loved the mountains. He'd gone there on vacations with his family. One summer when the children were still small, Thomas and Velma's brother John decided it was time that Velma and her parents saw the mountains. Thomas had a week's vacation coming, and he and Velma made plans to leave the children with his parents, go to the mountains for half the week with John and her parents, come back, drop off the Bullards, get the children and go to the beach for the rest of the week.

They left on Sunday. By the time they got to Asheville, where they spent the first night, Velma missed Ronnie and Pam so much that she was almost physically ill. The next day, they drove across the Smoky Mountains to Gatlinburg, Tennessee, but Velma couldn't enjoy herself for thinking about the children.

"I'd give half my life right now to be back there with those kids," she told Thomas that night. "I miss them so bad I can't stand it."

She wanted to cut the trip short and leave for home the next day, and the others gave in to her wishes. Although they didn't arrive until after midnight, Velma insisted on going to Thomas' parents' house and waking them to get the children. Only when she held Ronnie in her arms was she finally content.

When Ronnie started first grade at Parkton School, he was reluctant to go because he didn't want to leave his mother, so Velma went with him the first day and stayed all day to help him adjust. Ronnie's teacher, Mrs. Cooper, had taught his father, and she was so sweet and understanding that Ronnie took to her immediately.

He would come home every day telling new things about Mrs. Cooper.

Velma took her first job soon after Ronnie started school, mainly to provide more for her children. She worked third shift, midnight to eight, running a twisting machine at a textile plant in nearby Red Springs. She still served as a grade mother for Ronnie's class, though, and was there for every class party, field trip and special event.

After Pam started to school, Velma planned to rotate as grade mother, one year for Ronnie's class, the next for Pam's. But Ronnie got upset. Why couldn't she still be his grade mother, too? Velma gave in, and for all their years of elementary school she was grade mother for both.

She joked with her children that they had automatic arms. Anytime a parent was needed as a volunteer at school, Ronnie's and Pam's arms automatically shot into the air, and Velma never failed them.

By the time Ronnie started third grade, Thomas had a new job making more money driving for the Pepsi Cola bottler in Fayetteville. He moved his family out of the tiny, dilapidated house near his parents and into a big white house on South Fayetteville Street in Parkton.

Parkton had only a few hundred residents. The mainline tracks of the Atlantic Coast Line Railroad divided the town, and residents were as inured to the wail and rumble of passing trains as they were to the muffled thump of shells exploding in training exercises at Fort Bragg, the huge army base fifteen miles north of town.

The house into which Thomas moved his family had two stories, with dormers and a huge, columned and balustraded wraparound porch. Azaleas grew around the porch, and the house was shaded by big oaks, pines and dogwoods. It was just down the street from Parkton Baptist Church and the town's small business district: a grocery store, a cafe, a gas station, a drugstore with a marble soda fountain, a laundromat, a hardware store, a doctor's office and the tiny station for the town's single policeman. Parkton School was only a couple of blocks beyond, within easy walking distance.

The whole family loved the new house. It was spacious, with a big yard for Ronnie and Pam to play in, and other children, Alf Parnell's twins, were next door. Velma's brother John and his wife lived right across the street, and Velma's new house became a family gathering spot. She spent a lot of time in her big kitchen cooking and baking for her family. Her brothers and sisters often dropped by for a cup of coffee, a piece of cake, or a slice of pie. So did Wade Holder, a young coach at Parkton School who had moved into her parents' house as a boarder and had become one of the family. Velma was almost a second mother to her baby sister, Faye, who was only five years older than Ronnie, and Faye often stayed at the house. To Ronnie and Pam, Faye seemed more like an older sister than an aunt.

Since their house was so close to the church, the family's religious activities increased. Velma began teaching a children's Sunday school class, and helped with youth groups and vacation Bible school in the summer. Thomas became an usher. If something was happening at the church, the Burke family was sure to be involved.

Velma and Thomas didn't just participate in their children's church and school activities. Whatever the children wanted to do, they did with them. They went to movies, bowled, played miniature golf. Velma especially enjoyed playing basketball with her children. She never liked the beach, but Ronnie and Pam loved it, so she learned to like it, too. Carolina Beach, Kure Beach, Wrightsville Beach were just two hours away, and during the warm months Thomas, Velma and the children frequently spent weekends there, sometimes going just for the day. Every year they attended the Azalea Festival in Wilmington.

When he was ten, Ronnie decided to go to a week-long summer church camp in an adjoining county. His mother wasn't sure that she could stand to be separated from him for a week, but she took him. Once there, though, Ronnie was reluctant to get out of the car. He didn't want to leave his mother, and Velma had to talk him into staying. He cried when she left, and both had a difficult week.

"I wouldn't say I was a mama's boy," Ronnie would say later, "but I was close to it. I really loved my mama to death, a real adoring-type love."

Pam, on the other hand, adored her father. She wanted to go wherever he went, and he took her with him everywhere, even to the barbershop. She thought he was the funniest person who ever lived. He always thought up some new way to make her laugh. He loved to watch *The Three Stooges* and *The Andy Griffith Show* on TV, and Pam always climbed into his lap to watch with him.

Early in 1963, when she was thirty, Velma started hemorrhaging.

A gynecologist diagnosed fibroid tumors in her uterus and recommended a hysterectomy. Velma talked about it with Thomas. They had agreed that they wanted only two children, a boy and a girl. They decided Velma should have the surgery, but they had no way of knowing it would become a turning point in their lives.

"After she had that hysterectomy, seemed like she never was the same again," Velma's brother John would say years later. Doctors never warned her of the hormonal changes that the surgery could produce and how they might affect her moods. Sometimes she would be depressed for days. At other times she would feel edgy, nervous, and she didn't understand why. She would snap at the children, or at Thomas, then feel bad about it.

With time, she came to believe that Thomas thought that she was somehow less a woman now that she couldn't bear children and that she was not as attractive to him. She began to fret again about her weight. She normally weighed about 125, hardly fat. Yet she went to a doctor and got diet pills, which seemed only to make her edgier, more nervous. She would stay on her diet for a while, then go into a baking binge and gorge on sweets, feel guilty about it and get depressed.

Sometimes she would go on spending sprees. Mostly she bought things for the children, but she also bought for herself, clothes and jewelry, things she didn't need. The spending became so obsessive on occasion that she bought knowing she didn't have money in the bank to cover the checks she was writing. When they bounced, she kept it secret and somehow managed to pay off the merchants before legal action was taken or Thomas found out.

During that same year Thomas had a falling out at the Pepsi plant. Velma came home from work one morning to find a note from him saying that he had gone to Florida with his sister's husband to try to find a job. John told her that the two had stopped by his house that morning and asked if he wanted to go. Velma was baffled. Never before had Thomas done anything so impetuous and foolish. She was hurt and angry.

When Thomas called the next day from Jacksonville, Velma let him have it. She'd never heard of anything so stupid, and if he thought she was bringing those kids and moving to Florida, he had another think coming. Although his brother-in-law stayed, Thomas meekly returned home and got back his job at the Pepsi plant.

In 1964, Velma began having pains in her lower back. When

they grew severe, she went to a doctor. At first he thought she might have a simple muscle strain and prescribed pain tablets—she wouldn't remember later what they were. The trouble persisted, and Velma continued to take the tablets.

Ronnie entered seventh grade that fall. He was almost thirteen, and his interests were changing. Velma was on the second shift at the mill, had been working nights for six years. When school was in session she rarely saw her children during the week, except when she was called upon as a grade mother. She wanted more normal hours, more time with Ronnie and Pam, and although she had to take a cut in pay, she got a job as a clerk at Belk-Hensdale department store, usually called Belk's, in the Tallywood Shopping Center in Fayetteville.

An ominous sign of what was to come soon followed. Driving to work one morning, Velma blacked out at the wheel. Her car left the road, plowed through a woman's yard and nearly struck her house before coming to a halt. Velma said she didn't know what had happened, but Thomas and John thought they knew. They were sure that she had taken too many of those pain pills.

Another development, dark with portent, came at the same time. Thomas was talked into joining the Parkton Jaycees, a group of young men who undertook community projects. They also liked to have fun. They met weekly, and they sponsored regular weekend dances at the armory to raise money.

With Velma now home with the children in the evening, Thomas felt free to go off to Jaycee meetings. This was the first time since their marriage that he had undertaken any activity outside his family, and Velma didn't like it, although she said nothing in the beginning.

Everything was changing, she realized, and she sensed somehow that the only happy years of her life might already be behind her.

PART II

On the Wings of a Dove

CHAPTER 4

The sixties were turning into a turbulent decade, rife with assassinations, racial violence, riots, war in Southeast Asia, and a youth culture that seemed to be abandoning all that their parents held dear. All of that flickered across TV screens in Parkton to little effect. Change was slow in coming to rural North Carolina, and when it did, it often seemed to slip in insidiously. That would be the case with the single development of the sixties that would alter Velma's life most drastically.

In 1963 the Food and Drug Administration approved the marketing of a drug named Valium, which promised to relieve stress and deliver tranquility, and an anxious age embraced it. It was quickly becoming the most widely prescribed drug in the world, but nobody was aware then of the dangerous effects it could produce.

By the spring of 1965, as the first American combat troops were entering Vietnam, Horace Parnell, who owned the Corner Grocery in Parkton, gave notice to Thomas and Velma that they would have to move. The big house in which they had been living was the Parnell family home, the house in which Horace and his brother, Alf, who lived next door, had grown up. Horace had always intended to remodel it and move into it himself, and the time had come.

Nobody was happy about the prospect of leaving the Parnell house, but Thomas tried to make the best of the situation. He and Velma had been renting all along, he pointed out, and it was time they had a home of their own.

Thomas' parents had moved closer to town by this time, into a small white house with several acres on McCormick Road on the northern edge of Parkton. The health of Thomas' father, John, would no longer allow him to farm, and he was working at a pawnshop in Fayetteville owned by his brother-in-law. He offered to give Thomas a lot on which to build next to his own house.

That summer Thomas hired a local builder to begin work on a three-bedroom, brick ranch-style house with a single-car carport. The whole family was excited about the new house. They went almost every evening to check its progress.

More was changing than just their place of residence, however. The bonds that held Thomas and Velma together were about to unravel. The first crisis came that summer. One weekend when Velma took Ronnie and Pam to Carolina Beach, Thomas stayed home to help with a Jaycee project. On Saturday night he drove into Fayetteville. He was returning home alone after midnight in his black '62 Ford Galaxy when he apparently dozed off.

The car left the highway, hit a culvert, sailed into the air and landed on its wheels in the driveway of a house. Thomas' head banged the steering wheel, and he was knocked unconscious. Nobody saw or heard the accident, and because the car looked as if it had been parked in the driveway, no passersby noticed.

After Thomas came to, dazed and bloodied, he made his way to his sister's house in town, nearly a mile away. She called the rescue squad, and an ambulance took him to Highsmith Hospital in Fayetteville.

Nobody knew how to get in touch with Velma and the children. They didn't learn about the accident until they arrived home Sunday evening. Velma's brother John hurried across the street to tell them, then drove them to the hospital. Pam, who was almost twelve, was panic-stricken. She would never forget how horrible her daddy looked. His eyes were black and swollen, his head swathed in bandages, his nostrils clogged with dried blood. Pam was afraid he might die.

"I'm fine," he assured her. "It just looks bad."

In reality, he had suffered a concussion and his nose nearly had been severed. He was in great pain, but within minutes he was smiling and joking with Pam.

Thomas remained in the hospital for several days and was back at work within a week. But he complained frequently of headaches afterward, and they would increase in severity and number as time went on.

Although Thomas denied it, Velma was convinced that drinking had been the cause of his accident. She saw that as a perfect example of the horrors alcohol could wreak.

Velma abhorred alcohol. Her church did not preach against it without good reason, she was convinced. To Velma, there was no such thing as social drinking. Taking even a single drink was inviting the devil into your body. She had seen it in her father as a child.

One of the qualities she had most admired about Thomas when they were dating was that, unlike so many other boys, he resisted the temptation of alcohol. She had vowed that she would never marry a drunkard, never live with a man who drank.

Thomas had been perfect in that respect. So many men Velma knew still wanted to go out with their old buddies to drink and carouse after they were married, but not Thomas. He had devoted himself completely to family, work and church for fourteen years. Then he had joined the Jaycees.

Velma had been aghast when she had discovered that Thomas had been having a beer or two with his fellow Jaycees after their meetings, and she wasn't reluctant to let him know. Thomas, on the other hand, saw nothing wrong. Why shouldn't he have a beer, if that was what he wanted? He worked hard; he had a right to relax.

The friction quickly escalated into arguments, and both remained rigid in their positions. Ronnie and Pam were deeply distressed that their once happy and loving family had become tense and argumentative. They wanted things to be back as they were. They kept hoping that their parents would see what they were doing and change their ways, but that was not to be.

The new house was finished by fall. Thomas took out a loan of $11,500, with payments of $80 a month. He planted red maple saplings in the front yard and moved his family in mid-October. Two weeks later, Velma celebrated her thirty-third birthday in her own house, a house she couldn't have conceived in her childhood, with luxuries undreamed. She knew she should have been happier, but she wasn't.

A month after that, she and Thomas observed their fifteenth anniversary, but it was not the same as the anniversaries that had passed before. An edginess prevailed, a vague and unspoken uncertainty. A wedge had been driven between them.

Velma was certain about what was separating them: alcohol.

How could she hold her head up in church if people found out Thomas was drinking?

Thomas responded by cutting down on churchgoing. Eventually, he would stop altogether. To him, the issue was not whether he had an occasional beer or two, but his independence, his right as a man to make his own decisions. Neither would give in, and their arguments grew more frequent and intense.

"My mom would not leave any situation alone," Ronnie, her greatest defender, later would admit. "Daddy would just walk into the house, and Mama would find something to pick a fight about."

Not for many years would Velma realize that she was as much at fault as Thomas. Her chastising him for drinking unleashed something dark and suppressed within her. She was becoming just as short-tempered as her father once had been.

"Anything that my husband would do would agitate me," she said. "Coming home late. Being at a Jaycee meeting longer than I thought he should. Things like that really bothered me."

Even if Thomas hadn't been drinking, she would confront him, accusing, yelling. He'd make the slightest mess in the kitchen, and she would be on him. "In the house, I couldn't stand anything that was left out of place," Velma said. "I just couldn't take it. I liked for things to be clean, and I liked when I cleaned it for it to be left that way."

In the beginning, when her mother would start a fight with her daddy, Pam would try to stop it by pulling her mother into a bedroom and separating them, but it became more and more difficult.

"She wanted to stay and fight and yell," Ronnie said of his mother. "She was very combative."

The situation deteriorated further that summer. On July 18, 1966, just nine months after Thomas had moved his family into their new home, his mother came running across the field that separated their houses screaming for help. She had found her husband slumped dead at the breakfast table. John Burke was only sixty, and although he had suffered for years from emphysema, his death was an unexpected shock.

Thomas had always been close to his father, and he was overcome with grief. He became depressed and remained so for weeks afterward, gradually retreating deeper and deeper into alcohol.

Velma wasn't understanding of his loss. Any time Thomas came home with alcohol on his breath, a confrontation was certain.

Screaming and cursing inevitably followed. Thomas would stalk out, slamming the door and driving away, only to return drunk hours later, making his wife even angrier.

Neither Ronnie nor Pam could understand how things had spun so rapidly out of control. Their lives had been so happy in the big white house in town, but in this new house only misery reigned.

Pam had many friends at school and church, and she sought escape in activities with them. Other times she stayed with her grandparents, Murphy and Lillie, who had bought a house in Parkton beside the armory in 1958. When these sanctuaries were not available, she retreated to her room during the fights. Her father had bought her a set of drums, and she would put a stack of 45s on her stereo, turn up the volume and play along, shutting out the rancor beyond her door.

Ronnie, on the other hand, felt an obligation to intercede, to stop his parents from fighting, to try to make things right again. And although he rarely succeeded in bringing peace, he still felt the need to be close by in case things got out of hand.

As Thomas' drinking grew worse, his behavior became more erratic. Sometimes he would get so angry during the arguments that he would throw things. One night he threw a Pepsi bottle, which shattered on the floor. Then he passed out on the couch. The next morning, Ronnie got up and found that his mother had swept up the broken glass and placed it beside the couch, where Thomas might step on it when he got up.

"Why did you do that, Mama?" he asked.

"I don't know," she replied. "I guess I thought it might make him think about what he's doing."

Thomas had not yet become violent toward Velma, but he seemed constantly on the verge. Ronnie was afraid that he was going to hurt her someday.

At fifteen, Ronnie was tall, thin and rangy like his daddy at that age, hardly athletic, no fighter. He had no notion that he could whip his father, if it came to that, but that didn't keep him from challenging him. Several times he rushed to separate his parents when his father seemed threatening.

"You're not going to hit her," he yelled at his father more than once.

"He never did," Ronnie would recall years later, "but there was always the fear that he would, that he was going to do something really bad. I just wanted him to know that if he ever hit my mother, I was going to be glued to his butt."

Early in 1967, the inevitable happened. Thomas was charged with drunk driving. A judge gave him a suspended sentence, a warning, and took away his license, causing him to lose his job. He became despondent, seemed not to care anymore. His drinking grew even worse. As did the fights with Velma. The misery in the household increased. Pam and Ronnie dreaded going home after school, dreaded weekends. They were too embarrassed to have friends come to their house.

Eventually, Thomas got another job, back at the mill where he had worked when he and Velma had first married. Because he couldn't drive, he had to ride to work with others. He was a proud man, and this step backward was a great humiliation. Velma thought the shame might cause him to take stock, stop drinking and turn things around. But it had the opposite effect.

Velma had been telling Thomas all along that he was an alcoholic, that he needed to get help. He denied it. He could quit anytime he wanted, he told her. Drinking wasn't his problem, he insisted. His problem was her nagging, her belittlement, her constant badgering.

If he wouldn't get help, Velma finally decided, she would do it for him. She later claimed that she talked with two doctors, both of whom recommended that she have Thomas committed to Dorothea Dix State Hospital in Raleigh, known as Dix Hill, or more commonly as "the crazy house."

When she mentioned this to Ronnie, he argued against it. He knew how proud his father was, knew that he couldn't be forced to accept anything against his will, knew what a stigma commitment would be to him. He thought they should encourage his father to seek help on his own. But Velma was fed up. She couldn't go on like this, she said.

Ronnie begged her to reconsider, but soon after he entered the tenth grade, Pam the ninth, Velma went to the courthouse in Lumberton and signed the necessary paperwork. A court order was issued. Deputies stopped the car in which Thomas was riding to work one night and took him into custody. He was held overnight in jail and driven to Raleigh the next day.

Three days later, Thomas signed himself out of the hospital without treatment. He returned home and was waiting when Velma arrived from work.

"You put me in there with all those crazy people," he said to her. "I'm not crazy!"

He had already packed his clothes, and he took them and left. Several days passed before Ronnie and Pam learned that he had gone to Florida to stay with his sister and was looking for a job.

Pam was distraught. "I remember crying a lot," she would recall. She thought that her father was gone for good, that he didn't want to be with her, that she might never see him again.

But Thomas couldn't find work in Florida, and three weeks later he returned. Both Pam and Ronnie were relieved that he was back. They saw his return as a ray of hope that things might improve, but they were wrong.

Parkton was a town in which everybody knew everybody else and gossip was common. Thomas was so embarrassed about his admission to Dix Hill that he did not want to be around other people. He was sure that people were pitying him, and he left the house only to buy beer or vodka. He spoke to Velma only when necessary. If she criticized, or tried to pick a fight, he turned away, refusing to respond. Even when Velma found his hidden vodka and angrily poured it down the drain, he remained quiet. A sullen silence settled between them. As much as Ronnie and Pam had hated the arguing and yelling, they came to detest the unspoken hostility even more.

The strain wore on Velma as well. She got so she could hardly eat. Her weight had been dropping regularly, and by the late fall of 1967 she had gone from 130 pounds to only 103. One Sunday morning, Ronnie got up and found his mother passed out on the kitchen floor. He could not revive her. His father had gone to sleep drunk on the couch the night before and was of no help.

Frantically, Ronnie called Murphy, who rushed across town. By the time he got there, Velma had come around. She had just fainted, she said. She'd be all right.

Murphy insisted on taking her to a hospital in Fayetteville. On the way, she burst into tears. She didn't know why she was crying; she just was. And she couldn't stop. At the emergency room, when a doctor tried to question her, she couldn't answer for crying. He admitted her and ordered a sedative and intravenous fluids.

The next morning, another doctor examined her, but Velma was still crying and couldn't talk to him either.

"I'm not going to be able to let you out of here until you can tell me what's wrong," he told her.

When he returned later that day, Velma had calmed, though she still frequently burst into tears. The doctor questioned her gently. Velma had been brought up to believe that a person did not talk about intimate problems outside the family. She had adhered to that despite all the troubles of her childhood, despite the collapse of her marriage. But this doctor seemed so understanding that she began to respond, tentatively telling him what had been going on in her life.

"I think you've had a nervous breakdown," she would recall him telling her. The stress had built up until her body couldn't take any more, he explained. "I'm going to keep you here until we can build you back up." He prescribed vitamin shots along with sedatives.

Velma remained in the hospital for a week. Before she was released, the doctor recommended that she seek professional guidance for her marital problems. To help her until she could work her way through the situation, he gave her a prescription for tranquilizers. Later, Velma would remember only that they were "little blue pills." She was supposed to take them regularly, but she didn't in the beginning.

Nor did she seek professional help for her marriage, and as a new year began nothing had changed. During much of 1968 Thomas would be out of work. His drinking and withdrawal would grow even worse. When Velma felt really low, she would take one of the tranquilizers. "I found I could cope better if I took it," she later recalled. "And then not just one, I knew that two would be better than one. I could feel that."

When the prescription ran out, she got it refilled. And when she could no longer get it refilled, she went to another doctor and got more prescriptions for tranquilizers, first for Librium, a milder predecessor of Valium, then for Valium. On occasion, she also got Butisol, a barbiturate sedative.

When she began having frequent severe headaches and trouble sleeping, she sought out still another doctor, who prescribed not only painkillers but more Valium and sleeping pills. She told none of the doctors about the others, nor about the other prescriptions she was taking. Neither did she tell her family. But they were soon to realize that her medicine taking was getting out of control.

At times Thomas would go for periods without drinking, as if he were trying to prove to himself that he could.

In the summer of 1968, he decided that he wanted the family to go to the mountains, where they once had gone regularly on vacation. Ronnie was working six days a week on a tobacco farm to help out with family expenses and couldn't go. Pam went with her parents, but the trip was miserable. Her father wasn't drinking, but her mother had taken so many pills that she had trouble getting out of the car at overlooks. For the first time Pam realized that her family's problems had been compounded.

Later in the summer, both Ronnie and Pam went to the beach on a one-day trip with their parents, Faye, and Velma's brother Jesse. Thomas did drink on that trip, so Velma took the wheel on the way back. She didn't tell anybody that she had taken extra pills. In St. Pauls, not far from home, she lost control of the car, careening through a gas station lot, nearly clipping the pumps before coming to rest against a bridge railing. A quickly sobered Thomas took the wheel the rest of the way home.

The misery of that year still had not peaked. Ronnie was soon to see just how ugly his parents' substance-abuse problems could get.

Thomas' behavior grew more bizarre the more he drank. At times he would sit in his car in the carport, drunk, revving the engine at full speed, sometimes until the car ran out of gas.

One Monday evening that fall, Thomas came home and sat in the carport racing the engine over and over. Finally, Ronnie went out to get him. "Daddy, stop it and come on inside," he pleaded from the passenger door.

"Leave me the hell alone!" Thomas snapped at him.

Ronnie walked around the car to the driver's side, reached through the open window, shut off the engine and took the keys.

"What the hell do you think you're doing?" his father yelled. "Give me back those goddamn keys!"

"I'm not giving you the keys," Ronnie said. "Come on in the house."

Ronnie started to return inside, but his father caught him at the back of the car and grabbed him by the shoulder. When Ronnie turned to face him, he saw that his father had a hawk-billed pocketknife in his hand, the blade open.

"I told you to give me those goddamned keys," Thomas told him, holding the knife only inches from his chest.

Startled, Ronnie blurted, "Daddy, don't do this."

Velma had come to the door by this time and saw what was happening. "Thomas, what are you doing?" she cried. "Please, put it down."

"Mama, don't come out here!" Ronnie called frantically.

"Not until he gives me those fucking keys," Thomas told Velma.

"Have you gone completely crazy?" she screamed.

Ronnie was scared, but he stared straight into his father's eyes. Never before had he seen him with such a wild look. But he dropped the keys in his jeans pocket. "If you want to cut me, go ahead," he told his daddy, "but I'm not giving you the keys."

Suddenly, the look in his father's eyes changed, as if he had just realized what he was doing. The wildness instantly dissolved into an overwhelming sadness. He closed the pocketknife, and without saying another word he staggered into the house, collapsed on the couch and went to sleep.

Despite the problems in his family, Ronnie continued to make straight A's in high school and to help his sister, who was struggling with her studies. Ronnie also had discovered athletic talent. A chain of miniature golf courses called Putt-Putt had started in nearby Fayetteville, and Ronnie went there often with friends. He entered his first tournament that summer and placed fourth. He went on to play in others and was always a top contender. Trophies began to line his bedroom dresser.

Pam, too, had found a sport in which she excelled. Like her mother before her, she loved basketball. Lean and rangy, she would be nearly six feet tall by the time she finished high school. She became a starter on her school's team in her freshman year. When the season began in her sophomore year in the fall of 1968, she was elected cocaptain. A shooting forward, she quickly became the team's leading scorer.

Ronnie was immensely proud of Pam, and he became the team's scorekeeper. Velma never missed one of Pam's games, always sitting at the same spot so Pam would know where to look for her, always cheering loudly. Pam longed deeply for her father to be proud of her, but he never came to see her play. He was still too humiliated by his brief commitment to the mental hospital. When Pam led her team to the conference championship game, Ronnie begged his daddy to come, but Thomas refused.

"Someday you're going to regret not seeing this girl play," Ronnie told him disgustedly.

Early in 1969, after many months without work, Thomas got another job at yet another textile plant, working the third shift. He would do his drinking when he got off at eight in the morning, sleep through the afternoon and early evening, go back to work at midnight.

Usually, the uneasy silences prevailed between Thomas and Velma, but now and then she still managed to provoke hostile exchanges. When she accosted him about his drinking now, however, he had an easy comeback: "You're just as bad about taking pills as I am about drinking."

Ronnie and Pam had to admit that was true. They had seen their mother just as unable to function as their father. Several times Ronnie had spoken to her about it. She had to have the medicine, she told him. He knew how bad her nerves were. It was the only way she could get by.

But she didn't have to take more than the doctor prescribed, Ronnie pointed out. She knew that, she told him. And she would do more to control her dosage.

In March, after Thomas staggered home drunk one Saturday night and a shouting match ensued, Velma told him that she was leaving. "I can't put up with this anymore," she screamed.

Thomas passed out on the couch while Velma, sobbing, was packing her clothes. She was going to her parents' house, and Pam was leaving with her.

"What are you going to do?" Velma asked Ronnie.

"Somebody's got to stay here and look after him," he said.

Thomas woke up with a severe hangover the next morning and went in search of aspirin. "Where's Pam and your mama?" he asked.

"They left," Ronnie said. "Mama's left you. She wants a divorce."

Thomas couldn't believe it. He professed no memory of the previous night, and Ronnie knew this probably was true. His father rarely remembered anything that happened during his drunken bouts. He grew morose and quiet, and Ronnie suggested that they drive to Fayetteville to have lunch.

"I never thought it would come to this," Thomas told his son as he picked at his food.

"Your drinking is what's caused it," Ronnie said.

Thomas came back with his familiar line about Velma's pills.

"Yes, but she's working on it, and you're not."

Thomas grew contrite. He would change, he promised. "I'd like to see us try to make it as a family again."

"Pam and I would, too," Ronnie told him. "It's been tough on us, you know."

"I know it has, and I'm going to make it better."

Ronnie later reported this to his mother, and after several days she and Pam returned. Velma knew how desperately Ronnie wanted them to be a family again. For a few days the fragile peace held. Thomas didn't drink; Velma didn't take as many pills. But they seemed unable to communicate any longer. Within a week the anger and shouting had returned, but that soon would be ended by a silence that would last forever.

On the weekend of April 19–20, Ronnie stayed with his grandparents. When things got bad at home, he and Pam knew that they always could find refuge at Murphy and Lillie's house.

Ronnie got up Monday morning and went to school without going home. He was in his last class when the town's fire siren went off, summoning the volunteer firefighters. The siren caused Ronnie no concern, and when school let out a half hour later, he waited outside for Pam. They usually walked home together. The two had crossed the school's broad front lawn when they heard a car horn. Ronnie was surprised to see his mother sitting in the front seat of a car belonging to a local merchant, Fred Bodenheimer. Mrs. Bodenheimer was behind the wheel. Ronnie could tell that his mother had been crying.

"What's wrong?" he asked, bending to the open window, but she began sobbing and couldn't answer.

"Get in," said Mrs. Bodenheimer, who was serving as Good Samaritan. "Your daddy's been in an accident. We've got to go."

She seemed extremely anxious, and Ronnie and Pam obeyed. Both realized from their mother's distress that the situation must be bad, but despite repeated questions they couldn't find out what had happened. Ronnie figured his father had been in another wreck.

"He's going to be okay," Mrs. Bodenheimer kept telling Velma, but she could not be consoled.

"I know he's not, I know he's not," she kept repeating, still sobbing.

They went first to Highsmith Hospital in Fayetteville, only to be told that Thomas had been there but had been taken to Cape Fear Valley Hospital. "They're better equipped to handle this type of emergency," a nurse told them.

That gave hope to Ronnie. It meant his father was alive.

At Cape Fear Valley, emergency room attendants told them that doctors were with Thomas and one would come to talk with them as soon as possible. Velma sank into a chair, still too distraught to be questioned. Ronnie paced in a hallway nearby, while Pam and Mrs. Bodenheimer attempted to calm his mother. Within minutes, Faye burst through the emergency room doors. She had been close to Velma and Thomas all her life and she was extremely emotional. Ronnie couldn't tell her anything and took her to his mother. Velma and Faye fell into each other's arms and while they cried, Mrs. Bodenheimer slipped away.

A couple of minutes later, Ronnie glanced into the lobby and saw Mrs. Bodenheimer talking with Ernest Hagins, Parkton's sole police officer and the father of Ronnie's best friend, Julius. Ronnie seized his chance to find out what had happened.

There had been a fire at his house, Hagins told him. Apparently his father had gone to sleep with a cigarette. Because he had been found unconscious on the floor near his bed, it looked as if he had awakened and tried to get out but had been overcome by smoke. His father didn't appear to be burned badly, Hagins said, but there had been a lot of smoke.

Soon after Ronnie returned to his mother, a doctor appeared, looking grave.

"Mrs. Burke?"

"Yes," Velma said expectantly, struggling to stand.

"I'm sorry, but there's nothing we can do for your husband."

Velma began moaning and sank backward. Ronnie and Faye grabbed her to keep her from collapsing. Pam burst into tears. Faye was sobbing. Ronnie stood for a moment in stunned disbelief, but he knew he could not collapse. He was just seventeen, still had a year to go in school, and suddenly he was the man in the family.

He put his arm around his mother. "I'm still here," he said. "Pam's still here. We'll make it somehow."

"Mrs. Burke, would you like something for your nerves?" a nurse asked, and Velma nodded. Ronnie knew that this was not what his mother needed. He had no idea what she might have already taken. But he said nothing, and the nurse soon appeared with a needle to give Velma a shot.

On the way home, before the shot had taken full effect, Ronnie was able to get a little out of his mother about what had happened.

His father had come home from work that morning and, as he often did, downed a six-pack of beer before going to bed. Monday was Velma's day off, and after lunch she left the house to go to the laundromat. After putting the clothes in the machines, she drove to her mother's house. Olive's daughter, Robin, was there, and she went with Velma when she returned to the laundromat to put the clothes in the dryers. Velma drove home, less than a mile away, to wait until the clothes dried. When she opened the door leading from the kitchen to the carport, she discovered the house was filled with smoke. She slammed the door and ran into the yard yelling that the house was on fire.

Thomas' sister, Frances, who lived close by, was passing in her car. She stopped, and Velma frantically told her what had happened. Frances summoned the volunteer firemen and rescue squad.

The firemen and investigators had left by the time Ronnie, his mother and sister got home, but several cars were at Thomas' mother's house next door. Word of Thomas' death had preceded them, and family, friends and neighbors were gathering.

Ronnie sensed the tension in his grandmother's house as soon as they entered. Within minutes, Thomas' family began questioning Velma, and Ronnie could tell by their tone that they thought his mother's absence had contributed to his daddy's death.

"I've always done all I could for Thomas," Velma kept saying.

Ronnie's anger flared but he held his tongue. How could they blame his mother when it was his father's drinking that had killed him? He had to get out of that house, and the arrival of his friend Julius Hagins gave him the excuse. He stepped onto the porch with Julius, but as they stood talking, Ronnie's eyes were drawn to his house.

Unexpectedly, he found himself striding determinedly across the field toward the house, wishing as he went that he had not spent the weekend away from home. He couldn't even picture his last image of his father. What had he been doing? What had they last said to one another? Whatever it was, it hadn't seemed important at the time. Now it was vitally so, and he couldn't remember. He had reached the carport when a familiar voice stopped him.

"Ronnie!"

He turned and saw his grandfather hurrying toward him.

"Are you going in there?" Murphy asked.

Ronnie nodded.

"Are you sure you want to?"

"Yeah, I want to see it."

"I'll go with you then."

Ax marks scarred the kitchen door where the firemen had chopped it open. That was strange, Ronnie thought. Had his mother locked the door when she closed it?

The sun was setting, and electricity had been shut off to the house. Soot covered everything inside, making the house seem even darker. The acrid smell of smoke was nearly overwhelming. The floor was standing in water. No sign of fire damage was evident, however, until they started down the hallway and caught a glimpse of his parents' bedroom. The mattress where his father had been sleeping was as charred as a slice of burned toast. Ronnie's own room, just across the hallway, was blackened, all of his clothes and possessions ruined.

As Ronnie surveyed the damage, he suddenly remembered the pets, the family's Siamese cat, Sadie, and Termite, the poodle they were keeping for his mother's sister, Arlene. Nobody had said a word about them, and he hadn't seen them anywhere. He found them under Pam's bed, huddled side by side, dead, like his father, from the smoke.

Ronnie's first tears came as he carried Sadie from the house. She was his daddy's cat really. She loved to curl up in his lap while he watched TV, or lie beside him as he slept on the couch. She usually woke him, licking his face until he stirred.

With help from his grandfather and his friend, Ronnie buried Sadie and Termite in the back yard, and as he shoveled the dirt on the graves, he felt almost as if he were burying his father as well.

The funeral was at Parkton Baptist Church on Wednesday, one month before Thomas' thirty-eighth birthday. He was buried only a few feet from his father in the town's small cemetery, within sight of the big white house where he and his wife and children had spent the years of their greatest happiness.

Volunteers had cleaned and made emergency repairs to the Burke house, allowing Velma and the children to continue to stay there, and that night, in the lonely period after all the visitors had departed, Ronnie and his mother sat at the kitchen table drinking coffee and talking. His mother had taken his father's death hard, and Ronnie was worried about her. He knew that she would be looking to him for stability, for guidance, that she would be more dependent on him than ever.

She shouldn't pay attention to anything her in-laws had said, Ronnie told her. She couldn't have known that something like that might happen. And she shouldn't feel bad about not being able to save his daddy. If she had tried, she probably would be dead herself.

Ronnie thought that his mother should go back to work immediately. He and Pam would return to school. Resuming normal activities and staying busy would help to keep their minds off their grief.

"We've got to move on from this," he said.

And then words came that he hadn't intended to speak: "At least Daddy's drinking won't be a problem anymore."

Although he felt too much guilt to admit it, from the moment he had learned of his father's death, despite the pain, he had felt a wave of relief. Perhaps peace and happiness could now be restored in his family.

"I know," his mother said, "but I'd rather have him here drinking than dead."

For a moment Ronnie fell silent, ashamed of his thoughts. Then he took his mother's hand. "Mama, it's going to take time," he said, "but everything's going to be better."

CHAPTER 5

In the weeks following his father's death, Ronnie still had confidence that his mother could rid herself of drugs (the source of her problems was gone, after all). He pushed her into activity to take her mind, as well as his own, off what had happened. Together, they handled the estate, filed for Thomas' small life insurance policy, which barely covered the funeral costs, dealt with insurance adjusters, oversaw the repairing of the house, consolidated some of the debts that had piled up in all the months that Thomas had not worked, and applied for monthly Social Security benefits for Ronnie and Pam—Velma could collect those until each was eighteen.

Dealing with such matters helped Ronnie, but he still couldn't believe that his father was gone. He felt guilty that he had not been able to do more to help him see what his drinking was doing to him, where it was leading them all. Pam had a far harder time adjusting. For weeks she regularly closed herself in her room and cried.

After school let out in June, Ronnie returned to work full-time for the farmer who had employed him the year before. Pam got a summer job at the Belk's store with her mother. She had worked there during the two previous Christmas seasons. Velma still got up and went to work, but she had to fortify herself with pills to face each day.

Ronnie had no idea how many prescriptions she had from how many doctors, or how much of each she was taking every day, but he knew that too often she was taking too much. Despite his confidence that she wouldn't need so much medicine once the shock of his father's death had passed, she seemed to require more and more.

Pam knew that people at work were talking about her mother's drug taking. At times Velma seemed listless, disinterested, inattentive to her duties. Her speech was occasionally slurred. Velma's boss, D. N. Geddie, was aware of these problems as well, Pam knew, and she told Ronnie her concerns. Ronnie, too, had worked at Belk's during Christmas, and he knew Geddie thought highly of his mother. She'd always been a good employee. She even had risen to the position of buyer until the strain had grown too much and she had requested to be assigned again as a sales clerk. He was sure that Geddie was aware of all that his mother had gone through and would be tolerant.

Still, Ronnie gently warned his mother that she had better watch herself. She didn't want to risk losing her job. Velma assured him that while she was working she would never take more medicine than the doctor prescribed. But although Ronnie didn't yet realize it, that was something she no longer could control, for she already was addicted to her primary medication, Valium.

Although people around the world were now gobbling down Valium in ever increasing quantities (billions of pills each year, reaching a nadir of some seven billion by 1975 when one out of every dozen people in the United States would be taking it), another decade would pass before alarms would be sounded about its dangers and steps taken to curtail its usage. By then, millions of people, most of them women, including the former First Lady Betty Ford, would be addicted. Not until the eighties would it be fully understood that a normally prescribed dosage taken over a period of only four months could prove addicting to some people, and that combining Valium with alcohol and other drugs could be deadly.

Only then would doctors begin to learn that Valium accumulated in the fatty tissues of the body, creating a tolerance that demanded higher and higher dosages to achieve the same effect. And while the side effects of Valium usage—drowsiness, lethargy, slurred speech, loss of coordination, concentration, memory and sexual desire—were known (and Velma had suffered most, if not all), doctors were then unaware of some of its other effects on the addicted. Those included confusion, depression, nightmares, sleeplessness, suicidal thoughts, hallucinations, delusion, paranoia, hostility, and, for some, rage that could erupt in violence.

Withdrawal from Valium could be as difficult as withdrawing from heroin, causing headaches, nausea, insomnia, trembling, sweating, cramps, panics, even psychosis.

But in the early years of Valium's distribution, it still was seen as a harmless feel-good drug that relieved doctors of many problems, and they prescribed it freely. Anybody who went to a doctor with a complaint of anxiety was apt to leave with a prescription for Valium, refillable for up to a year. Bothersome patients who came frequently with vague maladies went away happy with Valium and often didn't return until the prescription needed to be renewed, making the doctor happy as well.

Velma never had a problem getting doctors to prescribe Valium for her, and as time went on and she needed more and more, she just acquired more doctors. Manipulating physicians became almost second nature to her. She became expert in describing symptoms and masking her drug intake. In the nine years between Thomas' death and her arrest, she would get prescriptions from more than two dozen doctors, not only for Valium but for nearly two dozen other drugs, most of them also addictive, including barbiturates, narcotics, sleeping pills, stimulants and antidepressants, all of them prescribed by doctors trying to be helpful, and all of them dangerous and unpredictable when combined with Valium.

On September 28, five months after Thomas' death, one of Velma's friends at Belk's, Pauline Barfield, who worked in the department next to hers, died suddenly from a cerebral hemorrhage. Older than Velma, Pauline had six children and six grandchildren. All but two of her children, both daughters, were grown and gone from home, and one of them soon would be entering college. Pauline's husband, Jennings, had been a civil service worker with the Army Corps of Engineers at Fort Bragg, but emphysema and diabetes had forced him to take medical disability retirement while he was still in his forties, and he had since developed heart problems.

Jennings had frequently stopped by Belk's to see his wife, and he often took time to chat with Velma. She thought he was a nice man, sweet-natured and good-hearted, and she knew how devoted he was to his wife. Ironically, Pauline had always worried so much about his health, but it was she who died unexpectedly.

Velma knew what a shock his wife's death must be to Jennings, and she went to the funeral home to offer her condolences. He was touched. He knew that she had recently lost Thomas.

Velma had no idea that she would ever see Jennings again after Pauline's funeral, but one day early in 1970 she glanced up and saw him standing there, looking forlorn despite his smile. They chatted about how each was doing, she would later remember, and talked about Pauline. Velma could tell that he missed her terribly and that he was lost and lonely without her. She was surprised that he'd even been able to come into the store because it had to stir memories of happier times.

Velma told him how thoughtful he was to come by, and that it was good to see him. As he started to leave, he turned as if he'd forgotten something, hesitated, then said, "Would you like to go get something to eat after work?"

Surprised, Velma told him that would be nice.

After that day Jennings began regularly dropping by to see her, and several times they went out to eat.

She didn't tell her children about it. She wasn't sure how they would react. After all, their father had been dead only a matter of months, and here she was going out with another man.

Seeing Jennings did not affect the cycle of Velma's addiction. She still had good days and bad, days when she took too many pills and days when she didn't. At times she seemed perfectly normal.

That fall she began complaining of a kidney condition. Once a week, sometimes more often, Velma would wake Ronnie at two or three in the morning and tell him she couldn't stand the pain. He'd have to take her to St. Pauls, ten miles away, to see a doctor who had been treating her for many years. Because he didn't feel comfortable leaving Pam alone, Ronnie would wake her and make her go with them. His mother would call before they left, and the doctor would be waiting on the curb in front of his house, satchel in hand.

"It's that ol' kidney colic again, Doctor," Velma would tell him.

The doctor would give her a shot, and often Velma would be asleep before they got back home.

Pam became especially irritated about these frequent middle-of-the-night trips. She had trouble enough in class without going sleepless, and she especially needed her rest during basketball season. She was leading her team to another conference championship, and during a home game against Magnolia High she scored forty-three points, a school record that would be standing nearly three decades later.

Velma still came to all of her games, but there were times that season when Pam wished that she hadn't. When she looked into the stands to see if her mother was in her familiar spot, she became anxious about the shape she was in. One night when the coach benched Pam after a foul, Velma made her way down from the stands and stood screaming at him. Pam wanted to run to the locker room and hide.

Velma always encouraged her children to talk to her about anything that was bothering them. As a girl, she had longed to have somebody to talk to about her own problems. Yet when Ronnie tried talking to her about her drug taking, she became defensive.

Doctors wouldn't prescribe that medicine if she didn't need it, she snapped at him. But doctors didn't tell her to take more than they prescribed, he countered calmly. Only reluctantly would Velma acknowledge that she sometimes took too much. She would promise to control herself, but the same patterns always returned.

"The drugs just helped me cope, I thought," Velma would say later. "I felt that I had to have them. I lived for them from day to day."

Ronnie and Pam began considering other measures for controlling their mother's drug taking. They tried seizing all of her medicines and doling them out only as prescribed. But they soon discovered that she was getting more prescriptions and hiding the pills. She hid them all over her body, in her bra, even in her hair curlers.

At one point that year, Ronnie and Pam drove to St. Pauls and talked to the doctor who seemed to be her major provider. They told him about the situation and asked him not to give Velma so many prescriptions. The doctor heard them out, then told them that their mother had conditions that required treatment and he could not ignore them.

Meanwhile, bills for medicines and doctors piled up faster than Velma could pay.

Perhaps if Ronnie hadn't had so much upheaval in his life, he would have been valedictorian of his graduating class. He missed by only a few points. Even so, as salutatorian he used his opening remarks at commencement to salute his mother. Tears flowed from Velma's eyes as Ronnie credited her for being responsible for all he was or ever would be. It was she who had stressed the importance of studying hard, who had instilled genuine values in him. He would be forever indebted to her. Nobody in the crowd was left with any doubt that Ronnie loved his mother dearly.

Traditionally, graduating students at Parkton School took off for a weekend of partying at Carolina Beach as soon as commencement ended. Ronnie had arranged a room with his buddies Julius Hagins and Oscar Everett. Juniors sometimes went, too, and Pam was going with a group of her friends.

She had already left when Ronnie's buddies drove him to his house to get his bag. Julius and Oscar waited in the car while Ronnie went inside. His mother had been crying.

"What's wrong?" he asked.

"Nothing."

"Something's wrong."

"I'm just a little bit sad."

"Why?" Ronnie said. "You've got every reason to be happy."

"I guess I just never wanted y'all to grow up and go away."

She burst into tears again and Ronnie embraced her. "I'm not going anywhere, Mama," he assured her.

A few minutes later, Ronnie went outside and told his friends to go ahead without him. His mother wasn't feeling well, he said, and he didn't want to leave her alone.

That night, they sat at the kitchen table talking. Velma told him how proud she was of him. "I know I rode you hard to make good grades," she said. "It'll pay off for you one day."

They stayed up late, reminiscing, laughing. Ronnie couldn't remember when he'd seen his mother happier. The evening was far more satisfying, he realized, than partying at the beach ever could be. A few weeks earlier, for Mother's Day, Ronnie had bought his mother a Jimmy Dean record called "I.O.U.," a country boy's recitation of lasting debt to his mother. Velma had cried when she first listened to it. Now Ronnie played it for her again, and she cried just as hard.

That was truly how he felt about her, Ronnie told her, holding her hand. Wherever their lives took them from here on, he assured her, he never would be able to repay what he owed her. She could always depend on him, no matter what. He could not have dreamed at the time what a price that promise would put on his future.

Ronnie got a job that summer at the Pepsi Cola bottling plant where his father once had worked. His supervisor had been his father's, and he still spoke highly of him.

"You sling Pepsis just like your daddy," he told Ronnie as he trained him.

Only a couple of weeks after Ronnie started the job, his supervisor met his truck when he came in at day's end.

"How about I give you a ride home today?" he said, a somber look on his face.

Ronnie was frightened. "Is something wrong? Is my mom okay?"

"Yeah, she's fine. There's been an accident. Your house has burned again."

The supervisor was concerned that Ronnie might not be able to handle another fire so soon after the one that had taken his father's life. They arrived to find Velma standing in the front yard with Jennings Barfield and his daughter Nancy. The smell of smoke hit Ronnie as soon as he got out of the car, and it immediately took him back to the day his father died.

This time the damage was far more extensive. The fire had been concentrated in Ronnie's room, and everything in it was destroyed: his clothes, books, typewriter, his golfing trophies, all his graduation presents, including the new set of golf clubs his Aunt Arlene and Uncle Erroll had given him. The volunteer firemen determined that the fire had begun near an electrical outlet under Ronnie's desk and theorized that a wiring problem had been the cause.

Ronnie could not understand how such awful things could keep happening to his mother. How much more could she take? Everything would be fine, he told her. The house could be repaired, the insurance would pay. It would just take time. This was not a disaster, only a setback. Meanwhile, Velma, Ronnie and Pam moved in with Murphy and Lillie.

By the spring, Ronnie and Pam had become aware that their mother had been seeing Jennings Barfield occasionally, but they thought this was just two lonely friends with similar losses comforting one another. Ronnie realized before Pam that the relationship was growing deeper than that, but he still was taken aback in July when Velma told him that she and Jennings were going to be married. Although years later Velma would acknowledge that she never loved Jennings, had merely felt sorry for him, she now assured Ronnie that she did. She knew that Ronnie would understand her desire to get married again—and he did—but she was concerned about telling Pam. And with good reason. Pam was outraged when she learned about it.

Her daddy was hardly a year in his grave and her mother was marrying somebody else! How could she do that? If it was her blessing that Velma was seeking, Pam made clear, it would be a long time coming. Nobody—*nobody!*—would ever replace her daddy.

Although Pam deeply loved her mother, she had always been strong-willed, and the two sometimes clashed. This was more than a clash, however. It quickly became a widening rift.

Ronnie didn't want any more discord. He was happy that his mother was moving on with her life. Perhaps a new marriage would bring her drug taking under control. After all, she always seemed to take less when she knew she would be seeing Jennings. Ronnie tried to win Pam over, but she remained adamantly opposed to the marriage, and she and Velma frequently had words about it.

Pam was as opposed for Jennings' sake as for her own. She was convinced that no matter how many promises her mother made she would not stop abusing drugs without far stronger intervention than she and Ronnie had mustered. Jennings, she knew, was a sick man. He wouldn't be able to deal with that. And while she knew Jennings was aware that Velma took medicines, she was certain that he had no idea how bad it was.

Pam felt that he should know, and she called Jennings and asked to talk with him. He came to her grandparents' house, and the two sat in lawn chairs under the pecan tree. Pam told him that she liked him, had nothing against him, appreciated the kindness he was showing her mother. But the marriage, she thought, was not best for either of them.

Jennings listened thoughtfully as Pam went on to relate her mother's problems, but she could tell that he didn't believe her.

"You know," he responded, "I have a daughter who's opposed to this marriage, too."

His eldest daughter, Ellen, was against it as much as she was, he told her, and while he and Velma respected both, they had to make the decision that they deemed best for them. He loved Velma, he said, and she loved him, and he was certain that they could make each other happy and handle whatever problems they might encounter.

Pam saw that her effort had been futile, but at least, she thought, he couldn't say he hadn't been warned.

The wedding was set for August 23, 1970. This time Velma would have the church wedding she'd dreamed about as a girl but had been denied when she married Thomas. Encouraged by Ronnie, Pam reluctantly accepted the inevitable and even agreed to take part in the ceremony at Jennings' church, Carroll Memorial Baptist in Fayetteville.

For her wedding dress Velma chose a pink suit, honoring the memory of her childhood pink dress. She also wore a pink pillbox hat with a veil, pink shoes and a pink corsage. Jennings, more than sixteen years Velma's senior, was only fifty-four, but he looked older, distinguished and grandfatherly in his light summer suit. Both families attended, as did friends of Pauline and Thomas.

Ronnie had cautioned his mother about getting nervous and taking too much medicine before the wedding, and he was pleased that she took his warning to heart. The ceremony came off without any hitches, and all of the guests gathered for a reception in the church fellowship hall, which was decorated with pink carnations, pink gladiolus and pink roses. The cake was trimmed with pink icing, and the fruit punch, too, was pink.

Velma's brother Tyrone took home movies of the reception. Throughout it, Velma was smiling and laughing. She looked almost radiant, Ronnie thought. He even allowed himself to hope that this new beginning might set her on a different path and bring her the happiness she deserved.

Jennings lived in a modest white house on Natal Street across from the Purolator plant in Fayetteville. Velma moved in with him and his daughter Nancy, who was sixteen. Velma's own house had been repaired by this time, and she had rented it.

Pam, who still had a year to go in high school, decided to live with her grandparents so she could stay in Parkton. Ronnie, too, was staying there temporarily. He soon would be going to college, something he had not dreamed possible. And he had his mother to thank for it.

Ronnie hadn't even applied to any colleges because he knew he couldn't afford tuition. Despite his good grades and the desire of some of his teachers to help him, scholarships were rare at that time for students at small-town schools in eastern North Carolina. Even so, before her wedding, Velma urged him to apply. She had talked to Jennings, she said, and he was willing to pay for at least one semester. Ronnie did as his mother said and was quickly accepted by the University of South Carolina. He had been a long-time fan of the university's basketball team.

Soon after the wedding, Velma and Jennings drove Ronnie to Columbia to enroll. But when time came to pay tuition, Velma looked at Jennings, who said nothing and made no move to produce the money.

Ronnie quickly realized that there had been a drastic misunderstanding. Jennings seemed unaware that he was to pay. And neither Ronnie nor his mother had the money. Not wanting to put any stress on his mother's new marriage, Ronnie moved to alleviate the uncomfortable situation.

"I'll talk to the financial aid office," he told his mother.

He went ahead and checked into the dorm, and Jennings and Velma returned home. Over the weekend Ronnie mulled over what to do. He wondered if in her desire for him to continue his education, his mother hadn't just fabricated the whole situation, thinking that if she got him there, Jennings surely would pay. Or perhaps the drugs she was taking made her delusional.

When Ronnie talked with the financial aid office on Monday, he discovered that no money was available. He had no choice but to withdraw. Not wanting to bother his mother and Jennings, he called Velma's brother Jimmy, who lived in Lancaster, sixty miles away, and asked if he would come to get him. When Jimmy asked why he was leaving, Ronnie told him that he was just homesick.

After returning to his grandparents' house, Ronnie called his mother to tell her he was back. "Don't worry," she assured him. "You'll get back there. I want you to go to college."

Ronnie, in the meantime, was faced with a harsh reality. The Vietnam War still raged, and many young men from Robeson County had already gone off to fight—and die—in it. Ronnie knew that without a student deferment he soon would be drafted. Though he went to work at a gas station in Parkton owned by Pam's basketball coach, he soon began talking to military recruiters. He wanted to see Pam through her final basketball season before taking any action. The coach let him remain as scorekeeper for the team. And his mother still continued to come to all the games, despite the long drive.

Velma's growing addiction compelled her to keep finding new sources for drugs, and just eleven days after her wedding, she went to Jennings' doctor, Neil Worden, complaining of migraine headaches. He gave her painkillers. A month later, Jennings had to bring her to the emergency room, and Worden was summoned. "She couldn't even stand up, and she couldn't talk," the doctor later recalled. "Her pupils were dilated." He diagnosed an overdose and admitted her to the hospital overnight. The next day Jennings drove Velma straight to her parents' house. He didn't know what to do with her, he told Lillie. He couldn't deal with it.

Ronnie was distressed when he found out what had happened. He knew that drugs kept his mother from considering the consequences of her actions, and he had another of his long talks with her, insisting that she had to get control if she wanted this marriage to succeed. She acknowledged that he was right and promised to try harder. After a few days Jennings came for her and took her back home.

Shortly afterward, Dr. Worden received a call from a pharmacist that Velma was getting refills on some of Jennings' medicines more frequently than he should be needing them. Certain that Velma was taking the medicines herself, Worden called Jennings to tell him, but Jennings didn't want to believe it.

In November, after Velma had been taken to the hospital with another overdose, Jennings called Ronnie and asked him to come over. Nancy was upset and wanted to talk to him. She and Ronnie had become friends—he had taken her to play miniature golf—and they got away from their parents to talk. Velma was drugged up all the time, Nancy told Ronnie. She staggered around and fell and sometimes couldn't talk. They couldn't keep pills away from her. They found them stashed all over the house. Ronnie knew that Nancy was undergoing what he and Pam had been suffering so long, and his heart went out to her. Her father was the sick one, Nancy went on. Velma should be looking after him instead of the other way around. He was too feeble to pick her up off the floor when she fell, too weak to drag her to the bed. Nancy was afraid that the strain of her father's struggle to care for Velma was going to kill him.

Ronnie apologized and promised to do what he could. Once again he talked with his mother.

"He still wants you to be his wife," he told her, "but he can't keep putting up with this. If you want this marriage to succeed, you're going to have to get yourself clean."

"I know I need to do better," she said, crying. "I do want it to work."

Even if his mother was floundering, early in December, Ronnie made a decision about his own life. With the draft closing in, he enlisted in the Army for four years, a year longer than the normal enlistment, so that he could be trained as an Army security specialist. But he had the enlistment deferred until the basketball season ended.

In February, Jennings took Velma to the hospital after yet another overdose. This time she was kept for nearly a week. When Ronnie went to see her, she told him that the marriage had been a mistake. Although Jennings had to use a respirator for his emphysema, he still smoked and sometimes passed out before she could get oxygen to him, she complained. He wouldn't watch his diet despite his diabetes, and that caused additional problems. Taking care of an invalid husband was more than she had bargained for. He wouldn't listen to a thing she said, and they frequently argued. She was clearly miserable.

Ronnie reminded her that she had known about Jennings' conditions before she got married. She had to expect some adversity. She needed to try harder.

Jennings took Velma back home from the hospital, but by this time he, too, had realized that the marriage was a mistake. He had led an upright life. He was a devout churchgoer, a Mason. He cared what people thought of him. He knew that people were talking about Velma's behavior and it bothered him.

After this overdose, Dr. Worden had another talk with Jennings about the seriousness of Velma's drug problem. This time Jennings did not doubt him. He told Worden that he was thinking about divorce.

In the meantime, Pam's team won the county championship for the third straight year, and Pam, at center, was named most valuable player. Ronnie couldn't have been prouder. Soon he would be leaving for the Army, and he knew that he would miss his sister deeply.

Velma grew more despondent as Ronnie's enlistment date neared, and she was even more unhappy in her marriage. Jennings was no less miserable. On Friday, March 19, he drove to a son's house and called a lawyer to talk about divorce. He made an appointment for Monday morning.

On Sunday night, Velma called Ronnie at her parents' house. She was at Cape Fear Valley Hospital again, but this time she was not the patient. Jennings had gotten very sick, she said, and she'd had to bring him to the hospital.

"Are you okay?" he asked. "Do you need me to come?"

"No, I'll be all right," she said.

Ronnie heard no more that night and assumed everything was okay. But the next day his mother called him at the gas station just before noon. She was crying. Jennings had died an hour earlier, she told him. His weakened heart had just given out. Ronnie, who ran the gas station alone, told her that he would be there as soon as he could arrange to get away.

How could one person have such an incredible run of misfortune? he asked himself. Why his mother? How much more could she be expected to endure?

CHAPTER 6

Disgust with the war in Vietnam was mounting early in 1971 as Lieutenant William Calley was tried for the massacre of civilians at My Lai three years earlier. In May, thousands of antiwar demonstrators would be arrested as they attempted to bring traffic and government activities to a halt in Washington. But in deeply patriotic Robeson County, with its close connections to Fort Bragg, the disgust was with the antiwar protestors and with an army that would make a scapegoat of a lowly lieutenant while exonerating his superior officers.

Ronnie was as patriotic as anybody in Robeson County and felt a deep obligation to serve his country, even if it meant going to war. But presented with a choice between his country and his mother, as he would be soon after Jennings Barfield's death, he had little doubt about which he would choose.

His mother was not handling Jennings' death well. She had been almost too drugged to attend the funeral, and afterward Ronnie helped her move back into her parents' home, where he and Pam still were living. Ronnie was scheduled to leave for basic training in only twelve days, but his mother took to bed with her medicines, pleading with him not to go. She needed him now more than ever, she said, and she didn't know how she could make it without him.

Ronnie didn't know what to do. He'd signed a contract. But he didn't want to leave his mother in this condition. Perhaps he could get a delay. He talked with his recruiter but got little encouragement. His enlistment had already been deferred. Still, Ronnie decided to try to get out of his contract. He got teachers, doctors and others to write letters to the Army explaining all the illness, loss and heartbreak his mother had undergone, asking that his obligation be dismissed. He even lined up a job at a furniture plant in Tabor City that would pay him $100 a week. His prospective boss also petitioned the Army on his behalf.

The Army was not swayed, and on April 7, nine days after Lieutenant Calley's conviction, Ronnie was sent to Fort Jackson, South Carolina, near Columbia. Velma was distraught when he left. How could the government be so cruel? How could the Army need Ronnie more than she did?

Jennings had bought Velma a car, a year-old Maverick, and three different times while Ronnie was in basic training, she drove to Fort Jackson to see him on the weekends that he was allowed visitors. No other recruit in his company had such visits from his mother.

When Pam's graduation from Parkton School came, Ronnie was in the last stages of his training and couldn't attend. He had to settle for calling to congratulate her. In mid-June, Velma and her brother John drove to Fort Jackson for Ronnie's graduation, and he returned home for two weeks of leave before reporting to the Army Security Agency School at Fort Devens, Massachusetts, in July.

By this time, Velma and Pam had moved back into the twice-burned house that Thomas had built for them. Velma's condition seemed improved while Ronnie was at home, but after he began training at Fort Devens to become a code interceptor, the situation quickly worsened.

Velma got one of her doctors, Roscoe McMillan of Red Springs, to write to the Army on her behalf.

"This certifies that Mrs. Velma Barfield is suffering from a complete nervous breakdown due partly to the sudden death of her husband and the induction into the Army of her son, Ronald," he wrote. "The purpose of this letter is to inform you of the above circumstances and if possible to work some solution out in which Private Burke can be discharged to support his mother and sister."

Ronnie's support was needed because Velma's drug swings had been interfering with her work. At Jennings' request, Velma had quit her job during their marriage, but now she was back at Belk's. Frequently, though, she was unable to go in because she took too many pills. And her doctor and drug bills continued to grow. In late July, she borrowed $800 from a Fayetteville bank to pay some of them.

In August Velma called the Robeson County Sheriff's Depart-

ment to report a break-in at her house. Alf Parnell investigated. He
found the screen cut on the window of Ronnie's bedroom, the window open, a pane broken. Ronnie's room was in disarray. Velma
told Parnell that five $100 bills—part of the money she had bor-
rowed—had been stolen from beneath the mattress in Ronnie's
room. Some of Ronnie's clothing and shoes also were missing, she
said. No charges would ever come from the report, but Velma filed
for homeowner's insurance.

Ronnie heard about this by telephone, as he was hearing of all
of his mother's problems, but it would be many years before he
realized that she likely was staging such events not only to get
money but to bring him back to her. This time she was even more
insistent that he try to get out of the Army and return home. Ronnie thought his chances of getting a hardship discharge unlikely but
promised to try again.

By fall, Velma's performance at work had grown so bad that her
boss, D. N. Geddie, removed her from contact with customers,
with whom she frequently was testy and argumentative. But Geddie was sympathetic to Velma, and instead of firing her, he reassigned her to the stockroom, marking prices.

Pam, meanwhile, had been unable to find a job since graduation.
On Thursday, October 14, Velma planned to take her to put in
applications at several businesses before going to work. Velma lingered inside after Pam had gone to the car, but Pam thought nothing about it at the time.

When they returned a couple of hours later, they found fire
trucks at the house and firefighters cleaning up inside. Pam could
not believe it. A third fire in just two and a half years. Surely, this
house was cursed. Velma went to pieces, Pam would later recall,
and neither she nor anybody else could console her.

Later, when Velma called Ronnie to tell him what happened, she
begged. "Can't you come home? My nerves are just completely
tore up."

Ronnie applied for emergency leave, and two days later he
arrived to his mother's welcome embrace. Velma and Pam had once
again moved in with Murphy and Lillie, but things were not well
there either.

During the summer Murphy had come down with laryngitis that
wouldn't go away. He had reluctantly gone to a doctor, who had
given him antibiotics and throat spray. Still, he had been slow to

recover, and even after the laryngitis passed, he had trouble swallowing and developed breathing problems and pains in his chest and right side. Doctors were uncertain about his problem, but for most of his adult life Murphy had smoked unfiltered cigarettes. He checked into a hospital for tests that fall and was told that his problems were due to angina. While Ronnie was at home, though, Murphy rallied. Velma was not rebounding, however, despite Ronnie's presence and his promise to press for a hardship discharge. While he was home, he began collecting the necessary paperwork for the discharge: letters from his mother, his grandparents, her doctors; death certificates for his father and stepfather.

His efforts became even more urgent after D. N. Geddie called to tell him that he was going to have to let Velma go. She was out of work too often, sometimes unable to function when she was there. She was even having prescriptions delivered to the store. He was sorry, he said. He'd given her every chance to work out her problems, but the situation appeared hopeless. Ronnie understood—he was beginning to feel the same way himself.

Ronnie did not want to leave his mother in this situation. It was not only her drug use, her poor health, the loss of her job, that concerned him. The latest fire and the break in before it made him wonder if his mother hadn't been targeted by somebody. But by whom? And for what reason? He questioned her, but she had no answers.

"I just can't understand why all these things are going on," she said.

Ironically, Velma's ploys to bring Ronnie back only led him further from her. On a Friday night while he was home he went to a high school football game between Rowland and Red Springs. One of his cousins played for Red Springs. At the game another cousin introduced him to a friend, Joanna McCollum.*

Joanna was a senior in high school. She had a thin, pretty face, straight brown hair to her waist, an artist's temperament and a dark sense of humor. Ronnie was taken with her immediately. He had dated in high school, usually double-dating with Pam, but he had never had a serious girlfriend. He asked Joanna out, and she accepted. When he had to return to Fort Devens, she told him she would write. He went back to his Army duties with another hopeful reason for seeking a discharge.

As soon as he got back, Ronnie arranged for an allotment from his pay to be sent monthly to his mother and informed his superiors that he would be seeking a hardship discharge.

At the beginning of November, Pam moved to Lancaster to live with Velma's brother Jimmy. He owned a Tom's franchise, selling peanuts, candies, crackers and other snacks, and offered her a job tending a vending machine route. She, too, would be able to send money back to her mother. With the income from her children and unemployment benefits, Velma could get by temporarily.

Before Ronnie could complete all the necessary paperwork to apply for his discharge, he got more bad news. His training was soon to be complete, and in mid-November he got orders for Vietnam. He was to report at the end of January. Although the United States was cutting troop strength in Vietnam, the long-promised end to the war was still not in sight.

Ronnie put off calling his mother. He knew this had been her greatest fear. Her best friend, Nellie Wallace, had lost a son in Vietnam, a helicopter pilot. He wasn't sure that his mother could take the news, but she had to know sooner or later, and after a few days he gathered his nerve and called home.

"Well, the thing we've been worried about has happened," he said. "I've got my orders. I'm going to Vietnam."

"Oh, no!" Velma cried. "No! I knew this was going to happen. I knew it." She burst into tears. "If you go over there, you're going to be killed!"

"You don't know that, Mama," Ronnie said. "You've got to have some faith. I'm in the Army and I've got to do what they tell me to do."

"You can't go!" she insisted. "I can't let them do that to you."

What about the hardship discharge? she wanted to know.

It hadn't gone anywhere yet, Ronnie told her. They still wanted more paperwork.

"You've got to get that."

On November 29, Ronnie completed the discharge application. His commanding officer approved it, noting that Ronnie was a fine soldier with excellent ratings in conduct and efficiency, and sent it up the chain of command. Now the anxious waiting began, and, the Army being the Army, nobody could predict how long it would last.

At Christmas, Ronnie went home again on leave and found the conditions of both his mother and grandfather greatly deteriorated.

His grandfather looked terrible. He was wasting away, and the doctors were unable to explain why. He had been forced to quit work a month earlier, but he didn't want to file for medical disability. He was not a man to accept "handouts," as he called it. Besides, he fully intended to return to work just as soon as he could get over whatever was dragging him down.

Murphy's illness and Ronnie's imminent departure for war threw a pall over Christmas. Velma's anxiety was causing her to take even more pills. At least Ronnie got to see Joanna a couple of times before returning to Fort Devens after New Year's, the only bright moments of his holidays.

After Ronnie's departure, Velma fell into even deeper depression. Her drug taking and despondency grew by the day.

Lillie, who had more than she could handle just trying to take care of Murphy, didn't know what to do. After Velma had been three days in bed, unable to get up, Lillie called the rescue squad. Velma was taken to the emergency room at Cape Fear Valley Hospital in Fayetteville on January 19, then transferred by ambulance to the mental health unit at Southeastern Hospital in Lumberton, where the county would help to pay for her treatment. There she told a psychiatrist that she had taken an overdose to commit suicide because she couldn't face seeing her son killed in Vietnam. After fifteen days she was released.

Ronnie's orders were put on hold until a decision could be reached on his discharge. Not until March 1 did he get a ruling. He called his mother to tell her that he had good news and bad. The bad news was that his discharge had been denied. His voice brightened as he told her the good news: He had been granted a compassionate reassignment to Fort Bragg. He would be there for her, after all! Hadn't he promised that he always would be?

By the time Ronnie reported for duty with the Army Security Agency at Fort Bragg on March 30, nobody held out any hope for his grandfather. In January, Murphy had developed more difficulty breathing. His minister helped get him admitted to a state hospital near McCain which specialized in respiratory ailments. Within a week, Murphy's condition had been diagnosed: lung cancer. He deteriorated rapidly and died at the hospital on April 15 at sixty-one.

Velma was greatly upset by her father's death, despite all the harsh feelings she once held for him. "I had learned to love him as much as I had hated him," she recalled years later. "He was so good to my kids. I think he tried to do with my kids like he wished he had done to us. He could not stand to see me correct them. If I would pick them up and spank them, he would ask me, 'Isn't that enough?' "

Her father was not Velma's only loss that spring. She had ceased making payments on her house months earlier. The mortgage company foreclosed, and the house was put up for auction.

After losing the house, Velma took a job at the textile plant in Raeford where she had worked years earlier when her children were young, back in the same department. But the job would last for only a few months before Velma was hospitalized again in Lumberton for an overdose, this time for three weeks.

If not for his mother, this would have been one of the happiest times of Ronnie's life. From the time he had been reassigned to Fort Bragg, he had been dating Joanna regularly. Just before Velma's hospitalization, Joanna had entered Pembroke State University, which once had been a Lumbee Indian college. She was planning to major in education and become an elementary school teacher.

One evening after finishing work at Fort Bragg, Ronnie drove for forty miles to the hospital in Lumberton to visit his mother. He had big plans for the evening, but he didn't tell her about them. As usual, he had trouble getting away from her. When he left, he was already late for his date with Joanna, and he still had sixteen miles to drive. In his rush to get there, he got stopped by a state trooper.

"What's the hurry?" the trooper wanted to know.

Ronnie showed him the diamond engagement ring he'd picked up at Tyndall's Jewelry in Fayetteville that afternoon, explaining that he was late for a date and was planning to propose.

"You'll have plenty of time to regret that later," the trooper said, opening his ticket book.

Joanna said yes, and Ronnie was overjoyed. But he decided not to tell his mother for now.

Unknown to Ronnie, Velma was beginning a romance of her own, bizarrely enough with a man named Al Smith, who was hospitalized in the mental health center undergoing treatment for alcoholism.

Velma was almost forty. Al Smith was sixty, a construction

worker from adjoining Columbus County. He was divorced, the father of a grown son and daughter, the grandfather of three.

Soon after Velma was released, Al began showing up at Lillie's house. Velma started going out with him, and for a period both seemed to be doing well. Velma had Al attending church, taking her to gospel singings and revivals, just as Jennings Barfield once had done.

Ronnie was wary of Al. Not only was he so much older, but he seemed a rough sort, and Ronnie couldn't believe that his mother was going out with a man who was a recovering alcoholic. He gently questioned her, but she was convinced that Al had overcome his drinking problem. Ronnie was dubious, but his mother seemed so pleased to have somebody paying attention to her that he reluctantly tolerated the doomed relationship.

That fall, Velma told Ronnie that she had taken a job at a textile plant in Whiteville, Al's hometown, in adjoining Columbus County. She found a small, furnished apartment above a garage behind an old house in Whiteville, and Al helped her move in. Although he didn't approve of the move, Ronnie was glad that his mother was showing initiative, doing things on her own. He also knew that his grandmother and the rest of the family were relieved that she was leaving.

Gaining Al didn't mean that Velma was willing to give up her son, however. Ronnie and Joanna had been discussing wedding dates, and early in November Ronnie decided to tell his mother. He and Joanna drove to Whiteville filled with expectation.

"Oh, that's nice," Velma said when Ronnie broke the news. The response was so cool and blatantly insincere that Joanna realized that perhaps Ronnie and his mother needed to talk. She excused herself and went for a walk. As soon as she left, Velma started on Ronnie.

How could he do this to her? Look at all the money he'd spent on that ring when he knew that she needed help. She didn't even have money enough to buy her medicine.

"I've always been the most important woman in your life," she said, breaking into tears, "and now you're going to have her and you won't even want to come around me at all."

"That's not true, Mama," Ronnie said, moving to console her. "I'll still be here for you. Nothing's going to change that. Just because I love Joanna doesn't mean I'm going to stop loving you."

He had not expected this. He had wanted his mother to be happy for him, to love Joanna, to grant her blessing. And although she seemed more accepting of the situation by the time he and Joanna left, her selfishness had stripped the occasion of any joy.

He and Joanna didn't talk much about his mother's reaction on the way back. He was embarrassed and didn't tell her what his mother had said. And Joanna, sensing his disappointment, didn't question him about it.

Ronnie knew that his mother's relationship with Al had grown volatile. He was not surprised when she called to tell him that Al had hit her and she had moved to an old motel that had been converted to efficiency apartments at Lake Waccamaw, a crater lake ten miles east of Whiteville. Ronnie went to see her and begged her to return to live with Lillie, but she was reluctant to give up on Al, and she still had her job at the mill.

"How's Joanna?" she asked as Ronnie was about to leave.

"She's fine."

"Are y'all still planning on getting married?"

They were, Ronnie said.

And even sooner, it turned out, than he expected. Early in December, Ronnie got orders to report to Fort Dix, New Jersey, in March for reassignment to Germany. He was surprised. He still had two years to go on his enlistment, and he thought his assignment at Fort Bragg was permanent. He talked to his commanding officer, only to learn that nothing could be done.

Ronnie and Joanna discussed the situation and agreed that they should get married before he left. Joanna could continue at Pembroke State until the end of her first year. By then Ronnie would be settled in Germany and could send for her. Joanna could continue her classes there through a University of Maryland extension program offered by the Army. They set February 9 as their wedding date.

Ronnie put off telling his mother until after Christmas. Her reaction was exactly what he knew it would be, but even he was shocked at the depth to which the news, combined with her other problems, pushed her.

Soon afterward, Pam called, distraught. "Well, she's finally done it," she said.

Al Smith had called Velma's brother Jimmy and told him that

Velma was in the hospital in Whiteville from an overdose, Pam said, and this time doctors were saying that she likely wouldn't survive.

Ronnie arrived to find his mother in a coma, breathing with a respirator, intravenous lines feeding fluids into her body. A doctor told him that his mother's stomach had been pumped, but too much of the medication had already made it into her system. They had done all that could be done. She might not make it through the night.

This was what Ronnie had feared all along, and it was the news of his imminent marriage and departure that apparently had pushed her over the edge. His guilt was overwhelming.

All the family gathered at the hospital, thinking this was the end. Velma remained comatose in intensive care for two days, then slowly began regaining consciousness.

Ronnie and Pam were at wit's end about what to do with their mother. After she got stronger, Ronnie went to the hospital and had another of his long, firm talks with her. He told her plainly that he did not approve of her relationship with Al. He wanted her back with her mother. He made it just as plain that he had no intention of backing away from marrying Joanna. She would just have to accept it, and he was sure that she would come to love Joanna as much as he did.

"It's all going to have to come from you," he told her. "You're going to have to take control of your life. Nobody can do it for you. Only you can make your life worth living."

Velma was released from the hospital less than three weeks before Ronnie's wedding. Although she still wasn't enthusiastic about the marriage, she wanted to take part in the ceremony. Ronnie was nervous about including her, worried that she might overdose and cause a scene, embarrassing Joanna and her family. He had another stern talk with her beforehand, and she did fine. Ronnie couldn't tell that she had taken any medicine at all.

The wedding was formal but held at Joanna's parents' house, because she wanted to be married at home. Joanna had chosen a beautiful gown; Ronnie wore a rented tux. Joanna's elder brother George* was best man. Joanna's pastor, for whose children she had babysat throughout her teen years, performed the vows, as friends and family of both Ronnie and Joanna looked on. A reception followed. Pam, who had arrived laughing and singing, "It's Too Late to Turn Back Now," caught the bouquet.

*   *   *

Ronnie and Joanna set up temporary housekeeping in a small furnished apartment upstairs in an old house not far from Joanna's parents' home. Ronnie had to drive more than eighty miles each day back and forth to his duties at Fort Bragg.

After Ronnie's wedding Velma took a job at a department store in the same town where he was living and seemed to be controlling her medicines better. Still, Ronnie was concerned about her, and after talking with Joanna, he began collecting new documents and renewed his request for a discharge.

"I feel that a hardship discharge would be of great benefit to Mrs. Barfield's mental health and would probably prolong her life," Dr. Robert Townsend of Raeford wrote on Ronnie's behalf.

Once again, though, the Army took its time deciding, and in mid-March, Ronnie reported to Fort Dix, his embarkation point for Germany. But soon after his arrival, a hold was put on his orders, and two days later he was sent back to Fort Bragg until a decision could be reached.

Only a few days after his return, Ronnie got a tearful call from his mother. She had been arrested in Red Springs and was being held at the jail. He rushed as usual to her aid. The charge, he discovered, was serious. She had attempted to pass a forged prescription at a local drugstore using a form she had taken from a doctor's desk. The pharmacist had recognized that the handwriting was different and had called the police.

Luther Hagins, the uncle of Ronnie's friend Julius, was the police chief of Red Springs, and he allowed Ronnie to take his mother home.

Velma's problems were no secret to Joanna, of course, but she did not know the severity of them. Ronnie had not told her much, fearing the effect it might have on their relationship. But that night, despondent, he decided the time had come to tell her everything. It was a long, sad story, one he'd never told to anyone. Joanna was understanding and reassuring. And Ronnie felt comforted having finally let it all out.

Velma did not tell Ronnie when the court date was set. She pleaded guilty on April 3 and was sentenced to six months, suspended for three years. She also was fined $100 and ordered to pay court costs. The judge warned that any future violations could put her in prison.

Three days later, Ronnie got the news that his discharge had been approved. He called both Joanna and his mother in jubilation. A day later, he was released, free at last from the Army. But not from his mother.

CHAPTER 7

Ronnie had never given up his dream of college, and in the fall of 1973 he joined Joanna at Pembroke State University, choosing history as his major. He arranged his classes so that he could continue to work full-time in his father-in-law's business, but strain soon took its toll.

For the first time, he was not making high grades. And tension was growing in his marriage. Money problems caused constant bickering. In the spring of 1974 one argument quickly got out of hand. Before it ended Ronnie grabbed a baseball bat and bashed the telephone, beating it into obliteration. Frightened, Joanna fled to her parents' house.

Ronnie was surprised and disturbed at the violence that had erupted from him. He always had been shy and pacific, and now this troubling force had boiled up. It scared and depressed him.

He thought his marriage was over, but he and Joanna soon worked out their problems and moved into a trailer park in Lumberton. Joanna got a job as a waitress at a steak house; Ronnie took a route for the morning newspaper in Fayetteville. That left him time to practice miniature golf. He had taken the sport up seriously again while he was stationed at Fort Bragg. Now a professional circuit had been organized and he joined it. By late summer he was making more money playing golf than working.

Joanna took an interest in the sport, too, and it brought them closer together. She soon started playing in the novice division. On one of the happiest days of their marriage, Joanna won a novice tournament at the same time Ronnie was winning in the professional division, and a story about them appeared in the sports pages of the newspaper Ronnie delivered.

Ronnie worried constantly about his mother, whose life was getting no better. Velma had remained with her mother, and during the previous year she had bounced between jobs at three different textile plants, holding none for more than three months. In November she was arrested again for passing a bad check for $115. The prosecutor failed to look up her prior record, and she was ordered to pay restitution and sentenced to thirty days in jail, suspended for six months, but she kept this from her mother and her children.

Her brother Tyrone had married and moved away, but he was in the National Guard and still came to Parkton once a month to attend drills. He always stayed with his mother, and she often complained to him about Velma and her drug taking. Velma staggered around like a drunk, Lillie said, sometimes falling, and she couldn't deal with it, couldn't understand why Velma was like this. She worried that something bad was going to happen.

Lillie also told Tyrone that her checking account was out of sequence. They discovered that some of her checks were missing. Later, the checks began showing up, signed with her name, but she knew she hadn't written them.

Clearly, Velma was forging the checks and using the money to buy her prescriptions. Lillie didn't want to take legal action. She didn't even want to confront Velma, fearful of stirring animosity. Tyrone took her to the bank to make certain that no future checks were cashed without her authentic signature. He also arranged for his mother to keep her checkbook under lock and key.

By early 1974, Velma had quit work, and her drug taking was at dangerous levels. One day Pam came and was met at the door by her grandmother.

"She's took a bunch of them pills again," Lillie said.

Pam found her mother in bed, foaming at the mouth, unable to speak, chewing her tongue. She forced a spoon into her mouth to keep her from further damaging her tongue and called the rescue squad.

After this trip to the hospital, Velma remained unemployed and seemed to have no interests other than maintaining her supply of medicines.

The relationship between Velma and her mother had been growing more strained. The two argued often. At times they didn't speak. Later, Velma would say that her mother treated her as she had when she was a girl, ordering her around and expecting her to be a slave. Anybody who came to the house was apt to hear a sharp exchange between Velma and Lillie. One day Ronnie was there when Lillie told Velma that she needed to do the laundry, and she exploded, cursing and throwing clothes. Ronnie tried to calm her, but she was defensive and didn't want to listen.

"I think there was more anger in my mom then than I had ever seen," Ronnie would say years later. "And it was a different type than I'd seen before, all directed at my grandmother. She just seemed to have a lot of resentment. She resented having to depend on her mother."

In the summer of 1974, Lillie was struck with stomach cramps and vomiting. The pain became so severe that she got Velma to take her to a doctor in Fayetteville who admitted her to the hospital but was unable to determine the cause of her problem. He theorized a virus. When the pain began to abate after several days, Lillie was released and returned home.

Not long after her mother's hospitalization, Velma was to be temporarily relieved of money worries by the death of somebody else close to her.

On Friday night, August 23, Ronnie and Joanna drove to Fayetteville to see a movie. On the way home, they encountered a traffic tie-up on U.S. 301. Flashing emergency lights. State troopers. An accident.

The next morning, Velma called, distraught. Al was dead, she said, killed in an accident.

Ronnie drove to his grandmother's house and found his mother high on pills and crying. He had to quiz her to find out what had happened.

She had gone the night before to see Al at a motel where he was staying while working on a construction project near Fayetteville. Al went across four-lane U.S. 301 to a convenience store for beer.

"I shouldn't have let him go, because he had been drinking," Velma said, "but he wanted to."

She hadn't worried at first when he didn't come back—sometimes he'd get to talking to people—but then she'd heard sirens, and she looked out and saw all the emergency lights, the traffic backed up. She hurried out and asked somebody what had happened. A man had been hit by a tractor-trailer, she was told, killed instantly, and she had started crying. She knew it was Al.

"When was this?" Ronnie asked.

"Last night, ten-thirty or eleven, I don't know."

Only then did Ronnie realize that he and Joanna had passed the accident without knowing that Al was involved and that his mother was by the side of the road, alone and in agony.

His heart went out to her. He held her and let her cry. What was it about his mother that drew so much tragedy, anguish and sorrow? Was it any wonder that she had to lean on her medicines to get by?

All the same, Ronnie could not bring himself to attend Al's funeral. He had never liked him and thought his presence would be hypocritical.

Not long after the funeral, his mother called again. She needed help. Al had left her the beneficiary of a life insurance policy. She had made several calls to the company without result. She wanted Ronnie to drive her to Greenville, South Carolina, to collect. Ronnie took her, and she returned with a check for $5,000. At least she wouldn't have financial problems for a while, Ronnie thought. Later he would realize that he should've known that it wouldn't be long before he would be having to rush to her rescue again.

That fall Joanna took a break from college, but Ronnie returned to class, although he would withdraw before the semester was over. He was still delivering newspapers and pursuing his dream of miniature golf riches. He had hopes of appearing in the TV matches, where the payoffs were as much as $50,000, and was working hard on his game.

One afternoon in October, Ronnie stopped to see his mother and grandmother on his way to Fayetteville to play golf. He usually dropped in a couple of times a week.

Nobody answered the door, and when Ronnie let himself in he froze in fear. His mother was sprawled on the dining room floor, a pool of blood beneath her head. Had she been murdered? Had she managed to get a gun and kill herself? Where was his grandmother? There was not a sound in the house.

He saw no gun when he reached his mother's side. She hadn't killed herself. "Mama, Mama," he said, touching her head. Suddenly, she moaned.

The front door opened, startling Ronnie, and his grandmother stepped inside, a paper sack in her arms. She had walked to the Corner Grocery.

"What in the world?" she said.

Velma had taken too many pills, fallen and struck her head on the corner of the table. Ronnie took her to a hospital in Fayette-ville, where her head was stitched and she was released.

Pam was dismayed when she heard about this incident. She was now living in the same trailer park in Lumberton where Ronnie and Joanna lived, driving a Tom's snack route. Early that year she had met Kirby Jarrett at a nightclub in Fayetteville. They began dating regularly, and that summer they set a wedding date: November 23. The wedding was now only weeks away, and she was sure that her mother was going to be in no condition to take part, afraid, as Ronnie had been, that Velma would do something to embarrass her.

But once again Velma did fine, even helping to arrange and host the reception afterward, and both her children were proud of her. Pam and Kirby went to Myrtle Beach for a brief honeymoon and returned to live in Pam's trailer in Lumberton.

Christmas had always been a big occasion for Lillie. She loved cooking and having her children and grandchildren gather. This year Christmas fell on Wednesday, and not everybody could come. Arlene and Erroll were in Greece. Tyrone and his family couldn't get there until the weekend. And John, who lived in South Carolina, planned to wait until New Year's. But all the other children would be there, as would many of the grandchildren.

Lillie didn't like the fancy Christmas trees that came from distant places. She still preferred a pine, the kind of tree she and Murphy had when her children were young and, a week before Christmas, Ronnie took his saw to the woods and cut a young pine for her, the fullest he could find. Velma joined in decorating it, and as Christmas approached she seemed in a good mood.

Lillie was never happier than when she was in her kitchen, cooking for her family. For Christmas, she baked coconut and German chocolate cakes, apple, pecan and pumpkin pies. She cooked a turkey, a ham, collard greens, speckled butter beans, sweet potatoes, made potato salad. Velma even helped, making a fruit and nut salad that always brought compliments. The last thing to the table was Lillie's hot biscuits. Everybody always raved about them.

Ronnie and Joanna went to her parents' house on Christmas morning, but they got to his grandmother's in time for the big dinner that afternoon. Everybody had a great time, even Velma, who laughed and gabbed with the others. After dinner they all gathered around the tree to open presents. Ronnie had bought his grandmother bedroom shoes and a nightgown, and she went on about how pretty they were and hugged him and Joanna. Ronnie left that night feeling good. It had been a great Christmas. He couldn't have imagined the bizarre turn of events that was about to take place.

When Tyrone brought his family to his mother's house on the Saturday after Christmas, Lillie pulled him aside. She had something to show him. The strangest thing, she said. A dun from a finance company had just come in the mail. It said that payment was overdue on her loan, and if it wasn't made promptly, her car would be repossessed. She hadn't taken out any loan, and there was no lien on the car. Murphy had paid off the car years ago. It had to be a mistake, Tyrone told her. She shouldn't worry about it. But if they kept dunning her, he'd look into it.

Whether Lillie talked to Velma about the dun, nobody would ever know, but on Monday night Joanna answered the phone shortly before ten and grew somber.

"When?" she said. "Where? . . . How is she?"

Ronnie tensed. He knew immediately that something was wrong.

"That was Lucille," Joanna said, hanging up "Your grandmother's at the hospital in Fayetteville. They don't know if she's going to live."

"We've got to go," Ronnie said.

After calling Pam, he and Joanna stopped to pick her up. Ronnie drove fast to Cape Fear Valley Hospital. Velma was crying in the hallway when they got there. Olive was with her; he'd been crying, too. John had just arrived. They looked stunned.

"Oh, Ronnie," Velma said, rushing to him. "She's gone."

Ronnie couldn't believe it. His grandmother dead? What had happened?

Velma was in no shape to talk.

Olive said his mother had become sick after lunch, had started throwing up, then developed diarrhea. Velma had called the doctor, who said a stomach virus was going around. He would call in something to the drugstore.

Velma called her niece, Robin, Olive's daughter, and asked her to go the drugstore for the medicine, which turned out to be paregoric and Dramamine. Velma gave it to her mother but it did no good. Lillie kept complaining of severe stomach cramps and pain between her shoulders. By dark she could no longer sit up. She writhed and moaned in pain and at one point threw up blood. Velma called Olive. When he came, he couldn't believe the condition his mother had fallen into so suddenly. They had to get her to the hospital. He called the rescue squad, then her doctor. Velma rode in the ambulance with her mother, and Olive followed in his car.

Lillie was in shock and cyanotic by the time she reached the emergency room, extremely restless, and she could barely tell the doctors where she hurt. She was taken to intensive care, and two hours later, at 10:30, she was dead. The doctors had no idea what had killed her.

What kind of illness could work so fast? That question was on the minds of all the family as they gathered at the house later that night, a house that felt eerily empty now with both Lillie and Murphy gone. Nobody slept. They sat up all night crying and asking what could have gone wrong.

Except for her migraine headaches, varicose veins, and phlebitis in her legs, Lillie had no health problems that anybody knew about. It seemed unreal that she could have fallen ill and died so quickly, especially when she had been feeling so well.

Everybody kept quizzing Velma for details. When had the attack started? Had she been feeling bad earlier?

Velma, who had received a shot at the hospital to sedate her, was as befuddled as the rest. "I did everything I could for her," she kept saying, "everything I could." And she would break into tears.

Everybody felt sorry for her. She had gone through so much. Tragedy and unhappiness seemed to stalk her. Even in their grief, they all reached out to her.

That night Lillie's children decided that they could never rest without knowing what had taken her life. They all agreed, Velma included, that they should request an autopsy.

Just twenty-one months after the family had gathered at Green Springs Baptist Church for Murphy's funeral, they came there again for Lillie's. She was buried beside her husband at LaFayette Memorial Park in Fayetteville. Velma stood sobbing at the graveside, comforted by her children.

"What am I going to do now?" she asked.

Don't worry, they told her. They were there. They would take care of her.

CHAPTER 8

Velma had no place to go after Lillie's funeral. Ronnie and Pam knew that she was in no condition to stay alone. Although Pam was only five weeks into her marriage, she allowed her mother to move in with her until another solution could be found. Her life quickly became a nightmare. Kirby was tolerant, pretending he didn't mind, but she knew that nobody could long abide the life her mother was forcing on them.

Velma was in a stupor every day, and Pam could not figure how she maintained it. She had searched her room for drugs, rifled all her possessions, even scoured her body. She had thought, as Ronnie had, that if she could just limit the number of doctors her mother was seeing, monitor the prescriptions she received, dole out the medications as prescribed, that Velma would be all right. But her mother had developed the slyness common to addicts and she always managed to get more pills.

Because Pam and Kirby had to work, Velma was alone during the day, but she was without money, so far as Pam knew, without transportation. How did she keep getting drugs? And how did she keep them hidden, no matter how hard Pam searched?

Pam beseeched her mother, lectured her, yelled at her, but nothing changed.

Ronnie had enrolled again at Pembroke for the spring semester, but stress was causing him to have trouble keeping up with his classes. One day in January, Velma came to him crying and said she had to have money to pay off some checks she had written on a closed account before her mother died. What had happened to all of the money she had gotten from Al's insurance? Ronnie knew that she had given him $700, but how could she have squandered all the rest so rapidly? She had no answer. It was just gone.

Ronnie felt obligated to help her. After all, she had given him money. Now she needed it back. He went to a bank in Lumberton where his uncle, Jesse, was now working, got a loan for $500 and gave it to his mother. Joanna was upset when she found out. They couldn't afford to keep getting Velma out of hock, she complained.

"If it was your mama," Ronnie said curtly, "you'd do the same thing."

A month after Lillie's death, Velma was in perhaps the worst shape that Pam had ever seen. She cared for nothing; she wouldn't eat; she soiled herself in bed. After her mother went without food for three days, Pam dragged her to the kitchen, sat her at the table, tied her in the chair with towels so she wouldn't topple over, and force-fed chicken soup to her.

"It always seemed to come back to Pam taking care of Mama," she recalled. "From thirteen on, I felt like I was her mother."

On February 3, Pam came home to find her mother unconscious from another overdose. She and Kirby took her to the emergency room. Velma was admitted, kept until she was sober and released again. What amazed Pam and Ronnie was that every time their mother was admitted for drug overdoses, she was always released with more prescriptions.

Soon after her mother's release, Pam began feeling not so well herself. Some days she was so sick to her stomach that she couldn't eat and didn't have strength to go to work. She finally went to a doctor, who quickly diagnosed her condition: she was pregnant. Her morning sickness just lasted all day.

This should have been one of the happiest moments in her life, but her mother's presence and hopeless condition gave little reason for celebration.

On the morning of Wednesday, February 12, a week after her release from the hospital, Velma appeared at Ronnie's door wanting to spend the day. Ronnie and Joanna had planned to play golf that day and were on their way to a nearby course. Velma seemed to be all right. They told her that she was welcome to stay. They'd be back when they finished their round.

They returned to find Velma unconscious on the floor in front of the washing machine. She'd broken her left collar bone and it was protruding through the skin. Ronnie called an ambulance. Velma was admitted once again to the mental health unit at Southeastern Hospital. She told the doctor who treated her that she had tried to kill herself, that she couldn't overcome her morbid thoughts. But she wouldn't tell him about the thoughts.

While Velma was in the hospital, sheriff's deputies came by Pam's trailer looking for her. They had more bad checks. Ronnie was flabbergasted when he heard. He'd just given his mother money to pay off bad checks, and here were more. The deputies went to the hospital to talk to Velma, warning that she would face arrest if she didn't make restitution.

Ronnie and Pam were more despondent than ever about their mother's behavior. They had been going through hell with her for more than seven years now, and she showed no sign of stopping. How much more could they take? How much more could they do for her? Would it ever end?

They had tried to control her medicines, had pleaded with doctors not to give them to her, had hidden them, flushed them down the toilet. But one way or another, she always managed to get more.

As painful as it was for both to accept, they had been coming to the same conclusion. Perhaps the only way they could save their mother was to force her to face the consequences of her actions. And that time seemed at hand.

Velma remained in the mental health unit until March 8, when she was given a weekend pass. She returned on Monday, March 10, and was discharged. Two days later, sheriff's deputies came to Pam's trailer to tell Velma that unless she paid off the checks, they would have no choice but to arrest her.

Velma turned tearfully to Pam for help.

"You got into this," Pam told her. "I tried to help you, and you wouldn't listen. Now you'll have to get out of it yourself."

When the deputies came a day later and Velma still couldn't pay, she was taken into custody and placed in the Robeson County jail. This time, as hard as it was for him to do, Ronnie did not run to bail her out.

On March 21, Velma appeared before a judge, alone in court, despondent and forlorn. She was convicted on seven bad check charges. The judge also revoked her suspended sentence for writing the forged prescription and ordered her sent to the North Carolina Correctional Center for Women in Raleigh for six months.

By the time Velma entered prison on March 27, she was agitated and irritable, suffering headaches, chills and muscle spasms. She was taken to the prison hospital, where she told the doctor about her "bad nerves" and how long she had been taking medication for the condition. The doctor recognized the symptoms of withdrawal and ordered a sustaining dosage of Valium, later changing to the highly sedating antidepressant Elavil. Velma would remain on one or the other throughout her stay in prison.

When Tyrone went to visit his sister, he brought the news that the autopsy report on their mother was finally back. An inflammation had been found in her heart, and her doctor thought that contributed to her lack of response to treatment and resulting death. It was too bad, Velma observed. If they'd known earlier, maybe something could have been done to save her.

Neither Pam nor Ronnie visited their mother. Pam was constantly sick with her pregnancy and having trouble maintaining her job. Ronnie was too busy. The top managers of Putt-Putt had taken note of him and offered an opportunity. The company had portable courses that could be set up on a vacant lot to test a market. They wanted to put one in Lumberton, and they asked Ronnie to set it up and run it for them. The situation was perfect, allowing Ronnie to combine work and pleasure. And he could practice all he needed, at no charge, for the weekend tournaments. He dropped his classes at Pembroke and went to work for Putt-Putt.

Velma hated prison, hated the noise, the crowding, the lack of privacy. She did her best to keep to herself and avoid trouble. Later, she would say that a war was going on within her while she was there. At times she thought that she had betrayed her children. At other times she felt betrayed by them. Her emotions swung from guilt to anger and back again. But one thing she was not fighting was her desire for drugs. She knew that she had prescriptions with refills left on them back in Lumberton. The fantasy of walking into a drugstore and being handed those refills pulled her through each day.

Velma was released at the end of June after serving three months. She moved back in with Pam and Kirby, but only, she cheerfully promised, until she could get back on her feet. Conditions of her parole required her to meet periodically with a probation officer and a social worker. On June 30, five days after her release, she met with Frederick Saravia, her social worker at the mental health center. She was upbeat. She planned to find a job, keep busy and stay out of the hospital, she told him. She realized, she said, that her abuse of medicines had caused her to waste some of the best years of her life, but all of that was behind her. From now on, things would be different.

Six days later, Velma was back at the hospital from an overdose. The next day a glum Ronnie and Pam met with Saravia and Velma's probation officer, Louise Sanderson. They'd had three months free of dealing with their mother's problems, and now the old misery had returned. Both were disheartened. Their mother was emotionally breaking up their lives, they said, and both admitted that they saw little chance that she would change. Clearly, Saravia and Sanderson told them, their mother could not function on her own; she needed a structured, supervised setting. Ronnie and Pam should consider a drug treatment program for her. Otherwise, Velma likely would be returning to prison to complete her sentence.

With help from Sanderson, Pam began looking for a program.

Meanwhile, Kirby was getting calls about bad checks. He discovered that Velma had written checks on an account he had closed long before, forging his name. That was how she had gotten the drugs. Kirby was furious. He wanted to let the checks go to the district attorney and force Velma to face the charges. But forgery was a felony, a far worse offense than writing bad checks. If Velma was charged, not only would her parole be revoked, but she also could receive a long sentence, as much as ten years.

Pam was distraught. She had not yet been married nine months. She was more than seven months pregnant. She'd had to give up her job because of her pregnancy. Her husband was angry and her marriage threatened because of her mother, who was at her trailer drugged out of her mind. Pam came to Ronnie in tears.

Ronnie found his mother in bed, barely able to understand what he was telling her. "Do you have any idea what's going to happen if that probation officer comes and finds you in this condition?" he said angrily. "You're going back to prison."

How could she do what she was doing to Pam? Didn't she know that she could cause Pam to lose her husband, maybe even lose the child she was carrying? Kirby and Pam had taken her in, given her a place to stay, fed her, and what does she do? Forges checks, overdoses, staggers around causing everybody misery. Didn't she understand that if Kirby pressed charges there would be nothing that he or Pam or anybody else could do? She would be back in prison— for a long time.

Velma cried uncontrollably and begged Ronnie to talk to Kirby. She couldn't go back to prison, she said. She'd rather die. She'd do better. They had to believe her. She would. Wait and see.

Velma knew her children wanted to believe her, and once again they did. Pam paid off the checks. A few weeks later, the probation officer found a halfway house in Charlotte that agreed to take Velma. It wasn't a treatment program, but it would be a structured environment, and her drug intake would be closely monitored. Pam was happy at the news, but when she brought it up to her mother, Velma's reaction was anything but positive.

She cried; she begged that she not be forced to leave. A halfway house would be like prison, she said, and she couldn't stand to go back to something like that, couldn't stand to be away from them again so soon. She wanted to be there when her first grandchild was born, not off in some institution. Wasn't she doing better? Hadn't she been trying to manage her medicines? She would get a job, she promised, get a place of her own, start going back to church, do whatever they wanted. Just give her one more chance, she pleaded, let her prove herself.

Both Pam and Ronnie felt sorry for her, and as they had done so many times before, they gave in. On September 3, Frederick Saravia wrote his final report on Velma, noting that she usually did a superficial follow-up after hospitalizations, then failed to continue needed treatment. She required live-in treatment, he wrote, but wouldn't accept it. "Patient doesn't appear amenable to outpatient treatment," he noted. Velma clearly didn't want to help herself, and there was nothing more that he could do. He was closing her case.

As it turned out, Velma did do better. Perhaps the change was due to the birth of her first grandchild the following month. Velma was at the hospital when Beverly Lynn* arrived. When she first held the baby, she later recalled, she was reminded of the time when she first took Ronnie into her arms. Tears came as she spoke to her first grandchild in the same baby talk she had used with her own children.

By this time Velma knew that another grandchild was on the way. Joanna, too, was pregnant, due to deliver in April.

The prospect of having a child had caused Ronnie to reassess his life. The Putt-Putt course that he had been managing had not brought in sufficient revenue to convince the company that one would thrive in Lumberton, and Ronnie could see that his chances of ever earning big money on the professional miniature golf circuit were scant, although he by no means intended to give up the dream. If he was going to adequately provide for his family, he realized, he had better prepare himself. That fall he enrolled at Robeson Technical Institute to study business and took a job on campus as a security guard.

Velma, at long last, also found work. Soon after Beverly's birth, Pam and Kirby moved to a small second-floor apartment on Seventh Street, not far from the trailer park, but Velma did not go with them. She had taken a job looking after an elderly woman who lived in the trailer park. The job provided a room, meals and a small weekly payment. But it was not without drawbacks. The woman had a mental disability that was rapidly growing worse, and looking after her proved difficult and frustrating. Velma had only one means of coping with difficulty and frustration. She soon was back to her old levels of medication, although she took care to make sure that neither Ronnie nor Pam found out.

Early in 1976, only a few months after Velma had taken on the role of caretaker, the woman she was attending had to be put into a nursing home. But the woman's sister, a county nurse who had hired Velma, recommended her to another family.

Montgomery Edwards was ninety-four. Diabetes had cost him his sight and both legs. He was bedridden, incontinent and suffered from bedsores. He couldn't feed himself, and all of his food had to be pureed. His second wife, Dollie, was eighty-four and could no longer take care of him. Dollie was short and stout and strongly opinionated. She was not in the best of health herself, having suffered intestinal cancer and undergone a colostomy. She offered Velma room and board and $75 a week to help her look after her husband and tend the house.

The Edwardses lived in a brick ranch house on the same street as Pam and Kirby, just a mile away on the edge of town. Pam was happy that her mother had found another position close enough that she could keep an eye on her. She was not working at the time and frequently dropped by the Edwards house to check on Velma. She enjoyed sitting and chatting with Dollie, and liked Montgomery's company, too, when he felt up to talking, but he slept much of the time. Ronnie came every Friday to take his mother to get her hair fixed, to run errands and pick up her medicines.

Both Ronnie and Pam thought that their mother was doing much better, although there were occasional lapses when both could see that she had overmedicated herself. Once Montgomery's son, Preston, called Ronnie to tell him that he'd taken Velma to Pam's apartment because she had seemed to be intoxicated. If this was going to become a habit, he threatened, other arrangements would have to be made. Ronnie had another of his talks with his mother, and she took heed.

She even started regularly attending the First Pentecostal Church in Lumberton. The church van came for her on Sunday mornings and Wednesday nights, and she seemed to be making friends there. Both Ronnie and Pam were heartened by this development. Maybe she really was turning her life around.

Velma was still regularly seeing the doctor in St. Pauls who had been treating her for years. On March 11, she called Ronnie and told him she had an appointment and no way to get there. Could he take her? Joanna, who was eight months pregnant, decided to ride along.

After Velma had seen the doctor, she asked if she could drive back. She rarely got to drive anymore. Ronnie was tired and his mother seemed fine. He let her have the wheel. They were headed back to Lumberton on a two-lane section of U.S. 301 when Ronnie saw the brake lights flash on the car ahead. "Mama, watch him," he said.

Velma, overreacting, locked the brakes. The car, a '67 Mercury Monterey, went into a skid and crossed the center line.

"All I could see was Ryder," Ronnie later recalled.

The driver of the big yellow rental truck heading in the opposite direction tried to swerve to miss the car, but one fender hit the car dead center. The truck went off the road, overturned and skidded into a bridge railing, almost toppling into a creek.

Ronnie's head hit the windshield, dazing him and leaving a big bow in the shattered glass. Joanna's screaming brought him around. As he climbed out of the car he heard what he thought was water splashing, but realized it was his own blood.

He tried the back door, but it was jammed. He had to pull Joanna over the front seat.

"You're bleeding, you're bleeding to death," she kept screaming as he led her to the side of the road. A small fire was burning beneath the hood and he realized if it spread his mother could be burned to death. He could see only from his left eye. His right was clogged with blood. He ran back to the car and found his mother rigid in her seat, her hands still on the steering wheel. He had to pry her hands from the wheel, but he managed to pull her out and drag her away.

He feared for the truck driver and had started toward the truck when one man grabbed him and another ripped off a T-shirt and started wrapping it around his head, saying, "Hey, man, you're bleeding bad." Then he saw the driver of the truck climbing out of the window, others rushing to help him, and he turned back to Joanna, who sat crying on the side of the road. That was when he remembered the baby.

Ambulances arrived and took all four to the hospital in Lumberton. Later, people who saw photos of the wreck in the newspaper would wonder how anybody had survived, but Velma suffered only minor cuts, bruises and cracked ribs, the truck driver even lesser injuries. Ronnie had glass fragments removed from his forehead and right eye and several cuts stitched. Joanna was uninjured, and the baby was fine.

Just over a month later, on April 14, Joanna returned to the hospital to deliver her child, a son, Michael James.* Velma was there when he was born, as was Joanna's mother. Ronnie was with the grandmothers when they first were allowed to see the baby in the nursery.

"Oh, Ronnie," Velma said. "He looks exactly like you did when you were born."

Then she noticed the red splotches on the side of the baby's head. They were in exactly the same spots as the cuts on Ronnie's head from the wreck, and she feared that she had "marked" the baby. But the spots later faded away along with Ronnie's scars.

With two grandchildren now, Velma seemed revived in spirit. Through the rest of spring and on through summer, she did better than Ronnie and Pam had ever dreamed. They even allowed themselves to think that maybe she could overcome her problems.

In September, Ronnie dropped by the Edwards house to visit and found his mother sitting at the kitchen table with a man. They were laughing and talking, and when his mother saw him, she said, "Oh, Ronnie, come here. There's somebody I want you to meet. This is Stuart Taylor, Dollie's nephew."

The man stood, greeted Ronnie, shook his hand. He was not quite as tall as Ronnie, about five feet ten, but bigger, stout, maybe 200 pounds. His hair, combed back, was dark with a little gray, and he looked to be in his fifties. He was friendly and pleasant, and they all sat and chatted for a while, Dollie joining them. Velma seemed happy, on her best behavior. After Taylor had left and Ronnie was alone with his mother, she smiled and said, "He's asked me to go out to eat with him."

"Do you know anything about him?"

"I know he's separated but not divorced."

"Well, are you going?"

She gave him another smile. "I'm thinking about it," she said.

Velma did go out to dinner with Stuart Taylor, and she had a good time. For more than a month, she went out with him once a week, usually to a fish camp, steak house or barbecue place. Several times a week he would drop by the Edwards house to visit, and Velma always looked forward to seeing him. His appearances broke up the drudgery of her life.

Then, at the end of October, Stuart suddenly stopped coming. Velma heard nothing from him. After a couple of weeks she mentioned his absence to Dollie. Stuart and his wife were trying to work out their problems and get back together, Dollie told her.

Later, Velma would acknowledge that she felt a twinge of disappointment at the news, but she accepted it, wished Stuart well and put him out of her mind.

Ronnie wasn't so certain that she had, although he didn't quiz her about it. He could see that his mother was much less happy than when she was going out with Stuart. But other factors also were affecting her mood. Montgomery Edwards' condition was getting worse, and caring for him was growing more trying. Velma's relationship with Dollie also was deteriorating.

On his regular visits, Ronnie could see that Dollie was becoming more critical of his mother. She frequently complained that Velma wasn't doing things right. She told her to do them in a different way, or made her do them over again. Velma was clearly resentful and snappish in return.

Ronnie heard some exchanges between his mother and Dollie

that reminded him of the tiffs between Velma and Lillie, and later Velma would realize that she was feeling the same acrimony for Dollie that she had felt for her mother two years earlier.

As the situation grew worse, Velma sought deeper refuge in her medicines. She was going to bed earlier each night, finding it harder to get up each morning. She lived for the moments when she could be away from the house, attending church, running errands, visiting with Ronnie and Pam.

Late in January 1977, Montgomery suddenly declined, and Velma called an ambulance. He died at Southeastern Hospital on January 29. He was ninety-five.

After the funeral, Velma remained with Dollie, but with Montgomery no longer there to occupy the time and efforts of both, their situation had changed. Dollie searched for new chores for Velma. And the more she found, Velma later claimed, the more she found fault with the way Velma did them. At times Velma wanted to scream.

On Saturday, February 26, Dollie started feeling bad. Preston Edwards came to check on his stepmother, as he did every day, and Dollie told him that she thought she was coming down with the flu. She was vomiting and had developed diarrhea.

By Sunday night, Dollie was so gravely ill that Preston decided she should go to the hospital. Velma summoned an ambulance and rode with her. Dollie was treated in the emergency room and sent back home. On Monday she was worse still, and on Tuesday morning she was returned to the hospital by ambulance. This time she was admitted. She died in intensive care at seven that evening.

Later that night, Velma called Ronnie to tell him of Dollie's death. Would he mind going with her to the funeral home to pay respects? She thought it important that her family show their sympathy.

That an old woman had died four weeks after her husband aroused no suspicions. What concerned Ronnie and Pam was where their mother would go now that she again had no place to live. More worrisome was that she would be at loose ends again. Her thirteen months with the Edwardses had given Ronnie and Pam hope. Despite occasional lapses, Velma had taken no severe overdoses during that time, had not been hospitalized once. Living with others, having responsibilities and work to perform, clearly gave her purpose and caused her to maintain a modicum of control over her drug intake. They knew that, without these restrictions, she was apt to quickly lapse into her old ways.

Pam and Kirby invited Velma to move back in with them until she could find a job and get a place of her own, though they had no extra bedroom and Velma had to sleep on a daybed in the living room. To the relief of all, the stay proved to be short. Only a week after Dollie's funeral, Velma got a call from a woman who identified herself as Margie Lee Pittman. The minister at Velma's church had recommended that she call.

Margie's mother, Record Lee, had fallen in her carport on March 1 and broken her leg. Being in a cast and using crutches was hard on a woman of seventy-six. Margie's father, John Henry Lee, a lifelong farmer, was eighty, and although he was still quite active, he couldn't give his wife the care she needed. Would Velma consider coming to work for them?

Velma went for an interview on March 10. The Lees could pay only $50 a week, but she needed income to pay for her prescriptions and she accepted, stipulating that she had to have Sunday morning, and Sunday and Wednesday evenings off for church. She wanted one weekend free each month and time on Saturday morning to have her hair fixed and run errands. That was fine with the Lees. She moved in the next day.

The Lees lived in a three-bedroom brick house in the country just north of Lumberton. With the Edwardses, Velma had been forced to be subservient to Dollie, but she quickly took charge of the Lee household.

Not only did she assist Record with bathing, dressing and any other needs, she endeared herself by daily making Jell-O, one of Record's favorite foods. Velma made the kitchen her own. John Henry had been doing the cooking until she arrived, but he was happy to get out of Velma's way.

The Lees' daughters, Margie, Sylvia and Frieda, couldn't have been more pleased with Velma. She kept the house spotless, cooked good meals, cared for their mother like a baby, and whenever any of them came to have a meal with their parents, Velma never failed to say grace. They trusted her so much that they approved when their father told them he was going to allow Velma to drive their mother to her doctor appointments in his Cadillac.

Velma was not nearly so happy with the Lees as they were with her, however. Record talked a lot, mostly about the past. Her mind had begun to fail, and she sometimes couldn't remember what had happened yesterday, or the day before. But the past remained as clear as the present. She talked so much that she began to get on Velma's nerves. She also bickered a lot with her husband, Velma later would say, always over pointless matters, and that too bothered Velma. When she reached the point that she couldn't stand it any longer, she took her pills, closed herself in her room and went to sleep.

Only a few weeks after Velma went to work for the Lees, Record Lee was looking through her returned checks when she spotted one she didn't recognize. It was made out to Bo's Supermarket for $50, and although it bore her name, she knew that she hadn't written it. She showed it to her husband, who called the sheriff's department. A detective was sent to investigate, but the Lees could think of no one who might have forged the check, or how it might have happened.

John Henry Lee had hardly been sick a day in his life. He had farmed until he was seventy-five, and even at that age he boasted that he could outwork a twenty-five-year-old. At eighty he still rode his tractor and raised a big garden each year. He was planning to paint his house as soon as the weather warmed a little.

On Wednesday, April 27, only a couple of weeks after John Henry Lee had called the sheriff's department about the forged check, Velma called Margie Pittman to tell her that her father was sick and vomiting. He was worse the next day, and Margie came to check on him. He thought it was something that would pass, but his daughter wasn't so sure. If he hadn't improved by the next morning, she said, she wanted Velma to take him to the doctor.

On Friday morning, before eight, Velma called an ambulance. The medics were unable to obtain a readable blood pressure as the ambulance sped to Southeastern Hospital.

John Henry spent four days in intensive care and gradually improved. His doctors had no idea what had caused his illness. A virus perhaps. He was released on May 2, weak, shaky and minus several pounds but thankful. His daughters came to the house that afternoon to celebrate his recovery. It was a warm day and they sat outside and talked. Velma served ice cream and Coke. The doctor had recommended soft foods and lots of liquids.

Throughout May, John Henry continued to be sick. For a few days he would be perfectly okay, then the vomiting, the diarrhea,

the cramps, the cold sweats, would start again. His weight continued to drop drastically. His daughters were very grateful for the
attentiveness that Velma showed him. She was so sweet to him, so
caring. They felt themselves lucky that she was there.

On Friday, June 3, Velma called Margie just as she was about to
leave work to tell her that her father was at the emergency room.
She'd had to call an ambulance for him again. Her father's condition was critical, Margie learned when she arrived at the hospital.
The prognosis was not good.

Years later, Margie recalled a few moments of the time she spent
with her father that night for *Fayetteville Times* reporter Priscilla
Brown.

"It was late. He was blue up to here," she said, drawing a line
across her chest with her finger. "He was limp and cold, and I put
my hand in his and said, 'Daddy, squeeze my hand if you can hear
me.' He didn't squeeze.

"Somewhere in the back of my mind I remembered the thing
about eyes blinking. So I said, 'Daddy, blink your eyes if you can
hear me.' His eyes were locked open in that—you know, that death
stare. With the greatest effort, they came down so-o slowly. Then
they flew open again.

"I said, 'He can hear me! He can hear me!' Frieda and the nurse
were standing there. I leaned over him, and I said, 'I love you,
Daddy. I love you and the Lord loves you!' "

A short time later, at 1:55 Saturday morning, June 4, John Henry
Lee died.

Velma was comforting to the family at the funeral, and they were
particularly taken with the wreath she sent. It had feathered doves
on it, winging toward heaven, one representing each member of the
family. After the funeral the Lee daughters thanked Velma for the
love and care she had shown their father. They gave her a small
bonus and told her that they wanted her to continue to look after
their mother. Velma agreed to stay.

A couple of weeks later, Velma saw a bright green pickup truck
turn into the concrete drive of the Lee house. She thought she recognized it, and she did, a pleasant surprise. Stuart Taylor got out.
It had been nearly eight months since Velma had seen him: She hurried to the door with a smile to greet her final victim.

CHAPTER 9

S tuart Taylor was a true son of Robeson County. If it wasn't in Robeson County, he didn't want it or need it. The farthest he'd ever gone was to Washington, D.C., to visit one of his daughters, but he only went once. While he was there he slipped on ice and broke his arm.

Stuart had grown up on a tobacco farm in Robeson County, one of five children. His mother had died when he was five and he was reared by a stepmother. At eighteen he married Leola Bentley, who had grown up on a nearby farm. She was three years older. They settled in a three-room house on his daddy's farm. Their first child, a daughter, Elizabeth Ann, was born three months after he turned nineteen. A son, Billy, followed fourteen months later. A second daughter, Alice, came two years after that.

Stuart was thirty when he got his first motor vehicle in 1951, an old Chevy pickup. Not until 1954 did he move his family out of the tiny, primitive house in which they had lived for fifteen years. The new house was bigger and nicer, with three bedrooms, but it had no bathroom. Stuart didn't think a toilet should be in the same structure where food was cooked, and his children would all be teenagers before he relinquished that point.

That same year, he took an eleven-year-old nephew, Marvin Bentley, into the family and made him a second son.

Stuart was a man devoted to family, his children later would say. Except for hunting, fishing and farming, he had no other interests. As his children grew older and moved away he doted on his wife. When she developed kidney disease and died at fifty-two on April 11, 1970, he was devastated.

"When my mom passed away, he fell to pieces," his daughter

Alice later would say. "Everything just crashed. I don't think there ever was a love like he had for my mom. My mom was his life. My daddy didn't even know where his underwear was. He didn't cook. Mom took care of him. And he didn't adapt to change too well. Daddy was the most unhappy person I've ever seen after my mom's death."

Leola never allowed alcohol in her house, but Stuart enjoyed drinking now and then. A few times a year he would go off hunting or fishing with buddies and drink his fill, but he never touched a drop the rest of the time. After Leola died, though, he sometimes drank for two or three weeks without letup.

Within six months of his wife's death, Stuart went to Dillon, South Carolina, and married a woman he'd known most of his life. His children saw it as an act of desperation, a hopeless attempt to replace the love and contentment he had known with their mother, and they were soon proved right. Within six months, the second wife was gone for good.

Stuart always had an exuberance for life. He was a man who rose singing every morning. He loved to pull practical jokes and tease his children. But that spirit was now gone, and as he sank deeper into loneliness and despair, his drinking binges grew longer and more frequent, causing his children great concern.

Several years after his divorce, Stuart's children saw signs that he was beginning to find some purpose in life again. He was dating the widow of an old friend, drinking less, and his children began to see the father they always had known. They were pleased when he married for the third time in 1975, hopeful that his loneliness and unhappiness might now be behind him. But that union, too, soon proved volatile and fraught with separations. And now it had come to an end.

Velma was unaware of this when she greeted Stuart at the Lee house on a June day in 1977. She really knew very little about him, had no idea even that he drank, despite having gone out with him several times the previous fall. Now they caught up on the months that had passed since. Stuart told her his marriage was over. Official separation papers had been filed in May. His divorce would be final a year from that day. Velma enjoyed his visit, and before he left, he told her he'd like to see her again. She'd like that, Velma said.

Stuart showed up again the next day. And the day after that. And every day for nearly three weeks. Several times Record Lee granted Velma time to go to supper with him. Then suddenly Stuart stopped coming. Velma heard nothing. When she called his house, she got no answer. After several days with no word, Velma called his stepmother.

Stuart wasn't well, his stepmother said.

Velma said she hoped it wasn't anything serious.

Well, to tell the truth, said his stepmother, Stuart was on one of his drinking binges.

That, Velma later would say, was the first she'd heard of Stuart's drinking problem.

Within a few days Stuart showed up, acting as if there'd been no break. He made no mention of his absence. Velma said nothing about his drinking.

By late summer, Velma was spending all of her weekends off with Stuart. "We would go on trips," she wrote two years later. "We would spend our nights together in a motel. But I kept this quiet. No one knew this was going on. I was attending church, and I mean regular, too. I was playing the role again of an ideal church member. The wrongs I was doing, I kept quiet, very quiet."

Although Velma didn't want others to know of her trysts with Stuart, both he and she were happily telling others of their relationship. He had introduced her to his family, and she took him to meet hers.

Velma's brother Jesse was living then in Hamlet, fifty miles west of Lumberton. His brothers John and Tyrone were visiting one Saturday afternoon when Velma arrived unexpectedly with Stuart. Her brothers had heard that Velma had a new boyfriend, but none had met him. They stood in the yard and talked. Stuart seemed a nice enough fellow, and Velma's brothers had to wonder if he knew what he was getting into. They were aware of Velma's many problems, and they knew, too, that every man she'd had anything to do with had come to a tragic end.

"He'd better watch it," Jesse remarked drolly to his brothers as Stuart and Velma departed, smiling and waving, "he might be next."

Stuart's friends knew that he was serious about Velma when they found out that he was taking her to gospel singings and even attending church with her. They couldn't believe it. They'd never known Stuart to go to church. "Going out with my Christian woman tonight," he'd tell them, laughing.

Early in September, Record Lee fell ill, vomiting, her stomach cramping. Velma called Margie Pittman, who took her mother to the emergency room. Velma couldn't take her because she had destroyed the Lees' Cadillac when she ran a stop sign and was hit by another car while coming back from church. Not until much later would Record's daughters learn that their mother, like their father, had been poisoned. But they had no reason to be suspicious when Velma told them soon after Record got out of the hospital that she could no longer care for their mother.

Had Velma become concerned that she was pushing her luck and might be caught? Later, she would never admit to poisoning Record Lee. At the time, she said that she quit the job because she found staying with others too confining and she didn't want to do that kind of work anymore. Ronnie thought there was another reason: that she wanted to have more time with Stuart Taylor.

Velma rented a trailer in the same park where Pam and Ronnie once lived and within a month she had found a job on the third shift at United Care, a nursing home within walking distance. Joanna was on the administrative staff and suggested she apply.

Before Velma started to work at the end of October, Ronnie stopped by for a visit. His mother met him smiling and holding out her left hand. On it was a diamond engagement ring.

"Are you sure about this?" he asked.

She was.

Ronnie had never seen Stuart drinking, or even under the influence of alcohol, but his mother had told him about his binges and he knew that they had argued about it. If she could not abide his father's drinking, if she had fought with Al Smith over his, how could she expect to live with a man who might regularly disappear on week-long drunks? But Ronnie didn't say that.

"What about his drinking?" he asked.

She was working on that, she said. She was sure he could overcome it. He went days, even weeks without touching a drop. Didn't that prove that he didn't need it?

"Does he know how much medicine you take?" Ronnie asked.

She resented the question, telling Ronnie she was taking no more than she had to have. Hadn't she been proving that she could control it? Hadn't it been nearly two years since she'd been hospitalized with an overdose?

Ronnie acknowledged that was true, and he was proud of her, but he pressed on anyway. Did Stuart know how much medicine she had to have?

He knew she took some, she said defensively, but she hadn't told him about the amounts or how long she had been taking it.

Ronnie was wary of this proposed marriage and didn't hesitate to say so. "You just need to be careful," he said. "Take your time. Make sure."

It would not come about until May, when Stuart's divorce became final, she told him. They'd have plenty of time before then to deal with any problems.

"Do you love him?" Ronnie asked.

She did, she said, but in only a few years she would admit that had been a lie. "Deep down inside I never really cared for him," she would say. "I never felt close to him at all. I can't comprehend why I wanted to be with him. Sometimes we're just lonely. Somebody to talk to, you know."

Whether she loved him or not, she clearly intended to get herself moved into his house. Velma got off work at seven in the morning. She usually walked home, showered, and slept until mid afternoon when Stuart would come by. Early in November, Kirby stopped to check on her on his way to work one morning. She had just arrived home and seemed fine. He was pleased that he would be able to give Pam a good report.

But at a little before five that afternoon, a call came to the Lumberton Police Department about an assault at Rowan Trailer Park. A uniformed officer was the first to reach Velma's trailer. He was met by a man who identified himself as Stuart Taylor. Stuart had gotten no response to his knock when he arrived to see Velma. He knew she should be there, and when he tried the unlocked door and called Velma's name he heard moans from her bedroom.

He found her on her bed in her underwear, feet and hands bound with duct tape, another slash of tape across her mouth, he told the officer.

Detective Benson Phillips arrived a few minutes later and questioned Velma. She had been crying, and she fought back tears while he pried information from her.

She had gone to take a shower that morning, she said, and as she stepped into the bathroom, a man tossed a towel over her head and forced her back to the bedroom. He bound and gagged her as she begged him not to hurt her. He left her there and departed. Later, she passed out.

She didn't see her assailant, couldn't identify him.

Did he say anything?

Nothing.

Neither had he molested her sexually.

Had he hit her, choked her, hurt her? Was anything missing? Had she seen or heard anybody inside before she went to the bathroom?

No to all.

Phillips checked the trailer and could find no signs of forced entry. How could somebody have gotten in?

Maybe with a key, Velma suggested. An earlier tenant perhaps. She didn't know.

But why would somebody lurk inside just to bind and gag her without doing any further harm or stealing anything? It made no sense, and Velma could offer no explanation. Phillips doubted that a crime had been committed. He suspected that Velma had bound herself, and he thought he knew why when he noticed how solicitous and reassuring Stuart Taylor was being. "You're not staying another night in this trailer," Phillips heard him say. "You're going home with me."

Both Ronnie and Pam were shocked when they learned that Velma had moved into Stuart's small white house on a country road near St. Pauls, ten miles north of Lumberton. They couldn't imagine their mother living with a man out of wedlock. How would she explain that at the Pentecostal Holiness Church?

Velma clearly was concerned about that as well, and she asked Ronnie what he thought when she next saw him. Times change, he told her. If she felt comfortable, she shouldn't worry about what others thought.

Later Velma would say that she and Stuart argued almost from the moment they began living together, usually about his drinking, which became more open and frequent after she moved in. Several times she felt threatened enough to call Pam and ask her or Kirby to come and get her, but every time she left, Stuart soon showed up, asking her to come back. She always returned.

Among the belongings that Velma had taken to Stuart's house were several letters she had received from acquaintances she made in prison. Velma often drove Stuart's truck to work, and one morning she came home to find him holding one of the letters and demanding to know why she hadn't told him she'd been in prison. Because she didn't want him to know, she said. She didn't want anybody to know. She was ashamed of it. And furthermore, she didn't like him snooping in her possessions; she had a right to some privacy. It was his house, he said, and he had a right to go through whatever was in it. He had a right, too, he claimed, to know that the woman he was planning to marry had been in prison. Velma realized that he had been drinking and an argument was inevitable.

From that point, she later said, every time they argued, no matter the reason, he always brought up her prison time, always found a way to use it against her.

Other ominous signs were also quick to appear. Soon after moving in with Stuart Velma wrote two checks to herself on his account without telling him, one for $100, the other for $95, and used the money to pay bills and buy prescriptions. When Stuart's bank statement came in December, he discovered the forged checks and another argument ensued. He demanded immediate repayment, Velma later claimed. If she didn't pay, he would turn the checks over to the police and have her returned to prison. She pleaded with him, promised to pay back the money, she later said. She went to work distressed that night, and the next morning, instead of returning to Stuart's house, she went to Pam's apartment.

Stuart showed up before noon, banging on the glass door.

"I think he was drinking," Velma later recalled. "I was asleep, and when I woke up he was there. He was upset and wanting to talk. He threatened me."

Later Alice would say that after her father learned about the checks and Velma's past, he cancelled his wedding plans, although Velma continued to wear her engagement ring. He wouldn't say that he would never see Velma again, he told his daughter—he was, after all, a man. But he would never marry her, he said. Never.

Despite his seeming resolve, Stuart asked Velma to come back soon afterward. Each seemed unable to stay away from the other. Later, Velma would say that Stuart had forgiven her and told her to forget about the checks. But early in January another fight erupted.

On a Saturday morning Velma turned up unexpectedly at Ronnie's apartment. She was upset, and she obviously had taken more of her medicine than usual. She had left Stuart, she told her son, and was never going back. She had no place to live. She couldn't keep moving in and out with Pam. Kirby was getting fed up with it. Couldn't she stay with him and Joanna for a while?

Ronnie and Joanna had struggles enough in their marriage without adding his mother to the mix. For a few moments he said nothing. Then words came from his mouth that he later said were among the hardest he'd ever spoken.

"Mama, I can't let you do that."

Velma looked shocked. She started crying. Ronnie moved to put his arm around her.

"If it was just me," he said, "it would be different. But I've got Joanna and Michael to think about. I can't do that to them. I'm gone a lot. Joanna can't look after you and Michael, too. I can't put that kind of burden on her."

"She won't have to look after me," Velma said, sobbing. "I can help out."

Ronnie reminded her of the time he and Joanna had gone out one night and left her to tend Michael, who was now twenty months old. They had returned to find her passed out on the couch and Michael crying in his crib. Pam and Kirby had had a similar experience with her and Beverly.

"You know how you are with that medicine," Ronnie said.

"I won't take too much medicine," she said plaintively.

"Mama, I can't trust you not to do that. I wish I could."

Velma pleaded, but Ronnie held firm. "It doesn't matter what you say, you're not going to stay here," he said.

He promised to help her find a place.

"I know you're my mother," he told her, "but I've got a family of my own now, and I've got to put them first."

"Fine, if that's the way you feel," Velma said, her anger suddenly flaring. "I just can't believe you're treating me like this."

She whirled and was out the door, then turned and, saying nothing more, gave Ronnie a look he would never forget.

"It was a mean, mean look," he later recalled, "real angry, unlike any I've ever seen before."

As Ronnie watched his mother drive away in Pam's car, he was overcome by guilt. He had promised her that she always could count on him, and now he had turned her away.

Pam took her mother back in, and on Wednesday, January 25, Velma entered Southeastern Hospital for minor surgery. She had been complaining of pain in her left shoulder and an enlargement of her left breast. A reduction mammaplasty was performed.

Velma was released from the hospital on Saturday with new prescriptions for painkillers. She had called Stuart before going to the hospital to tell him about the operation, and he came for her and took her home with him.

Velma was scheduled for a checkup on Tuesday morning, January 31, and Stuart drove her to Lumberton. After leaving the doctor's office, they stopped at Eckerd's Drugs to get a prescription filled. While they waited, Stuart went to look at the fishing tackle. Velma picked up a can of hairspray and a few other items.

As they were leaving, Stuart suggested that they drop by Alice's house. He wanted to see her baby. Alice suffered from multiple sclerosis and wore a steel brace on one leg. Her pregnancy had been difficult, but she had delivered a healthy son, William Norman Storms IV, her first child, on October 9.

Alice knew that her father and Velma had broken up again, and she had thought that it might be permanent this time.

"Look who I found," Stuart announced when he got to his daughter's house, and Alice was surprised to see Velma smiling behind him.

Alice had the flu, was feeling terrible, but she sat to chat. Both Stuart and Velma held the baby. Alice showed off snapshots, and that led to looking at old family photos and reminiscing. Velma laughed and told Stuart she wanted to see his "dead" picture. He'd told her about it, but she'd never seen it.

At a family gathering when Alice had her camera out, her father, as a joke, had stretched out on the couch, folded his hands across his chest and closed his eyes as if he were laid out in a coffin. Get a picture of him like this, he told Alice, he'd always wanted to see what he would look like dead.

Now Alice fetched the photo for Velma, and they all laughed about it, although Alice soon would view the incident in a totally different light.

A nationally known evangelist, Rex Humbard, was holding a crusade in Fayetteville, and Stuart had promised that he would take Velma to hear him that night. A little after five, he put on his good clothes and got ready to drive the twenty miles to Fayetteville.

He had a beer before supper, but Velma didn't object. After eating, they drove to the Cumberland County Civic Center. Soon after the service began, Stuart said that he was feeling sick—maybe it was something he ate. Within a half hour, he needed to go outside. Don't worry, he told her; stay until the service is over, but he was going to the truck and lie down.

Stuart was having such severe pains that Velma had to drive home. Before they got there, she had to stop so he could vomit.

By 2:30 in the morning, Stuart was so sick that Velma called Alice's house. Her husband, Bill, answered groggily, and Velma told him she hated to call at such an hour but she thought they ought to know that Stuart was very sick. She didn't know if it was worth bothering Alice. She knew Alice was sick herself.

A short time later, Alice called for details. Did she need to come? No, honey, Velma told her, no sense in coming out in the cold in your condition. She was on leave from work because of her surgery, so she could care for him. He probably just had the same flu Alice had.

If he gets worse, Alice told her, do whatever you can to get him to the doctor. Her father hated doctors, and he had to be nearly dying before anybody could convince him to see one.

Alice called Velma again as soon as she got up the next morning. Stuart was no better. He hadn't eaten anything, hadn't slept at all. But he didn't want to go to the doctor. Velma assured Alice that she was looking after him and would call if any problems developed.

Later in the morning, Velma appeared at the home of Stuart's good friend and neighbor, Sonny Johnson. Johnson had known Stuart for forty years and had lived only a hundred yards away for the past fifteen. During quail season they hunted together almost every pretty day.

On Monday the two friends had gone together to check their tobacco beds. Soon the seeds would be sprouting. The young plants would grow under white muslin until the weather was warmer and they could be set in the fields. Both men looked forward to spring when they could get back to the fields. Stuart had been fine when they had separated that day.

Now Velma was telling Johnson that Stuart was sick and wanted to see him.

"I went down and he looked terrible," Johnson later told *Fayetteville Times* reporter Dennis Patterson. "Had a wash basin there by the bed and he was throwing up and seemed real weak. He asked me if I'd take care of his pigs for him till he got over this touch of flu he had."

Alice called several more times Wednesday to check on her father, always to be told by Velma that there was little change.

At 9:30 Thursday morning, a cold and rainy day, Velma and Stuart showed up at the emergency room at Southeastern Hospital in Lumberton. Stuart complained of pains in his chest, stomach, arms. He was dehydrated, his blood pressure low. The emergency room physician started him on intravenous fluids and vitamins. The doctor questioned Velma about his medical history. She knew of no previous illnesses, nothing chronic except his drinking. He was an alcoholic, she noted. The doctor questioned Stuart about his drinking. Stuart acknowledged it but said he hadn't been drinking recently.

Velma called Alice from the emergency room, frightening her. Alice knew her father had to be desperately ill to go there. She was too sick to come to the hospital, but she called her brother Billy, who hurried over.

Stuart remained in the emergency room for nearly three hours while tests were conducted. When they were completed, the doctor came out to talk to Velma and Billy. His diagnosis was gastritis. He suspected it had been triggered by Stuart's drinking. He prescribed Mylanta and lots of fluids and told Velma she could take him home.

Sonny Johnson came by to see him that afternoon. "He said he'd gone to the hospital and gotten a shot and some fluid," he later recalled. "He was sitting up on the edge of the bed and smoking. I just stood in the doorway and talked to him because he thought it might be the Russian flu."

When Alice called on Friday, Velma told her that Stuart was doing better. He was talking, sitting up some. He'd been able to go to the bathroom by himself. He hadn't eaten anything yet, but he was thinking about it. He'd said he'd like to have some oyster stew.

Alice relaxed. If her daddy was talking about oyster stew, he definitely was getting better. It was one of his favorite foods. Velma said she had to run into Lumberton and she would pick up some oysters.

Yet at eight Friday night, Velma called a neighbor and told him Stuart needed an ambulance. The rescue squad was dispatched.

John McPherson, who lived nearby and had known Stuart for fifteen years, got to the house within five minutes. He found Stuart on his bed, the sheet marked with feces. Stuart was moaning and flailing, unable even to tell him where he was hurting. Velma had put kitchen chairs around the bed to keep him on it. The rescue squad members had to restrain Stuart's arms to take his blood pressure. It was dangerously low and falling rapidly. "Let's go, boys," McPherson said, "we've got to get him to the hospital now!"

They raced to Southeastern Hospital, Velma following in Stuart's truck.

An hour after they got there, Stuart Taylor was dead.

Stuart's children were stunned when Dr. Richard Jordan came to the small waiting room where they had gathered with Velma and told them of Stuart's death. They couldn't understand how this had happened. Their father had never been sick. He was only fifty-six. He'd always been strong and healthy. Dr. Jordan admitted that he was as puzzled as they were. He suggested an autopsy. The children included Velma in their decision. She told them that if they didn't do it they'd always wonder, and all agreed.

The telephone beside the bed of Lumberton Police Detective Benson Phillips rang at 5:30 Sunday morning, stirring him from sleep. A woman was on the phone, crying, hysterical. She sounded drunk and at first Phillips couldn't make out anything she was telling him. He attempted to calm her with little success. He finally got from her that a murder occurred the night before and she knew who did it. He'd heard of no murder, and if one had happened in Lumberton, he would have been called; he investigated all homicides. He tried to get details but failed. "Somebody's got to stop her," the woman kept saying. She wouldn't tell him who she was, wouldn't say who needed to be stopped, wouldn't even reveal who had been murdered. Just another crazy, he thought.

But just to be safe, he said, "Look, I'll be going to the office at eight o'clock. Why don't you give me a little time to check things out and call me back there." He gave her the number, thinking he'd never hear from her again.

At the office, he found that no homicides had been reported in town or in the county. Just as he suspected. He was certain that he wouldn't hear from the woman again.

But at nine o'clock she called. This time she was calmer, more coherent. She still didn't want to give details, but Phillips gradually coaxed them from her. She revealed that she was calling from South Carolina, but she couldn't give her name, she said. She didn't want anybody to know that she had called. The man who was murdered, she said, was the boyfriend of Velma Barfield, and she had killed him just as she had killed her own mother. The name triggered no immediate reaction in Phillips. It would be weeks before he would connect it to the incident he had investigated at Rowan Trailer Park three months earlier.

The caller admitted that she could offer no proof, but she was sure that what she was telling him was true. She was sure, too, that Velma's boyfriend and mother weren't the only ones. Too many other people close to Velma had died, she said, including two elderly people Velma had worked for, but she didn't know their names. When Phillips pressed for evidence, she could offer none.

How did she know about all of this? Phillips asked.

"Because," she said, "Velma is my sister."

CHAPTER 10

Velma went home from the hospital with Alice after Stuart's death Friday night. When the family received guests at the funeral home Sunday, Velma stood before the open coffin with her arm around Alice. "He's in a far better place," Velma told her, and Alice took comfort from the words. Velma remained at Alice's house until the funeral on Monday. Ronnie attended the service with his mother, both sitting with the family.

Ronnie had to take off from work for the funeral. "You know, it's the saddest thing," he said to a colleague as he was leaving, "but it seems like everybody my mother ever gets close to dies."

Stuart was buried in the cemetery at Great Marsh Baptist Church, not far from his house. Nearby was the grave of his Aunt Dollie, who had introduced him to Velma. Later, Stuart's friend, Sonny Johnson, would remember looking across the cemetery as he was departing and seeing Velma standing alone by Stuart's grave, the last to leave.

Stuart's children were deeply moved by the care that Velma had given their father and the comfort she offered them, despite her own apparent grief. She had prayed with them and for them, and they were especially touched by the wreath she sent, featuring doves flying toward heaven, one for each member of the family.

On the day after the funeral, Velma went to Stuart's house with his children to get her belongings. The children wanted to begin sorting through their father's things. Estate matters were looming. As they went through the house, Alice asked Velma if she would like to have anything of Stuart's.

Just one thing, Velma told her, and a misty look came to her eyes.

The wedding ring Stuart had bought with the engagement ring she wore, the ring he now would never get to place on her finger.

The children had no idea where the ring was, but Velma knew. Stuart had had a burglary, had lost his hunting guns and other valuables, and he was wary of thieves. He had hidden the ring on a nail inside the wall behind a closet, and Velma went right to it.

Velma told Stuart's children that she was planning to set up housekeeping alone again, and they gave her some kitchen appliances and several other items. Later, back at Alice's house, the children and Stuart's adopted nephew presented Velma with another gift: $400, $100 from each of them, a token of their affection. Velma cried and hugged each in turn. Such good people, she said. How lucky Stuart had been to have them.

Benson Phillips did not know what to make of the two strange calls he'd received Sunday morning. The charges the caller had made were so vague and uncertain. She might have been somebody with a grudge, telling lies in hopes of creating trouble for Velma Barfield. He had no way of knowing if she actually was Velma's sister, but even if she was, she could just be paranoid, imagining things, especially considering her condition during the first call.

Still, he was intrigued enough to find out if any deaths actually had occurred over the weekend. He called the hospital and got the name of Stuart Taylor. He had been brought to the emergency room Friday night and had died a little later, apparently of natural causes, Phillips learned. Certainly no indication of murder, but he couldn't rule it out.

Phillips called the hospital's pathology department to see if an autopsy had been ordered, and, if not, to alert the medical examiner that one should be considered. An autopsy, he discovered, had been done the day before by Dr. Bob Andrews, the regional medical examiner, who had been a pathologist at the hospital for more than twenty years. The results, however, were not yet complete.

If Taylor had been murdered the autopsy would show it, Phillips figured. And even if somebody had killed him, the case would not be his. He had discovered that Taylor had been brought to the hospital from the countryside near St. Pauls. That would put any investigation under the jurisdiction of the sheriff. He had no responsibility. Still, he made a note to call his old friend Wilbur

Lovett at the sheriff's department on Monday to tell him about it. As police chief, Lovett had given Phillips his job.

Lovett, too, was intrigued after talking to Phillips. He couldn't reach Andrews on Monday, but he left a message requesting the results of the autopsy when it was complete. That was all he could do until he knew whether a crime had in fact been committed.

Although Dr. Andrews had received no word of suspicions about Stuart Taylor's death, he was also intrigued, because he could find no real cause. The only disorder he found was gastroenteritis, a severe inflammation of the stomach and intestines, but that wasn't enough to kill an otherwise healthy man of Stuart's age. Andrews cut out a portion of each of Stuart's organs and kept them for later examination, hoping for an answer.

When he returned to work on Tuesday, the day after Stuart's funeral, Andrews began examining the tissue under a microscope. On Wednesday, February 8, he discovered what he thought was an abnormality in a bit of liver tissue. He didn't know what it was, but he packed all the tissue into five plastic bags and sent it to the office of North Carolina's chief medical examiner in Chapel Hill with a request for further tests.

A week after her father's death, Alice Storms called the hospital to find out if the autopsy results were complete yet. The answer was no. Later, she went to the hospital for a copy of the death certificate. In the block marked "cause of death," three words had been scribbled: "undetermined, pending autopsy." That first word stuck in Alice's mind and gnawed at her. What undetermined force had killed her daddy? She wanted an answer and she kept calling the hospital trying to get one. A month after her father's death she was forwarded to Dr. Andrews, who told her he was still waiting to hear from tests he had ordered.

After talking with Alice, Andrews called Page Hudson, the state's chief medical examiner, to see if any progress had been made on the tissues he'd sent. The family was pressuring, he noted. Hudson hadn't heard of the case and asked Andrews about it. Later Hudson would recall that after Andrews had related Taylor's symptoms, reporting that he'd been brought twice to the emergency room by his girlfriend, Hudson interrupted: "I said, 'Where'd she get the arsenic, Bob?' "

Hudson had schooled himself in death by arsenic. He'd had to.

In the ten years since he had set up the state medical examiner's office and become its first chief hardly a year had passed when he hadn't had to deal with at least one arsenic murder. The use of arsenic as a murder weapon was more common in the South than in any other part of the country, Hudson had learned, and probably more common in North Carolina than in any other state. Sixteen arsenic deaths, mostly homicides and suicides, had occurred in the state just since 1971, when records began being kept, six in a single year—and those were just the confirmed cases. Hudson was sure that many others went unsuspected and undiagnosed. Most of North Carolina's arsenic murders took place in the eastern part of the state, partly because arsenic was so commonly used to control pests and was so easily accessible.

One reason for that was a one-man company run by Fred B. Singletary in Rocky Mount, 125 miles up I-95 from Lumberton. The company produced Singletary's Rat Poison, a clear, odorless and tasteless liquid, which contained a high concentration of arsenic trioxide, the deadliest form of arsenic. In 1976 the North Carolina Pesticide Control Board had tried to outlaw it, but Singletary, who died later that year, had blocked the effort. The board had succeeded only in passing a regulation that anybody buying Singletary's had to sign for it, but no identification was required, and any signature would do. Singletary's was available in almost every country store in eastern North Carolina and had been for many years. In 1977, when the regulation requiring customers to sign for it went into effect, the proprietors of most stores selling it were still unaware of the new rule.

To some, the effort to stop the sale of Singletary's seemed pointless. After all, Terro, an ant poison, also colorless and tasteless, contained arsenic too, and anybody with sixty cents could walk into almost any drugstore or hardware store in the state and buy enough to kill almost any adult.

After Andrews' call, Hudson found the tissue he had sent still waiting to be tested. Hudson could tell from a slide of liver tissue whether arsenic was present in appreciable quantities. Arsenic attacks cells, especially in the central nervous system, causing them to weaken and break into nuclei. Hudson looked for those meiotic traces in the liver, where they never should be. He quickly found them in the tissue that Andrews had sent and called to tell him that he was fairly certain that Stuart Taylor had been poisoned. More extensive tests would confirm it, but this was Friday and they couldn't be done until Monday.

On Monday, March 6, Hudson called back. Stuart definitely had been killed by arsenic.

"What do I tell the family?" Andrews asked.

"Don't tell them a damn thing. Call the D.A."

Joe Freeman Britt had never prosecuted a poisoner. After talking with Andrews Monday afternoon, he immediately called Hudson and got a twenty-minute course in arsenic poisoning: where the deadly potion could be purchased, how it killed, how much was required, the symptoms produced. Death by arsenic was torturous, Hudson said, slow, agonizing, extremely painful, horrible to witness. Near the end of their conversation, Hudson told Britt one thing to keep in mind: in perhaps half the cases of arsenic murders he'd examined, the killer had done it before—and that pattern and the ease with which arsenic murders escaped detection left him with little doubt that many of them would do it again.

Britt often padded about his office in his socks, his shirt collar unbuttoned, tie askew. Now he pulled on his shoes and, puffing on an ever present cigar, took the elevator from his second-floor office in the shiny new courthouse to the sheriff's department in the basement. He walked into the office of Malcolm McLeod, who had been sheriff of Robeson County for twenty-seven years and was beginning his last year before retirement.

"Sheriff," Britt said, "we might have us an arsenic murder."

McLeod called in his chief investigator, Hubert Stone, who soon would become sheriff, and Stone summoned his two homicide investigators, Wilbur Lovett and Alf Parnell.

As soon as Britt told the officers about his conversation with Andrews, Lovett brightened. That was the call he'd been waiting for. He already had reason to believe that Stuart Taylor's death was murder, and he had a suspect as well. Her name was Velma Barfield.

He told about the calls Benson Phillips had received a month earlier. If the caller was right, they didn't have only one murder. Velma might also have killed her mother and a couple of elderly people for whom she'd worked.

Alf Parnell could not believe the way this was unfolding. Not only had he known Velma Barfield for most of her life, he also knew Stuart Taylor. He'd met him when he was a patrol deputy in St. Pauls, though he had no idea that Velma had become involved with him. He had known all of Velma's family and her first husband, Thomas Burke, who had died in a fire. He knew, too, that Velma had married again, an older man from Fayetteville he'd never met—he didn't remember his name, didn't know what had become of him. But he did know the identity of one of the elderly people for whom Velma had worked. He was John Henry Lee.

Parnell had been the detective who had gone to Lee's house to investigate a forged check just before his death. He had been surprised to find Velma working there. She had seemed a likely suspect for the forgery, but when he questioned the Lees about her, they wouldn't hear it. Velma was an upstanding Christian, they said. She would never do something like that.

For his part, Lovett had known the other elderly couple for whom Velma had worked, Montgomery and Dollie Edwards. Montgomery's son, Preston, Lumberton's fire chief, was one of his closest friends.

And everybody in the room knew Stuart Taylor's son-in-law. Bill Storms, the husband of Taylor's daughter, Alice, worked right there in the courthouse with them. He was the court reporter, a quiet and gentle man liked by all.

Not an hour had passed since Bob Andrews' call to Britt, and an investigation of Velma Barfield was already under way. Nobody in the room had to be told that this very well might become the biggest murder case that Robeson County had ever seen.

The detectives began with basics, gathering records, collecting the easily available information that would guide them to people who could help their investigation. Parnell even went shopping, searching out places that sold Terro and Singletary's to see how easily Velma could have obtained it.

By Wednesday, Parnell and Lovett had assembled the death certificates of Stuart Taylor, Lillie Bullard, Dollie and Montgomery Edwards, and John Henry Lee (Jennings Barfield's identity was not yet known to them), and delivered them to the district attorney.

"We spread them out across the desk," Britt later recalled, "and it was just like a damn suit of cards: gastroenteritis, gastroenteritis, gastroenteritis. . . ."

"Gentlemen," said Britt, running a hand through his curly dark hair, "I think we have a serial killer on our hands."

By this time the detectives knew that Velma had been in prison, that she had a history of writing bad checks (thirty-one charges in two counties going back to 1968), forgery and wrecking cars. They also knew that seven bad check charges were still outstanding against her, that she worked on the third shift at United Care, a local nursing home, and that she lived in the home of an elderly woman on Franklin Street, Mamie Warwick, a woman, they realized, who might be in danger, as perhaps could be the patients in the nursing home. This potential danger lent an urgency to their investigation.

The detectives wanted to pick up Velma and question her, see her reaction when they told her they knew Stuart Taylor had been poisoned. If she was willing to talk, they could at least stake out her position, which could prove helpful later. They might even startle her into a confession, which would make their case much easier. They could bring her in on the ruse of the bad checks, then spring Stuart on her.

Britt thought the plan worth a try.

Velma had passed the bad checks in Lumberton, so Benson Phillips, who had been brought into the investigation because of the calls he'd received about Velma, was sent to bring her in on Friday afternoon.

Later, Velma would say that when Phillips surprised her from sleep that day, she asked for a few minutes to get ready and during that time had downed two Valium, two Tylenol with codeine, a Sinequan and an Elavil, both antidepressant sedatives, but the detectives would say that she had not appeared to be under the influence of drugs.

Phillips talked to Velma alone at first, advising her of her rights, going over the checks with her. They then were joined by Lovett and Parnell. Lovett told Velma that they understood she knew Stuart Taylor. When she acknowledged that she did, he asked if she knew that he'd been killed by arsenic.

Velma seemed shocked at the news. The detectives asked about their relationship. Had they argued? Fought? Was Stuart's drinking bad? Had he ever hit her?

Velma broke into tears. "Y'all think I poisoned Stuart, don't you?" she said. Then, with bite in her voice, she asked, "What would I have to gain by poisoning him? I was going to marry him."

She was the one who had taken care of him when he was sick, she went on, the one who had taken him to the hospital for help.

Was anybody else with him during that time? she was asked.

No, she acknowledged.

How could he have gotten the poison?

She didn't know.

The detectives were more certain than ever that Velma had killed Taylor, but she steadfastly denied any involvement.

Would she be willing to take a lie detector test? Lovett asked. She most certainly would, she assured him, and it appeared to be no bluff. They would arrange one and get back to her. She was free to go. Phillips would take her home.

Velma was clearly shaken, and as she was leaving, Parnell said, "Velma, you know, this can go all the way back to your mother." He wanted her to realize that they knew about the others, wanted her to worry about it. She gave him a sharp look, then turned away, saying nothing.

On Saturday morning, Lovett and Parnell went to Bill Storms' house to give Alice the information she had been seeking for more than a month: the autopsy results.

They were sorry to have to tell her that her father had died from arsenic poisoning, they said, and they felt certain he'd been murdered. Alice burst into tears and nearly collapsed. "Who in heaven's name would have given it to him?" she asked when she had recovered enough to speak.

"We suspect Velma Barfield," Lovett said. He and Parnell went on to explain why and to question her about her father's relationship with Velma.

Alice told them about her father's last days, the checks Velma had forged, Stuart's discovery of her prison sentence, their arguments and breakups. As she did, her fury was growing. All she could think about was how she had trusted Velma, how she had taken her into their family, how sweet Velma had always seemed. Velma had called regularly during her most difficult times with her pregnancy and her M.S., Alice said, calling just to say that she was praying for her and requesting prayers for her at church. And when she had given birth to her healthy, beautiful child she had been convinced that those prayers had helped to make it possible. Alice and her family were Catholic, and she remembered, too, how Velma had prayed with their priest right in this room on the night of her father's death, prayed for Stuart's soul and for peace for them all, and how later Alice had stayed up all night, unable to sleep, but

Velma had slept soundly in the room beside her child, Stuart's grandbaby, snoring all night. Poor Velma, she had thought, she's so exhausted from looking after Daddy. Velma had made fools of them all, she now knew, and her sense of betrayal was beyond expression.

Velma still called regularly, innocently asking if she'd heard anything about the autopsy, saying how good Stuart had been to her and how much she missed him, Alice told the detectives.

Before they left, the detectives asked Alice and Bill not to talk about the investigation to anybody. They could let Velma know that they were aware of the autopsy results, since she already knew that herself, but they shouldn't say anything else.

Later that afternoon, Velma called, asking if Alice had heard about the autopsy. When Alice replied that she had, Velma went on to reveal that the police had come to inform her the day before, that they had questioned her with seeming suspicion, upsetting her greatly, and how indignant she was that they could think that she would hurt Stuart when she was the one who had cared for him and loved him. She thought the sheriff's department was trying to cover up wrongdoing at the hospital by blaming her, she said, and she didn't appreciate it one bit.

Alice went along with her, hearing her out as if nothing was wrong, but it wasn't easy. "I put a crease in my lower lip," she later said. "I was about ready to come out with a few choice words."

On Monday, Bill Storms came to the sheriff's department carrying a check that Alice had discovered in her father's most recent bank statement. The check was for $300, payable to Velma. But the signature on it clearly was not Stuart's, and Bill brought other checks signed by Stuart that proved it. The check was dated January 31, the day Stuart fell ill. It had been cashed February 2, the day before Stuart's death. Bill had just handed the detectives and Joe Freeman Britt a motive for murder.

Wilbur Lovett was at First Union Bank later that day trying to find the person who had cashed the check Bill Storms had brought him when Ronnie Burke called Alf Parnell and told him that he was on his way to the sheriff's department—and he was bringing his mother.

Bob Jacobson was driving to work Tuesday morning, March 14, his radio tuned to Lumberton station WTSB when he heard a news report that a woman had been charged in the poisoning death of her boyfriend. In North Carolina, murder by poison was automatically a capital case, and only a few lawyers in Lumberton who accepted court-appointed cases met the criteria for trying capital cases. Jacobson was one, although he had not yet tried one. Robeson County courts had a rotating system for appointing lawyers in major cases for indigent defendants and this was Jacobson's week. He just caught the woman's name—Velma Barfield. If she didn't have the money to hire a lawyer, he knew, she was about to become his client. A short, sandy-haired man in his mid-thirties, with an open, freckled face, Jacobson stopped by his office, then walked to the courthouse.

Ronnie and Pam were already at the courthouse with Velma's sisters, Arlene and Faye, all of them still reeling from the events of the past twenty-four hours. They had gone to the jail earlier and learned that Velma was about to be taken to the courthouse for her first appearance before a judge. At the courthouse, Ronnie saw Alf Parnell, who told him he would try to arrange for her family to see her afterward.

Ronnie would never forget how his mother looked when she was led into court that morning: befuddled, depressed, sick, angry. She was only forty-five, but she looked like an old woman.

District Court Judge Charles McLain asked if she had a lawyer, or the money to hire one, and Ronnie could barely hear her as she answered no. McClain appointed Jacobson to represent her, then ordered her sent to Dorothea Dix Hospital in Raleigh for psychiatric evaluation, a standard procedure in cases of such gravity. Ronnie was pleased that Jacobson would be representing his mother. Jacobson taught night classes at Robeson Tech, where Ronnie worked, and he liked him.

After the judge's rulings, Jacobson led Velma to a small room off the courtroom for their first meeting. Later, he would recall that he got very little from that encounter. Velma was in no shape to be questioned. She kept saying that she hadn't meant to kill them, only to make them sick. *Them?* thought Jacobson. She was charged only with killing her boyfriend. Not until later would he learn that his new client had already confessed to killing four people. That was going to make his job extremely difficult.

After Jacobson finished, deputies allowed Ronnie, Pam, Arlene and Faye into the room to see Velma. The meeting was brief and awkward, a gathering of strained faces and sad eyes that didn't want to meet. Questions raged in the minds of Velma's children and sisters: Why? How could she have done these horrible things? What had been going on in her mind? But nobody asked them, and Velma offered no apologies, no explanations.

Hardly anything was said, for nobody knew what to say. For Velma's children and sisters, their very presence said everything that was important at the moment: They were still family. They were there for her. They hugged her. Then the deputies took her away. The next time Ronnie and Pam saw their mother she would be in the depressing and frightening ward for the criminally insane at Dorothea Dix Hospital, and she would be in pain, angry, bitter and crying, going through the agonies of withdrawal.

That afternoon Lumberton's daily newspaper, the *Robesonian*, carried its first notice of Velma's arrest, a brief, single-column report buried on page two under the obituaries. It was headlined, "Woman Charged in Poisoning Murder." Near the end, a single sentence gave the sole hint that this could develop into a bigger story. It quoted Hubert Stone, the chief of detectives, as saying the investigation was continuing and that it could shed light on three other suspicious deaths.

By the following morning, the *Fayetteville Times* had made Velma's arrest a page-one story, and the sheriff was quoted as saying that his officers were trying to link her to at least three other deaths, including her mother's.

Reporters had discovered that Velma had worked at a nursing home, where an official called her "very neat, conscientious, intelligent, a good, dependable, capable worker," while being careful to emphasize that no questionable deaths had occurred during her employment. Reporters also had learned that Velma previously had worked for John Henry and Record Lee and for Montgomery and Dollie Edwards, but no officials would acknowledge any of the other deaths to which Velma might be linked.

That morning, Velma was taken to the hospital in Raleigh, and late that afternoon Joe Freeman Britt drove through a blinding rainstorm to Fayetteville to get Superior Court Judge Maurice Braswell to sign exhumation orders.

The story grew daily in the newspapers for the rest of the week, anonymous courthouse sources being the most widely quoted, and

TV crews chased futilely after Joe Freeman Britt, who refused all comment.

On a chilly Saturday morning, work crews, funeral home employees, sheriff's deputies and medical examiners descended with backhoes, shovels and hearses on two cemeteries in Robeson County and a third in Fayetteville, and, under the watchful eyes of Page Hudson and Joe Freeman Britt, unearthed the graves of Lillie Bullard, Dollie Edwards and John Henry Lee. The three bodies were taken to the University of North Carolina Medical Center in Chapel Hill.

On Sunday morning, the *Robesonian* offered no news about the Velma Barfield case for the first time since Tuesday, but it did contain two stories noting the beginning of National Poison Prevention Week.

The barrage of reports about their mother's case on radio, TV and in newspapers made Ronnie and Pam want to hide, yet even worse were the tormenting questions thrust upon them by the revelations that came with their mother's arrest.

Why had he not seen? Ronnie kept asking himself. It was he, after all, who had thought himself closer to his mother than anyone else. How could she have looked him right in the eye and lied to him? He had always trusted her so completely, had been so devoted to her. How could she have fooled him so? Had she done so all of his life? Were there signs that he had not recognized that might have led him to intervene in some way, to have stopped this nightmare before it started?

As he wrestled with these questions, he had trouble sleeping. When he did sleep, he was sometimes jerked awake by disturbing dreams—dreams of fire.

Despite his questions and his haunting dreams, Ronnie remained determined to support his mother and do whatever he could to save her.

"I knew I'd be behind my mom, probably even if it wrecked my marriage," he later would recall. "I knew I'd be behind her whatever it took."

Pam, like Velma's brothers and sisters, found the knowledge that Velma had killed Lillie particularly difficult to handle. Accepting her grandmother's death had been hard enough, but to know that the life of such a gentle and loving spirit had been taken by her own daughter was almost more than heart and mind could bear.

Pam received an even more troubling shock when Kirby reminded her of the time three weeks earlier when they both had been sick. Her mother had been staying with them again after Stuart's death, and she had been reverting to old patterns, taking her medicines in greater quantities than before. One afternoon after Pam and Kirby arrived home from work, Velma asked to use the car.

"Where do you need to go, Mama?" Pam asked.

Velma wouldn't say. Pam knew, of course, that she likely wanted to go for pills. She had that panicky look about her.

"If you need to go someplace, we'll take you," Pam told her, "but we can't let you use the car. We don't want you hurt and we don't want the car tore up."

Velma was indignant. They didn't have to take her anywhere, she huffed; she was sorry she'd asked. She sulked.

Pam was working at a shirt plant then, Kirby at a textile mill. Both went to bed early because they had to be up early for work, but before midnight both awoke with severe cramps and stomach pains. They spent the night retching and running to the bathroom with the diarrhea that soon hit, growing sicker and weaker by the hour. By daybreak they were so sick that they went to the hospital emergency room.

Flu was suspected.

"I thought I was dying," Pam recalled years later. "I'd had the flu before, so I knew it wasn't the flu. I couldn't lie still in the emergency room bed. I was just moving from side to side. It was really just excruciating pain."

They were kept for a while, administered fluids, given shots and released with pain tablets. Velma had returned from work when they got home, and she showed concern. Had to be the flu, she said. There was a lot of it going around.

Pam and Kirby had remained sick, unable to eat and out of work for three days. They even had to return to the hospital once during that time. And in the middle of it Velma announced that she had found a new place to stay. A woman from her church had offered her a room. The church van came for her, and she took her clothes and left.

Not until Kirby brought it up after Velma's arrest, though, did Pam even think about the illness. Remember the tea? Kirby had said. Instantly Pam realized that her mother had poisoned them.

Velma had cooked for them that night, and Kirby had noted that the iced tea seemed different.

"Oh, that's saccharine tea," Velma had said. "We're out of sugar."

It had to be the tea, they knew, because that was the only thing they consumed that Beverly didn't—she had milk—and Beverly had not gotten sick.

Clearly, Pam saw, she and Kirby barely missed being her mother's final victims.

The question she now had to answer was this: How do you forgive a mother who attempts to kill you for no greater reason than petty spite?

In time, both Pam and Ronnie would come to the same conclusion about the questions that troubled them. Although they knew she had done evil things, they could not accept that their mother was evil. They were certain the drugs were at fault. Who knew what awful chemical reactions were set off in the brain when a person combined so many drugs in such great quantities over so long a period? Who knew what bizarre thoughts they created, what instincts they released, what qualities they suppressed? Pam and Ronnie simply could not believe that the mother they had known before their father started drinking, before she turned to doctors and drugs for relief from her stresses, could have done these horrible acts. They had to honor the mother who had nurtured, loved and encouraged them, the mother who had read to them, taken them on their class trips and made certain they were in church every Sunday, the mother they credited for every virtue they possessed. They would stand by the mother who had made their lives miserable for so many years because they could not abandon the mother who had given them so much. And they could only hope that the mother they once had known might yet return, might still be saved.

Velma's brothers and sisters also struggled with some of the same questions that troubled Pam and Ronnie, as well as with their anger over their mother's murder, but in the end most of them, too, would stand behind their sister. Velma's brother Tyrone would sum up their thinking succinctly: "If the Lord could give his life to forgive us, how could we not forgive her?"

On March 26, Joe Freeman Britt went before the grand jury and, using Wilbur Lovett as sole witness, got an indictment against Velma for only a single count of murder, that of Stuart Taylor.

One month later, Velma was released from Dorothea Dix Hospital and returned to the Robeson County Jail. On Friday, May 5, she stood before Judge Hamilton Hobgood for arraignment.

"The defendant is charged with murder in the first degree," said the judge. "How does she plead?"

"Not guilty," replied Bob Jacobson. "Let me add to that plea, not guilty by reason of insanity."

Jacobson requested that an independent psychiatrist examine Velma, and that was granted. He also asked that Velma's trial be moved to the western part of the state, where public attention had been slight and potential jurors would be less likely to know any of the people involved. The judge, however, set the trial in Laurinburg in adjoining Scotland County in the same judicial district. Earlier, Jacobson had asked for additional counsel to assist in Velma's defense, but that was denied.

Ronnie spent many hours with Jacobson, providing background and gathering information and evidence that might prove helpful. When he had gone to clear his mother's belongings from her room at Mamie Warwick's house, he discovered dozens of empty medicine vials and delivered them to Jacobson (he also had found among her possessions Dollie Edwards' driver's license and checkbook). Although his mother's arraignment came during his final exams, he made time for both.

He was determined that nothing would keep him from getting his degree, however. Just as he long had dreamed, he donned cap and gown and was awarded his diploma at Pembroke State University on Sunday afternoon, May 14, honored as a dean's list student. But one important aspect of his dream was missing.

Sunday was the only visiting day at Robeson County Jail, and after the ceremony Ronnie rushed to Lumberton, diploma in hand, hoping to get there in time. He was waiting at the big, thick window where visitors congregated when his mother was brought down from her cell. As she was being led to one of the tiny visiting cubicles, he held his diploma up against the window, grinning broadly. Velma saw him, gazed at the document as if she were momentarily puzzled, realized what it was, and for the first time since her arrest, Ronnie saw her smile.

A few minutes later, peering through the glass in the cubicle, Velma broke into tears.

"Ronnie, you know I wanted to be there," she said.

"You were," he told her. "I felt your presence."

PART III

A Death-Qualified Jury

CHAPTER 11

Joe Freeman Britt hadn't intended to become "the world's deadliest prosecutor," or even a prosecutor at all, for that matter. He hadn't even planned to be a lawyer.

A dozen years earlier, if anybody had told him that he would be living out his life in Robeson County, the place that in his youth he had found so bleak, dreary and boring that he couldn't wait to leave, he would have laughed.

Only the sky had ever truly called him. At twelve, he had taken a paper route—the biggest bicycle delivered route in the county, he later would boast. At fourteen, he had become a bag boy at the Colonial Store in Lumberton. And his only goal was to earn and save money for flying lessons. He soloed at fifteen.

He couldn't explain this yearning for flight. Neither could he fully explain the satisfaction it gave him—the serenity, the security, the sense of freedom, command, order, and, yes, beauty; for from the air even Robeson County took on a resplendence he'd never imagined. He just knew that flying always would be part of his life.

He didn't finish high school. After completing eleven grades, he discovered that he already had enough credits to go to college so he enrolled at Wake Forest, a small Baptist college near Raleigh, his father's alma mater. His would be the last graduating class before the college moved to Winston-Salem and, with Reynolds tobacco money, became a major university.

Even after college, he had no idea what he wanted to do with his life. His father was a prominent lawyer in Lumberton, his mother a teacher, but he was drawn to neither field. Because he had been an ROTC student, he had a two-year military obligation, which would give him a chance to decide what he wanted to do. He spent a year in New Orleans and another with the Twenty-fifth Infantry in Hawaii, and all he got from it was a desire to live out his days with palm trees, sunshine and balmy breezes.

An unexpected scholarship allowed him to attend graduate school at the University of Tennessee in Knoxville. He studied business, but found it boring, and after holing up in the Smoky Mountains town of Gatlinburg to sweat out his thesis, he fled to the palm trees and sunshine of Florida, enrolling in law school at Stetson University.

One reason he had shied from law was that public speaking flustered him, but he forced himself to face it. After graduation, he took the Florida bar exam and, to please his father, flew immediately to North Carolina and took its exam. He passed both and returned to work for a big law firm in Tampa.

After a year and a half, his father's health began to fail, and he had to go home. His plan was to stay maybe a year, get things under control, and return to palm trees and balmy breezes. But family problems kept him in Robeson County, and he opened an office in Lumberton where most of the lawyers were long established and fiercely territorial. Still, he picked up a few cases.

"First time I walked into a courtroom I didn't know when to stand up, when to sit down or what the hell to do," he would recall with a chuckle.

He learned quickly, though, and discovered that he liked it. After he'd won a few cases, the solicitor, John B. Regan, came to talk with him. Regan was an elected official, but his job was only part-time. He was paid twenty-six weeks a year to prosecute all the criminal cases in Robeson and Bladen counties. The job was getting to be more than he could handle, and he was trying to talk the county commissioners into hiring a part-time assistant. Would Britt be interested?

Britt had been uncomfortable having to defend guilty people, and he was more than happy to move to the other side. As a prosecutor he found his calling. It was as natural as flying.

"It was shoot-from-the-hip," he would recall, "not a lot of preparation time. Flew blind through it. You learn an awful lot from that. Anybody can prepare a case. The test is what you can do extemporaneously. It teaches you to seize opportunities."

Within a year of becoming a prosecutor, Britt married a local teacher, Marlyn Linkhaw, and found himself settled even more deeply back into Robeson County. Although he didn't have palm trees and balmy breezes, he still had flying. He'd never stopped that. He was always learning more, getting new licenses. He was qualified for instrument flying, commercial flying, multi-engine planes, seaplanes, gliders, licensed as an instructor in many fields of aviation. But helicopters became his passion, and he acquired his own.

In his helicopter he was no longer a prisoner of the air. He had complete power. He could hover, move forward, go backward, do whatever he wanted. "In that bubble," he said, "you're like a little tin god." Later, there would be those who would claim that he was much the same in the courtroom.

After John Regan developed cancer early in the 1970s, Britt had to take on more and more of the workload, and it was clear even before Regan entered the final stages of his illness that Britt had been anointed his successor. He had already taken the necessary political steps in the Democratic Party, becoming precinct chairman, a member of the party's executive committee, president of the Young Democrats. He announced for election in February 1974, only days before Regan's death, and was appointed to fill his unexpired term.

Ironically, Britt had once opposed the death penalty. At Wake Forest, he had gone to Raleigh with a group of fellow students to pass out leaflets in front of the state capitol in opposition to a pending execution. But that, he later realized, was typical, starry-eyed, youthful liberalism entertained without great thought and with no experience with harsh reality.

Crime and punishment in Robeson County had brought Britt a different viewpoint. In seven years, he had tried criminal acts too horrendous to believe. He had encountered people so vicious, so evil, so utterly irredeemable that he had become convinced that society had no other choice but to eliminate them. To do otherwise was to ensure that some other innocent person would suffer down the road.

As that view had grown, he had become frustrated by his subservient role. John Regan thought that going for the death penalty was a waste of time. Under North Carolina law at the time, juries had the right to recommend mercy in capital cases, and, far more often than not, they did. A dozen other cases could be tried in the time a capital case took. There were only two prosecutors to try all

136 • J E R R Y B L E D S O E

the cases in two counties, and those cases accumulated in appalling abundance. The courts had to keep moving. Far better to accept a guilty plea and get a murderer into prison, Regan thought, than to squander time and hold up the system to no greater effect.

Britt, though, saw killers going off to prison vowing to return to kill again, and he knew that they meant it. He knew, too, that a life sentence was far from that. He was acquainted with families who lived in terror of the day a killer would be released, because they knew they would be next. By the time he was sworn in as prosecutor at age thirty-nine by Judge Henry McKinnon, he had decided that he would do something to help those people.

By then Robeson County was aligned in a new judicial district with Scotland County and his job title was district attorney. "Lot of people didn't know what a solicitor was," he said. "They thought you were a damn vacuum cleaner salesman." Britt had two assistants, but he had already decided that when first-degree murder cases came along, he would be the one who tried them. And he would go for the death penalty in every one, no plea bargains accepted.

Britt was well aware that in the past the first-degree murder cases that usually went to trial were high-profile cases with white victims. Blacks killed by blacks, Indians killed by Indians, Indians killed by blacks, and vice versa, never had been deemed as important as whites murdered by killers of whatever race. Britt made known that distinction would be no more. A victim's rights were the same, no matter race or class, and his job was to see that justice was done on behalf of all.

Britt had read a lot about capital punishment, but he had never seen convincing evidence that it actually deterred other murderers. He had made the acquaintance of Frank Schmalleger, a criminologist who was the head of the sociology department at Pembroke State University (Schmalleger later would become a noted author of criminology textbooks), and the two teamed up to conduct a study to determine if Britt's planned "blitz," as he called it, would show any effect on the first-degree murder rate in Robeson County, where nobody had received the death penalty since 1946.

But even as he embarked on his course, Britt knew that chances were good that nobody he sent to death row ever would be executed.

*   *   *

In 1972, more than two years before Britt was appointed district attorney, the U.S. Supreme Court, in a five-to-four vote, wiped out all the nation's death statutes, ruling that capital punishment was "so wantonly and so freakishly imposed" as to make it "cruel and unusual punishment." The nation's death rows, which had held more than six hundred people—only ten of them in North Carolina—were emptied.

In the wake of the decision, Raleigh's *News & Observer* carried a lead editorial headlined: "Capital Punishment Is Now Dead." Many were pleased, including North Carolina's commissioner of corrections and his boss, the secretary of social rehabilitation and control, both opponents of the death penalty.

Although public sentiment against the death penalty had been growing—just a year earlier the North Carolina House had beaten back by a single vote an attempt to repeal it—most voters in the state still favored it. Within days movement was underway to introduce new capital punishment laws in the next general assembly.

The same grassroots support rose elsewhere, and eventually thirty-four states reinstated the death penalty, taking two divergent routes to ensure more equitable enforcement. More than half of these states, including North Carolina, chose to make death mandatory for persons convicted of certain crimes: a wide range of killings as well as the rape of children and rapes committed in the course of other felonies. But nobody knew whether the new laws would stand up to the scrutiny of the Supreme Court, or whether the court had actually meant to eliminate the death penalty in its 1972 ruling.

Nevertheless, North Carolina's new law became effective in 1974, just as Joe Freeman Britt became district attorney of the Sixteenth Judicial District. Whether the U.S. Supreme Court approved or not, North Carolina was about to begin filling its death row at a rate never before seen. Britt, with his planned "blitz," was determined to do his part.

Within seventeen months, he had conducted thirteen first-degree murder trials and won thirteen convictions, a national record for a single prosecutor. *Newsweek* took note of his accomplishment in an article on July 21, 1975, in which Britt, in explaining his success, was quoted as saying, "You try to re-create just what happened, and you make the jury identify with the victim. Sometimes it's difficult to re-create the savagery that took place."

Britt, who was away on Army Reserve duty when the story appeared, was inundated with laudatory mail from across the country. Students from prestigious law schools sent applications for jobs. A district attorney in Alabama called wanting to bring his entire staff to watch his next trial.

Joe Freeman Britt at work in a courtroom was indeed a sight to behold, for in first-degree murder trials he had found his purpose. He loved the spectacle, the drama, the tension, the challenge, and just as in the cockpit of his helicopter, he controlled and directed it all.

He had discovered a simple truth: a murder trial was story-telling—and he was a born storyteller. He had overcome his early fear of public speaking to find an orator lurking inside, and not an Old-South bombastic orator, but an orator in the finest tradition of the region, where storytelling was prized and good storytellers held power.

The power that Britt held over juries was mesmeric. His hulking presence commanded the courtroom. And his stentorian voice, rolling like thunder, compelled rapt attention. His trials unfolded like stories, with vivid scenes that reached right into jurors' hearts and guts, and made them see, hear and feel a victim's terror, degradation and agonies—feel it to their very sinews—leaving them with images they could never forget.

He liked nothing better than getting a defendant on the stand and going straight for the jugular, exposing him for the merciless and vicious killer he was. "You never get the truth by kissing 'em on the cheek," he said. "I like to heat 'em up, like a crucible, boil the truth out of 'em."

Britt's crowning glory was his closing argument. His voice rose and fell, now in wonder, now incredulous, indignant, angry, filled with wrath, eyes rolling, arms flailing, pointing, pacing. He would slam a fist into a table, wave bloody clothing, brandish a murder weapon. Trial was theater, Britt knew, and dramatic effects made good theater. Nobody came away from a murder trial conducted by Joe Freeman Britt without realizing that he, or she, had seen a hell of a show.

Yet, despite his unprecedented success, Britt was not without detractors, defense lawyers primary among them. Some resented his style, power and achievement, while others, sensing his disdain, simply disliked him.

"He doesn't like defense lawyers," Velma's lawyer, Bob Jacobson, would later say. "The feeling is mutual."

Britt lumped defense lawyers into two categories: nice guys and acid assholes. "The acid assholes are always sniping at you to get you off track," he told journalist Pat Jordan, "and the nice guys are trying to take you home for dinner so they can rub up against you and take off the cutting edge of your personality. I used to get antagonistic with them, but now I just stay the hell away from them. They're the enemy."

Although none of the lawyers who had to try cases against Britt would admit to being intimidated by him, few relished the prospect. "You get your ass kicked so much, you don't want to go back for more," one later remarked.

Not only defeated defense lawyers and embittered defendants sniped at Britt, though. One killer he sent to prison would be charged with attempting to hire a hit man to assassinate him. Sometimes appellate judges went after him.

In 1976, Susie Sharp, chief justice of the North Carolina Supreme Court, took the unusual step of publicly upbraiding Britt for his zeal and for courtroom tactics that "transcended the bounds of propriety and fairness." The court overturned a rape conviction because Britt reminded the jury that the defendant's wife had not testified on his behalf. Under North Carolina law, spouses could not be required to testify against one another, and the comment was considered to be prejudicial. The chief justice noted that the court had earlier overturned one of Britt's death penalty convictions for his excessive and prejudicial language and criticized him in another case for telling the jury that the defendant's lawyers "would do everything they can to sway your mind from justice in this case and get their clients off if they can." Later the court would accuse Britt of "gross improprieties" for telling a witness in a drug trial, "You are lying through your teeth, and you know you are playing with a perjury count, don't you?"

"I deserved it roundly," Britt said years later of the court's criticism. "I just got carried away. You ignore the opinions of the Supreme Court at your peril. It caused me to be a hell of a lot more careful. It made me a better lawyer because it caused me to sit down and think through arguments that were powerful but could be prejudicial, and made me present them in a way that would be legally acceptable."

When newspaper editorial writers fumed about his overzealousness, however, Britt responded less contritely. "It doesn't disappoint me to be called zealous," he told a reporter. "They can't call me stupid, and they can't call me crooked, and they can't call me lazy. As long as I can be called zealous, I'm very happy with it."

Britt did not allow any criticism to quell his zeal for prosecution. He went right on sending murderers to death row. At one point reporters calculated that of all the people occupying death rows across the country, nearly four percent had been personally put there by Joe Freeman Britt.

Then suddenly all his effort was for naught.

In June 1976, the U.S. Supreme Court ruled that mandatory death sentences were unconstitutional, and 120 people on death row in North Carolina celebrated their new life sentences. In the same ruling, though, in a seven-to-two vote, the court decided that it had not intended to outlaw capital punishment in 1972 and decreed that new death penalty statutes enacted after that ruling by three states—Georgia, Florida, and Texas—were acceptable. Those states had chosen to break death penalty trials into two phases, one to determine guilt, the other to set sentence. To be tried as a capital case, a murder had to meet at least one of a set of so-called aggravating circumstances (that a murder was particularly heinous, that it was committed for pecuniary gain, to avoid lawful arrest, etc.). Once guilt was found, the trial then moved to the penalty phase, where aggravating circumstances would be weighed against an almost unlimited number of mitigating circumstances (that a person was impaired, under duress, mentally disturbed, had no previous criminal record, etc.) to determine if death was the appropriate punishment.

North Carolina legislators moved quickly to write a new law in line with those of the three states that met the court's approval. The new law went into effect on June 1, 1977.

Not until October would North Carolina's Central Prison reopen its death row, however. The first person to occupy it under the new law was James C. Jones, age thirty-six. Jones had been on pass after being returned to prison for a parole violation on an armed robbery charge when he shot Jimmy Locklear, age sixty-eight, in the back, killing him. The shooting took place in Pembroke in Robeson County, and Jones, of course, was sent to death row by none other than Joe Freeman Britt.

Britt would not have another first-degree murder trial for more than a year, and if the study undertaken by Pembroke University political scientist and criminologist Frank Schmalleger was any indication, he would be having fewer and fewer. The study, published in the October 1978 issue of *Carolina Politics*, showed that the murder rate in Robeson County had plummeted dramatically in Britt's first two years in office while it had climbed in adjoining Cumberland County, in another judicial district. The conclusion was that the certainty of facing a death penalty was deterring murder in Robeson County.

But at least one murder had not been reported in that study because nobody had known about it: that of Velma Barfield's mother, Lillie. Britt's "blitz" hadn't deterred Velma from killing then or later. Now she would be facing Britt, who still hadn't failed to win a death penalty in twenty-two trials. But this case might well be the one to break his string. He had never tried a woman for her life, and he knew that jurors weren't just reluctant to sentence women to death, they almost never did.

Velma Barfield, Britt knew, would be his greatest challenge.

CHAPTER 12

The Bladen County courthouse was thirteen years old, a two-story red-brick structure with a wide lawn facing Broad Street on a bluff above the Cape Fear River in Elizabethtown. It was here that Joe Freeman Britt brought Velma to trial eight and a half months after her arrest. A special court session had been ordered, and 150 citizens had been summoned as potential jurors.

Four weeks earlier, Judge Henry McKinnon moved the trial from Scotland County because the docket there was overburdened. Bladen County adjoined Robeson County on the east, and Elizabethtown was twenty-five miles from Lumberton.

The courtroom on the second floor was huge, with walls of robin's egg blue, wainscoted with lustrous cherry. Bands of morning sun streamed through tall, narrow windows that faced the courthouse lawn. The area behind the bar was immense, as big as a stage, appropriate for the spectacle that was about to open. The fourteen rows of dark wooden pews were jammed with people called for jury duty when the trial opened on Monday morning, November 27, 1978.

Joanna, Pam and Kirby sat in the first row behind the bar, on the same side as the defense table where Ronnie sat with Bob Jacobson. Family members of Velma's victims occupied the first two rows on the opposite side of the aisle.

Velma was led into the courtroom by bailiffs from a side door. She looked tired, haggard, ill at ease. Dark circles framed her eyes. Her skin was pallid and pasty, her makeup too heavy, her hair stiff with spray. She'd had no appropriate clothes for court, and Pam's in-laws had borrowed several outfits from a woman in their church who was about Velma's size. For opening day she wore a blue skirt with a blue jacket and a white blouse.

Remarkably, few reporters were in the audience, and those present were only from area newspapers, radio and TV stations. Velma's trial wouldn't get the sensational national attention that a serial-killer grandmother might be expected to receive. In part, this was due to Robeson County's isolation—and the even greater isolation of the trial site in rural and heavily forested Bladen County. Perhaps in larger part it was because Velma, despite her admission to killing four people, was charged with only a single murder, that of Stuart Taylor.

The reason was simple. Stuart was the only person she had killed after the enactment of the new death penalty statute. John Henry Lee had died just three days after the law had gone into effect, but the criminal act, the administering of the poison, had first taken place more than a month earlier, and the state had no evidence that Velma had given him poison after June 1.

If Britt failed to win a death sentence in this case, he could try Velma for the other murders one by one, winning life sentences in each and preventing her from ever being paroled.

Ronnie and Pam had already accepted that their mother would spend the rest of her life in prison. Bob Jacobson had told them as much at their first meeting in the spring. His best hope was to save her life. And in that, he knew, the odds were with him.

Jacobson was as much aware as Britt that women rarely received the death penalty. He knew that Velma also had another powerful advantage: she was a grandmother. Sending a grandmother to the gas chamber was practically unheard of, no matter her crimes.

Pam trusted in that. But Ronnie tried to view the situation realistically, and he was dubious about his mother's chances. On one side, as he saw it, were the power and resources of the state and "the world's deadliest prosecutor." On the other was his obviously addled mother with no resources other than the assistance of a soft-spoken young lawyer who had never handled a capital case and was far less experienced and dynamic than his adversary. Despite his respect for Jacobson, Ronnie realized that the matchup was less than even.

Like Britt, Jacobson had had no particular desire to be a lawyer. He had grown up an Air Force brat, the eldest of four sons of a bomber pilot. His high school years had been spent in California and Kansas.

His father had been a native of Iowa and still owned a family farm there, so Jacobson attended the University of Iowa, a political science major, an ROTC student. Following his graduation in 1964, his military obligation awaited, and with it the near certainty of being sent to Vietnam. He chose law school to postpone it.

With his law degree in hand, he became a first lieutenant in the Air Force and was sent not to Vietnam but to North Carolina, to the Judge Advocate General's office at Pope Air Force Base adjoining Fort Bragg, where at the officers club he made the acquaintance of a couple of lawyers from Robeson County who were military reservists. One was Joe Freeman Britt. The other was John Campbell, a past president of the state bar association. Through Campbell he met Judge Henry McKinnon, who like Britt was a native of Robeson County and the son of a lawyer. A World War II combat veteran and graduate of the Duke University Law School, McKinnon had been on the bench since 1958.

Campbell offered Jacobson a job in Lumberton when he was released from the Air Force in 1971, but Jacobson already had a position lined up with the Iowa attorney general's office, where for the next two years he represented the state on criminal appeals before the Iowa Supreme Court. But the winters were bitter in Iowa, and when John Campbell called with another offer in 1973, Jacobson took it. He had been licensed to practice in North Carolina for just under four years when he was assigned to represent Velma.

Now, as court was called to order and Jacobson's friend Henry McKinnon, fifty-six years old, tall and angular with kind eyes and a thin, patrician face, took the bench, Jacobson's mind was concentrated on one thing: picking a jury that would be sympathetic enough to allow Velma to live out her days in prison.

"Ladies and gentlemen of the jury, this is a special session of Superior Court for the trial of criminal cases," McKinnon intoned, "and the case that is expected to be begun at this time is a case in which Margie Velma Bullard Barfield is charged with first-degree murder, it being alleged that she killed one Stuart Taylor under such circumstances as to constitute first-degree murder about January 31, 1978."

He moved quickly to picking the jury. Earlier, in chambers,

Jacobson had requested that the jury pool be sequestered during selection and McKinnon had granted the request, ruling that candidates for the jury would be questioned in groups of twelve. Now the courtroom largely emptied as all but the first twelve potential jurors called to the box departed.

Joe Freeman Britt didn't hold with modern, so-called scientific methods of jury selection. "Courtroom voodoo," he called them. Law schools taught to look for affluent, educated people. Not Britt. Such people had been exposed to too many specious sociological and psychological theories, he thought, were too easily swayed by sad stories, carried too much secret guilt about their advantages.

"I like my jurors to be kicked around a little bit," he later would say. "I want a guy who drives an old car, not one who reads psychology books. That way, when some fast-talking defense attorney starts telling how his poor client was beaten by his daddy as a child and how that makes him not responsible for what he's done, my juror's going to think, 'Shoot, my daddy beat me, too, and I never killed nobody.' "

Britt even looked for jurors who'd had brushes with the law. "I just happen to like tattooed jurors," he would tell reporter Dee Reid, only half joking. "They know why he did it. He's just mean as hell, that's why."

In this jury pool, all of them rural and small-town people, many wearing work clothes, Britt had no doubt that he could quickly assemble a panel that suited him.

Britt wasted no time getting to the crucial question with each juror. How do you feel about the death penalty?

"I am opposed to it," said the first person he asked, a woman.

"Is your opposition such that you could not vote to impose the death penalty regardless of the evidence and circumstances?" Britt asked. "Is that what you are saying?"

"Yes, sir."

She was excused, and the next juror was more to Britt's liking, a truck driver who said he thought the death penalty was necessary in some cases. Another, a construction worker, was even more Britt's kind of juror. "I believe I feel for it," he responded.

A farmer who followed thought the law necessary but said he'd have to have proof "beyond a shadow of a doubt."

What about beyond reasonable doubt? Britt asked.

"I would have to know they deserved it. Couldn't say without hearing the case."

"Well, assume . . ." Britt said and went into a litany of assumptions.

"That's a lot of assuming," said the farmer, drawing chuckles from the courtroom.

It went on like that, but by day's end, ten jurors had been chosen. Before the lunch recess on Tuesday, the second day of the trial, the panel was complete, seven men, five women, nine white, three black. The two alternates were white, one male, one female. The members included a former waitress, a retired Navy flight engineer, a timber buyer, a secretary, a factory worker, a forest service employee, even a member of the National Guard who had been in classes taught by Joe Freeman Britt.

Every person on the panel had agreed that he or she could vote for the death penalty. All who had expressed opposition to capital punishment had been excused. This was, in modern legal parlance, "a death-qualified jury."

Conventional wisdom among lawyers was that the opening statement was one of the most important aspects of a trial. Britt didn't hold with that. He didn't see the point of telegraphing his intentions to the opposition, for one thing. Keep them guessing. But mainly he didn't want to waste his story, didn't want to roll it into a tight little summary, squeezing out its vital juices. He wanted it to unfold full-bore, with all its shocking horror. As usual, he declined to make opening remarks, and Jacobson followed his example.

After lunch, Britt began his story by calling Billy Taylor, who described his father's condition on his first visit to the emergency room.

"Occasionally he would groan or complain and he would try to sit up and he would sit up for a short period and then he would try to lie down and he would fall down. He couldn't stop moving. He would hold his stomach and he was just continually moving."

Jacobson, on cross-examination, made certain the jurors knew that Velma had brought Stuart to the hospital.

"Did she seem concerned about his condition?" he asked.

"At that time, yes."

*　　　*　　　*

The next witness, Leland Jones, an emergency room physician, told of his examination of Stuart on his first visit. "I felt he had gastritis. He had admitted to drinking but not recently, and he was very dehydrated."

Stuart didn't vomit in the emergency room, Jones said. "He had writhing movements."

"Beg your pardon?" said Britt, seeing a chance to emphasize his victim's agonies.

"Writhing."

"Writhing around?"

"Yes."

How many poison cases had he seen in his work? Jacobson asked.

"Well, probably over a hundred."

"This did not appear to you to be that type of case?"

The symptoms were quite common, said the doctor. "There was nothing that would tip you off to anything unusual."

"Are you familiar with the drug Valium?" Jacobson asked.

"Yes."

"What is it used for?"

"Well, it is used for sedation and tranquilization and a number of other things."

Jacobson went on to ask about a long list of drugs that Velma had taken over the years. He would repeat this with every doctor who took the stand. He wanted to plant drugs in the minds of jurors early as the source of Velma's problems, and before they reached any decisions he wanted them to be thoroughly familiar with the names and effects of all that she had taken.

Britt called rescue squad member John McPherson to tell about taking Stuart to the hospital on the night of his death.

"He was breathing really rapid—really fast and his color was real gray-looking. He just couldn't be still. He would try to turn over. He would try to sit up. Of course, all the time we were trying to get him to stay on the litter."

"Was he making noises?"

"Yes, sir, he was moaning and groaning all the way over there."

McPherson said he and two other squad members stayed with Stuart at the hospital for more than an hour. "He seemed to get more restless, seemed to hurt more. I'm sure they gave him a shot, maybe two. We were holding both hands and arms and legs, trying to hold him in the bed. He was trying to move his hands, but we did our best to hold him down."

"And how long did you and the other attendants stay there holding him immobile?" Britt asked.

"Until such time as he threw back his head and gave a long, hard scream. I dashed out and got the nurse and the nurse and doctor came in and started to administer a tracheotomy on him."

"How loud was the scream that you say he uttered?"

"Fairly loud."

"Can you duplicate it here?"

"Object," said Jacobson.

"Overruled, if he can," said McKinnon.

"Well, he just threw back his head and said . . ."

And McPherson threw back his own head and let out a blood-curdling scream that echoed through the big courtroom, leaving no person in the room with any doubt about Stuart's final agonies.

"Object," Jacobson called testily. "Move to strike."

"Overruled," said the judge. "Motion denied."

McPherson went on to briefly describe the doctors' efforts to save Stuart after the death scream.

"What eventually happened?"

"After several tries of resuscitation and CPR, they decided it was of no use, that he had passed on."

"Your witness," Britt said.

Jacobson had little with which to counter. He asked if McPherson had spoken with Velma at the hospital.

"I believe that at one time after I stepped out in the hall she asked me was he going to be all right."

"Did she appear to be concerned about him?"

"At the time, yes, sir."

John Larson, a physician from Sanford who had been working relief at the emergency room when Stuart was brought in the second time, described the treatments he started, the tests he began. "I was very puzzled, because I thought that he had just not had enough fluids," he said. "I had gone out and talked to the physician that was on call . . . and I told him that he would have to hurry because the man was dying and I didn't know really what he was dying from."

"Did the possibility of arsenic poison ever occur to you?"

"No, sir, it did not."

"If that had occurred to you, and if it had been arsenic poisoning, could you have saved the life at that time?"

"Not at that time, no. I believe he was dying before he actually got there."

On cross-examination, Larson told Jacobson that he had treated hundreds of poisoning cases in his thirty-six years of practice.

"What would you have done in a case of arsenic poisoning?"

"Well, if I had known, you give BAL, British antilewisite."

"That is a type of medication?"

"Yes."

If it had been administered a day before, would it have saved him?

"I have never treated a case of arsenic," said the doctor. "I have no idea whether it would or not."

Velma scribbled in a spiral-bound notebook as Richard Jordan told of hurrying to the hospital and attempting to revive Stuart. Britt used him to verify the symptoms of arsenic poisoning: vomiting, diarrhea, severe abdominal pains, restlessness, mental confusion.

"Do you know this lady here?" Jacobson asked, pointing at Velma.

"Yes, sir."

"The fact is, you have treated her, have you not?"

He had treated her for a neck injury following a car accident, he said, and again for tension headaches, giving her a prescription for Tylenol with codeine.

Did he recall speaking to her at the hospital on the night of Stuart's death?

He had told her that Stuart was dead.

"You don't recall what her reaction was, do you?"

"She appeared to be grieved."

Alice Storms was a frail, intense woman, and she seemed nervous as she took the stand.

She told about her father bringing Velma by her house on January 31. "He seemed to be in very good health and very happy acting, playing with my baby and looking at some old pictures of the family," she said.

She went on to describe her father's illness and the events of the next three days. She was relieved, she said, when Velma told her on Friday that Stuart seemed to be improving.

"Sometime in the afternoon I got a call and she said that he was complaining of aching," she said. "She asked me if she should give him an aspirin."

"What?" asked Britt, as if he hadn't heard correctly.

"She asked me if she should give him an aspirin. I told her if he had a fever that it certainly wouldn't hurt, that it normally makes the aching better."

About six or seven, Alice said, she called Velma to check on her father and Velma told her that she fixed oyster stew for him.

"Did Velma Barfield tell you whether or not your father ate the oyster stew?"

"She said she prepared it and he ate it."

Alice said she'd been "really surprised" when Velma called later that evening to tell her that her father was back at the hospital. "I think she told me that he had flared up in bed—sat up—was talking out of his head and that she had, could not keep him on the bed. She had gone and gotten chairs from the dining room and put them beside the bed to hold him on and had gone to the phone and called the rescue squad. I told her I was on my way to the hospital."

She had seen her father only from a distance in an examining room, she said. "I could see him from the shoulders up. He just looked to me really bad off and kind of gray, pale."

"How long did you stay there, please, ma'am?"

"We were called back in the little room and told that he had died."

The family had approved an autopsy, she said, and all of them, Velma included, had gone to her home in shock.

The judge interrupted for a recess, and, afterward, Britt asked Alice if she was familiar with her father's handwriting.

"Yes, sir."

"Had you had occasion to see his checks from time to time?"

"Yes, sir."

Jacobson quickly objected, and the judge asked the jury to leave.

Velma was not on trial for forging checks, Jacobson pleaded, hoping to keep out the exhibits Britt was about to produce.

"Let's see what you are going to show, Mr. Britt," said the judge.

He produced four checks in plastic bags. These bore Stuart's verifiable signatures. Then he brought forward three more checks bearing signatures purporting to be Stuart's, all made payable to Velma. One, for $100, was dated November 4, 1977, and had been cashed November 8. The second, for $95, was dated November 23, cashed November 25. The third, for $300, was dated January 31, 1978, cashed February 3.

"This," Britt said of the final check, "is a very critical piece of evidence."

Jacobson protested that Britt had to be able to show that Stuart had not authorized Velma to sign the checks on his behalf, and that obviously wasn't possible. "To allow these to come in would be pure speculation," he said.

"I do not intend to introduce them," Britt responded. "I merely want them marked for identification. Obviously, if I could not establish these things that the lawyer is talking about, I would not be entitled to introduce them."

McKinnon allowed Britt to proceed, and the jury returned.

Alice looked at the first four checks and said they all bore her father's signature. Britt showed her the other three. Did she recognize those?

She did indeed, but Britt asked her nothing about the signatures.

"Your witness," he said, turning to Jacobson.

Jacobson handled Alice cautiously, quizzing her about how she had come to know Velma, how often she had seen her.

"Did you ever see her take any medication?" he asked.

"No, sir, I did not."

"Did you ever ask Mrs. Barfield her opinion about whether or not an autopsy should be taken?"

"I am quite sure we did at one time."

"Do you recall what she said?"

"No, sir. I can't really say exactly what she said. But she never did object to one."

"No further questions," said Jacobson.

As his final witness of the day, Britt called Bob Andrews, the pathologist who had performed the autopsy on Stuart. Andrews said he had found nothing unusual and couldn't determine the cause of death. No toxicological screenings were done at first, he noted.

"Is this a routine thing in autopsies?" asked Britt.

"It is not routine to screen for arsenic poisoning."

Andrews told the jurors that he continued to work with tissues from Stuart's organs because he was mystified, and that he finally sent them off for tests. Those tests showed that Stuart had high concentrations of arsenic in both his liver and blood.

"It is my opinion," he said, "that Stuart Taylor's death was from acute arsenic poisoning."

"Take the witness," said Britt.

Did his opinion about the cause of death rule out any other cause? Jacobson asked.

"Yes, it does."

The doctor stepped down, and Judge McKinnon recessed court for the day.

In just a half day's testimony, Britt had established murder, let the jurors see, feel—and especially hear—the victim's dying agonies, and had hinted at a motive. Next, he would show the jury that Stuart Taylor had not been Velma's only victim.

CHAPTER 13

When Joe Freeman Britt called Margie Lee Pittman on the third day of the trial, Jacobson objected and asked that the jury be excused.

"Your Honor, the state is bringing up evidence about offenses that are not charged," he told the judge. "Anything about the death of John Henry Lee would be irrelevant in this trial."

"I'd better see what your intent is, Mr. Britt," said McKinnon. "What do you propose from this witness?"

"Boiling it down to its essence, Your Honor, I can say this. The state is in a position to prove conclusively that this defendant murdered John Henry Lee by arsenic poisoning, that the symptoms were the same as the symptoms of the Taylor case, that there was a motive involved in killing him and that related to a check that she had written on Mrs. Lee." He went on to tell the judge that Record Lee, too, had fallen ill, and a sample of her hair and fingernails, tested months later, also contained arsenic.

He planned as well to demonstrate conclusively that Velma had killed her mother and Dollie Edwards, he said, and would further show that she had killed Jennings Barfield, although that evidence would be circumstantial. Velma frowned, shook her head, and whispered to Jacobson when Britt spoke of Jennings.

As precedent for allowing evidence of the other deaths, Britt cited a 1938 case in which a man was tried for giving strychnine to his daughter to collect insurance. In that case, in order to establish intent, the state had been allowed to show that the defendant previously had murdered his two wives for the same purpose, and that case had been upheld by higher courts.

"You have identically the same situation here, if it please the court," Britt argued. "From the very outset of this case, the crux has been intent."

He cited Velma's contention that she hadn't intended to kill Stuart, only to make him sick. "That makes that the central issue. For that reason the state should be allowed to show these other killings."

In addition, Britt noted, Velma had entered a plea of not guilty by reason of insanity, maintaining that she didn't understand the nature of her act. "And I want to be in a position to show that she did very well know the nature of her act. As a matter of fact, she probably knew more about arsenic poisoning than most physicians. I think the law is clear, and I feel that the state should be able to go into these matters."

"Mr. Britt is trying to try five or six cases here rather than one," Jacobson responded, "and it is purely a matter of giving the defendant a fair trial."

"Gentlemen, I think we are previewing right much that is yet to come, and properly so," said the judge, going on to allow Britt to proceed with evidence of the earlier deaths.

The jury returned to hear Margie Lee Pittman describe how she had hired Velma to look after her mother and how her father had become sick soon afterward.

"I stood over him when he was sick on the potty chair because he was too weak to go to the bathroom," she said. "I wiped his head from sweat pouring out all over him. He would groan, and if you had been in the yard you could have heard him, it was so hard. Daddy was the kind that went, 'Oh me, oh me.' "

She went on to describe being summoned to the hospital on the night of her father's death. "When I got there and ran into the room where he was, the first thing I saw were his two feet out of the cover, like halfway up his leg. They were bluish-green-looking to me. I went on up and he was pale—an ashen color is what I would say, and I called him, 'Daddy, Daddy,' and the third time I said, 'Daddy,' I started crying and I turned around and walked out."

"Did he recognize you?"

"He did not. I went back out to the hall and Velma was standing in the hall. I said, 'Velma, Daddy is dying. Daddy is dying.' Well, they went on and put him in ICU and, of course, we saw him later on and he was—he couldn't be still. He was all over the bed. His legs were going this way and that."

Britt got her to describe her father's death and tell how Velma had sat with her mother at the funeral. Then he handed her a check made out to Bo's Supermarket and signed Record B. Lee.

"Is that your mother's signature?" he asked.

"No, sir, it is not."

Jacobson moved that all the testimony about John Henry Lee be stricken.

"Denied," said McKinnon, who then instructed the jury that the testimony had been allowed solely to show intent and could only be considered for that purpose. "The evidence of her commission of some other crime is not evidence of her guilt of the crime with which she is charged here," he said.

Britt now called Frieda Monroe, another of John Henry Lee's daughters, to tell about an incident at the hospital on the night of her father's death.

"The doctor told us that he would have to admit him to intensive care. He was critical. When Velma went to leave the hospital, she looked at me and said, 'Frieda, I do not believe your daddy will go home alive.' I said, 'I don't think so either, but why do you say this?'"

"Object," said Jacobson. "Move to strike."

"Motion denied," said the judge.

"She said, 'I have seen it happen too many times.'"

"Your witness," said Britt.

"No questions."

Joe B. Alexander, a Lumberton physician for more than twenty-five years, took the stand to describe his treatment of Lee. He was familiar with arsenic poisoning, he said, and Lee had the symptoms.

"Did that occur to you at that time?" Britt asked.

"No. I knew Mr. Lee and his family quite well. His recovery from the illness in April was good, and the diagnosis of gastroenteritis seemed perfectly logical. No one came forward with a suspicion that poisoning might have occurred."

Alexander said that he'd seen Lee again when he was brought to the hospital June 3 and that he was deeply cyanotic and unresponsive.

"The skin was cold, sweaty," he said. "The sheet beneath him was wet with sweat. His blood pressure was fifty over twenty, which would not support cerebral circulation."

"Dr. Alexander, do you know this defendant?" Jacobson asked on cross-examination.

"Yes."

"She has been a patient of yours, hasn't she?"

"Yes."

He'd first seen her on January 13, 1977, he said. She'd complained of ulcers, and he had prescribed Maalox, Robinul, which cuts acid secretions, and Valium.

"How much Valium?" asked Jacobson.

"She was given one hundred tablets, five-milligram, to take one three times a day with the Robinul."

She returned a month later complaining of severe headaches with nausea and told him that other doctors had given her shots for it. He prescribed a potent painkiller, Mepergan, and Equagesic, which contained the tranquilizer Equanil. At the end of March, she had been seen by his assistant and given more Mepergan. Four times after that, Alexander said, he had prescribed Valium at telephone request, each time for a hundred tablets, the last on the day that Velma had first been brought in for questioning about Stuart Taylor's death.

Jacobson went on to inquire about other drugs and how they affect the brain, then asked if Alexander had known that Velma was seeing other doctors.

"She referred only to Dr. McCormick."

"What is your practice with regard to represcribing drugs such as Valium?"

"If the request is legitimate, I will refill them up to one year as a standard procedure, if I have no reason to suspect that there is some unusual circumstance about it."

Jacobson named other doctors Velma had been seeing at the same time, asking Alexander if he had known that she was seeing them.

"No, she referred only to one physician, which satisfied my mind."

Would he have prescribed Valium if he'd known Velma had been on other drugs?

"No."

Britt had a few more questions.

"Whether or not she was receiving any other medications, you don't know, do you?"

"No. I had no warning or reason to suspect that something unusual was behind her request."

"Do you know what BAL, British antilewisite, is?"

"I sure do. It counteracts poison by heavy metal."

"In your opinion, how much lead time does a physician need before the terminal onset of arsenic poisoning in order to save a human being by administering BAL?"

"Not to be vague, but in acute arsenic poisoning, death will occur within six to forty-eight hours . . . so the physician is pressed for time. It should be started as soon as the diagnosis is even legitimately suspected."

After lunch, Velma's twenty-year-old niece, Robin Bullard, told about going to her grandmother's house on the day of her death and finding her sitting on a stool in her bedroom wearing only a shirt and retching while Velma was putting plastic sheets over her bed.

Had she ever seen Velma under the influence of drugs? Jacobson asked.

"Yes. I couldn't begin to tell you how many times."

"How did she act on these occasions?"

"She would respond to some things you would say to her, and then again she would act like she didn't know you were in the room."

Weldon Jordan, Lillie Bullard's physician, spoke of her symptoms and how puzzled he was about her death.

"Did you call for an autopsy after she died?" Jacobson asked.

He did, he said, and it was Velma who granted permission.

Edward Fonvielle, Jr., who had been a loan manager with Commercial Credit in Lumberton in 1974, would be the last witness the jury would hear this day. He testified that on November 12, 1974, Velma had taken out a loan for $1,048 under the name of Lillie M. Bullard. No payment was ever made, he said, and a delinquency notice was sent on December 27, just four days before Lillie's death. The loan was repaid by life insurance.

*   *   *

The jury remained out of the courtroom after a fifteen-minute recess because Jacobson told the judge that he anticipated evidence of a confession and was moving to suppress it.

"Do you propose to offer a confession, Mr. Britt?" the judge asked.

"We propose to offer several statements of the defendant."

The judge wanted to preview the evidence, and Britt called Wilbur Lovett to describe his two interviews with Velma and the four signed statements she had given.

"No promises were made to her in any way?" asked Britt.

"No, sir."

Velma nodded affirmatively at Lovett's answer and silently mouthed, "There were."

"Didn't you tell her that it would go easier on her if she made the statement?" Jacobson asked.

"No, sir. I did not."

Jacobson called Velma to give her version of the interviews and followed with Ronnie, who told what had happened when he brought his mother to the sheriff's department.

Jacobson maintained that Velma's statements were not voluntary because Velma was under the influence of drugs and couldn't understand her rights at the time. He asked that they not be admitted.

McKinnon was quick in his decision. "The Court finds the facts to be as testified by Mr. Lovett, and not as by the defendant and her witness. Motion denied."

The hearing had gone longer than anticipated, and the judge brought the jury back and dismissed them. They would have to wait another day to hear Velma's admissions of murder.

The first witness Thursday morning, the fourth day of the trial, was Jennings Barfield's eldest daughter, Ellen Mintz, who told of being summoned to the hospital because of her father's illness, only to learn when she got there that he was dead.

"I said to Velma that I was really sorry he had died and not one of his children could be there. She told me that she had stayed with him and done everything she could for him and I shouldn't feel bad about not being there, that Daddy had said not to leave him, that he did not want to die alone and she had not left him but had taken his hand and held it and stayed with him until he died.

"She told me that Daddy had gotten real sick, that he thought he had the flu and she thought it was something like a stomach virus, that he had gotten sick after supper and vomited and couldn't breathe and was very cold. He had chills and he seemed to be in a great deal of pain. She said he had a rough night."

"What was the general condition of your father's health prior to his death?" Jacobson asked.

"Very bad. He suffered from emphysema. He had diabetes. He had an awfully strong constitution and was always able to rally and stay going, but he was not in good health."

Neil Worden, Jennings' physician, described his symptoms, and his puzzlement over Jennings' death. On cross-examination, he acknowledged treating Velma for dizziness and headaches.

"She called me on several occasions for medications, but after I had prescribed for her on one or two occasions, I told her I would not be able to treat her any longer," he said.

William Hamilton, a Duke University pathologist, who performed second autopsies on both Jennings and Lillie, testified that both had consumed enough arsenic to cause death. And Page Hudson, the state medical examiner, confirmed that John Henry Lee and Dollie Edwards had also died from arsenic poisoning.

Next Britt called Wilbur Lovett to tell about his two interviews with Velma and the confessions she had made. Britt produced the four statements Velma had signed, and all were admitted as evidence. Lovett read aloud the statement about Stuart's death.

Britt then produced an empty brown bottle with a label faded by weather and asked Lovett to identify it. The detectives had found the Singletary's Rat Poison bottle in a field behind Dollie Edwards' house after Velma told them she'd thrown it there, Lovett said. It, too, was admitted, as was a bottle of Terro that Alf Parnell had bought and shown to Velma during questioning.

After a recess, Alf Parnell told the jury that Velma had denied poisoning Stuart or forging checks on his account during her first interview, but that she changed her story after Ronnie brought her to the sheriff's department three days later.

"She said that she just intended to make him sick, that she didn't intend to kill him," he said.

Asked what she'd said about the other cases, Parnell replied, "She said in each of them she knew what the results would be. She said she knew what she poisoned them with, that the result had been death before."

He then read the remaining statements to the jury.

Britt recalled Page Hudson and handed him the two-ounce bottle of Terro that had been introduced into evidence.

"Can you state whether or not that bottle contains sufficient arsenic to kill a human being?"

"Yes, it does."

"Approximately how much dosage would have to be administered to kill a human being?"

"Oh, half of it would be extremely dangerous."

Britt now handed him the larger, empty Singletary's bottle and asked about that.

"As with Terro," Hudson said, "I believe an ounce or so could be lethal."

"Let me ask you about arsenic poisoning. Is it the type of poisoning that accumulates or can you recover from it?"

"Oh, one can certainly recover from it. I have had experience with several nonfatal cases, but it is usually the effect of one or two or several doses over fairly short periods. For example, having one now after having one six months ago, neither one would have much effect on the other. It would really be the effect of the last dose when they are that far apart."

"But if you had one today and one, say, Saturday or Sunday, they would accumulate, would they not?"

"Yes, sir. There would be an additive effect then."

"Could half an ounce kill?"

"Depending on the person. I certainly wouldn't take half an ounce of it."

How long would it take for an ounce of Terro to kill somebody? Jacobson wanted to know.

Some could survive it, he said. Others might die within a day or so. But there could be considerable variation, depending on how much was held down after vomiting began, how much was absorbed into the bloodstream, and how healthy the person was.

Britt came back to get Hudson to describe the effects of arsenic on a human body, then asked about BAL. Was it effective if given in time?

"Yes sir, it is the one fairly specific antidote to arsenic poisoning."

"No further questions."

"You may be excused," the judge said to Hudson.

As Hudson left the stand, Britt rose.

"The state rests," he said.

After lunch, Bob Jacobson began by calling Dr. Arthur Douglas, the psychiatrist who had been appointed at Jacobson's request to perform an independent evaluation of Velma. Douglas had interviewed her on May 29, during a period in which Velma was several times taken from jail to the emergency room with severe headaches and nausea. But before Douglas could answer a single question, Britt objected and requested that the jury be excused.

Britt contended that during Douglas' examination Velma had made self-serving statements that should not be allowed before the jury except as corroboration of her own testimony.

"That is exactly why I want to have it introduced," Jacobson countered.

The judge asked the attorneys to approach the bench. When they did, he turned to Jacobson.

"Is it your purpose to offer the defendant as witness?"

"Absolutely."

"I think from that the doctor, without any special instructions, may go ahead, Mr. Britt," McKinnon said.

The jury returned, and Douglas told them about his interview with Velma. She had indicated that for many years she'd had a nervous condition that included anxiety, depression, difficulty sleeping and headaches, he said, and she blamed it on her husband's drinking.

When he asked about Stuart Taylor, he said, she admitted that she had given him poison.

"She indicated that they had had an argument and that he had been drinking and that he had threatened her, and then she said, 'I thought it would make him sick but not kill him.' "

Asked his diagnosis, Douglas replied that he thought Velma was depressed, which was appropriate to the circumstance in which she found herself. He also concluded that she had a passive-dependent personality disorder and a history of multiple drug abuse.

Asked to define a passive-dependent personality disorder, Douglas replied, "They tend to cope very poorly with stress, and frequently are dependent upon drugs."

Britt went straight to the point on cross-examination:

"You don't consider this woman to be mentally ill, do you, Doctor?"

"No, sir, I don't."

Britt read several passages from Douglas' report. " 'No evidence of illusions or hallucinations. Memory is intact. Her judgment is immature. Intellectual function at least average. This patient is considered competent to stand trial and to participate in her defense. There is no evidence to suggest the patient was mentally ill at the time of the alleged crime, and it is felt that the patient was able to distinguish between right and wrong at that time.' "

Had he written all of this? Britt asked.

"Yes."

"Thank you, Doctor. No further questions."

Next, Jacobson called Dr. R. E. Hooks of St. Pauls, who had been a general practitioner for thirty years and had treated Velma since 1966. He had last examined her on October 18, 1977, he said, three and a half months before Stuart's death, treating her for nervousness and headaches.

"What did you prescribe for her?" Jacobson asked.

"Valium, five milligrams, four times a day. No refills."

"Did she return?"

Monthly, he acknowledged, and each time he gave her a new prescription.

"And each time you put 'no refill' on this bottle?"

"Yes."

"Was there a particular reason for that?"

"Yes. I had had trouble in the past with her taking too much medication and having prescriptions filled at more than one place."

Was he aware that she was seeing other doctors and getting other prescriptions during this time?

"I was led to believe that she was not. I was aware that she had been under the care of other doctors in the past."

Jacobson named some of the other drugs Velma was taking, including the sedative antidepressants Sinequan and Elavil, the sleeping pill Dalmane and the tranquilizer Tranxene.

"Had you known she was being treated with these other drugs, would you have prescribed for her the Valium that you did?"

"No, sir."

"If you had known that Dr. Alexander was also prescribing Valium, would you have prescribed it?"

"No, sir."

"Had the family members of Mrs. Barfield ever approached you about her problems?"

"Yes, they did."

"Could you say who?"

"I think it was her son that talked to me."

"Do you recall the substance of the conversation?"

"I believe that dates back several years when she was having kidney colic, or supposedly kidney colic. There was quite a bit of late-night shots I was giving her, and it reached the point where you could not determine if it was the kidney colic or a nervous problem, and I think that is the discussion that I had with her son."

On cross-examination, Britt inquired about the reason Hooks had Velma coming back month after month.

"You were rationing the medication, is that what you were saying?"

"Right."

"Would someone become intoxicated taking Valium according to prescription?"

"No, sir, not that alone."

"What if they had been taking that in combination with other medication?" Jacobson asked on redirect.

"You could have any state from slightly intoxicated to a coma, depending on the dosage," Hooks replied.

When Hooks had stepped down, Jacobson called the witness most people in the courtroom were waiting to hear, but none more so than Joe Freeman Britt.

"Mrs. Barfield, would you please take the stand?"

CHAPTER 14

Bob Jacobson felt he had no choice but to have Velma testify. He had two hopes to save her life. First was to win a conviction for second-degree murder. From the beginning Velma had unwaveringly maintained that she never intended to kill anybody, only to make her victims sick. Even if that seemed irrational, he needed her to tell it to the jurors. Intent was a necessary element of first-degree murder. If he could get the jury to believe that it was never there, they could only find her guilty of second-degree, and the maximum penalty for that was life.

If that failed, his other chance was to persuade the jury that Velma's long history of drug abuse had left her unable to comprehend that she was committing a crime when she gave Stuart poison. That might also win a verdict of second-degree, and even if it didn't it still would be a strong mitigating factor for the sentencing phase. Velma could be a powerful voice in her own defense, confirming her drug problem and relating the reasons behind it.

Jacobson was well aware, however, that calling her could be dangerous. From the beginning she had been testy, argumentative and uncooperative, and that was a side of her that he didn't want the jury to see. He had mentioned this to Ronnie, who talked with his mother about it. But she didn't understand the legal system, was angry and resentful about her situation. She didn't like Jacobson either, didn't think he was doing enough.

"I think he's doing the best he can," Ronnie said. After all, he hadn't exactly been handed an easy case, and the court had denied him any assistance. "He's all you've got, and you've got to do everything you can to help him."

Jacobson asked Ronnie about putting Velma on the stand, and

he agreed it was necessary, even though he worried that Britt might tear her apart.

"Your appearance, the way you conduct yourself, is going to be of utmost importance," Ronnie told her. "It could be the difference between life and death."

Both Ronnie and Jacobson counseled her on how to act. She had to control her anger, be remorseful and polite, answer only what was asked, keep her hands in her lap.

Jacobson wanted her to look as grandmotherly and sympathetic as possible. "If you feel like crying," he told her, "by all means cry." He was hoping that she would.

Pam had picked a beige dress with a broad collar and puffed sleeves for her mother to wear on the stand, and because Velma was worried about dry mouth, she had given her gum.

When Jacobson called her Thursday afternoon, Velma walked heavily to the gray vinyl-covered chair in the witness box. She seemed calm and in control, but Ronnie knew that she was frightened.

"You are the defendant in this case, are you not?" Jacobson asked.

"Yes, sir," she said meekly.

"And when did you meet Stuart Taylor?"

"In September 1976."

Guided by Jacobson, Velma told how she had been introduced to Stuart by his aunt, how they had gone out for a while, stopped, then resumed months later. She spoke softly at first but seemed to gain confidence as she went on. She said Stuart had a problem with alcohol and wouldn't come around while he was drinking.

"On the weekend prior to the death, what had you and Mr. Taylor been doing?" Jacobson asked.

"Well, we had an argument. He was drinking and we had had an argument, and I would threaten him, you know, to come back to Lumberton, and this is when, every time he would always say, 'If you leave, the law will pick you up,' due to this forged check."

"Had you forged a check on him?"

She had, she admitted. She went on to tell about her breast surgery and Stuart taking her back to the doctor on Tuesday. Afterward, they'd stopped at Eckerd's to get her prescription, she said, and she had bought the poison while Stuart was looking at fishing tackle.

"Why did you purchase the Terro?"

"Well, I thought it would make him sick."

"But you intended to give it to him?"

"Yes, I did."

When they got home, she said, she put the Terro on a table on the back porch where Stuart kept pesticides.

"Tell me what you did with it."

"Well, on Tuesday afternoon he came in and he had been drinking, and when he went to the bathroom, I put some in his beer. It was approximately 3:30, and then about six, I would say, at supper, I put some in the tea."

"What happened then?"

They went to Fayetteville to a revival meeting, she said, and he got sick when they returned. Later she called Bill Storms and told him that Stuart was sick and didn't want to go to a doctor. Soon afterward, Alice called, and she promised to keep her informed about her daddy's condition. Stuart remained sick all day Wednesday, she noted.

"He still was not any better Thursday morning so he finally gave in to go to the doctor, but he said, 'I cannot sit up to go to Lumberton,' and I said, 'Well, there's means of getting you there rather than having to sit up.' "

She called for an ambulance and followed in Stuart's truck, she said.

"Did you tell the hospital people what you had done?"

"No, sir, I did not."

"Why not?"

"Because I was afraid."

"What were you afraid of?"

"Well, I was afraid of what they might do."

"Might do to who?"

"To me."

Jacobson led her to the day of Stuart's death, and she said that he was feeling better that morning, although he developed diarrhea and continued vomiting in the afternoon. "About seven o'clock he got up off the bed, and when he did, he fell in the floor, so I put some chairs there to keep him, you know, from getting off again. And a little later he tried again, and he just fell backwards, so then I ran to the phone and called K. K. Daniels, who was a neighbor, and asked him would he summons for some help, the rescue squad, whatever would be quick."

"What happened at the hospital?"

"I got there as they were taking him in, and I went on into the room with him, and they were asking me, you know, had he been drinking and had he taken an overdose of medicine, and these things. And I told them no, he had not, so then they asked me out of the room. I called his daughter to tell her that I had Stuart at the hospital and he was under oxygen."

Jacobson asked about her own medical problems, and she said that she had been seeing five different doctors in January and getting prescriptions from each. She was taking Sinequan, Elavil, Tranxene, Valium and Tylenol with codeine, she said, and doubling the doses.

"Did you ever run out of this medication?"

"No, sir, not going from one doctor to another. I never was out of it."

"How long had you been taking medications like this?"

"I would say from six to ten years really."

Jacobson then asked about John Henry Lee.

"This is very vague," she answered. "I don't remember very much about it. I had written a check on him, and I had put some of the roach poison in some cereal and coffee."

She had forged the check, she said, to buy medicine.

Why had she poisoned Stuart? Jacobson asked.

"Same thing."

"Tell me what happened with Mrs. Edwards."

"I put some in her cereal and coffee, but there was nothing really between her and I."

"Can you offer an explanation for it?"

"No, sir, I cannot. My mind was really fuzzy. I do not know. There was no reason."

"You didn't write a check on her?"

"No, I did not."

"You weren't afraid of her?"

"No, I was not. There was times that I was thoroughly confused."

When Jacobson asked about her mother, she told about taking out a loan in her mother's name without her knowledge.

"You used this money for doctors and medications?"

"The majority of it, yes."

"Your own mother?" Jacobson asked incredulously, referring to the poisoning.

"Yes, I did not realize my mother would die. I have never intended to kill anyone."

"Surely you must have suspected?"

"Object to form," said Britt.

"Sustained to the form," said the judge, and Jacobson did not pursue the question.

"What about Mr. Barfield?" he said.

Velma shook her head and denied any memory of poisoning him.

Jacobson took her through the first interview with the police, then asked about the second on March 13.

"It is hard for me to really tell exactly what I did tell them. I do not remember my rights being read to me. I made a statement that I didn't mean to kill him. Mr. Lovett said, 'It will make it easier on you, tell everything you know.' I told everything I knew."

To reemphasize her abuse of prescription drugs, Jacobson got her to tell about her hospital stays for overdoses. Then, wanting to leave nothing for Britt to accuse them of hiding, he asked, "You have been charged with worthless checks many times, have you not?"

"Right."

"Have you ever been charged with forging a prescription?"

"Yes, sir."

"You served time in prison for that, did you not?"

"Yes, I did."

Jacobson thought he had gotten in every point that he wanted Velma to make, and she had done fine—so far. But now would come the real test.

"Your witness," he said, turning to Britt.

Cross-examination was not something that was easily planned, Britt believed. Mainly, it consisted of seizing opportunity. But in Velma's case Britt had been planning, because he knew exactly what he wanted from her: anger. And from reading her psychiatric reports, he thought he knew how to get it.

"I liked what her shrink had said about her," he later recalled. "Passive-aggressive. When she was confronted or felt threatened, she became very aggressive."

He wanted the jurors to see that aggression, that hostility, that desire and ability to kill, and from the first question he bore in, his tone sharp and indignant.

"So you can't recall poisoning your second husband, Jennings Barfield?"

"No, sir, I do not."

"Had you ever bought any poison in 1971?"

"Uh, 1971, no, I had not."

"When was the first time you ever recall purchasing any poison?"

"Before my mother died."

"How long before?"

"The day that she died."

"What type of poison was that?"

"It was Singletary's."

"Had you ever had any experience with poisons before?"

"No, I had not."

"Thereafter, you switched to Terro ant poison, did you not?"

"Later, yes, I did."

"Did you ever give any poison to Record Lee?"

"No, I did not."

Velma's responses were growing sharper. Ronnie could tell that Britt's tone and the hard, fast questions were beginning to get to her, and he was worried.

"Have you ever given poison to anyone who recovered and survived?"

"No, I haven't, but could I state one thing, please, sir?"

"Yes, ma'am."

"What I would like, Your Honor, to say to the jury and all, these autopsies—let me say first of all, when a person dies, one of our loved ones, friends, whatever dies, and they ask for an autopsy to be performed, is it not true that we have an autopsy performed to find out the reason of the death? Is this true or not?"

"Let's not argue with anybody," Judge McKinnon said to her. "You may make a statement and respond to the question."

"So I don't believe it killed them really," Velma went on emphatically, ignoring his admonition. "That is exactly the way I feel about it." She stared at Britt with an air of smugness.

"Beg your pardon?" he said, his voice filled with wonder.

"I don't think it killed them."

"You have heard the testimony in the courtroom, have you not?" Britt asked, his voice bristling.

Ronnie had seen his mother's rage building many times. He saw it in her eyes now, and his heart began to sink.

"Yes. I said I heard the testimony," Velma snapped at Britt. "What testimony are you talking about?"

Later, Jacobson remembered cringing at this point. He put his hand over his eyes and turned to Ronnie with a look of dismay. Velma was reacting just as he had feared. "Her eyes turned as flinty as steel," he recalled later.

"Let me ask you this," said Britt. "In the five people that it is alleged you killed, autopsies were performed in four of them, were they not?"

"Every one. I never objected to any of them."

"That's right. And the reason you didn't object is because the first time there was an autopsy performed, you slipped by. You thought they couldn't pick up arsenic poison in an autopsy. Isn't that correct?" He was practically yelling at her.

"No, indeed not," Velma said, her anger apparent. She crossed her arms defiantly and chewed her gum fiercely.

"She's blowing it big-time," Ronnie whispered to Jacobson, his face a picture of despondence, and Jacobson could only agree.

"Now you say you started giving Taylor poison on the thirty-first of January," Britt said, "is that correct?"

"It was on a Tuesday."

"To make him sick?"

"Right."

"Had you ever made anyone sick with Terro before?"

"No, I had not made anyone sick with Terro."

"Well—"

"Except Mr. Lee," Velma quickly added.

"You made Mr. Lee sick with it?"

"Right."

"Did you make Mrs. Edwards sick with it?"

"No, I did not."

"You made Mrs. Edwards sick with Singletary's rat poison, did you not?"

"No, I thought it was roach and ant poison," said Velma, with a look of satisfaction, as if she had scored against Britt.

"So you knew these compounds would certainly make people sick?"

"I knew it would make them sick."

"You knew it would kill them, too, didn't you?"

"No, I did not."

"Did you tell Frieda Monroe at the hospital, 'You needn't look for recovery of Mr. Lee because I have been through this before and I know they don't recover'?"

"I did make that statement, and I had stood by a lot of people that had died that had not had ant or roach poison also."

Ronnie sat looking at the table top, no longer able to watch what his mother was doing to herself.

Britt went to Velma's interviews with the detectives and asked if she was under the influence of drugs during the first on March 10.

"I was under the influence every day."

"Well, were you—"

Velma cut him off petulantly. "If I was under the influence every day, I was then."

When Velma said she didn't recall signing a waiver of rights, Britt carried it to the stand, handed it to her and got her to admit that it bore her signature.

"Do you write that plainly when you are under the influence of intoxicating drugs?"

"I sure do," she said with a tone of self-satisfaction.

Still she maintained that she didn't recall having the waiver read to her. She did, however, remember denying to the officers that she had anything to do with poisoning Stuart.

"Your denial was not true, was it?" Britt said. "You had killed these people, hadn't you?"

"No. I didn't think that I had killed them," she said adamantly. "No, I did not."

Britt moved on to the $300 check that Velma had forged on Stuart's account. She took the checkbook from a dresser in his bedroom before she poisoned him Tuesday and wrote it when he went to fix a hog fence, she said. She kept it in her pocketbook.

"When did you cash the check?" Britt asked.

"On Friday," she said, the day he died. She drove his truck to the bank.

"And left him there at the house?"

"He seemed better."

She was gone for about an hour after lunch, she said.

"So it wasn't true when you told the officers that you killed him because you were afraid that he was going to have you arrested for cashing a forged check, was it?"

Velma looked as if she'd been caught off guard. "Would you repeat that, please?"

"In other words, you cashed the check just before he died, didn't you, lady?" Britt said sharply.

"Yes, sir. I sure did."

"And you wrote it the very day you put the poison in his food, didn't you?"

"I sure did."

"And kept it while he suffered through three days?" he said indignantly, his voice thundering through the courtroom.

"Object," said Jacobson.

"Sustained to the hollering."

Ronnie could tell that his mother's wrath was reaching explosive levels again, but Britt didn't press further, turning instead to another check Velma had written.

"And in Mr. Lee's case, you wrote the check on Record Lee, his wife, didn't you?"

"Yes, I did."

"They caught up with you on that, didn't they?"

"No, they didn't."

"Then why did you put poison in his food?"

"I thought he would find out."

"Were you just going to make him sick because you thought he would find out?"

"Yes, sir. I never intended to kill him."

"Let me ask you this: What was your purpose in making Mr. Lee sick if you thought he was going to find out?"

"Well, I thought in the meantime I could have paid the money back."

"Now, Mrs. Edwards, the reason you poisoned her was because she was just a cantankerous old lady, wasn't she?" Britt said, his voice again loud and antagonistic.

"At times she was difficult."

"Extremely?"

"No, not extremely."

"Made life miserable for you, didn't she?"

"No, she did not."

"Well, can you give us any reason whatsoever for giving poison to poor old Mrs. Edwards?"

"No. I was under a lot of drugs again all this time."

Britt shifted to the night of Stuart's death, getting her to admit that she was standing by, watching his agonies.

"Able to talk, weren't you?" he asked with heavy sarcasm.

"I was able to talk," she said defiantly.

"Did you ever tell anybody that you had given him poison?"

"No, sir. I did not."

"Why?"

"When I went into the room, as soon as they would let me go in, they asked me had he been drinking much, had he taken too much of his medicine, and I said no. Then they told me I would have to leave out, so I left out."

"Did you ever tell anybody, doctors, family, anybody that you had given him poison?"

"No, sir, I did not."

"Why not?"

"Because I was afraid."

"You were afraid they would save his life?"

"No, I wasn't afraid they would save his life. I was hoping when I brought him in Thursday that he would be kept. I asked them to keep him."

Britt turned to the loan Velma got six weeks before her mother's death. She admitted that she never made a payment and was there when Lillie got the past due notice.

"And there was the dickens to pay around that house, was there not?"

"No. She did not say anything at the time."

"Well, why did you decide to make her sick?"

"Because I was afraid that she would find out, and I was hoping that I could get the money and pay it back to her. I did not mean to kill her."

"Would you explain that, please?"

"Borrow the money from someone to pay the loan back."

"Well, explain to us what you mean when you say that making her sick would allow you to borrow money."

"Well, if she had to be in the hospital for a while, I would have had the chance," Velma said, making little sense to anybody in the courtroom.

Britt handed Velma the two-ounce bottle of Terro and began asking about the amounts of poison she had given to each of her victims.

"You know that both Singletary's and Terro are completely taste less, didn't you?"

"Yes, sir, I did."

174 • J E R R Y   B L E D S O E

"You knew that because nobody had ever complained when you put either one in their food."

"Could you repeat that please?"

"Well, you knew that Jennings Barfield had never complained," Britt said, trying to slip one by her.

"I beg your pardon!" she quickly interrupted. "I didn't put any in Jennings Barfield at all."

"Didn't you?"

"I did not." Her contempt for Britt was transparent.

"You are now saying you did not at any time give Jennings Barfield any poison?" Britt said, his voice rising.

"That is what I am saying."

"All right. Thank you, ma'am," Britt said with a look of satisfaction. "I believe originally you didn't remember."

Velma was looking withered by Britt's unrelenting assault, but he didn't stop, going on to ask about her call to Alice Storms the day after her first interview with the police.

"Do you recall telling her it was all the fault of Southeastern General Hospital that her father had died?"

"I did not say it was the fault of them. I said, 'It looks to me like they could be more prompt in the way they handle cases.' Mrs. Storms, on Saturday morning after her daddy died on Friday night, she had gone out to get her hair fixed. When she came back home she made the remark about how many cases that have been taken into Southeastern General Hospital and people had died on their way back home. She was saying that as she drove into her driveway. This is why I commented to Mrs. Storms like I did. We were all making comments about it the whole time."

"No more questions," Britt said, and as Velma walked back to the defense table, he looked at her and smiled.

Ronnie was devastated. His mother's irritability and combativeness had made her appear to be a harridan, perfectly capable of cold-blooded murder. "I was wanting to see the remorse," he later recalled. "She seemed to have no remorse about what she had done. I saw a mean person, a callous person who didn't seem to care what happened. She was just like Britt later pictured her, cold and calculating."

Court adjourned early to allow the judge and lawyers to drive to Fayetteville to take the testimony of one of Velma's doctors, who was hospitalized with a fatal illness.

But before his mother was returned to jail, Ronnie was allowed to speak with her in a holding room. He was angry, and he didn't conceal it.

"That was horrible," he said of her response to Britt.

"Well, he's the one who started it," she said. "He was yelling at me. No one's going to yell at me like that."

"It doesn't matter who started it," Ronnie said. "Don't you understand? That was exactly what he wanted you to do."

He was certain that she had put herself on death row, but he didn't want her to be completely without hope, didn't want to affect any slight chance she might have during the remainder of the trial. "If you keep on with this kind of display, it's going to seal your fate," he told her. "You won't have a chance."

CHAPTER 15

Bob Jacobson was dispirited after Velma's performance Thursday, almost certain that she had ruined any chance of a second-degree conviction. Although he still had to cling to that hope, he knew that he had to emphasize her abuse of drugs even more strongly to have a chance of saving her life.

He opened the fifth day of the trial Friday morning by calling Dr. Bob Rollins, a forensic psychiatrist who was the former superintendent to Dorothea Dix Hospital. Rollins described Velma's six weeks of testing and evaluation after her arrest. Although she was not very cooperative, he said, he determined that she was depressed and had a passive-dependent and inadequate personality.

Jacobson brought out the long list of drugs Velma had been taking at the time and asked if they affected the mind.

"Yes," Rollins replied.

Britt kept his focus on Velma's insanity plea on cross-examination. "Dr. Rollins, you are not saying that the defendant was insane, are you?"

"No, sir."

"Is the word insanity a legal term or a medical term, sir?"

"Well, I think lawyers think it is a medical term and doctors think it is a legal term."

"Can you give us a definition?"

"Well, the one I use in this particular case is when the patient is able to distinguish between right and wrong, and generally, insanity is thought of as being the same as a very serious mental illness."

Britt read from Rollins' report: " 'Based on the limited information I have, I believe she should be considered responsible for her actions.' "

Rollins acknowledged that. "But I would say Mrs. Barfield is a limited individual in that her personality structure is immature and restricted, and I think that could be considered a form of mental illness but not one that interferes with her ability to stand trial."

A court clerk, Mildred Simmons, took the stand to read answers given by Anthony Sainz in a deposition taken by the judge and attorneys from his hospital room the afternoon before. Sainz, a neurologist with a Ph.D. in philosophy who also had a psychiatric practice, had treated Velma since 1975, first at the mental health center at Southeastern Hospital. She had continued as his patient after her arrest. Indeed, even as Velma sat listening to the transcript, she was under the effects of tranquilizers and sedatives prescribed by Dr. Sainz.

In response to questions from Jacobson, Sainz told of treating Velma for a severe overdose early in 1975 when she was brought to the hospital unconscious. He had diagnosed her as having a "well-established depression with underlying passive-aggressive neurotic reaction," a person who abused medicine without justified motive. Her depression, he said, was organic, a disease of the body that affected the mind, leaving no initiative and an inability to cope. She was unable to establish an equilibrium between being hostile to her environment or becoming dependent on it.

"In other words," he testified, "she is either a parasite or a destructor."

He told of the drugs he had prescribed for her, including Elavil, an antidepressant, and the tranquilizer Tranxene, in January when Stuart was murdered.

Jacobson asked if any of these were habit-forming. "I have to give you a highly personal opinion," Sainz answered. "I would say that any drug is addictive regardless of the chemical constitution." He had seen addictions to all the drugs he had prescribed for Velma, he said, sometimes psychological, sometimes physical.

In all the years he'd known her, Sainz said, Velma had "never been without a good bull pen so that she can substitute if she needs a relief pitcher to get somebody to give her a prescription in a hurry."

"Are you saying that she has a history of abusing drugs by going to other physicians to obtain them?"

"That is right."

Sainz told of seeing Velma in jail after her return from Dorothea

Dix. She was complaining of gross memory defects, severe headaches, insomnia, lack of appetite, inability to cope. "Her ideas were just jumbled in her mind," he said.

Had that caused him to alter his earlier diagnosis?

"No. What I saw was a patient who hadn't had any medication for several days, and the symptoms are congruent with the illness that she had."

"Did she require the medication?"

"Oh, yes."

"And she requires it now?"

"Oh, yes," he said, going on to add that depressive patients have to have maintenance doses to function properly.

Had Velma told him anything about the crime for which she was being tried?

"She told me that she did not remember any of the allegations, that she did not remember making any admissions and she was very vague in her reminiscences, but on this she was definite. She remembered that the doctor who examined her at Dorothea Dix saw her on only two brief occasions, and she complained very bitterly of her physical symptoms."

"Doctor, you are not saying that the lady is insane, are you?" Britt asked on cross-examination.

"There is no such thing as insanity."

"You understand the meaning of the legal term insanity, don't you, sir?"

"I understand it, but I don't feel qualified to pass on it."

Jacobson now called Ronnie to tell about discovering that his mother had poisoned Stuart and about taking her to the sheriff's department. Then he asked about his mother's drug abuse. "How far back does this go?"

"At least to 1969, when my father died."

Ronnie outlined her many overdoses and told of taking drugs away from her on the day of her arrest. Jacobson handed him a wad of tissue. "Would you unwrap it, please?"

Ronnie did and described the pills inside. They were the ones he had taken from his mother that day, he said, and Jacobson had them admitted as evidence. Then Jacobson produced the grocery sack of medicine vials Ronnie had taken from his mother's room after her arrest and they, too, were admitted.

"Can you tell us how your father died, sir?" Britt asked after Jacobson had surrendered the witness.

"His death certificate said the cause of death was smoke inhalation," Ronnie replied. Britt knew that to be the case because he had had the body of Thomas Burke exhumed at the end of May, and Page Hudson, the state medical examiner, had found no arsenic but heavy soot in his lungs and trachea.

"There was a fire in the trailer, is that correct?"

"In the house."

"Your mother was just outside the door when that occurred, is that not so?"

"I don't know where she was at."

Had his mother ever told him that the reason she had the pills that had earlier been put into evidence was because she intended to commit suicide but decided she wasn't ready to leave this world yet?

"Yes, she did make that statement."

Britt had no more questions, and the judge declared a fifteen-minute recess.

When court reconvened, Jacobson brought forth a succession of doctors to relate the drugs they had prescribed for Velma in December 1977 and January 1978. One was Dr. Horace M. Baker, who had performed breast surgery on Velma on January 25. He didn't have a record of the drugs he had supplied her, he said, but normally he gave Percodan, Dalmane, and Tylenol with codeine. Velma had returned to have the incision dressed on January 31, he revealed, and again on February 2, the day before Stuart's death.

Did Velma appear to be under the influence of drugs on January 31? Britt wanted to know.

No, said Baker, not on any of her visits.

Pharmacists from four different drugstores began the afternoon's testimony, all describing prescriptions they had filled for Velma in December and January, a total of thirteen. Then Jacobson called Velma for a question he'd failed to ask the day before. He knew that he was taking a chance, for he would be submitting her to another verbal assault by Britt. But it was important, and he hoped that she would control her temper after being admonished both by him and Ronnie the day before.

On the day she had poisoned Stuart, he asked, what medications had she taken?

Three Sinequan, three Elavil, six Valium and four Tranxene, she answered.

"Did you take it all at once?"

"Yes, I did."

Such a dosage of sedatives and tranquilizers would render many people unconscious, and Britt thought she was just trying to make the jurors think that she was completely incapable of knowing what she was doing when she poisoned Stuart.

"You took this around eleven-thirty a.m., you say?" he asked on cross-examination.

"Yes, sir."

That was the day she had written the check on Stuart's account, he noted.

"Did you write the check before you took the dope?"

"Yes, sir, I did, the best I can remember."

But then she said she wasn't sure. She did remember taking the medicine, did remember going to see Dr. Baker, but she said it was in the morning, and Britt pointed out that Baker said she'd come in the afternoon.

"He testified to that, but I truly couldn't say," Velma said.

So far, Ronnie thought, she was restraining herself, doing okay.

"You are not getting tangled up, are you, ma'am?" Britt asked tauntingly.

She recalled Dr. Baker testifying that she had not appeared to be under the influence of drugs when she came to his office but she maintained that she was.

Britt took her again through the events of Thursday, February 2, the day she first took Stuart to the hospital, and this time she included going to see Dr. Baker that day, something she hadn't mentioned earlier. She acknowledged that she left Stuart alone when she went.

"He was extremely ill at that time, was he not?" Britt asked antagonistically.

"He was feeling better when I left."

Hadn't she testified earlier that she had stayed with him all day because he was so sick?

"I don't recall. I'm not going to say."

"The only reason you are telling the jury now that you went to Dr. Baker's office on Thursday is because you heard him testify to that effect, is that not so?"

"No, it is not," Velma said curtly, and Ronnie could see her anger boiling again. Britt could manipulate her at will, and she seemed not to be aware of it.

Britt went on to her activities on Friday, the day of Stuart's death. She'd gone to Lumberton to cash the check she'd written on his account that morning, she said. While there, she'd called Dr. Sainz for more medicine, and later she had returned to Lumberton to get it. Stuart was still sick, she acknowledged, but feeling better.

"Didn't you tell us earlier that your whole purpose was to make him sick so that you could cash the check and pay the bank before he got well?"

"I vaguely remember what I said about that," she said uncertainly, glancing at Jacobson.

"Now you say he was getting well. Weren't you afraid to cash the check?"

"No, I wasn't."

"You cashed the check because you knew there was no recovery to be had for him at that time, did you not?" Britt practically shouted, his voice filled with righteous anger.

"No, sir, I did not," she said, her own anger flashing.

Britt asked when she had returned to Lumberton that day to pick up her prescription at Eckerd's, and Velma said it was about three-thirty or four.

"Did you buy any more poison then?"

"No, I did not," she said indignantly.

"Well, it was within four hours of Mr. Taylor going to the hospital for the final visit, wasn't it?" Britt said, knowing he was antagonizing her.

"Approximately," Velma replied, glaring at him.

"When you got back home, was he sick?"

"He seemed about the same as when I left."

"When did this sudden onset of violent sickness take place?"

"I would say around seven o'clock."

"Had he eaten the oyster stew at that time?"

"Yes."

"You fixed that, didn't you?"

"Yes."

"As soon as he ate the oyster stew, then he really started getting sick, didn't he?"

"No, sir, he did not," Velma answered sharply, her disdain for

Britt plain in her expression. "In fact, he did not vomit anymore at all from the time I got back from Lumberton with my medicine and oysters. He never did vomit anymore. He had diarrhea, but he didn't vomit."

Velma said that Stuart was taken to the hospital about eight-thirty that evening and that she was under the influence when she followed the ambulance there, driving his truck.

"The truth of the matter was that you just simply did not get under the influence of any drug until after Mr. Taylor died, did you?" Britt demanded.

"No, sir, that is not true."

Ronnie thought his mother looked as if she might spring off the stand and throttle Britt, which was just what Britt wanted the jurors to see, he knew. Clearly, nothing Ronnie said to her the day before had the slightest effect.

Britt took Velma back again to her first interview with the police on March 10.

"You had denied any knowledge or complicity in the death of five people, had you not?"

"I sure did—" Velma said, then caught herself, "—not in five people."

"Four people?"

"No, sir," she said challengingly.

"How many?"

"One was all that was mentioned."

"You knew it was going to lead to more people, didn't you?"

"No, sir, I did not."

"You knew that things were closing in on you, didn't you?"

Her expression remained defiant. "No, sir, I did not."

"Isn't that why you started to take all those pills and do away with yourself?"

"I did take them with me to work on Sunday night, and I did think about doing it but I did not—"

"Do you remember telling them, 'If I had done that, nobody would ever know what had happened except you and me'?"

"No, sir."

"No further questions," Britt said disdainfully.

Velma had performed no better than she had the day before, had appeared no more sympathetic or remorseful. She despised Britt so much that she couldn't keep from responding with anger and scorn no matter how important it was to saving her life. Later, she would say that she had wanted to hit him.

"Is there further evidence for the defendant?" Judge McKinnon asked after Velma had made her way back to her seat.

"Nothing further," Jacobson said dejectedly.

"Any further evidence for the state?"

"Yes," said Britt, calling Alf Parnell in rebuttal. Had Velma said anything to him about the pills Ronnie had taken from his mother?

They had been talking after Velma had given her statements, Parnell said, when Velma mentioned that she had taken the pills to work the night before with the intention of taking all of them, but she couldn't get up nerve enough to do it.

"She said she knew she was not ready to leave the world at this time."

"Did she say anything about what would have happened to this case had she had nerve enough to do that?"

"She said that if she had taken the pills that the three of us would be the only ones that really knew what happened."

"The state rests," Britt said, and McKinnon called the lawyers to the bench, then asked the jury to step out.

After denying Jacobson's standard motion for dismissal, the judge said he wanted to go over the instructions he would give the jury. Jacobson asked that the jury be allowed to consider verdicts of guilty to second-degree murder and not guilty by reason of insanity in addition to guilty of first-degree murder and not guilty. The judge was willing to allow second-degree and skeptical on not guilty by reason of insanity, as Jacobson had expected he would be.

"Do you care to be heard?" he asked.

Jacobson said he realized that three doctors had testified that she wasn't insane and knew right from wrong. "I feel that just by the very reason that we have had some testimony that she was under the care of a psychiatrist, that she had a mental illness or an emotional problem that would be enough for the court to consider instructing on it."

Britt countered that the burden was on the defense to prove insanity and all of the expert witnesses had testified to the contrary.

"I agree," said the judge. "There is no evidence of insanity."

He would, however, allow the jury to consider self-induced

intoxication as a factor negating intent for a verdict of second-degree murder.

After a recess, Bob Jacobson began his final argument talking about the verdicts the jury could render.

"I am not one to hide anything from you," he said. "You have heard all the evidence. It is all here—every bit of it. Mrs. Barfield has testified that she put Terro ant poison in Stuart Taylor's tea and beer, so technically you have got guilty of first-degree murder or guilty of second-degree murder because you can't consider insanity anymore.

"What my purpose here right now is to convince you that Mrs. Barfield is guilty of second-degree murder, and I want you to give consideration to all the evidence."

He went on to explain reasonable doubt and the elements of first-degree murder. "But the state must prove beyond a reasonable doubt that the defendant intended to kill Stuart Taylor," he told them.

"Now, you have heard evidence of other crimes. You are not convicting her of five different murders. If you convict her of first-degree murder, it is one murder, but I submit to you that you should convict her, if at all, on second-degree murder because she didn't intend to do it."

The judge would instruct them about how drug intoxication and mental illness could negate intent, he said.

"In other words, in simple terms we are saying that you should consider her mental condition and you should consider her use of drugs in determining a specific intent to kill. We are submitting to you that because of these conditions she could not form that intent to kill Stuart Taylor."

The jurors should consider Velma's mental condition and drug abuse in two ways, Jacobson contended, first to determine if she had an ability to form an intent to kill, and second whether she was too intoxicated to understand what she was doing, thereby making intent impossible. In either case, he pointed out, she would be guilty of second-degree murder, not first-degree.

Jacobson summarized the testimony about Velma's long drug abuse and mental instability, noting that she took the drugs to cope, but the more she took, the less she was able to cope.

"These things that I have gone over have been to convince you

Velma Barfield thought she had escaped the misery of her childhood when she married Thomas Burke. She was newly married when she posed for this photo. (*Courtesy of Tyrone Bullard*)

Years later, Ronnie and Pam would long for the days when their parents were still happy, as they were on this trip to the North Carolina mountains when Ronnie was four, Pam three. (*Courtesy of Ronnie Burke*)

Velma Barfield was already the mother of two when she posed for this family snapshot with all her brothers and sisters. Back row (left to right): Olive, Velma, John, Jesse, and Jimmy. Front row: Arlene, Tyrone, Faye, and Ray. (*Courtesy of Tyrone Bullard*)

Velma Barfield was so
attached to Ronnie and
Pam that she could not
stand to be apart from
them even overnight.
(*Courtesy of
Ronnie Burke*)

Ronnie and Pam loved to
play on the Dr Pepper truck
their father drove.
(*Courtesy of Ronnie Burke*)

Ronnie poses with his
uncles Jimmy and Ray
at his grandparents'
rented farmhouse.
(*Courtesy of Tyrone Bullard*)

After his mother was sent to death row, Ronnie found it harder and harder to visit her, saying he could not stand to see her trapped and facing death.
(*Photo by Elin Schoen Brockman*)

On her final Easter, Velma Barfield presenting Easter bunnies she made to her granddaughters, Beverly (sitting on her mother's lap) and Sarah Sue, as Ronnie looks on, in March 1984. (*Photo by Elin Schoen Brockman*)

Velma Barfield's family watching her return to her cell block after the Easter visit, 1984—Ronnie and Faye are on left.
(*Photo by Elin Schoen Brockman*)

Velma Barfield in her cell at Women's Prison, in fall 1984, where she was affectionately called Mama Margie by other inmates. (*Courtesy of Fayetteville Observer-Times, photo by Cindy Burnham*)

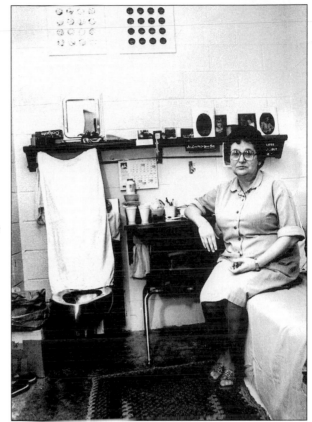

LEFT: The gurney on which Velma Barfield died by lethal injection.
RIGHT: The death chamber where Velma Barfield was executed.
(*Photos by Patty McQuillan*)

Velma Barfield's execution drew unprecedented attention from around the world, and hundreds of reporters and photographers gathered outside the gates of Central Prison.
(*Courtesy of* Fayetteville Observer-Times, *photo by Johnny Horne*)

Attorney Jimmie Little fought until the last day to save Velma Barfield in the courts. (*Courtesy of* Fayetteville Observer-Times, *photo by Cindy Burnham*)

Velma Barfield's impending execution brought demonstrators both for
and against capital punishment. ABOVE: Vigil keepers held candles and
hummed "Amazing Grace," Velma Barfield's favorite hymn.
BELOW: Death-row supporters cheered and shouted "Die!" when
the execution hour arrived. (*Courtesy of* Fayetteville Observer-Times,
photos by Johnny Horne)

Stuart Taylor invited Velma Barfield to move into his farmhouse near St. Paul's. Three months afterward she put arsenic in his beer and iced tea. (*Photo by Jerry Bledsoe*)

At Stuart's funeral, one of his closest friends saw Velma Barfield standing alone by his grave, the last to leave. (*Photo by Jerry Bledsoe*)

Ronnie and Pam wanted their mother buried alongside their father, within sight of the big white house in Parkton where they all had shared the happiest years of their lives. (*Photo by Jerry Bledsoe*)

that you should be convinced to a moral certainty that she is guilty of every element of first-degree murder before you can convict her. Review the evidence. Discuss it. Ask yourselves, 'Am I fully satisfied? Is there a reasonable doubt?' If you give consideration to the evidence that the defendant has presented, I believe you will find that this woman did not intend to kill Stuart Taylor. Thank you."

Jacobson had begun his argument so late that Britt had figured he wouldn't have to present his until the next session of court. But Jacobson had spoken for only about thirty minutes, and it was only four-thirty. Suddenly, Britt found himself having to present his case. He rose slowly, his suit coat unbuttoned. He checked his watch and turned to the jury.

"The defense counsel has been very brief, and I promise you I am not going to trespass on your time one minute longer than is necessary either," he said. "I won't talk past five o'clock."

The reason Jacobson had been so brief, he said, was simple. He suddenly whirled and pointed a long arm and accusing finger at Velma. "There is no doubt whatsoever that that woman sitting right there," he said, his voice rising dramatically, "is guilty of murder in the first degree!"

The crucial question in this case, he said, was intent, and that was why he had introduced the evidence of the others Velma had poisoned.

"Now, you know it's going to be very easy to say, 'My goodness, let's don't talk about those other cases. We are only trying this case concerning Stuart Taylor.' Let me say this. Those other cases should be uppermost in your mind because those other cases demonstrate without any doubt that she knew precisely what she was doing when she put the poison in his beer and tea.

"She now says, 'I didn't mean to do it.' Well, isn't that just a little bit silly, ladies and gentlemen? Didn't mean to do it, when we know from the evidence that just six short months before, she had done precisely the same thing to John Henry Lee?"

And before that to Dollie Edwards and her own mother.

"I say to you that ordinary intelligence and ordinary experience tell you that someone who would commit these kinds of horrendous crimes over and over and over again knows precisely what she is doing each time she does it."

He briefly reviewed the evidence before moving on to Velma's mental condition. "There are people out there with all kinds of infirmities, people with all kinds of hang-ups and problems. But if you start giving everybody with some kind of hang-up or little personality problem a license to start killing, we might as well hang it up because it is going to be a mighty chaotic society. The law doesn't intend that."

If the jury bought Velma's contention that she was too drugged to know what she was doing when she gave poison to Stuart, they would have to believe her as a person, he said.

"You observed her there on the witness stand. I suggest to you it was a cold, hard woman, a woman who was calculating and cunning. Did you see that Terro ant poison when it got passed around, and the little skull and crossbones on the back? She knew what that stuff would do.

"She tells you now, 'Oh, I didn't mean to do it. I had all that nasty old stuff in me, and I just did it and didn't know about it.' Is that consistent with what Dr. Baker tells you? Of course it's not."

Velma, he said, was a master of deception who could give poison to people, pretend to care for them, and console their families without anybody becoming suspicious.

"She was over there in the house with Stuart Taylor while he was puking his guts out, and she was standing there watching the whole time knowing what she had done. I suggest to you that Stuart Taylor's life could have been saved if some doctor could have given him British antilewisite. Right there she had the key to his life, but she intended to kill Stuart Taylor, ladies and gentlemen, because she sat on that information."

She knew that arsenic poisoning would not show up in autopsies and thought she was home free, he said. But Stuart's death had been different from the others. He was younger and in better health, and his family and the doctors couldn't understand why he had died. "And that's when the medical experts got into it, and the long arm of justice got into it, and the truth finally came to the surface."

Her motive, he said, was simple: to get money to satisfy her craving for drugs.

"No wonder she wants and craves and needs drugs to allay anxiety. No wonder she needs those to have lived with the deaths she has lived with for the last seven or eight years. Who wouldn't?"

Britt checked his watch.

"I told you I would quit at five, and I will. Your job is a very simple one—to return a verdict." The word verdict, he explained, was derived from Latin—veritas, truth; dictum, speak.

"That's all the state of North Carolina wants you to do is to render a verdict, to speak the truth, and the verdict that speaks the truth is guilty. I am asking you to find her guilty of murder in the first degree."

Not one of his better arguments, Britt thought later, but he had no concern about its effect. That Velma would be found guilty of first-degree murder was a foregone conclusion. He would save his fire for the sentencing argument.

As Britt turned back to the prosecution table, Velma, a smirk on her face, raised her hands in silent applause. None of the jurors could have missed it, and Bob Jacobson's spirits suddenly bottomed. What little hope he'd had for a verdict of second-degree murder suddenly dissipated because of a single, stupid act.

But the jurors would have overnight to overlook that and to think about their decision. Judge McKinnon recessed court for the day and ordered everybody back for an unusual Saturday session.

CHAPTER 16

After an hour of instruction from Judge McKinnon Saturday morning, the jurors elected as their foreman Ronald Tuton, an auditor for the North Carolina Department of Revenue who was the same age as Velma. Tuton, who lived in Clarkton and worked in Whiteville in Columbus County, had been surprised to find himself on the jury. He had grown up in Lumberton, and although he was three years older than Joe Freeman Britt, he had played in the high school band with him. Although younger than Judge McKinnon, he had lived near him and known his family. He had made all of that known during jury selection, but he was chosen anyway.

Tuton began the discussion by announcing that no arm twisting would take place. Everybody had to reach a conclusion on his or her own, and everybody's position would be respected. He soon discovered, however, that everybody appeared to be in agreement. Although some jurors were timid about speaking up, nobody seemed to think that Velma had been so heavily under the influence of drugs when she gave poison to Stuart that she didn't know what she was doing. And the notion that she had done it just to make him sick seemed absurd to all. Everybody thought that she fully intended to do what she accomplished.

The factor that sealed intent, as far as Tuton was concerned, was that Velma might have saved Stuart's life if she had told the doctors about the poison when she first took him to the hospital. That she didn't was clear evidence that she wanted him to die.

Tuton decided to take a secret ballot. Each juror was to write a verdict. He opened them one by one, read each aloud and placed it on the table in front of him. The reading became a litany. "First-degree . . . first-degree murder . . . first-degree . . ."

The vote was unanimous. But Tuton wasn't willing to accept it.

"I want us to make sure that we're all satisfied," he said, and the jurors went through the discussion and vote again. The result was unchanged.

"Okay, if that's it, let's go let them know," Tuton said, and he notified the bailiff.

They had been gone from the courtroom only an hour and ten minutes.

"Has the jury reached a verdict?" asked Judge McKinnon.

"We have, Your Honor," said Tuton.

"Will the defendant please stand."

Velma stood expressionless, wearing a pink-and-navy suit, still chewing gum, as the verdict was announced.

Few in the courtroom were surprised. Certainly neither lawyer had doubted the outcome. Nor had Ronnie, who already had resigned himself to it after his mother's performances on the stand. Velma showed no emotion as the verdict was announced.

Bob Jacobson had one more opportunity to save Velma's life during the sentencing hearing, and the judge moved swiftly to that phase of the trial. Did Jacobson want to offer evidence?

He did. He called Diane Hayes, an old friend of Velma's, who had worked with her at Belk's. Ironically, Hayes was now employed in the administrative offices of Central Prison in Raleigh.

She described Velma as "a very happy person" when she first met her in 1964. "Velma was always talking Thomas this and Thomas that—just a very happy relationship with her husband. And then he started drinking."

Velma changed after she started taking tranquilizers, Hayes said, and after Thomas' death she frequently came to work "glassy-eyed" and with slurred speech. "Shaky," she said. "She was real shaky."

Jacobson called Pam back to reemphasize her mother's drug abuse.

"I have seen it for the last ten years," she said. "I have lived with it most every day."

"Do you understand what has happened here this week?" Jacobson asked

"Yes, I do."

"And it is a very, very serious matter?"

"Yes, it is."

"You love your mother, don't you?"

"Very much."

Ronnie, too, came back to talk about his mother's drug use.

"Have you ever tried to do anything about this problem?" Jacobson asked.

"Yes, sir," he said, then went on to tell of taking her to the hospital and the mental health center, of talking to physicians and asking them not to prescribe drugs for her.

"You love your mother, don't you?"

"Yes."

"How do you feel about the punishment?"

"Object," said Britt.

"Sustained," said the judge.

"No further evidence," said Jacobson.

Joe Freeman Britt never underestimated the task that lay before him. "You can have twelve clones of Attila the Hun in the jury box, and they're still going to look for a reason not to give the death penalty," he said later. "You're asking a jury to do an unnatural act to kill a person, and that's a hell of a burden. Jurors just look for reasons—some of us would say excuses—not to give the death penalty."

Experience had taught him what he had to do to overcome that. "You don't send a prisoner to the gallows with sweet reason. Freud says that when emotion and reason compete, emotion will always win. Perception is reality. It doesn't matter what the facts are, doesn't matter what the evidence is. Jurors are guided by their perceptions. And that's where the advocacy comes in, molding and manipulating those perceptions."

Standing now before the jurors, he began his molding and manipulating in a low-keyed monotone, speaking slowly, as if he were attempting to lull them.

In trials such as this, with the lawyers orchestrating everything, he noted, it was easy for jurors to rock back in their comfortable chairs and begin to look upon the proceedings as a melodrama.

"They wait to see what happens next, and they are concerned with following the factual situation, and they tend to forget the most important part of the case. You know what I am talking about," he said, his voice quickening.

"I am talking about the fact that a living, breathing human being, who I would suggest on the thirty-first of January and up to the third of February, wanted to live just as badly as any one of you sitting in that jury box. He is dead! He is gone! He is gone forever, and he lies out there in that cold, damp sod wrapped in his shroud because of the callous, indifferent, malicious act of this woman sitting right here at this table."

His voice had become a tornado ripping through the courtroom as he whirled on Velma. "She killed him dead! And sent him to meet his maker! And he is gone for an eternity because of that act of *this* woman!"

Suddenly, he changed pace, spoke in a more solemn tone.

"I want to point it out to you, ladies and gentlemen of the jury, so that when you get back there in that jury room, you don't have that feeling in the back of your head that this has just been some little old floor show we have been watching and Stuart Taylor never lived, that he was a figment of some scriptwriter's imagination, because he wasn't, my friends.

"He was a fifty-six-year-old man, an innocent human being who was just snuffed before his time. Now, for God's sake, when you get back there, remember that because you know what it is like in the twentieth century where every time you turn on the tube or every time you pick up a newspaper, what are they talking about? The rights of the poor defendants in our society today!

"Well, when are we going to start worrying about the victims?" he asked, his voice back in the higher decibels. "They had a few rights, too, you know. Stuart Taylor had a few rights on the thirty-first of January, but who was there to protect his rights on that occasion? Did he have a lawyer, judge or jury? Or did he just get executed that week?"

Britt believed that argument had to find a rhythm, and when it did, he later would say, "You can almost see the jury begin to sway."

The jury was beginning to sway, and Jacobson knew it.

"Objection," he sang, hoping to break the rhythm.

"Overruled."

"He is gone, my friends. He is gone forever, and it is because of this woman sitting over here at the next table.

"It is truly impossible to demonstrate in a well-lighted, orderly courtroom like this the agony and the pain and suffering that Stuart Taylor went through those three or four days. How in God's name can I do that? I didn't have a camera on him as he writhed in pain and clutched his stomach and vomited and had diarrhea and went through that for several days. I don't have a time machine where I can poke a button and you go back to the emergency room at Southeastern Hospital and see him rolling around there and when he dies, the final gasp and throws back his head and screams . . ." He was practically screaming himself now. "There is no way I can bring home to you the true inhumanity of what was going on then.

"Stuart Taylor did not die at the end of a double-barrel shotgun. He didn't even know he was facing his murderer. He didn't have a chance to grapple with his assailant and try to save his life, because she was doing to him some nefarious act in secret, and he didn't even realize what was happening to him.

"She used a weapon, I would suggest to you, much more horrible than a shotgun. It is a weapon that creates incredible torture. I had it here in my hand, state's exhibit number nine."

He carried the bottle of Terro to the jury box. "Do you know what that is? That is arsenic poison. It is designed and bottled for a reason. It is put in that bottle to kill things, whether they be ants or mice or human beings. This is a killer, and it is a killer that creates excruciating pain as it works its way into the human body. That isn't something that makes ants sick or mice sick or human beings sick. That is something that does away with them forever!"

Velma couldn't plead self-defense or insanity, he noted.

"What excuse does she have? There is no excuse!" he yelled. "There is nothing there for you to hang a cloak of life imprisonment on. I argue to you strongly that if there has ever been a case that deserved the imposition of the ultimate penalty, this is such a case."

He reminded the jurors of the others who had died at Velma's hand. "Now, the defense attorney will get up here and cry and tell you, 'Oh, you saw the two children, and how can you do that to this poor woman?' This poor woman sitting over there at that table," he went on, his voice dripping with disdain, "according to the evidence has done away with at least four people in the last ten years—*killed her own mother*!"

His voice reverberated through the courtroom as he went on to explain why this trial was being held in two stages because of rulings by the U.S. Supreme Court, and to explain about aggravating and mitigating circumstances.

They would be considering three aggravating factors, he said. Number one was that the crime was committed for pecuniary gain. Clearly that was the case, he pointed out, because of the check Velma forged. Number two was that the crime was committed to hinder enforcement of the law. They should say yes to that as well, because Velma killed Stuart to prevent him from prosecuting her for the forgeries. The third factor was that the murder was especially heinous, hateful, odious, greatly reprehensible, atrocious, extremely shocking, wicked or cruel. That she used poison and remained indifferent to Stuart's pain proved that without question, he maintained.

"Could it be that she does get her kicks from this type of thing?" he asked the jury. "The Lord knows that the evidence would show that she had done enough for a cheap enough price—"

"Object," said Jacobson.

"Sustained," said the judge, then instructed the jury, "Don't consider that statement."

"Would you say she was hardhearted to watch the man lie there and suffer as he did?" Britt asked. "Have you seen the first tear of remorse in this defendant's eyes? Have you seen the first flinch of contrition? Has she ever seemed to be sorry for what she has done? What you have seen, I suggest, has been a cool—yes, cold!—individual fighting to avoid the supreme penalty in this case."

This was "a hard woman" who "coolly and cold-bloodedly" poured poison into Stuart's drinks, he said.

"Can you think of a more atrocious act in your life? Can you think of a more malicious act?"

After poisoning Stuart, he pointed out, she had watched his agonies while deceiving his family and his doctors.

"Do you think she has tried to deceive you in this courtroom this week?" he asked, going on to detail her lies to the detectives and Stuart's family.

"Let me ask you something, ladies and gentlemen of the jury. Can you be satisfied that a recommendation of life imprisonment for that woman will protect society in the future from her? I suggest to you that there is one recommendation that will protect society from Velma Barfield, and it's the ultimate penalty!

"When you go to the jury room, just take one picture back there with you. Picture Stuart Taylor lying on his deathbed at Southeastern Hospital. Mr. McPherson said he threw back his head and made a scream and he went to get the doctor. Picture him lying there clutching his stomach. Do you recall what Dr. Page Hudson said about death by arsenic? He said there was an agonizing, hot, burning sensation in a person's insides and that you threw up and had diarrhea until you were dehydrated and eventually died in pain. Take one picture with you, please, as he lay there dying, knowing that his Florence Nightingale was beside him but not knowing that his Florence Nightingale was in truth Lucrezia Borgia."

"Objection," said Jacobson, hoping to deflect his crescendo.

"Overruled," said the judge.

After that performance, Jacobson was thankful that he wouldn't have to face the jury immediately. It was well past noon, and the judge recessed for lunch, telling the jurors that they would have to remain together. They would be taken to the Tory Inn, he said, and fed at the state's expense.

Jurors would later say that they thought Jacobson appeared nervous and uncertain when he began his argument after lunch.

"I have never had to ask anybody for anybody else's life before," he said in a quiet, almost tremulous voice. "It's hard to do, and I don't imagine any of you have ever had to decide whether to give anybody else their life or death, so this is not something that you can go in there and in five minutes decide."

He urged them to take their time, give their opinions, discuss it thoroughly.

Britt had talked for an hour, he noted, and he didn't know how long he would take. "It's so important to me, if I had to talk forever to convince you to give this woman her life, I would do it."

He went over the mitigating circumstances: that the murder had been committed while Velma was under mental or emotional disturbances, that her capacity to appreciate the criminality of the act was impaired, plus any other mitigating factors that the jury might want to include.

"Now you say, 'Mr. Jacobson, this is a first-degree murder case. How can anything make it milder or less severe? Murder is murder.' Mr. Britt has suggested the three aggravating circumstances and there is, admittedly, evidence that tends to show all three of them. You say, 'Mr. Lawyer, what have you got to offer us to support your contentions that there are mitigating circumstances that outweigh those aggravating circumstances?'

"I submit to you there is a very serious mitigating circumstance."

He went on to encapsulate Velma's life, Thomas' drinking, their fights, his death, the medicines she started taking as a result, the growing abuse of those medicines and all the problems that ensued.

"This really isn't one case," he said. "This is five cases, maybe six, maybe seven. It's not just murders, it's forgeries, worthless checks."

The jurors might ask, "Why are you telling us all that?" he said.

"The problem goes back to the medications, the dope, the problems that she had coping. She is an inadequate personality, passive-aggressive, unable to cope. She is a poor person, not enough money for doctors and pills. She forged. She tried to cover up, and she used the poison. And this didn't happen one time. It happened in a series of poisonings, but I submit to you that it goes back to the dope.

"These bottles over here aren't figments of my imagination," he said, indicating the empty medicine vials that had been introduced into evidence. "And these doctors that came in, even the state's doctors, many of them had prescribed drugs for her. It goes back to the dope, more dope, more dope, more forgeries, more covering up, more poisonings."

He went back over all the doctors who had testified, all the drugs he'd asked them about, pointing out how easy it was to get the doctors to prescribe them.

"These drugs have reduced Mrs. Barfield to the point where she can't reason," he said. "The thing that separates a human being from an animal is the ability to reason, and Mrs. Barfield, because of these narcotics over here, was not able to reason. You have seen her testify. Does she look like a person with a problem?

"Mr. Britt pointed out how cold and calculating she was. That looks mighty bad, and I submit to you that's part of the problem. It's part of the dope that for years and years she has been taking, and it is due from the many, many doctors giving her many, many medications.

"You convicted her of first-degree murder, and I am not suggesting to you for one moment that she shouldn't be punished. But I think she has got mitigating circumstances, and it's really not two or three. Her capacity was impaired, and you can see it. I don't have to tell you that. I submit to you that her emotional disturbance caused her to do this."

Jacobson recalled that in questioning potential jurors, one had said that he felt capital punishment was a necessary law but that he might feel different if life imprisonment really meant that.

"I want to submit to you in this case that it will mean life imprisonment," he said, getting a quick rise from Britt.

"I object to that argument."

"Overruled," said the judge.

"And you know who has the power over that?" Jacobson went on, his voice rising for the first time. "Do you want to know who can determine that and who has had the power to determine that all along?" This was his first real display of emotion, and now he turned and pointed. "That man right there, Mr. Britt."

"Now, I do object to that, Your Honor," Britt said.

"Objection sustained," said McKinnon, turning to the jury. "Don't consider the last portion of the attorney's statement."

If Velma had committed five murders, as Britt had contended, Jacobson pointed out, then he could charge her with five, win five convictions and five life sentences, and they could run consecutively. A life sentence was considered to be eighty years, and in North Carolina a person could become eligible for parole after serving a fifth of the total maximum punishment. "If the total is four hundred years, one-fifth of four hundred years is eighty years, and eighty added to forty-five . . ." he said, noting Velma's age, although she had turned forty-six a month earlier. "You add it up."

"Your Honor," said Britt, "I object and move to strike."

"Motion denied," said the judge.

"Consider that, ladies and gentlemen of the jury. It is a viable alternative. Go back there, discuss the issues, ask yourselves, 'Am I doing the right thing? Am I convinced beyond a reasonable doubt?' Express your opinions. When you come out here, each of you personally will be asked what your verdict is. Ask yourselves if you can live with it. I am not asking, I am begging you to give this woman her life."

Jacobson didn't have to win all twelve jurors. Just one strong juror holding out for life would do. A hung jury would bring the same sentence as a unanimous verdict for life.

After a brief recess, the judge instructed the jurors on their deliberations, and they filed out.

Velma remained in the courtroom, her family gathered around her. Three of her brothers and her sisters were there, as well as Ronnie and Pam and their spouses, and others. Ronnie and Joanna, unable to find a babysitter, had brought Michael to court. He was two and a half, and he ran to his grandmother and climbed into her lap.

Ronnie and Pam were anxious and tense, but Velma didn't appear ill at ease. "She didn't seem to be worried at all," Ronnie later recalled. "I think she enjoyed the trial. She enjoyed all the attention she was getting."

The longer the jurors took, Jacobson had told them, the better, and Ronnie couldn't keep his eye off the clock.

As soon as the jurors had taken their seats in the jury room, one man announced that he was ready to vote. "I'm for the death penalty," he said.

Tuton, who thought this far too grave a responsibility to be handled hurriedly or flippantly, asked instead if anybody objected to a prayer. Nobody did, and he called for a minute of silent prayer.

The jury had been given a verdict sheet, and on it were four questions that had to be answered: (1) Did the aggravating circumstances exist? (They could say yes or no to any of the three.) (2) Did the mitigating circumstances exist? (They could say yes or no to either and add any that they pleased.) (3) Did the mitigating circumstances outweigh the aggravating? (4) Were the aggravating circumstances sufficient for the death penalty?

Tuton led the group through all the issues, discussing each. And although some jury members initially seemed to have trouble fully grasping the concept of mitigating and aggravating circumstances, he continued the discussion until he felt that all understood before taking a secret ballot. This time the jurors would answer all the questions as they appeared on the verdict sheet. As he opened and read each, he was amazed. All the answers, he later would recall, were identical.

But once again he wanted to make sure that if anybody had reservations there was ample opportunity to make them known. He wanted everybody to be completely certain of his or her decision. So he went through the discussion and vote again. And again.

And still again. Later, he would lose count of how many votes he took, but he thought it could have been as many as seven.

The afternoon had stretched on agonizingly for Ronnie. His only real hope was that the jury might spare his mother because she was a woman, a grandmother; and, as the jury's deliberations had gone past an hour, then two hours, he had begun to allow himself to think that it might happen. Then darkness came, and still the jury was out, and Ronnie felt certain that at least some of the jurors must be tormented by their decision, and that could only be seen as a good sign.

At 5:50, nearly three hours after the jury had begun deliberating, word filtered through the courtroom and hallways that the jury was returning. Court quickly reassembled. Pam joined Ronnie at the defense table. The judge took the bench and called for order.

"Ladies and gentlemen, the jury indicates that it has some report," he said. "We do not know what it is at this time. If it should be a verdict, or regardless of what it is, this remains a court of law in which order will be kept and no one should make any visible, audible outburst in response to the report of the jury."

As the jury filed back in, both Ronnie and Pam noticed that a young woman juror, about Pam's age, appeared to have been crying.

Once again the judge asked if the jury had a verdict, and Ronald Tuton said they did. McKinnon asked for the verdict sheet, and the clerk handed it to him. He read it silently, then requested that Velma stand while he asked Tuton each of the questions. The jury had found that all three aggravating circumstances existed, but found against both the mitigating.

Were the mitigating circumstances insufficient to outweigh the aggravating?

Tuton answered yes.

Were the aggravating circumstances sufficient to call for the death penalty?

"Yes," said Tuton and a gasp came from the audience where the victims' relatives were seated.

"You return as your recommendation, 'We the jury, based upon the answers to the above issues, and as evidenced by the signature of the undersigned foreman of the jury, unanimously recommend to the court that the punishment for the defendant, Margie Bullard

Barfield, be the death penalty, this the second day of December, 1978. Ronald Clay Tuton, foreman of the jury,' " said the judge. "Mr. Foreman, is that the verdict as the jury returned it?"

"Yes, it is."

Pam began sobbing uncontrollably; Ronnie sat slumped in his chair, his arms folded, despondent. But Velma stood mute, as stoic as a statue.

Jacobson requested that the jurors be polled, and each in turn agreed that this was his, or her, verdict.

The judge thanked them for their service and dismissed them, then declared a brief recess.

"Mr. Jacobson, are there any motions prior to the sentencing?" the judge asked after court had reconvened.

"Well, I would like to make a motion for mistrial on account of the misconduct of the prosecutor during the closing arguments."

"Motion denied and exception noted," said the judge.

Jacobson also offered motions that the verdict be set aside because it was contrary to the law and the weight of the evidence, and that a new trial be granted for errors assigned, both of which were denied.

"Will the defendant please rise," said the judge, and Velma stood, a blank look on her face.

"Do you have anything to say before sentencing, ma'am?"

Velma shook her head, and the judge went on to read the long and repetitive sentence.

"It is therefore ordered and adjudged that the defendant, Margie Bullard Barfield, be, and she is hereby, sentenced to death by asphyxiation. . . ."

McKinnon set the date of execution as February 9, 1979, a little more than two months away, a date that had special meaning to Ronnie. That would be his sixth wedding anniversary.

"Mr. Sheriff, she's in your custody," the judge said.

Bailiffs quickly took Velma back to the jail, and the judge closed court.

It was over now. Ronnie turned to Jacobson, who looked as despondent as he felt, thoroughly beaten. ("You really can't lose a bigger case than that," Jacobson would say much later. "There isn't anything more devastating than losing a capital case.") Ronnie offered his hand and assured Jacobson that he'd done the best he could.

Kirby put an arm around his still sobbing wife and led her from the courtroom, avoiding reporters and their questions.

At the prosecutor's table, Joe Freeman Britt began assembling his papers. He was not flush with victory. Instead, he looked drained. "When you finish that last argument," he later would say, "you're dead. You're so damned tired. You don't feel anything. If you did it right, you'd train for murder trials just like an athlete. It's a very debilitating activity."

Britt seemed surprised when he looked up and saw Ronnie standing before him.

"I know you were just doing your job," Ronnie told him. "I just want you to know that I and my family don't hate you for it."

"I wouldn't want anybody to hate me," Britt said, and thanked him. The two shook hands.

"I think respect sent me over there," Ronnie later would say. "I respected what he was doing. I had been taught some good qualities in my life, and strange as it might seem, it was my mother who had taught them to me."

Ronnie remained silent on the long ride home. He wanted no supper. He sat in his favorite chair, staring into space.

"Are you okay?" Joanna asked.

"Yeah," he said, "I just need to let it sink in, I guess."

The week had seemed unreal. His whole life was beginning to seem unreal. How had it come to this point? he kept asking. And what might he have done to change it? A pointless exercise, but he couldn't stop himself.

At eleven, he turned on the TV to see the news about the trial, and as he watched, it was almost as if it really didn't involve him. It seemed like every other awful event he saw on the news. It was happening to somebody else.

On Sunday morning, Ronnie took Michael and drove back to Elizabethtown to visit his mother. Velma broke into tears when she saw them, and she didn't stop crying. She was upset that she wouldn't get to see her grandchildren as often, upset that she wouldn't be allowed to return to the Robeson County jail to pick up her things and to say good-bye to people she'd left behind, to thank the jailers who had been kind to her. She seemed to be upset about everything but the thing that should concern her most: that she had just been sentenced to death, which she never mentioned. Ronnie couldn't help but wonder if she was truly aware of what had happened.

He hadn't expected to find her like this, and it hurt. "That was a tough, tough day," he would say years later.

Velma was to be taken to Raleigh the next day, and Ronnie returned with Michael to see her again Monday morning. She was still upset, still crying when Ronnie was told that their visit had to end.

He went outside and stood on the sidewalk, waiting for his mother's departure. She soon emerged with two deputies, still crying. She looked up and saw Ronnie holding Michael and raised her cuffed hands in a sad attempt at a wave.

The car pulled away from the jail at the back of the courthouse. Ronnie could barely make out his mother's head in the backseat as he hurried to the corner and stood watching until the car disappeared.

"Daddy," Michael asked, "why are you crying?"

"I'm crying for your grandmother," he said.

"Where's she going?"

"She has to go away," he said, "but you'll see her again. She still loves you."

PART IV

A Mother Again

CHAPTER 17

The North Carolina Correctional Institute for Women did not look like most prisons. A collection of low, red-brick buildings in east Raleigh, its grounds blooming with dogwoods and azaleas each spring, it might have been mistaken for a community college if not for the high, barbed-wire–topped fence that surrounded it.

The state's only prison for women, it had no death row, the need for one usually being scant. Instead, those sentenced to death were housed in Dorm C, which held prisoners on lockup for disciplinary infractions or emotional problems as well as new arrivals being processed into the open dormitories where most inmates lived.

The cell to which Velma was assigned was designed for four but she occupied it alone. Steel bars separated it from a common area where inmates—residents, they were officially called—who were not on lockup could mingle and watch TV at certain hours.

John Frazier, the prison chaplain, came to call on Velma on her first afternoon there. He held a master's degree in clinical psychology and had studied therapeutic counseling of the mentally ill at Oxford University in England. Frazier, who was black, realized that some white inmates of Velma's age and circumstances were reluctant to talk with him, but Velma was not. She was very talkative, although not particularly coherent. She would be speaking about one thing, then suddenly go to something that was completely disassociated. She frequently would forget what she was about to say. She would start talking about her childhood without prompting or logical transition. She told Frazier that she had bizarre feelings that she couldn't control and that her mind and body sometimes seemed to be separated. She clearly was depressed and confused. She'd been accused of killing people, she said, but didn't remember much about it and didn't think that she had. She'd only tried to care for people. Her confusion seemed sincere and he thought Velma showed signs of serious psychological disturbance. He suggested to the prison physician that she be evaluated for schizophrenia.

What Frazier didn't realize on that first visit was that Velma was beginning withdrawal from drugs she'd been supplied in jail. Shortly after her arrest, Alf Parnell had called Dr. Anthony Sainz and he had prescribed the tranquilizer Tranxene and the sedative antidepressants Sinequan and Elavil, which she had taken until she was sent to Dorothea Dix Hospital two days later.

During her six weeks at the hospital, she had complained daily of headaches, nervousness and insomnia. Initially, she had been given only buffered aspirin, the antidepressant Tofranil, Dalmane for sleep, an occasional shot of Benadryl (an antihistamine), and infrequent dosages of the heavily sedating antipsychotic agent Thorazine. Six days after her admission she was trembling, dizzy, complaining of headaches, back pains, cold sweats and blurred vision, and she was diagnosed with acute drug withdrawal. For the next three days she was given heavier dosages of Thorazine and the barbiturate Phenobarbital. For the last four weeks of her hospitalization, however, she was allowed only buffered aspirin and Tofranil.

Back at the Robeson County Jail, Velma was taken on several occasions to the emergency room at Southeastern Hospital with severe headaches, nausea and other signs of withdrawal, and Dr. Sainz again gave her Tranxene, Sinequan and Elavil. In July he started her on the tranquilizer and antispasmodic drug Librax, along with the Elavil and Fiorinal, a painkiller. From the first of September, she had been given all that plus Tranxene and Equagesic, a sedative pain killer, and during her trial she was also given Gantrisin for a urinary tract infection.

But Velma's drugs were not transferred with her to prison, and she soon was complaining of nausea, severe headaches, cold sweats. She was unable to eat or sleep. When Frazier went to see her again, she was trembling uncontrollably, her eyes darting wildly. He recognized drug withdrawal, and she was taken to the infirmary and started on Tranxene, Librax, Endep, a highly sedating antidepressant, and Vistaril, an antianxiety drug. Later, she would receive only Valium and Vistaril in gradually decreasing amounts, but it would be sixteen months before she would be completely free of drugs.

That didn't stop her from telling a reporter she was "drug free." Three days after her arrival at the prison, Velma agreed to an interview with Ginny Carroll of Raleigh's *News & Observer.* The story appeared across the top of the front page on Sunday a week after her conviction. In it, Velma spoke not only of being free of drugs and filled with the Holy Spirit, but proclaimed her readiness for the gas chamber.

"I am guilty," she told Carroll. "I don't want an appeal. Personally, I'd rather go ahead. The day is February ninth."

The story was picked up by the Associated Press and appeared in other newspapers across the state. It came as a shock to Ronnie as well as to Bob Jacobson.

"All I could think was Gary Gilmore," Ronnie later recalled.

Gilmore had been the first person executed after the U.S. Supreme Court had approved the resumption of capital punishment in 1976. He had died early in 1977, within months of the holdup murders he committed. He had dropped all appeals and demanded that the state of Utah put him before a firing squad. Utah had accommodated him.

Could his mother actually do this? Ronnie wondered. Might she end up going to the gas chamber on his anniversary after all?

Ronnie called Jacobson, who assured him that under North Carolina's new capital punishment laws, an appeal to the state Supreme Court was automatic and Velma couldn't stop it. Her execution date was a fiction. The court had appointed Jacobson to handle her appeal, and he hadn't even begun getting it together. He wouldn't complete it for months, and more months would pass before the Supreme Court ruled on it. Velma was in no immediate danger, no matter her public pronouncements. But Jacobson wasn't pleased about them.

Once again Velma was undercutting him and hurting her own chances. If he should win a new trial or new sentencing hearing, her admissions to a reporter could be used against her, and she had for the first time professed vengeance as a motive, telling Carroll when asked how she felt while giving poison to her victims, "It was kind of like something they have done to you and you want to do something back." Jacobson also was keenly aware that the Supreme Court sat in Raleigh and its members likely read the *News & Observer.*

Jacobson immediately wrote to Velma: "I have read in several newspapers where you have said that you did not want to appeal this case and that you were guilty of four murders. An appeal in a capital case is automatic. In order for me to do the best possible job that I can for you, please do not make any more statements to the press."

Velma's profession of her newly found religion in the *News & Observer* was the first time she had made that public. She had come to know the Lord, she later would reveal, on a hot and particularly desolate Saturday night at the Robeson County Jail in July. She had been at her lowest ebb, she said, wanting desperately to die, but she couldn't figure out how to kill herself. She was alone in her cell. No other women were prisoners. At nine o'clock, the guard turned out the light, and she lay on her bunk in abject despair, unable to sleep.

The guard had a radio tuned to a gospel music station in Laurinburg. At eleven, Velma heard what she later would describe as "the sweetest sounding music" coming from the radio and she began to weep. Then came a man's strong and enthusiastic voice saying, "No matter where you are tonight or what's happening to you, somebody loves you!"

The man was J. K. Kinkle, who operated a Christian bookstore in nearby Laurinburg. His weekly radio program was called "The Way of Jesus Broadcast."

"Yes, somebody loves you and His name is Jesus! He loves you tonight no matter where you are or what you've done. That same Jesus is standing at the door of many hearts tonight, knocking, waiting to come inside, and wanting to put a new spirit within you."

Those words struck Velma as none ever had, she later would say. Could she be forgiven despite all she had done? Could she actually be freed of guilt, anger, bitterness, hatred? Could she truly know peace? She had gone to church for years, had proclaimed herself a Christian, but she knew it all had been a facade. She had never truly opened her heart to Jesus.

Now she realized that Jesus was there in this awful place. His arms open to her, willing to forgive, to love her without reservation, prepared to grant her a whole new life, ready to accompany and comfort her through whatever lay ahead. As undeserving as she felt herself to be, all she had to do to receive that was to open her heart to Him. She began to pray as she never had before, begging forgiveness, reaching out, and while J. K. Kinkle preached on, she began to feel a new presence within her. She started to cry again, but this time the tears were from joy, and she knew that she would never be the same.

At first she didn't say much about this experience. When Ronnie visited the next day, she asked him to bring her Bible, and she read from it for hours at a time, understanding for the first time, she later claimed, verses she had recited emptily before. She wrote to J. K. Kinkle, and he sent material for her to study. She wrote, too, to the Billy Graham ministry, never dreaming that a day would come when this famous man, this friend of presidents and the rich and powerful, would take a personal interest in her. His group, too, sent material, including several books that helped her along her fledgling path toward redemption.

No mention of Velma's newfound religion was made at her trial, and she didn't carry her Bible to court, as defendants often do. This, she later would claim, was deliberate, because she didn't want anybody to think that she had grasped religion in a desperate attempt to get a lighter sentence.

At one of the low points of her trial, Velma told Ginny Carroll, she had returned to the jail to find another packet of materials from the Billy Graham ministry and that had helped her through that dark time.

"I had strength I didn't know existed," she said. "It lasted even through the trial. I didn't shed a tear through it all. When the jury came in with the death penalty, the lawyer had my two kids at the table. I begged the Lord to help me hold up for their sakes. When they announced the death penalty, my daughter broke. I hated so much to see her hurt like that."

Velma's religious conversion would quickly gain strength in prison. On her second Sunday, she met Sam and Gales Roane. Sam was retired from his hospital supply business. He and Gales had four daughters and nine grandchildren, a fine home in Raleigh and an apartment in Myrtle Beach. Their good fortune and their many years at Raleigh's First Presbyterian Church had convinced them that they needed to give something back, to share their faith with those less fortunate. They chose to do that at Women's Prison, where they came regularly to conduct Sunday school classes in Dorm C. Sam, a big, white-haired man with a huge voice, conducted the Bible studies and prayers, and his bubbly wife played a portable organ while Sam led hymns. The Roanes wrote to Velma each week, encouraging her, and their Christian friends around the country began writing as well.

Because she was sentenced to death, Velma was not allowed to attend chapel services (she could only leave her cell to shower and to exercise for an hour alone each day on a small, fenced concrete pad). John Frazier, a Unitarian, realized that he could not adequately minister to Velma's fundamentalist beliefs. He suggested that she might want to have a minister from outside the prison, and she agreed. Since she had been a member of a Pentecostal Holiness church in Lumberton, Frazier asked Tommy Fuquay, the pastor of Trinity Pentecostal Holiness Church in Raleigh, to call on her. He came for the first time in January.

Fuquay, who was forty-five, had previously ministered in prisons. Sometimes prisoners had fooled him, and he was wary of them. But Velma impressed him as genuine in her faith from the beginning. "I don't think I had ever seen anybody who had the repentant spirit she had," he recalled years later.

Fuquay began visiting weekly. "I could see her growing and her attitude changing," he said. "The faith in her just grew and grew each time I would see her. I would feel refreshed when I came out."

In their talks Velma expressed concern about her children and family and the pain and disgrace she had brought them. She worried, too, about the families of her victims. She asked Fuquay's advice on making amends. Did he think the families might reject her if she wrote asking forgiveness? She could only try and see, he suggested.

Velma did write to Alice Storms. "I hardly know the right words to say to you," she began. "I am truly sorry for all the hurt that I have caused all of you. When you wept, you didn't weep alone. . . ." She went on to ask forgiveness and signed the letter, "May the God of love shine upon you. Velma."

She got no response. The Velma Alice knew before her father's death had been just as pious as the Velma who wrote the letter, Alice said later. She couldn't believe that Velma had undergone meaningful change. Velma was a person without a conscience, she thought, and the only reason she would seek forgiveness had to be self-serving.

In May, five months after she had entered prison, Velma's

youngest brother, Ray, was killed in a traffic accident, sending her into despondency. The following month, she got another blow. Tommy Fuquay accepted a new pastorate in Stanley, in the western part of the state, 150 miles away. For nearly two months he made a three-hundred-mile round trip to minister to Velma, but the strain grew too great, and he asked his replacement at Trinity, Hugh Hoyle, if he would consider becoming Velma's pastor. Hoyle agreed and Fuquay took him to see her in August. The two hit it off, and Brother Hoyle, as Velma called him, not only became her closest spiritual adviser but a good friend as well.

Hoyle was thirty-five, a man of high intelligence, vigor and enthusiasm. He was a preacher's son who had committed his own life to God at the age of fifteen and had gotten his license to preach upon his graduation from high school in Greensboro. He had graduated from Guilford College, a Quaker school, and had pastored a church in Greensboro while doing graduate work at the University of North Carolina. He had married at thirty-three, and had come to Raleigh from a church in North Wilkesboro, in the foothills of the Blue Ridge Mountains.

Hoyle felt an obligation to be up front with Velma from the beginning about one matter: he was not opposed to capital punishment. That didn't matter, Velma told him. She understood; she'd always favored it herself. She wanted him to be her minister, and he began coming to see her every Thursday afternoon.

Hoyle guided Velma in her Bible studies, prayed with her, listened to her problems, gave her communion, and soon started her on a long-term, eight-step, self-examination study program that was designed to allow her to discover her defects, accept herself, deal with her problems. He found her to be an eager and receptive student, and he looked forward to their visits.

As Velma's outlook changed, so did her attitude about her sentence. She found new reason to live and placed hope in her appeal. So far, five other cases under the new death penalty law had come before the state Supreme Court, and it had found error in all, granting a new trial, a new sentence, or a new sentencing hearing in each.

Hugh Hoyle was returning from a funeral on Tuesday, November 6, 1979, three months after becoming Velma's minister, when he heard on the radio that the Supreme Court had upheld her conviction and sentence.

Bob Jacobson had focused his appeal on two main issues: whether the insanity plea should have been allowed, or the evidence of the previous deaths admitted. He also raised ten other points, but the court, in a twenty-one-page opinion, rejected all, finding sufficient evidence to uphold the conviction and justify the aggravating circumstances.

"We find nothing in the record which would suggest that the sentence of death was imposed under the influence of passion, prejudice, or any other arbitrary factor," stated the opinion. "The manner in which death was inflicted and the way in which the defendant conducted herself after she administered the poison to Taylor leads us to conclude that the sentence of death is not excessive or disproportionate."

Hoyle drove straight to the prison after hearing the news. He knew Velma would need him, as indeed she did. She was concerned about how Ronnie and Pam would take the news, but she was especially worried about Pam, who was expecting her second child.

Hoyle consoled Velma—"He always has just the right words to say for everything," she later would say—then prayed for Ronnie and Pam and the safe delivery of Pam's baby.

The baby was born, healthy and strong, a day and a half later on Thursday morning. Pam and Kirby named her Sarah Sue.*

"I will never forget how my heart ached to see this child," Velma later wrote. Pam would bring the baby for a visit two Saturdays later. "I held her almost the entire two hours," Velma scribbled afterward in a notebook where she kept a record of important events. "To me she was a living doll. As I looked at her I cried inside because I couldn't be home with her."

Ronnie had received word of the Supreme Court's decision before it became news, and it meant a new source of worries. Jacobson, in calling to tell him, said that he would be happy to continue with additional appeals, but the family would have to pay. The state had paid him $3,500 dollars for Velma's defense and another $3,000 for the appeal. But that was all the state allotted. From this point, Velma was on her own.

There was no way the family could come up with the money, Ronnie told Jacobson, who would be filing for a stay of execution pending an appeal to the U.S. Supreme Court (it would be granted on November 14), then would be finished with Velma's case—or so he thought.

Ronnie had no idea what to do. He fretted for two days, uncertain where to turn. He was to play in a Putt-Putt tournament in Greensboro that weekend, and he drove there early Friday and called the local office of the American Civil Liberties Union from a telephone booth, explaining the situation to director George Gardner.

"Don't worry," Gardner said to Ronnie's immense relief. "We'll see that your mother has a lawyer."

That lawyer, Ronnie later would learn, would be Richard Burr III, who knew little at the time about appealing death penalty cases, although Ronnie didn't know that. He was just pleased to know that his mother had somebody to defend her.

Velma, too, was pleased, and she went into her second year in prison with renewed confidence. But she confided to Hugh Hoyle her fear that she was losing close touch with her son. In the beginning, either Ronnie or Pam had gone every week to see their mother, then a couple of weeks passed between visits. By the end of Velma's first year in prison, she sometimes went a month without seeing either of them. Ironically, it was her very improvement that was keeping her son away.

Year after year, Ronnie had fought to get his mother off drugs, had dreamed of the day when she would be free of bitterness, anger and despair. As Velma was weaned off drugs, her disposition grew brighter by the month, the rancor and resentment dissipating as her mood improved. When Ronnie visited now, his mother seemed cheerful. She giggled and laughed.

"She was my old mom," he later said. "It was like she had been taken out of her body and returned."

But the change did not bring him the happiness he had imagined it might. Instead, he left after each visit with a profound sadness. "Seeing her trapped, it kind of sank in what had happened. She wasn't the same person who had done what she had done. I began to wonder if she didn't understand the gravity of what was going on, if she just didn't know. Every time I left, I knew I was leaving her on death row, and it was getting harder to handle."

But Velma did understand. Several years later, she would write about that period when so many changes were taking place.

"As I began to dry out, I began to have a clear mind and started remembering and facing reality and I began to think of the horrible nightmare experiences that brought me to prison. It was so frightening. I would lay on my bunk for long periods going over and over the past ten years, crying, really wanting to scream. . . .

"I relived days, months, and years that all the deaths had occurred, how I had hurt not only the victims, but how I had crushed the lives of the victims' families and brought so much hurt and disgrace to my own family. I kept praying, asking God to help me overcome these bad memories. I knew He had forgiven me but at this period of my life I had not forgiven myself, and this is why I couldn't rid myself of these thoughts."

Velma would not slip back into despair this time, though. She would reach out to others. Combining a mother's instincts and her newfound religion, she would start making a difference in the lives of other prisoners.

"There are lots of girls here who cannot read or write," she wrote in her first year in prison. "I couldn't believe this to start with. I mean, these girls tell me that they finished through nine, ten, and eleven grades and still cannot read or write. It's really sad. I write a lot of their letters home for them. . . .

"Another sad thing is that such a small number claim Jesus as their Savior—very few. My heart goes out to them because I know the feeling of living with bitterness and hatred inside. The feeling of being unwanted, unloved and lonely—not caring if they live or die. . . . I just want to reach out to them."

Although Velma had begun remaking herself, finding new strength in religion and new purpose as she reached out to help others around her, none of this would yet be of concern to the courts that would be deciding whether she would live or die. Still, her new lawyer had given her great reason for hope.

CHAPTER 18

Richard Burr was thirty and brimming with idealism. He had grown up in Lake Wales, Florida, and graduated from Vanderbilt University in Nashville before going to law school at the University of Kentucky. He was committed to the great social issues of the time, and in February 1979, he had become the sole, underpaid lawyer for the Southern Prisoners Defense Committee in Nashville, an outgrowth of the Southern Coalition on Jails and Prisons started by a North Carolina minister, Joe Ingle. His job was to work on prisoners' rights cases, but a greater need quickly presented itself.

Many cases tried under the new death penalty laws were just reaching the end of state appeals, and those defendants, almost all without resources, were finding themselves facing death with nobody to carry on their cases. Within a matter of days in November, Burr got three calls from the NAACP Legal Defense Fund about such cases and he decided he'd better learn something about death-penalty appeals.

A seminar on the death penalty was being held in Charlotte by North Carolina trial attorneys in early December. Burr attended, then drove to Raleigh to meet Velma, the first of more than two hundred death-row inmates he eventually would defend. Nice lady, he thought, pleasant and sweet, hard to picture as a murderer. She talked freely and seemed happy to have his services. After their visit, Burr drove to Lumberton and introduced himself to Bob Jacobson, who gave him free access to his files on Velma.

Burr's first official act on Velma's behalf was to appeal her case to the U.S. Supreme Court, but in June, 1980, the court declined to hear it, indicating that it found no fault in the constitutionality of North Carolina's new death penalty statutes.

In response to the ruling, Burr told reporters that despite earlier press reports, Velma wanted to live.

"She is resolved to fight," he said, "and she and I both believe that she will get a new trial at some point and won't get the death penalty."

Although he asked the Supreme Court to reconsider its ruling, Burr had concluded that the best chance to save her lay in the state courts. There he had a problem. He was not licensed to practice in North Carolina. He needed a local lawyer to be her attorney of record, and in September, seeking help, he called Mary Ann Tally, the public defender in Fayetteville, whom he had met at the death penalty seminar in Charlotte the previous December.

Tally called her friend Jimmie Little, the former public defender, who now was a partner in his own law firm in Fayetteville, and explained the situation. If Little had heard of Velma Barfield, he couldn't remember. He had been living in Fayetteville during her trial, but he had paid little attention to the news coverage.

Later, Little would marvel at how casually he stepped into a role that would come to dominate his life. "I didn't think a whole lot about it," he said. He agreed to help until another lawyer could be found, and he assumed that one would be. He and Burr began talking about the case by telephone.

On September 17 the Supreme Court declined to reconsider Velma's case and a new execution date was promptly set for October 17. On Friday, October 3, Little filed motions in Bladen County Superior Court asking for a new stay of execution and a hearing to determine whether Velma had received a fair trial.

The motion for a new hearing listed twelve reasons why Velma should be granted another trial—the primary one being ineffective counsel. Bob Jacobson, Velma's new lawyers claimed, had spent only a few hours with her before trial, had failed to present the right witnesses, hadn't had her fully examined psychologically, hadn't put on appropriate psychiatric testimony, hadn't offered testimony about the effect of her drug use, hadn't made proper motions, and failed to make Velma appear human and sympathetic in the penalty phase, among other things. Jacobson, the motion charged, had himself dehumanized Velma.

In the fight against the death penalty, the charge of ineffective counsel was becoming a standard tactic, but that didn't keep Jacobson from being shocked and upset.

The motion was persuasive, however, to Judge Maurice Braswell of Fayetteville, who had signed the order to exhume the bodies of Velma's victims, and on October 9 he granted both the stay of execution and the hearing for a new trial. Velma was exultant, as were Ronnie and Pam when they heard the news.

The following day, Velma held her first news conference at Women's Prison. She laughed and joked with reporters, and a photograph of her smiling broadly appeared in newspapers across the state.

Her new faith had given Velma new reason to live and confidence that she would be allowed to. "At times I think of death in the gas chamber, but I never dwell on it," she said. "Who am I to say I am going to die in the gas chamber? I don't know that I am going to be here tomorrow. My life is in the hands of God and I have great faith in Him. He won't fail me."

A week later, Jimmie Little drove to Raleigh to meet Velma. "She was deferential, demure, shy, very pleasant," he recalled. "I couldn't imagine this nice person about to be executed."

He left Women's Prison that day knowing he had to do everything he could to keep that from happening.

Mary Ann Tally knew from the moment she called Little that was how it would be. She knew the kind of person he was. "He's cause oriented," she later told a reporter. "It doesn't make any difference if it is an unpopular cause or an unpopular client. If he believes in it, he'll do it."

At thirty-six, Little had been involved in many unpopular causes. As a student at the University of North Carolina, in a free-speech issue, he fought against North Carolina's so-called speaker-ban law, enacted in 1963, which prohibited communists from speaking on state university campuses. He had attempted to change his church's stand on civil rights and had opposed the Vietnam War while serving as an Army officer.

In 1972, after law school, he became an assistant prosecutor in his hometown, Fayetteville. The district attorney then was Jack Thompson, whose father was his father's business partner. Little's heart, however, was not with the establishment, but with the disenfranchised, the poor, the uneducated, who often, he thought, got a raw deal in the courts. A year after he became a prosecutor, the public defender's job came open. He put in for it and, to his surprise, got it.

As public defender, he remained an activist. He pushed to start one of the country's first pretrial release programs, worked on a North Carolina Bar Association committee to provide legal services to the indigent and helped to start the movement to form a State Appellate Defender's office, also one of the first in the country.

After three and a half years as public defender, he joined Fayetteville's biggest law firm and later went out on his own. When Mary Ann Tally called about Velma, she had no doubt that he would say yes. She knew that he was opposed to the death penalty and that, once he got involved, he would not quit; he would throw his whole being into the battle and fight to the end.

Bob Jacobson had never been in a more awkward situation as a lawyer. When Velma's hearing for a new trial opened before Judge Braswell on Monday, November 17, 1980, at the Robeson County courthouse in Lumberton, there he sat with his longtime antagonist Joe Freeman Britt and Donald W. Stephens, an assistant attorney general who handled death penalty appeals for the state. "It was kind of like fraternizing with the enemy," Jacobson later recalled. "You get to see things from a different perspective."

Even though Britt would be defending him, Jacobson realized that he couldn't allow himself to start feeling too warmly about it. "You know that before long, he's going to be across the table tearing you up again," he said years later.

At the next table now were Dick Burr and Jimmie Little, who were charging that Jacobson had been incompetent in Velma's defense, and Jacobson's attitude left no doubt how he felt about that. "I don't think any defense attorney has any business going into some other county and saying another attorney didn't do his job," he would say later. "Maybe I didn't do the best job that ever was done in this world, but it certainly was the most I could've done at the time."

Joe Freeman Britt found the whole procedure repulsive, all the more reason to hold defense attorneys in contempt, and he would make no secret of that either. "Self-appointed experts who ride up and shoot the wounded," he would later snort of Velma's new attorneys and some of their witnesses at the hearing. "What you have to realize is that this was a new law when this trial was held. Nobody knew how to try these things. We were all just feeling our way along, but they wanted to come in and tell us how it should have been done."

Little and Burr were contrasts in style. Little was short with thinning hair, almost prim in appearance. Burr was big, six feet tall and 200 pounds, but teddy bearish, with long, curly hair and full beard to hide his baby face. Little was intense, highly strung; Burr soft-spoken, seemingly more relaxed, and openly emotional.

Velma sat with her lawyers, looking much different than she had at her trial two years earlier. Life had returned to her face, and she seemed relaxed, no longer angry and bitter. Later, Ronnie would say that even her animosity toward Britt appeared to have dissipated. She clearly was happy to be away from the prison, back in Robeson County amongst family and friends. Both Ronnie and Pam had taken off from work for the hearing, and other family members and friends would come to visit during the breaks.

The hearing got under way with Bob Jacobson on the stand. Had he been satisfied with his handling of Velma's case? Little asked.

"Yes, sir," he replied.

Would he like to retry it?

"Object," said Britt.

"Sustained," said the judge, and that would set the tone of this hearing. But neither Burr nor Little could imagine then how Britt's objections would come to plague them, flying through the courtroom in such quantity that they would eventually feel obligated to object to the objections.

"Everyone has to try a first capital case," Jacobson said when he finally was allowed to answer. "I would say as to whether I would approach it differently that I would try harder and that I did work harder."

Jacobson went on to explain why he had put Velma on the stand, hoping to save her life with a second-degree murder conviction or to make her drug use a mitigating factor in the sentencing phase should she be convicted of first-degree.

"I counseled her on trying to be a sympathetic witness. I wanted her to look like somebody's mother. Here was this poor lady and look what she was going through. I counseled her that she could very much help herself in the manner that she testified, and very frankly I was afraid that she was going to get into an argument with Joe Freeman Britt and look very bad. My fears came to pass. I told her many times I wanted her to cry, and at no time did she do that. In fact, she just seemed to stick her chin out and just wanted to go at it with the D.A. I was very disappointed."

"What made you think she would go at it with Joe Freeman Britt?"

"Every time we got together, she wanted to argue with me about the cause of death of all the decedents. She was not satisfied that the arsenic had caused the death and we ourselves would argue about it, and I was afraid that she was going to do that, and that is what she did. She would get argumentative."

Jacobson stayed on the stand for two days explaining his actions, and he grew testy about the implications of some of the questions.

"I don't think it's fair for you to give me a bar exam up here," he told Little at one point.

At another, when Little began, "Did you consider asking the judge—" he was interrupted by Judge Braswell.

"I feel compelled to make a gratuitous comment," said the judge. "The phrase 'did you consider' has been asked many times. It has been the opinion of the court that it has been worded so as to give the impression of 'have you stopped beating your wife?' Therefore the court registers its disapproval of the language."

The next witness was Selwyn Rose, a psychiatrist who also held a law degree and was a frequent expert witness, usually for the defense. Velma's new lawyers had hired him to examine her and he had spent two hours with her on September 13. Later, he had psychological tests administered.

While reading through his notes on the stand, Rose revealed one thing that Velma had never made known before.

"I asked her very specifically whether her father had ever made a sexual assault upon her and she admitted that he had at one time when she was about thirteen or fourteen, coming in to the bed with her, was naked and she was in a state of complete terror and they heard somebody outside, some noises occurred and he quickly got out of the bed and did not have intercourse or complete any assault upon her."

She told him that she'd never thought of poisoning her father despite his abuse, he said. She also said that she had been "numb" from drugs when the idea came to poison her mother.

" 'It didn't bother me then,' " he said she'd told him, " 'but it did after I began to think about it.' "

When Little tried to get an opinion from Rose about Velma's mental condition at the time of the murders—which he and Burr considered to be important new evidence—he was stymied by consistently sustained objections from Britt. Little finally asked that the answer be allowed for the record, for the benefit of appellate judges, although it couldn't be considered as evidence, and the judge agreed.

In his opinion, Rose said, Velma was not sane, but he was uncertain if she was sufficiently disturbed to meet the legal definition of insanity. She had three types of "severe psychopathology," he said. First was organic depression. Second was drug abuse. Both could impair her thought processes. Third was a personality disorder that was "of such magnitude as to make her, or as to allow her, to pour poison into people's drinks without any clear understanding of what that means."

Mary Ann Tally was helping Little and Burr with Velma's case, and Little wanted her to testify as an expert on the defense of first-degree murder. Although Tally had been practicing for only six years, her credentials and accomplishments were impressive. She was a member of the board of governors of the North Carolina Trial Lawyers, president of the North Carolina Association of Public Defenders, a member of the criminal code commission. She had attended seminars on the death penalty and had represented people charged with capital crimes.

Britt wanted to cross-examine her before she was qualified as an expert, and he asked how many of her capital cases had gone to the sentencing phase.

Three, she said.

And how many of those defendants had gone to death row?

Two, she answered.

Britt inquired about her interest in this case.

"I am interested that Mrs. Barfield have adequate representation and that she be given the kind of open and fair hearing that she deserved."

"Well, do you feel then that she did not receive adequate representation at the prior trial?"

"Yes."

"And this is based on your experience where two-thirds of your clients with capital cases have gone to death row, is that right?"

Little quickly objected, and the judge sustained.

Over Britt's objections, Tally was declared an expert.

Although little of her testimony would be allowed except for the record, Tally read from notes as she listed twelve motions that should have been made in Velma's case. She also criticized several of the motions Jacobson had made. Little then asked the judge to allow her testimony to be interrupted to accommodate an out-of-state witness who had just arrived and whose time was limited.

That witness was John Ackerman, dean of the National College for Criminal Defense at the University of Houston, which held seminars for defense lawyers throughout the country. Ackerman lectured on capital cases and was editor of *Death Penalty Reporter*.

The judge allowed him to testify as an expert, but because of Britt's objections most of his answers were only for the record. Jacobson, Ackerman maintained, was "absolutely ineffective" in both stages of the trial.

"There is just no coherent theory of defense," he said. "It was in effect a slow plea of guilty. It was not a trial."

He went on to list all the many ways Jacobson had failed before the judge declared a break at four o'clock.

After the recess, Britt had his turn.

"Mr. Ackerman, would it be fair to say that you make your living by contemplating in the cool of the evening what better men have done in the heat of the day?" Britt asked.

"No, I don't think that is how I make my living."

His job was trying to improve the competence of trial lawyers, he said. "And I think we are succeeding."

"What percentage of the total national bar would you say is competent?"

"I hesitate to even say, but Justice Burger, I think, his estimate is around fifty percent, or something like that."

After more fencing, Britt asked if he had an opinion about the percentage of lawyers who were competent to try capital cases. "Surely you have an idea about that."

"Yes, I'd say one or two percent. Maybe five percent."

"You are saying then that it is virtually impossible for anyone in the United States to get a fair trial in a capital case unless he has a lawyer from this one or two percent sample that you are talking about, is that correct?"

"I think there are two hundred and fifty thousand lawyers who are members of the ABA, and I don't know how many more that are not. So that one percent would include quite a few people."

Ackerman's testimony closed the third day of the hearing, and it had not been a good one for Velma. Little that her lawyers had attempted to get into evidence had been admitted.

When court opened Thursday morning, Burr requested that the judge require that grounds for all objections be stated at the time of the objection.

Britt, of course, was opposed, saying, "I just object very strenuously to conducting a law school seminar for two lawyers who are floundering around over here at the other table."

"While we appreciate Mr. Britt's concern about our being educated," responded Burr, "we don't think that is the problem. We think the problem is one of having adequate notice and an opportunity to respond and to have the issue focused."

The judge declared a recess to look up the rule. He returned and read it aloud. It did not require the reason for an objection to be stated.

When Burr suggested that the rule denied Velma's constitutional rights, the judge sharply denied his motion.

Little was astounded at the turns this hearing was taking. He knew Judge Braswell, who was the senior resident superior court judge in the Twelfth District. When Little had been public defender he had worked closely with Braswell on administrative matters. "I always knew when it came to the crunch I could count on him," Little said. But this seemed to be a Braswell he didn't know.

"He thought of himself as a fair man, but he was prosecution oriented," Little said later. "I was surprised and appalled at the rulings he made. He was not there as a finder of fact."

Little suspected that Braswell was intimidated by Britt, but to Britt that was nonsense. Little and Burr simply weren't laying the proper foundation for their evidence, he later said, and for that neither the judge, nor he, could be blamed.

Now Little brought Mary Ann Tally back to continue her criticism of Jacobson. Among other points, she claimed the penalty phase of the trial had been disastrous for Velma. Jacobson had presented too few witnesses and no evidence of Velma's background, personality, humanity. The evidence of her mental state was not effective, she said. Doctors should have been called. And perhaps worst of all, Jacobson failed to tell the jurors that their decision on the penalty didn't have to be unanimous (at least one juror had told a defense jury poller that he thought it had to be).

After a recess, Britt had some questions for Tally.

Was she saying that if Jacobson had done all of the things she talked about, the outcome would have been different?

"Sir, I cannot presume to talk about what twelve jurors might decide," she replied.

Britt brought up one of Tally's own death penalty cases. Did she do in that case all that she claimed Jacobson should have done in Velma's?

No, she answered, explaining that each case had to be handled on an individual basis.

"In your expert opinion, did you rise to the level that you have advocated here in that case?"

"I certainly hope so, but that will be something for someone else to judge, Mr. Britt."

"Went to death row, didn't he?" said Britt.

"Yes."

Britt brought up another of her cases and went through the same questions.

"Went to death row, didn't he?" he asked again.

"Yes, he is currently on death row."

After Tally had stepped down, Little called a series of people, family and friends of Velma, as examples of witnesses who could have testified in Velma's trial but were never asked. More expert witnesses also were called but little of what they had to say was allowed into evidence. One, because of Britt's barrage of objections, got to speak only her name.

Little and Burr had only five more witnesses, and they presented them on Friday morning, the fifth day of the hearing. Two were expert witnesses, a political scientist and a law professor, neither of whom was allowed to speak for evidence. Three were family members, Ronnie, Pam and Velma's brother, Jimmy.

As he had done at the trial, Britt asked Ronnie about his father's death. When Ronnie replied that he had died in a fire that started on his bed while he was sleeping, Britt asked, "Did that raise any suspicions in your mind as to what may have happened or what might have set that blanket on fire?"

But Little quickly objected.

"Sustained," said the judge. "Don't answer that."

Following a recess, Velma's lawyers began their final arguments. Burr left the matter of Jacobson's competence to be argued by Little and concentrated on the other issues that had been raised about Velma's trial. Many had yet to be looked at by any court, he noted, although they could have been if Velma had had effective counsel. "In a sense, ineffectiveness is all," he said. "It encompasses everything."

He also argued that Velma should have a new trial because of newly discovered evidence presented by the psychiatrist, Selwyn Rose, and the character witnesses.

After listing all the issues, Little began by going step by step through what he considered to be Jacobson's errors in handling Velma's case and finally got to Velma's performance on the stand. If Jacobson had asked for a pretrial hearing to suppress Velma's statements, Little said, he could have put Velma on the stand and seen how she reacted to Britt, thus avoiding the disaster of her testimony before the jury at her trial.

He moved on to what he called "the psychiatric mess," Jacobson's insanity plea, which, Little claimed, gutted his credibility with the jury. The psychiatrists he presented, Little said, were in effect state witnesses, although much psychiatric evidence was available that wasn't presented.

Jacobson should have done more to keep out the evidence of the earlier deaths, Little maintained, and should have limited what was admitted once it was allowed. "The impact of the four other deaths cannot be understated," Little said. "Mr. Jacobson was in effect trying five murder cases in one because he did not effectively move to limit the evidence that was presented as to the other deaths."

Many witnesses could have been called in Velma's behalf, especially in the sentencing phase, Little said, and by limiting his witnesses, Jacobson had limited his argument. "In the sentencing phase and in the guilt phase, it is our contention that Mr. Jacobson failed to argue effectively to the jury even the evidence that he had."

In closing, Little stressed that he was not attacking Jacobson personally.

"This was his first capital case and everybody that tries capital cases has their first. We would submit that the fact that it is a person's first capital case gives no lesser degree of effectiveness for which he is responsible, that the question is not whether or not Mr. Jacobson did his best. The question is whether he effectively represented Mrs. Barfield and we submit Mrs. Barfield has been prejudiced to the point that her rights to a fair trial, her rights to due process and other constitutional rights including the right to effective assistance of counsel were denied."

It was four-thirty when Britt's turn finally came. He went straight to basics. The new ideas presented in Velma's behalf were not grounded in the fundamentals and practicalities of trying cases, he said.

"I love to hear them talk about the far-flung ideas that they dream up at these seminars they go to, but as they concentrate more and more on that, they lose sight of the business of the court itself, and the hands-on experience that is necessary, and the difficulty of getting some of this material into evidence."

He went on to point out the many witnesses Little and Burr had presented whose testimony was not allowed. "Yet I would argue in a way they are some of the most important witnesses in this courtroom this week. They were presented to demonstrate the method in which a lawyer humanizes his client for the jury. Were they able to get any of that evidence in? No.

"What they have to learn is that all of these ideas are great, but they have to fit within a framework of rules of evidence. You can't just go to some seminar and say, 'Hey, humanize your client,' and expect to walk into a courtroom and make it suddenly be part of the evidence. It is not that simple as—and I don't mean to cast aspersions—certain counsel in the courtroom have found out this week.

"Talk is cheap and you can dream up all of these ideas and try to force them off on people and point the accusing finger at people like Jacobson and say, 'Gee, you just didn't do your job,' but when you get down to the practicalities of it, when you get down to real life and the mano-a-mano confrontation in the courtroom, it ain't quite that simple anymore."

Britt moved on to the expert witnesses, noting that Little and Burr should have known that type of evidence wouldn't be admissible. "They presented Brother Ackerman, who was an interesting, friendly little fellow in his alligator shoes, but I suggest to Your Honor that Mr. Ackerman sees himself as a guru of the new wave of how to try capital cases. I'm not belittling the fellow, Your Honor, but he had one death case, and he went to death row. He's got him a good thing going, I guess, with his National Defense College and all that business, but I suggest that you don't prove this type of case the way they have attempted to prove it here this week."

Next he brought up what he referred to as "the juxtaposition of Madam Tally and Mr. Jacobson." He had no quarrel, he said, with Tally being declared an expert. "At this stage of evolution of capital trials in North Carolina, I suppose anybody who has tried a capital case and read a few articles is an expert."

It was her criticism of Jacobson, he said, that was the trouble. "There is something about it that just kind of rankles me. It galls me. If she has all these magic answers, they don't seem to work for her very well because she's got two people up on death row out of the three that she's tried, and yet she says that Mr. Jacobson did it wrong some way. Monday morning quarterbacking. Anybody can do it.

"I suggest that Mr. Jacobson did everything that he could to protect the rights of his client and protect her life. He tried the case on the theory he set out to try it for, a poor woman completely soaked up in drug abuse, wallowing in depression and not responsible for her actions even though it didn't quite meet the test of legal insanity."

Then perhaps realizing that he seemed to be arguing in Velma's behalf, he quickly jumped to the subject of trial tactics. "Nobody, and I don't care how smart they are, can sit down with a cold record and second-guess what some trial lawyer fighting down in the trenches thought and felt and did in the performance of his duty," he said.

The rules of evidence that controlled Jacobson during the trial had applied equally during this hearing, he pointed out.

"And I think when you compare what's happened here this week with what happened in *Barfield,* Your Honor will see that there is no comparison between the effectiveness of counsel."

*   *   *

Judge Braswell continued the court session into the following week and said he would try to have a ruling at 2:30 on Wednesday afternoon. Velma would be allowed to remain at the Robeson County Jail until then.

As he read his thirty-seven-page decision four days later, Braswell began telling about a football game between the Steelers and the Browns that he had watched on TV ten days earlier. The game went down to the last six seconds, the judge read, going on to describe the final play. "The Monday morning quarterbacks and the TV announcers were saying that the world champion Steelers blew it, meaning that they did not take advantage of their opportunities or perform as professionals. . . ."

Ronnie sat listening in disbelief. His mother's life was at stake, and the judge was talking about football.

"While football and a person's life are not to be equated in value," the judge went on, "the perfect game in sports or life is yet to be played. Success—and failure—always look different in hindsight."

Braswell agreed on every point with Britt, noting that Velma's new lawyers were guilty of some of the same failures of which they had accused Jacobson.

"There is no believable evidence to support the allegation that the defendant was denied effective assistance of counsel," Braswell ruled. "The defendant had a fair and impartial trial. None of her constitutional or other legal rights were denied or violated."

He denied all motions and set a new execution date: December 12, little more than two weeks away. But Velma's lawyers soon would get another stay and embark on new appeals.

CHAPTER 19

Ronnie fell into depression after his mother's hearing, and his pessimism about her chances of escaping her death sentence was reinforced two months later when he picked up the Sunday *Fayetteville Observer-Times* and saw a full-page story headlined "On Death Row" by Tim Pittman.

Velma told Pittman that she had been depressed about the outcome of the hearing, but she refused to give in to it.

"When I begin to feel that way, I get up and start reading or writing letters," she said. "I work with yarns. I keep myself busy. I refuse to be depressed. I think depression just invites defeat. I can't afford to give in to doubts and fears right now."

The story only fed Ronnie's doubts and fears, though, for in it an unnamed lawyer summed up the situation much as he suspected it to be: "You've got to remember, this is a state that has yet to prove it will enforce its own new death penalty. This state needs to kill somebody. Because of the number of people she has confessed to killing, Velma Barfield is a likely choice."

Oddly enough, such thoughts were far from Velma's mind on the day this story appeared, for just the evening before she had received an assignment that was fully occupying her time and energies.

In October, while Velma was waiting for her hearing to begin, a bright and positive new force had come to Women's Prison. Jennie Lancaster had become interested in prisons when she had taken a criminology course at Meredith College. An idealistic, self-styled "child of the sixties," she was searching for a career in which she could help people. During her senior year, she got an internship at a youth center and decided that here was a place where her hope-filled attitude could be put to the service of good. After her graduation in 1972, she got a job as program director at Umstead Youth Center, where she would be the only female employee for the next eight years and in the beginning the only female in the Department of Correction with a college degree. When she was offered the job of assistant superintendent for treatment and programs at Women's Prison, Lancaster leaped at it, although some warned her against it, for women's prisons were then considered to be the backwater of corrections, a career killer. That Women's Prison was looked down upon within the system was something that needed changing, Lancaster thought, and she was up to the challenge.

Contrary to accepted beliefs, Lancaster thought that correction officials had to become involved with inmates and their families if they hoped to make any genuine differences in their lives. She had made Velma's acquaintance and taken an interest in her case soon after taking her new job (she even had read the transcript of her trial). She realized that Velma was doing good within the prison and could do even more. On the day before the story about Velma appeared in the Fayetteville paper, Lancaster had come to her cell and asked a favor. A fifteen-year-old girl had just arrived, convicted as an adult of being present at a murder and sentenced to thirty years. She was scared, confused, distraught. She was too young to be in the general population, where other inmates might take advantage of her youth, and Lancaster had no choice but to place her in lockup for her own well-being. Lancaster told Velma that she was going to put the girl in the cell next to hers. Would she talk to her, help her through this difficult time?

Her name was Beth, and later Velma said that as soon as she saw her, she knew that nobody would have had to ask for her help. Even if Beth had been involved in a murder, Velma realized immediately that this was just a lost child, and her heart went out to her.

At first she could not get through to her, because Beth lay on her bunk, sobbing uncontrollably. As she told the story later, Velma began to pray for the means, the strength to help this child, and she was moved simply to call out to her and put her hand through the bars toward the adjoining cell and hold it there. The girl grasped her hand with a desperation Velma never had felt.

"Is it okay if I pray for you?" Velma asked, and the girl agreed.

Afterward, they began to talk, and they continued into the night, both at times in tears, as Beth poured out her heart until both collapsed, exhausted, into restless sleep. Velma knew that a bond had formed between them that could not be broken.

In the weeks to come, as they learned more about each other, Velma began to think of Beth almost as a daughter. And Beth made no secret of her feelings. In prison, Velma was known by her first name, Margie. Beth would be only the first to call her Mama Margie.

Velma urged Beth to begin studying for her high school equivalency test, and she was pleased that she did. More important, Velma worried about Beth's spiritual shortcomings. She introduced her to the Roanes, who took her into their hearts as well. Velma rejoiced when Beth started taking part in the Roanes' Sunday services.

Jennie Lancaster had been trying to get Beth into a training school, a more appropriate setting, but under state law that had to happen before she turned sixteen. The order for her transfer came only hours before her birthday on April 16, and for the next two years the only contact between Velma and Beth would be by mail.

The effect Velma had on Beth came as no surprise to Lancaster. Velma was not just a model prisoner; she had an encouraging influence on other inmates. She always referred to them as "ladies," and she treated all with equal respect. She was always open to any who sought her out, and although she was eager to share the joy and peace she claimed to have found in religion, she did not push her beliefs on anybody. One by one, inmates in Dorm C came to talk about their troubles, to ask advice, to get her to write letters for them, to seek her prayers or her guidance in their own religious quests.

During this time, Velma continued the course of self-discovery and healing on which her minister, Hugh Hoyle, had started her and, by the spring of 1981, they were on the subject of forgiveness. Velma was learning to forgive all whom she had perceived to have done her wrong in her life.

But she was still having trouble forgiving herself. To do that, she needed forgiveness from others. She and Hoyle had lengthy talks about it. And he urged her to seek forgiveness from those from whom she most wanted it: her family and the families of her victims.

She had never apologized to her family, never mentioned her crimes to them. And none of her family, not even Ronnie and Pam, had ever asked about them. The subject simply was too painful and awkward. They talked about anything and everything else, always carefully avoiding the one issue that most troubled them—the need to resolve Lillie's death. Velma recognized it even if she couldn't bring herself to talk about it.

By this time she had reached her own resolution with her mother. It had been a very real, face-to-face experience, as she later described it. Her mother had come to her in a dream so vivid that when she awakened she still felt her presence in the cell. Velma had begun crying, begging forgiveness. Soon a sense of peace and comfort came over her, a feeling not unlike the one she had gotten as a child when her mother had gone from bed to bed each night to check on all the children, to kiss their foreheads and tuck their covers, before she could find peace in sleep. Velma knew then that her mother had forgiven her. And she wanted the rest of her family to do the same.

Hoyle suggested that she write to her family, as well as to the families of the other victims, asking forgiveness. Two years earlier, Velma had written to Alice Storms offering apologies, but she had received no response, so she had no idea what reaction such letters might bring. She intended to go ahead until she mentioned the plan to Jimmie Little, but he quickly ended it. He wanted her making no admissions to anybody as long as she had a chance for a new trial or sentencing hearing.

Her need for absolution frustrated, Velma still wanted to set down her feelings so that at some point they could be known, and she and Hoyle came up with a compromise.

On May 27, 1981, she wrote two letters addressed to Hoyle, instructing him that, in the event of her death, he was to read one to her family, the other to the Edwards, Lee and Taylor families (she didn't mention the Barfield family).

"God has convinced me of how wrong my acts were, how I have wronged each of you, so now I come to you asking you to forgive me," she wrote. "I know He has forgiven me and my heart's desire is that you will forgive me. My prayer is that God will bless each one of you real good each day of your life."

She said the same in the letter to her own family, adding, "Please tell them that I have lifted them up before the throne of grace each day—and as I lifted them up, my prayer was if there was one among them unsaved that they would be saved. I love them dearly."

Hoyle promised that he would see that her wishes were carried out and put the letters in his files.

In the meantime, Ronnie was now working three jobs. He was employed full-time as a cost accountant by a manufacturing plant in Clio, South Carolina. On weekends, he helped a certified public accountant. And three nights a week he taught business classes for four hours at Robeson Tech.

Ronnie and Joanna had moved from the apartment off Snake Road where they had been living when Velma was arrested and tried. Pam and Kirby and their two daughters had taken that apartment. Ronnie, Joanna and Michael had moved to Laurinburg, where, after living in an apartment for six months, they had bought a three-bedroom, two-bath brick house in Country Club Estates. Joanna was working in the office at a construction company, and it took all the money both could make just to meet their bills.

Calm by nature, Ronnie prided himself on his ability to maintain control. But for several years he had felt on edge, tense, nervous, easily irritated. He seemed never to be able to relax, and he had trouble sleeping.

Worry about his mother, stress from striving and overwork were all part of the problem, Ronnie knew. But his marriage also played a role. It had become highly volatile, with lots of bickering, accusing, yelling, storming out. Clearly it was disintegrating.

Before the move to Laurinburg, Joanna had told Ronnie that she wanted a divorce, but she had later changed her mind. They always found the same reason for working things out and staying together. His name was Michael—he was now five—and neither thought that they could get along without him.

Buying the house had been one of their attempts to improve the marriage, but like all of their efforts it had turned out to be a temporary and inadequate fix. The strain was ever present, the anger and bitterness just under the surface waiting to erupt. Many times during their frequent arguments Ronnie was reminded that this was how it had been with his parents.

Ronnie's depressions usually vanished with time, but the one that set in after his mother's hearing continued and grew, compounding with his anxiety until the tension was more than he could bear. He went to a doctor seeking relief and was prescribed Valium, which seemed to work at first. It made him less tense and irritable. He could sleep better.

But after a couple of months he began having headaches so severe that they disabled him. He returned to the doctor, who gave him Tylenol with codeine. The pain tablets not only relieved the headaches, but combined with the Valium, Ronnie discovered, they allowed him to sleep even better.

As time went on, however, neither seemed to help as much as they had in the beginning, and he began taking more than had been prescribed. By the spring of 1981, he found that he was having to take more and more just to stay on an even keel.

He didn't tell his mother about this, nor did he let her know about any of his problems. He didn't want her worrying. She had enough on her mind.

By the fall of 1981, Ronnie had lost twenty pounds and he had taken on such a gaunt and haunted look that he didn't want his mother to see him. He felt bad all the time, and he frequently took several Valium and Tylenol with codeine at a time. He knew that he couldn't go on that way, that he was heading down the same path that had led his mother to disaster. Something had to change. He had to give up the drugs, but he knew, too, that they were simply a symptom of deeper problems.

His worry about his mother had grown with each setback in her appeals. And the problems in his marriage were worse. He frequently slept on the sofa, and he and Joanna barely talked. The conversations they had often degenerated into fights.

One night Ronnie became upset because Joanna kept finding fault with Michael. "You need to stop fussing at him, or he and I are going to leave," he told her.

"You're not taking him anywhere," she snapped.

When he tried to get Michael, she grabbed him first, and they found themselves in a tugging and screaming match that ended when Ronnie slammed his fist through the Sheetrock wall.

Not long after that, Joanna followed him into the bathroom, yelling during an argument. "Stop it!" he shouted, grabbing her by the shoulders. "Stop it now!" She tried to jerk away and fell backward into the fiberglass tub, striking with such force that her elbow knocked a hole in it. Sobered, Ronnie tried to help her up, saying, "I'm sorry, I didn't mean to do that," but she grabbed a handy canister, sprayed him in the face and stormed out.

Both were miserable, and they knew that they could not continue like that. Both could see that the strife and misery were affecting Michael, who was becoming fearful and withdrawn.

They began talking about separating, and Ronnie decided that he needed to get away for a while, to clear his system of drugs, to try to come up with some solutions. He called his aunt Arlene, who was still living in Charleston, and she invited him for a visit. He packed the car and was about to say good-bye when Michael started crying.

Soon all of them were crying, and Ronnie and Joanna began talking about working on their marriage again, trying to save it for Michael's sake. Ronnie called Arlene to say he wasn't coming. And as he unpacked the car he resolved that he would stop taking drugs completely. He took none that night and felt good about his willpower. But he didn't sleep well, and the next day he felt terrible. His head hurt, and he was nervous and scared, overcome with feelings unlike any he'd ever known.

A day later, he collapsed, unconscious. Joanna called an ambulance, and he was taken to the emergency room at the Laurinburg hospital, where he was revived.

He told the doctor about the drugs he had been taking and how he had stopped two days earlier. "What you did was very dangerous," the doctor told him, going on to say that the body adjusted to the level of drugs it was receiving and that stopping cold could create problems severe enough to kill. He could need help coming off the drugs, the doctor said, and suggested that he talk with his own doctor to create a plan.

Ronnie thought he had been through the worst of it. He went home to rest after being released from the emergency room. But he began feeling worse, and Joanna called a friend who was a nurse. She recommended that Ronnie admit himself to the mental health center at Southeastern Hospital in Lumberton, where a close watch could be kept on him while he underwent withdrawal.

Ronnie signed himself in later that day, was given vitamins and a shot that knocked him out for the night.

The irony of his situation overwhelmed him when he awoke the next morning. How many times had he been to this place to visit his mother? How many times had he condemned her weaknesses for putting her here? And now he was a patient himself. He couldn't believe how easily he had fallen into her patterns. The irony was only reinforced when he met later that day with Dr. Malcolm Kemp, who had treated his mother after she overdosed in 1972.

"Why shouldn't we be having this conversation?" Dr. Kemp asked. "Can you think of a reason why you shouldn't be here?"

Ronnie nodded. "I know what my mom's been through, and now I've ended up the same way," he said.

"That's the way I see it," the doctor agreed. "I'm glad you do, too."

Ronnie checked himself out of the hospital after three days. He was feeling much better, and he wanted to get back home and back to work. Joanna was upset that he didn't stay longer, but he was determined to quit drugs and do something to relieve the stress in his life.

He would beat the drugs with nothing more than vitamins, aspirin and determination, although it wasn't easy. "I could feel the drugs coming out of my system," he later recalled. "I could literally smell it."

Soon after leaving the hospital, he quit teaching, cut back on his part-time work, and left his job for a less stressful position as an accountant at a plant in St. Pauls. But other troubles were soon to come. Joanna lost her job and they had to sell their house and get a bill-consolidation loan. They moved into an apartment and started over again.

Velma learned nothing of any of this, however, because Ronnie didn't want her worrying about his problems.

All during this dark year, the appeals process kept grinding onward. The state Supreme Court upheld Judge Braswell's findings on July 9, and once again Velma faced another hearing and a new execution date. On July 23, she was taken to Whiteville, where she had nearly died from an overdose, to face Judge Braswell again. He set her execution for October 21, 1981.

That date was as meaningless as the others, for Little and Burr would now be going back to the U.S. Supreme Court. Little asked for another stay of execution on October 1, and it was granted eight days later.

The court took little time with this appeal, however, again declining to review her case. When Burr asked the court to reconsider, it declined again on December 7. Three days before Christmas, Velma was taken back to Elizabethtown to have yet another execution date set: March 22, 1982. That date was as meaningless as the others, for the appeals through the federal courts had not even begun.

To file an appeal in federal court, Velma's lawyers had to show violations of her constitutional rights during her trial and subsequent hearing. On March 12, 1982, Little and Burr took Velma's case to U.S. District Court Judge Franklin Dupree in Raleigh, claiming several such violations. Their motion came with more than 2,000 pages of court documents. Dupree, as expected, granted another stay until he could review all the material.

Two weeks later, Dupree asked Burr and Little to provide a more extensive list of what they claimed to be errors in the 1980 hearing before Judge Braswell. Clearly, here was a judge who was going to look carefully at all the issues, and the lawyers were heartened that Velma might now be on her way to a reprieve. They were surprised when Dupree issued a thirty-six-page opinion two months later, May 21, ruling against them on every count.

"The evidence against her was overwhelming," Dupree said. "She was convicted and sentenced in strict compliance with a constitutionally sound statutory scheme by twelve of her peers who unanimously concluded that, beyond a reasonable doubt, the death penalty should be imposed in this case."

Dupree said that Judge McKinnon had not committed any constitutional violations by allowing the jury to hear about Velma's previous crimes or by his instructions to the jury. Neither, Dupree ruled, did Velma receive ineffective counsel.

"The case which Mr. Jacobson was called upon to defend was an almost hopeless one from the beginning," he wrote.

Velma was not surprised by the ruling. She had become accustomed to judicial rejection. But now the rejections were growing more serious. The appeals process was winding down. Only two more basic steps were left, a plea to the Fourth U.S. Circuit Court of Appeals in Richmond, and a final plea to the U.S. Supreme Court, which had refused to consider Velma's case four times already.

The reality of Velma's situation was brought into sharper focus less than three weeks later when, on August 10, Virginia executed Frank J. Coppola, who had robbed and murdered a woman in Newport News in 1978. Coppola was only the fifth person to be executed in the country since the Supreme Court decision in 1976.

Like all but one of the others who had been executed, Coppola had dropped his appeals and asked to be allowed to die. But his attorneys still had fought to the end to save him, and death-penalty opponents, including many from North Carolina, had made last-minute appeals to Governor Charles Robb asking for clemency.

The following day many North Carolina newspapers carried stories saying that Governor Jim Hunt might soon be facing the same situation in Velma's case as had Robb in Coppola's. The stories quoted Hunt's press secretary, Gary Pearce, as saying that the governor supported the death penalty because he believed it to be a deterrent. He would not hesitate to allow it to be carried out if he thought the case warranted it, said Pearce—and that included executing a woman.

North Carolina's death row had been growing steadily in the five years since the new death penalty had been enacted. Twenty-three people now faced execution, but Velma was the only woman among them, and her case was farthest along. Still, many people could not believe that Hunt would want the distinction of allowing the first woman to be executed in the nation in more than twenty years. He, after all, was a progressive Democrat who obviously had higher ambitions.

Shortly after Judge Dupree's ruling, Velma received another setback that brought her far more sorrow. Hugh Hoyle arrived for their weekly session subdued, not his cheerful and effusive self. Velma knew immediately that something was wrong. He was reluctant to reveal what it was, but she had to know. He had accepted the pastorate of a much larger church in Wichita, Kansas. He would be leaving soon. Velma began to cry.

In the three years that Hoyle had been ministering to her, Velma had become closer to him than to anybody outside her family. He seemed like family. When he and his wife, Lois, adopted a son, Benjamin, in March, they got permission to bring him to see her, and she took the infant into her arms and cooed over him as if he were a grandchild.

Velma didn't know what she would do without Hoyle to guide her spiritual growth, to inspire and cheer her when she was low, and she told him so. They would still write regularly, he assured her, still talk by telephone. They just wouldn't get to see each other so often, although he would come whenever he returned to North Carolina to visit family.

Velma wanted only one promise from Hoyle. More than a year earlier, she had started talking with him about her funeral. Already she had picked hymns to be sung, scriptures to be read. Now she asked Hoyle to promise that he would return to conduct her service. Knowing that he would be there would mean everything to her, she said. If it was possible, he promised, he would be there.

Phil Carter had replaced John Frazier as chaplain at Women's Prison. He had a special empathy for the inmates because he once had been one himself, having served a brief term in a youth center for a drunken misdeed as a teenager. He had redeemed himself by graduating from the University of North Carolina and working with deprived children before attending seminary and entering the ministry. A former member of a rock-and-roll band, Carter was an anomaly: a liberal Southern Baptist.

Carter had been serving an internship at Women's Prison when Velma arrived, and he met her soon afterward. He rarely saw her during her first year there, but after he was named chaplain at age twenty-seven in December 1979, he began going by to see her regularly. He enjoyed talking with her. They rarely discussed religion, talking instead about whatever was on Velma's mind, and they soon developed a closeness. After Hoyle left, Velma decided that Carter would be her spiritual guide as well as friend and confidant.

Ronnie's marriage had lapsed back into anger and animosity by the fall of 1982, and the strain continued to grow. Joanna was like his mother in some ways, Ronnie would later say. Once she started, she would not let up. But unlike his father, who had never allowed himself to be provoked into violence, Ronnie had gone past that point.

On two occasions he had lost control and hit Joanna, once leaving her with a swollen eye, another time with a cut lip. Both times he had been ashamed and frightened of the fury within him and his inability to restrain it.

After she was struck the second time, Joanna rented a small apartment in another town and took Michael when she left. Although she and Ronnie talked about getting back together afterward, it was clear that their marriage was a shambles that couldn't be made whole again, that trying to hold it together for the sake of their son was only doing him harm.

At the end of 1982, Ronnie quit his job and gave up his apartment. He could not afford to store his belongings, and he tossed his golfing trophies and college textbooks into a dumpster, along with other items that had meant a lot to him. He was going to Charleston to stay for a while with his aunt Arlene and to try to start a new life, taking only some clothing and a small stereo.

Joanna kept their only car, and he had no means even to get to his sister's apartment, where he was to meet his aunt. He had to call Joanna to ask for a ride, and the trip was a sad and silent one.

Michael didn't understand what was happening, and when they got to this place where Ronnie and Joanna had lived when he was born, it was almost more than Ronnie could stand. Michael was six now, in the first grade, and Ronnie led him to the front stoop and sat with him in his lap to talk.

"I'm not going to be able to see you as much anymore," he said. "I've got to go away. It may be for a long time. I want you to help look after your mama and promise me you'll be a good boy."

"I don't want to be away from you, Daddy," Michael said, tears coming to his eyes.

"I don't want to be away from you either," Ronnie said, holding back his own tears. "It's just something that has to be. Someday maybe you'll understand."

Then he kissed his son on the forehead, hugged him tightly and carried him back to the car.

"I love you," he told him, "and I'll call and see how you're doing."

Joanna left hurriedly, Michael's face pressed to the car window looking back, as Ronnie stood waving in the driveway, tears streaming. When the car disappeared from sight, Ronnie sank slowly to the pavement and sat sobbing quietly.

Ronnie knew that he probably couldn't keep his mother from finding out about his separation, but he tried. In March 1983, she fell ill and had to be taken to the prison hospital, where she remained for eight days being treated for angina, the same condition that had plagued her father in his final years. Ronnie drove from Charleston to see her. He had not visited for many months, and had regained most of his lost weight by drinking high-calorie, vitamin-enriched supplements. He tried to put on a cheerful front.

"Where are Joanna and Michael?" Velma asked after he hugged her.

"Oh, they couldn't come today."

"Ronnie, something's wrong, isn't it?" she said, catching him off guard.

"No, why?" he insisted.

"I can tell just by looking at you. What's wrong?"

Suddenly, Ronnie felt a surge of emotion that he couldn't suppress. He burst into tears. "Joanna and I have separated," he said. "I didn't want you to know. I didn't want to hurt you."

She went to him and held him as she had when he was a boy. For more than an hour she listened and consoled while he poured out his pain and fear—he was scared that Joanna was going to try to keep him from seeing Michael, and that he wouldn't be able to bring him to see her.

"It's times like this," she told him, "when we have to rely on faith to get us through."

Ronnie left feeling better than he had in a long time.

When Velma talked with Jimmie Little the following week, she couldn't wait to tell him what had happened.

"Ronnie let me be his mother again last Saturday," she said.

A month earlier, Little and Burr had filed their appeal with the Fourth Circuit Court in Richmond, listing eight issues. They went to Richmond to argue their case on March 8.

Burr was no longer with the Southern Prisoners Defense Committee. He now had two small children, and the work demanded too much time and travel. Late in 1982, he had taken a job in the public defender's office in Palm Beach, Florida, where a staunch conservative Republican named Richard Jorandby had assembled what many people considered to be the best team of anti-death-penalty lawyers in the nation. But before taking the job, Burr had insisted that he be allowed to remain on Velma's case, serving without pay and at his own expense.

Little, too, had changed jobs, but unlike Burr he was now closer to Velma, not farther away. At the beginning of the year, he had become chief counsel of the Public Staff of the State Utilities Commission and had moved to an apartment in Raleigh. He was now an employee of the state that was doing its best to kill Velma, but, like Burr, he had told his new bosses that he was committed to her case and would continue to work on it in his free time, also without pay, as he had done all along.

Summer came and passed without a decision from the Fourth Circuit Court.

On Tuesday, October 4, guards came to bring Velma to the administration building without telling her why. Richard Burr had called, she discovered when she got there. She knew then that the appeals court had finally reached its decision. The procedure had become routine, and the outcome had become so common that she dared not allow herself to be optimistic.

As usual, she had no right to be. The court had rejected all of the issues her attorneys had raised.

Velma was in a low mood when she called Pam and Ronnie to tell them the unhappy news. She explained that Burr would be asking the circuit court to reconsider. After that, he would take the case back to the U.S. Supreme Court, the final step in the appellate process. The timetable for all of this was uncertain—perhaps five or six months at most.

Later, she wrote to give Hugh Hoyle the news. "During these difficult days, I'm just asking God for His mercy. God is using every pain and heartache and tear to bring me so very close to His precious side. He is using this to take me inwardly apart, fiber by fiber, giving me 'a broken and contrite heart,' and teaching me to walk softly before the Lord and more tenderly with others."

As 1984 began, a year in which executions would become common across the country, a remarkable thing happened. For three years the state's legal establishment and news media had been predicting that Velma would be the first to die under North Carolina's new death penalty, but suddenly somebody moved ahead of her.

James Hutchins, a fifty-four-year-old alcoholic with little education, had been largely unemployed for five years after getting hurt on his job as a tree trimmer. On May 31, 1979, he had gotten into an argument with his eighteen-year-old daughter on her graduation day. He hit her and she fought back. When he began choking her, his wife rushed to her daughter's aid, and she broke free and fled to a neighbor's house, where she called the sheriff's department.

Deputy Roy Huskey, who lived nearby and was the brother of the county sheriff, arrived and attempted to talk to Hutchins, but Hutchins opened fire with a high-powered rifle, hitting Huskey twice, leaving him dead in the yard. Moments later, Sgt. Owen Messersmith arrived to assist Huskey. He was fatally shot through the chest as he got out of his patrol car.

Hutchins fled in his Ford Galaxie, and a state highway patrolman, Robert Peterson, who was thirty-seven, spotted him and took up the chase. Peterson radioed that Hutchins had stopped and was fleeing toward the woods. Then his radio fell silent.

The next law enforcement officer to reach the scene where Hutchins had abandoned his car was another state trooper, Dan Good, a close friend of Peterson. He found his friend still seated in his patrol car, part of his head blown away, a chunk of his skull lying in the road.

Trapped in the nearby woods, Hutchins held more than 200 law enforcement officers at bay through the night. He surrendered to Dan Good when a pack of attack dogs flushed him the next morning.

When Hutchins was sentenced to death in September 1979, the presiding judge called him the most dangerous man he'd ever seen.

Many people thought that the reason Hutchins was pushed ahead of Velma was because state officials did not want to return to executions by beginning with a woman. North Carolina had executed only two women in this century, both in the forties, neither of them white.

Whatever the case, the state appeared to be in a special hurry to be rid of Hutchins and, in January 1984, his lawyers twice snatched him back from imminent death, once by six hours, again the same day by only an hour.

After all of Hutchins' appeals were finally exhausted two months later, Governor Jim Hunt denied clemency, saying it was an extraordinary power to be used only under exceptional circumstances, such as the discovery of new evidence casting doubt on guilt.

Velma had been closely following Hutchins' case, praying daily for him, his family and lawyers. On the night of March 15, Jimmie Little called the prison to tell her that this time nothing was likely to stop the execution. Sam Roane had already realized that, and he was there with Velma, as was Phil Carter.

"I asked God to be with those who made the decisions on James Hutchins and to forgive them," Velma told Little.

In 1983, the North Carolina legislature had approved execution by lethal injection, which was assumed to be a more humane means of killing, and Hutchins had chosen it.

At 1:50 on the morning of March 16, Hutchins was rolled into the death chamber covered with a pale green sheet. At 2:17, he was declared dead. Fifteen witnesses, many of them law enforcement officers from Rutherford County, watched him die. One of the witnesses, a friend of the victims, said beforehand that Hutchins' death would be too easy. "I think he should suffer," said the sheriff's deputy. "Let him do a little struggling."

Hutchins became the fifteenth person to be executed in the nation since the Supreme Court had reinstated capital punishment in 1976, the third to die from lethal injection.

North Carolina was back in the killing business, after an absence of nearly twenty-three years, and Hutchins' execution proved to be relatively painless for the state, drawing little protest and garnering almost no attention in the national news. But that would not be the case with the next person the state intended to kill. Velma Barfield would soon be the center of an unprecedented, worldwide protest against her execution and the death penalty.

PART V

On Sinking Sand

Twenty-two people would be executed across the nation in 1984, far more than in all of the seven and a half previous years since the death penalty had been revived. Many killers' appeals were running out, and the mood of the Supreme Court had hardened in favor of death. Velma's attorneys, like other lawyers fighting to save death-row clients, had little real reason to believe that the court might consider the issues they'd raised.

Jimmie Little had thought all along that Velma's case eventually would come down to clemency. To have any hope, Little knew that he had to bring pressure on the governor. He had to turn to television, newspapers, magazines to stir public opinion on Velma's behalf. He had to make her a sympathetic figure, had to let people know the kind of person she was before drugs took over her life, had to let them see what she was like now, redeemed and remorseful, serving a useful purpose in prison.

If enough people came to think that Velma was worth saving and made their feelings known, perhaps the governor would spare her. Unfortunately for Velma, the timing was bad.

Just five weeks before the state killed James Hutchins, Governor Jim Hunt had officially filed for the U.S. Senate seat held by Jesse Helms.

Hunt, a pious, clean-living Presbyterian, was completing his second term as governor, the state's only two-term governor in this century. He was a rising star of the Democratic Party, frequently mentioned as a future presidential candidate. An admirer of Franklin D. Roosevelt and John F. Kennedy, he was considered liberal by North Carolina standards. Actually he was a moderate.

Helms, a staunch Baptist who made his fundamentalist, Old Testament religion a strong part of his politics, was finishing his second term in the Senate. He had become a powerful figure in Washington, credited with reviving Ronald Reagan's national political career, thus a favorite at the White House. A strong supporter of right-wing causes—and of fascist dictators around the world—Helms had built a national following of ultraconservatives who funneled vast amounts of campaign money his way.

The campaign upon which Hunt and Helms were embarking as spring arrived in 1984 would become the most expensive, and most widely watched, Senate race in the country's history—also one of the nastiest.

Jimmie Little realized that he would have to seek clemency for Velma during the heat of the Helms-Hunt campaign, and that could only diminish her prospects. Already Helms was trying to paint Hunt as "wishy-washy," a "weak-willed liberal," and any action that made Hunt appear to be soft on criminals, particularly multiple murderers, would be put to good use by the Helms camp. A poll made at the time of the Hutchins execution showed that two-thirds of North Carolinians approved the death penalty, and other polls put the figure at seventy percent and higher.

Hunt had not always been in that number. "As a college student I was opposed to capital punishment," he said, explaining his position. "But in later years, after I read a lot of theology, I came to realize that human beings have an awesome responsibility to maximize love and to minimize hurt, and especially death. I believe that capital punishment is a deterrent in most cases. If the law is enforced fairly and people are made aware of that, I believe it will result in fewer murders and thus more lives will be saved."

Clearly, Hunt had lived up to his convictions in Hutchins' case, and that promised little reason for hope in Velma's.

Still, it was possible that the governor's decision on Hutchins had freed him to show mercy to Velma. Hunt could point to Hutchins to demonstrate that he was willing to take strong stands against crime. If he could be convinced that Velma's condition at the time of her crimes had not truly been made known at her trial and that she was now a different person, perhaps he would want to prove that he also could be humane and forgiving when it was warranted.

In January, Little had begun organizing a support committee to rally people to Velma's cause and to raise money for the clemency effort. Its members included opponents of capital punishment, ministers, and friends of Velma. Among them were Wade Holder, the teacher and coach who once had lived with Velma's parents, and John Lotz, the assistant athletic director at the University of North Carolina, who taught Bible studies in prisons and was the brother-in-law of Billy and Ruth Graham's daughter, Anne Lotz.

Another member of the committee was Phyllis Tyler, a writer, who was on the board of the American Civil Liberties Union in Wake County. She had been visiting Velma in prison for four years. She kicked off the campaign for clemency in February with a column on the Sunday editorial pages of the *News & Observer*.

She had been anxious about visiting Velma in the beginning, she wrote. "I didn't think I would like her or that I could relate to her. Velma Barfield was the surprise of my life. She is warm and kind; she is funny, real and very human. . . . I consider her one of my best friends."

She went on to tell about Velma's effect on other inmates, then related an incident that had happened when she had gone to see Velma after one of her appeals had been rejected and she was low.

"Come on home with me, Velma," she'd told her as she was leaving, "Climb into my pocket, and we'll beat it out of here."

"She laughed," Tyler wrote, "then she became serious. 'If I thought I could go out into the free world,' she said, 'back to the life I used to lead, I'd say, Shut them gates! I've never been so useful as I am right here in prison. People need me here. This is where I belong—and I wouldn't choose to be anywhere else in the world.'

"That's why I believe the world needs Velma. There aren't too many people like her and almost nobody like her in prison.

"She's on the side of the angels and she is strategically placed. To execute her to fulfill a point of law is not just a personal tragedy, it is a terrible waste."

In March, after Hutchins' execution, Little stepped down as chief counsel of the Public Staff of the State Utilities Commission to give more time to saving Velma. He remained a staff attorney.

Another state employee had joined Little in his fight. She was Mary Teresa Floyd, who had worked as a counselor to long-term inmates at Women's Prison for seven years. Although she didn't counsel Velma, she talked with her often and Velma valued her advice. "She is the one who taught me trust," Velma said. "She taught me to care, to reach out." A nun of the Good Shepherd Order, Sister Teresa was a native of Robeson County who had been affected by its tradition of violence. Her father had been murdered by a tenant on his farm in 1935, shortly before her birth.

Sister Teresa became the support committee's most energetic member, organizing fund-raising and letter-writing campaigns and preparing brochures to be mailed nationwide.

Easter came late in 1984, on April 22, and Jimmie Little put it to use for Velma. He called her family urging as many as possible to visit on that Saturday because he needed to talk with them. He also had another purpose. He and the support committee were planning to make a videotape to present to the governor during the clemency plea, and he wanted to do it on this weekend so it would show Velma with her family, especially her grandchildren.

Velma's brother John was driving from Hartsville, South Carolina, stopping in Red Springs to pick up his older brother, Olive, and in Fayetteville for their long-time friend Wade Holder. Pam and Kirby would be there with their daughters. Ronnie was coming from Charleston with Faye and her two daughters, but he was not able to bring Michael.

Little and volunteers from the support committee set up a video camera in a prison conference room to record an interview with Velma before her family arrived. Several times she fought back tears while answering their questions. Asked how she felt after her mother's death, she started crying and paused to lift her glasses and dab at her eyes before answering.

"I was so drugged at the time I don't even remember part of the funeral. There have been times when it's been almost unbearable to think about, but it's there. If I could undo any of it I would. I would gladly take it on myself. Nobody knows. When I look at my family and think about what I've done to them—and that's only the beginning of what I've really done. . . ."

She couldn't go on and asked that the tape be stopped until she could recover.

Had she sought her family's forgiveness, she was asked, when she was able to resume.

"I feel they just haven't wanted to talk about it," she said. "They have never talked with me about it. I know it would be painful. I believe it would be good for all of us."

Asked what she would say if she could speak directly to the governor, Velma replied, "I would ask Governor Hunt to please spare my life, to leave me here with my children and grandchildren. . . ." Once again she paused, fighting tears. "They're my life," she said, her voice choking.

Velma's family had arrived outside, and as she waited for them, her mood brightened. She chatted easily with the guards and volunteers.

Laughing, Velma said that on a recent visit her granddaughter Beverly, now eight, had asked, "Ma-ma, why do you wear the same dress all the time?"

"I told her, 'I guess you could say because I love brown,' " Velma said to laughter.

Suddenly, the door opened and Beverly burst into the room, racing for her grandmother.

"My baby!" Velma cried, her face aglow.

Sarah, now four, was close behind, both dressed in new yellow Easter dresses trimmed in white lace. Velma gathered them into her arms as Pam and Ronnie entered and hugged their mother.

"The Easter bunny is coming," Beverly was excitedly telling her grandmother. "We've got to go to sleep so he can come."

"Can Ma-ma show you what he left here at her house?" Velma asked, reaching for a cardboard box beside her. From it she took big-eyed, fluffy-tailed Easter bunnies she'd made, a pink-faced one for Beverly, lavender for Sarah.

"Oh," said Beverly, hugging the bunny. "Can I kiss him?"

"Tell Ma-ma what you've been doing," Velma said.

"Playing," said Beverly.

"Getting in trouble mostly," Pam put in.

Velma was running her fingers through Sarah's hair.

"You are really getting to be big babies," she said wistfully.

Velma's visit with her family lasted several hours—all of them trying to keep it as light and happy as possible, denying the reality that lay so heavily over them—and when her family left, they hurried to wait outside the prison fence to watch as Velma was returned to the building called Single Cell, where she had been moved after the aging Dorm C had been closed the previous year. She emerged holding a pale orange orchid corsage that Faye had brought, accompanied by a guard. She was fifty-one now, and she had gained more than forty pounds in prison, a short, plump, sweet-faced woman. Faye clung to the fence looking sadly at her sister. There had been something she had wanted to tell her on this visit but she couldn't bring herself to do it. "Bye, Velma," she called in a small voice.

"I love y'all," Velma called back with a forlorn smile as she walked slowly past pink azaleas.

"We love you, too," several responded, as the children stood waving.

"Oh, Lord, oh, Lord," Faye said and burst into tears, Ronnie taking her into his arms. Pam began to cry, too, burying her head in Kirby's chest.

Velma had to pause to pass through a gate, and she looked back over her shoulder and gave a little wave. As she walked past a dormitory, voices began coming from the windows.

"Miss Margie, Miss Margie . . . We're praying for you, Miss Margie."

The tough part for Jimmie Little came now. While others watched the children, he took the adults to a nearby house on the prison grounds for a talk about reality.

He thought that perhaps some of the family had grown so accustomed to the seemingly interminable appeals that they believed they could go on forever. He explained the situation and said he expected the Supreme Court to reject the appeal filed two weeks earlier. That could come within weeks. And it could be the end. Reality was that Velma could be dead at the hands of the state before summer's end.

The only recourse would be clemency. He would arrange for all who wanted to meet with the governor to do so in the final two weeks.

"So this is serious now?"

"Yes, it's very serious."

He wanted them to be thinking about what they would say to Governor Hunt when the time came.

"What we have to do is show the governor that not only has Velma turned her life around, but that the compassion he could show her would not be misplaced. We have to convince him that if she spends the rest of her life in prison he could expect her to have a positive influence. And lastly, we have to convince him that the Velma her friends and family love today is the Velma they knew and loved before all of this happened."

There was one more thing that they needed to be thinking about, Little said. If clemency failed, family members could witness the execution.

"I know Velma would like some of you to be near her if this happens," he said, and Faye was crying as he spoke. "But you all ought to talk about this. I want to deal with it only when it's necessary."

Little had invited a reporter to be present this day. Her name was Elin Schoen. She wrote for the *Village Voice*, a weekly paper in New York. Schoen remained in Raleigh over the holiday and later spent several hours interviewing Velma in Little's presence.

The Hutchins execution five weeks earlier was still much on Velma's mind, and she talked at length about it. "It was just such a sad occasion," she said.

She was thinking mostly of Pam at the time, she said. Pam was having an extremely hard time accepting the possibility of her death, and she knew that Pam had to be identifying Hutchins with her.

Velma had been as saddened by the bitterness the Hutchins execution had stirred as by the execution itself. So many people had said so many bad things, she said, and some even cheered when it happened. "I really did pray for those people," she said. "And I prayed for his family. I don't know if you can take the hurt and sting of death away. I think death is bad any way you look at it, but when someone is sitting there waiting, you know the very hour that it's scheduled by man. . . ."

Little allowed Schoen to probe deeply into Velma's life and crimes, and Velma later would say that she found the experience, coupled with the emotional strain of seeing her family for the holiday, especially wrenching. Several times she broke down during the interview.

Perhaps the most difficult burden of her life had been the guilt that she had carried for so long, Velma told Schoen.

"I think that that's the most horrible type life to live, is loaded with guilt twenty-four hours a day. To me the number one pain in getting a life straightened out is admitting guilt and ridding yourself of it."

Velma talked about her unhappy childhood, but she said that she could not hold that experience responsible for her present situation.

"We sometimes have a tendency to lean on what happened, life as a child. It does have a lot to do with our adult lives, but I think we all become responsible for our own lives, and we're accountable for it. I don't blame my childhood. I realize that it fed into me a lot of hatred and bitterness. And it's not easy to break out."

When she had spoken with Faye earlier, Schoen told Velma, Faye said that when she was fifteen and her mother was away visiting Arlene that her father had made a pass at her, and she had locked herself in her bedroom and gone the next day to stay with Velma until her mother returned.

"Did anything like that ever happen to you?" she asked.

"Yes."

"Do you want to talk about it? It would really be important. This happens to millions of women, girls, all over the country. It's a horrible thing, and I think if you could tell me about it it would help me to understand you."

"I think I was maybe thirteen when he came to where I was in the bedroom and I knew what he was after and he was forceful and I was frightened, but this I had never said to you all"—she turned to Jimmie Little—"but this happened a few times when we were swimming."

"Like what, for instance?" asked Schoen.

"Feeling, you know. And I was so frightened of him, so I couldn't tell anybody. I had nobody to say that to. My aunt who lived next door would never have believed that."

She hadn't told anybody about it until she told her lawyers before her hearing for a new trial three and a half years earlier, she said.

"And that was the first time you told anybody in your life?"

"My minister, I had told him, but I had never told anybody else."

"Did he actually rape you in the bed?" Schoen asked, turning back to the incident.

"Yes, he did. My minister used to ask me if I had ever thought of telling my mother, but I never did. I just couldn't make myself do that, and I don't think she would have believed me either, she just wouldn't have believed."

"Did your mother know what had happened to Faye?"

"Faye told her."

"But you never told her what happened to you?"

"I never told her."

"Did you feel angry at your mother?"

"Yes I did feel angry at her. I couldn't understand why she could not protect us. As a child, I could not understand that. After I got grown, I began to see and especially since I have been here and just took my life apart, I know that she was just as afraid of him and more so maybe than we were. But I do feel bitter toward her."

Schoen asked only one later question about sexual abuse: Had there been more than the one incident? No, Velma said, but she never mentioned that she also had told a psychiatrist, Selwyn Rose, prior to her 1980 hearing, but that she had told him a different version, that a noise had frightened her father away before he had done anything to her.

Later, what Velma had told Schoen about her father would send angry reverberations through her family.

Velma had not asked Ronnie about Michael during the Easter visit. She knew it was a sore subject. Ronnie's fear that Joanna might prevent him from seeing Michael had come true, and Velma had not seen her only grandson for nearly a year and a half. His absence tore at her, but not nearly as much as it troubled Ronnie.

After his arrival in Charleston in January of 1983, Ronnie stayed with Arlene for three weeks, then moved in with Faye, her husband, Clifton," who was in the Navy, and Faye's two daughters. He soon found a job at an interior decorating company, but it was a while before he had enough money coming in to send any to Joanna. Their every attempt at communication had ended in bitter arguments about money and Michael. After Ronnie started sending money for Michael's support, he later claimed, Joanna still wouldn't allow him to see his son. He stopped the payments hoping to force Joanna's hand, but that only resulted in more bitterness and acrimony.

In January, Ronnie filed for divorce on grounds of a year's separation. In his complaint he claimed that he had been prevented from seeing his son for a year and sought a regular schedule of visitation. Ronnie's lawyer advised him to resume sending support payments, even though none had formally been agreed upon, and Ronnie did. Joanna denied in her answer to the complaint in February that she had kept Ronnie from seeing Michael, and when next they talked by telephone, her attitude seemed to have softened.

Ronnie wanted to take Michael to see his mother, and in March Joanna okayed a visit. On a Friday afternoon, Ronnie drove to the cottage where Joanna lived, arriving at the appointed time. Nobody was home. He waited, growing more upset as time passed. After more than a hour, Joanna appeared in the Pinto station wagon that once had been his. A friend was with her. Michael was in the backseat.

Ronnie walked over to the car smiling at his son. As he remembered the incident later, Joanna asked, "What are you doing here?"

"What do you mean?" Ronnie replied. "I came to get Michael. I told you I wanted to take him to see my mom tomorrow."

"I've changed my mind."

"You can't do that. That's not fair. I told my mom I'd bring him."

"I'm the one who decides what Michael does now. You don't have any say in it."

"I'm taking him with me," Ronnie said angrily, reaching for the car door, and Joanna's friend started to get out.

"Look," Ronnie told him, "this is between me and Joanna. I don't want any problem with you. I didn't come here for trouble. I just came for my son."

"You're not taking him anywhere," Joanna said.

Ronnie was so angry that he was afraid of what he might do. He didn't want to make things worse for himself or for Michael. He left and went to a friend's house in Laurinburg where he brooded until after midnight. Despite his friend's attempt to get him to stay the night, Ronnie declined, saying he wanted to drive on to Raleigh. Instead, he returned to Joanna's house, arriving about two.

He stepped onto the small porch and knocked. The door had no window. He knocked louder. No response. He continued beating on the door until he heard somebody on the other side.

"Joanna, it's Ronnie, open the door."

Still no response.

"I've thought about this," Ronnie called, "and I'm really upset. You need to just open the door and let me take Michael and be done with it."

"I want you to leave right now," Joanna said. "If you don't leave, I'm calling the police."

Enraged, Ronnie stepped back and kicked the door with all his strength. The door flew inward in a great shattering of glass, one hinge breaking free from the frame. A mirror had been mounted on the other side of the door and it had broken. Joanna stood in her nightgown screaming, blood running from a cut on her leg where a piece of the mirror had hit her. Ronnie caught a glimpse of Michael crying. But he did not see Joanna's friend. He only saw a baseball bat suddenly coming toward his head.

He ducked, and the bat hit the door frame with a resounding whack. "Goddamn it, you're going to jail," he could hear Joanna shouting. "You broke into my house."

The next blow caught Ronnie across the shoulder, knocking him backward. The man came onto the porch, still swinging.

"You son of a bitch, you're not hitting me with that bat again," Ronnie yelled, lunging for it. Both toppled from the porch, cursing and gasping for breath. At one point Ronnie had the bat, then the other man had it, swinging wildly, hitting Ronnie on the back and legs.

"Don't swing that damn bat at me anymore," Ronnie yelled. "I'm leaving, I'm leaving."

With his fury spent, he was ashamed and frightened that he had again reacted with violence. He realized that if he didn't learn to control himself he could end up in jail—or worse. He drove to the police station and reported what had happened. The officer was sympathetic. He said he would drive out to Joanna's and try to smooth things over. He got Ronnie's address and told him to go home and wait to see if charges developed. He also strongly advised him not to try to get Michael again without a court order.

Ronnie did not get such an order until the divorce proceedings on May 14. He was ordered to pay fifty dollars a week in child support and was allowed to have Michael for one weekend each month, one week at Christmas, and two weeks each summer beginning in 1985. His first visitation would not be until Saturday, June 2, when he could see Michael for six hours at the home of his mother-in-law. On the following day, he could take him for three hours. It would not be until the second monthly visitation in July that Ronnie could take Michael to Raleigh to see his grandmother—and that, Ronnie knew, might be the last time that either would get to see the other.

That possibility became all the more real only a week after Ronnie's divorce when the U.S. Supreme Court, in a seven-to-two vote, refused to hear Velma's appeal. The decision was expected, and Velma tried to take it in stride.

"Now all that's left to do is go to the governor for clemency," she wrote to a friend. "I know my Lord is still in control. I won't question this. My daughter and youngest sister are really finding it difficult to cope with what my future holds."

What she didn't know was what a difficult time Ronnie was having. She thought that he was stronger, better prepared than Pam. But after Velma called to give him the news, Ronnie dealt with it by doing exactly what he had done almost every night for more than a year. He went out and got drunk.

His drinking was as bad as his father's ever had been, and he had no desire to control it. He looked forward to leaving work every day and heading for the bars. He sometimes drank until two in the morning, slept a few hours and always made it to work on time, usually with a hangover.

He would stop drinking a day or two before he was to see his mother, however, and brace himself to appear strong for her sake, and for Pam's. He didn't want his mother to find out that he was drinking, didn't want her to know that, deep down, he felt weak, hopeless and guilt-ridden.

"Does This Woman Deserve to Die?" read the big, bold headline on page one of the *Village Voice* in its June 5 edition. "A Grandmother on Death Row."

Elin Schoen's story, along with a photo of a benevolent, slightly smiling Velma, took up two-thirds of the front page and continued over nine pages inside. It was the longest and most thorough story about Velma's life and troubles yet written, the first to appear outside of North Carolina, and the first to reveal Velma's claim that she had been raped by her father. Schoen also wrote about the political race between Governor Hunt and Jesse Helms and its potential effect on clemency.

Appearing with the story was an informational box offering instructions for readers who wanted to write to Hunt to urge clemency.

The effect of the story was immediate—and stunning to Jimmie Little. All three TV networks wanted interviews. Reporters from major newspapers and national magazines called, as did reporters from other countries. Letters pleading for Velma to be spared began arriving at the support committee's post office box. They soon would number in the hundreds, then the thousands. Other letters and calls went to the governor's office.

Until this point Little had been laboring to get reporters from regional TV stations and newspapers to interview Velma to get her story known. Suddenly, he was deluged with so many requests that coordinating them became a problem. Would CBS get the first interview, or NBC?

After the Supreme Court had again refused to hear Velma's case, the state asked Judge Franklin Dupree to set aside the stay of execution under which Velma had been living since March 1982. On Friday, June 8, Dupree issued a one-paragraph ruling that the stay had been automatically dissolved by the Supreme Court's refusal to hear Velma's case on May 21. The state wasted no time in scheduling a hearing for a new execution date. It would be Wednesday, June 13, in Elizabethtown.

On the morning of the hearing, Velma was seen on both *The Today Show* on NBC and the *CBS Morning News,* talking about her addiction to prescription drugs and her remorse about the murders. Pam, too, was interviewed on CBS. "She's a warm person whose family loves her dearly," she said of her mother. "I'll support her to the very end."

Not surprisingly, Joe Freeman Britt had a different opinion. "Velma Barfield is a sweet little old lady in appearance, and underneath she is a cold-blooded merciless killer," he said. "She is dangerous to society and don't let anybody kid you. She wears this nice little grandmother cloak and her religiosity as a kind of protection."

Velma had a doctor's certificate allowing her to miss the hearing because of her angina, but about a hundred people were present, including Ronnie, Pam, Faye, and many from the families of Velma's victims. Under North Carolina law, the execution date could be set for as early as sixty days but no more than ninety. Jimmie Little asked Judge Robert L. Farmer to grant the full ninety days to give him and Dick Burr time to file for a reconsideration by the Supreme Court as well as to work on Velma's clemency appeal.

"This matter has lingered as long as it took Mrs. Barfield to kill her victims—about six years," Joe Freeman Britt responded, asking for sixty days. "Enough is enough."

The judge compromised, but in Velma's favor, setting the execution for August 31, seventy-nine days away.

After the hearing, reporters cornered Pam in a hallway. She had spoken to reporters before, usually by telephone, or in one-on-one interviews, but here she was surrounded by cameras; microphones were thrust in her face; questions were coming from all directions; and it rattled her. Little waded through the crowd to her rescue, leading her and the rest of the family into a private room. Later, they emerged as a group, and Little told reporters they would speak with them outside. Pam and Faye fought back tears as they tried to answer questions, both trembling.

When a reporter asked Faye if she'd ever suspected something was wrong with Velma, she didn't want to answer. "I saw changes," she said, and hesitated. "But I love her. She's my sister and she raised me. I'll love her forever."

The new execution date, presumably Velma's last, brought her even more attention, not only nationally but internationally. Requests for interviews continued to pour in. Governor Hunt was regularly being asked about Velma at press conferences and campaign stops, and he refused to answer, saying that it was a matter that was still before the courts.

Hunt's race against Helms was reported to be a draw, and his aides and handlers were clearly irritated by the distraction Velma's case was causing, the unfavorable attention it was bringing, and the pressure it was putting on Hunt. And, five days after Velma's execution date was set, the state moved to curtail the attention she was getting.

CHAPTER 21

On Monday evening, June 18, five days after the new execution date was set, Jennie Lancaster came to Velma's cell with bad news. Lancaster, who had become superintendent of the prison in 1982, was clearly unhappy about what she had to do. A call had come from the Department of Correction, she told Velma. She was to be transferred immediately to death watch at Central Prison. She had thirty minutes to prepare herself.

Velma was stunned. This was unexpected and unprecedented. Normally, a person facing execution was not put on death watch until five days before the event at most.

Living under death watch was a grim existence in a tiny, bare cell just beyond the execution chamber. Lights burned around the clock, and prisoners were completely isolated, denied personal items and kept under constant observation.

Velma's execution date was still seventy-four days away, and she could not understand why this was happening. She stood watching helplessly as guards tossed her family photos, books, letters, writing materials, her scripture placards and other belongings into plastic garbage sacks. When they were finished, no sign remained that she had made this cell her home.

Velma was allowed to take only her Bible, a few toiletries and a letter that had arrived that day from Ruth Graham. After reading an article in the *News & Observer* about Billy and Ruth Graham, Velma had written to Ruth to say how much she admired her dedication to family, how she wished her own family could have been like hers. Ruth had answered and they had been pen pals for more than three years. Velma always found comfort and inspiration in Ruth's letters, and this was a moment when she needed both.

Ruth had written that she was praying for Velma and her children, and she thanked Velma for being a blessing to her. Her hope, she said, was that Velma would reach many others at Women's Prison with the message of God's love. But now, Velma knew, she would not be reaching anybody.

The death-watch area was separated by a hallway from the execution chamber. It contained four cells, all identical, facing a glass-enclosed control booth, where a guard kept watch around the clock. A stainless steel table with four seats occupied the area between the cells and the control booth, where another guard was stationed. A shower stall with a plastic curtain was beside the control booth.

Velma was placed in Cell C, the same cell, a guard told her, in which James Hutchins had spent his final days. The cell was ten feet long and six feet wide. A steel cot with a thin mattress was attached to one wall. A window four inches wide and four feet long in the center of the electronically operated steel door allowed guards to see inside. A drawer for passing food and small items divided the window near the top.

Things would be much different for Velma here. She would never see another inmate. She would have no familiar guards.

Warden Nathan Rice came to her cell soon after her arrival to instruct her on the rules. Her visits would be restricted to two persons, and they would be held in a tiny booth, separated by glass and steel. If she wanted writing or reading materials other than her Bible, she would have to request them from a guard and return them when she was through. Whenever she met with her lawyer, she would be handcuffed and escorted by four guards who would remain present during their conversations. She would be stripped and searched upon her return.

After the warden departed, Velma collapsed onto her bunk in despair.

Jimmie Little was informed about Velma's move Monday night, and he was furious. He had been repeatedly reassured by the Department of Correction that Velma would not be transferred to Central Prison until three days before her execution. He drove straight to the prison and demanded to see his client.

Prisoners on death watch were allowed to see their attorneys in a parole hearing room adjoining the execution chamber. The room also served as a staging area during executions.

A rusting hospital gurney with a black vinyl-covered cushion and olive drab restraining straps was parked in the hallway when Velma was escorted the short distance —only twenty feet or so—to the hearing room to see Little. She thought the gurney was there in case of a medical emergency—perhaps they feared she'd have a heart attack. Actually, this was the gurney on which James Hutchins had died. Usually it was kept in the chamber's preparation room. Later, after she realized what it was, Velma could only wonder if it hadn't been deliberately left in the hallway as a macabre reminder of what lay ahead.

Little had never seen Velma as despondent as she was that night. "I don't think I'm ever going to see my grandkids again," she told him tearfully. It hadn't been so bad for them at Women's Prison, where she could hold them, but this would be much different. "I just can't let them see me here and wonder why Ma-ma is in a cage," she said.

Little could only reassure her that he would do everything possible to overcome this outrageous act and see that she was returned to Women's Prison where she belonged.

Phil Carter did not learn of Velma's move until the next morning. He called the chaplain at Central Prison, Julian Moorman, to arrange to see her. Moorman told him that wouldn't be possible. Henceforth, he said, Central Prison was assuming all responsibilities for Velma's welfare, including her spiritual guidance.

Carter was flabbergasted. "In other words, you're telling me she's going to be cut off from everybody she's spent the last six years with?"

"That's right."

"I've got one thing to say to that," Carter said. "All hell's going to break loose. I will resign and go to the press about being denied access to a parish member."

Carter stormed into Jennie Lancaster's office only to discover that she was as angry and upset as he.

Word was not long in reaching the prison administration about the disgruntled staff at Women's Prison, and the command manager, Gene Cousins, was sent to meet with them. The staff's primary concern was that Velma was isolated from all the people she knew and trusted, that she had been put into conditions that amounted to cruel and unusual punishment.

Carter was certain that the embarrassment Velma was bringing to Governor Hunt's campaign was the reason she had been moved, and he made clear that he intended to add to it if he were not allowed to continue ministering to her.

After that meeting, the prison administration changed its position and allowed the people who had been working with Velma at Women's Prison to continue seeing her at Central. But all were instructed that they were to say nothing about the situation to anybody.

"We got a gag order," said Carter.

It had not escaped Jimmie Little's attention that Velma's move to Central Prison had come just days after she had appeared on two national TV networks causing embarrassment to the governor. What he didn't know was that Secretary of Correction James Woodard had called a meeting of his top subordinates, and the following day, the warden of Central Prison had been summoned back from vacation to create a plan for isolating Velma. If higher political pressure hadn't been at play, he might have asked, why such urgency?

But he could not voice his suspicions. If the move had been ordered by the governor's office, he couldn't prove it. And he didn't want to make Velma's situation any worse by making wild charges. He also had to be especially sensitive not to offend Hunt, who was, after all, not only his boss but his only real hope for saving Velma.

On the morning after Velma's move, Little met with James Woodard to appeal for her return to Women's Prison, but he had no success. "It doesn't look good," he told a reporter at noon. "We'll talk some more this afternoon. This whole thing just makes me sick."

When later talks provided only more frustration, Little called the governor's legal counsel, Jack Cozort, to ask for intervention. Cozort called back, Little later said, to tell him that the governor could not involve himself in a matter that was strictly up to the Department of Correction.

On Tuesday morning, a press release from the Department of Correction announced that the reason for Velma's move was security. Patty McQuillan, the department's spokesperson, reminded reporters that an inmate had escaped from Women's Prison earlier in the year. That prison had no guard towers, she noted, but nobody had escaped from the new Central Prison since it had opened a year and a half earlier. "Central is much, much more secure," McQuillan said.

This was patently absurd to Little. Velma had never been cited for a single infraction in her five and a half years in prison. And unlike other inmates at Women's Prison, she did not have the run of the yard and potential access to flee. To escape, she would first have to break out of lockup—something that had never happened. Then she would have to scale a twelve-foot, barbed-wire–topped fence—which seemed unlikely for a fifty-one-year-old woman who stood five feet three and weighed 168 pounds.

The real reason for Velma's move became clearer on Wednesday when the Department of Correction announced that, henceforth, reporters wanting to interview Velma would be restricted to a one-hour press conference on Friday mornings. Only eight reporters would be allowed, two from newspapers or other print media, two from wire services, two each from TV and radio.

Jimmie Little had been carefully arranging and controlling all of Velma's interviews. Now he had been cut out. And he was not about to take it quietly. He called a press conference and charged that Velma was being held under conditions unlike those for any other prisoner.

"I'm sure that there are people who could care less how Velma is treated," he said. "The question is: Should the state make her go through these extraordinary conditions under a cloak of security concerns that have never before come up until Velma's side has finally begun to emerge?"

Little followed up by calling the presidents of the state press association and the association of radio-TV news directors. Both withdrew from the plan for interviewing Velma. The Department of Correction announced that it would choose the reporters itself. But when the first press conference was arranged for Friday, June 22, Velma refused to participate.

On Saturday, Ronnie and Pam came to Central Prison and spent two hours with their mother in one of the tiny booths in the visiting area on the top floor. They had not seen her so depressed in years. Pam left crying, and both talked with a reporter afterward.

"I'm not sure she has hopes of getting back to Women's Prison," Ronnie said. "I understand that she's a death-row prisoner and she's not going to get treated nicely all the time. But to move her this far in advance, that's what gets to me."

Pam said that she didn't want her children to remember their grandmother locked in a concrete and glass box and wouldn't be bringing them to see her for now. Beverly, she said, had seen a TV news report about Velma's recent hearing and had come to her to ask what "execution" meant.

"I told her it meant her grandmother might die," she said. "She sat in my lap and we both cried for about ten minutes. There's very seldom a day goes by I don't cry. It's on my mind in the morning when I get up and in the evening when I go to bed. I've tried to prepare for it, but how can anyone accept the death of their mother?"

Little's efforts to get Velma's story known not only got her moved into isolation, they also produced other unexpected results.

On the morning of Velma's hearing on June 13, relatives of Stuart Taylor and John Henry Lee gathered in Lumberton to watch the two reports scheduled that morning on CBS and NBC. Alice Storms, Margie Pittman and Sylvia Andrews watched tensely, gritting teeth and suppressing tears whenever Velma's face appeared on the screen.

Both reports used snippets of the videotape shot at Easter of Velma and her granddaughters supplied by Jimmie Little. Everybody at the gathering was resentful at seeing Velma happily playing with Beverly and Sarah. Stuart Taylor had grandchildren he'd never seen because of Velma, and John Henry Lee had great-grandchildren who would never know him because of her. That Velma could be playing happily with her grandchildren was an insult to the families of these two of Velma's victims, prompting anger and disgust.

They did not trust her supposed religious conversion—she had pretended to be just as religious when she had stood watching their fathers' agonizing deaths. They thought her professions of sorrow for all the hurt she had caused were self-serving and insincere. They did not believe that Velma had killed because she was so addled by drugs that she didn't know what she was doing. They thought that she had killed because she enjoyed it, that she took pleasure watching the agonies of her victims as she feigned caring for them, enjoyed the pain of their families while playing out her spurious role as comforter.

To them Velma was a person without a conscience, a charmer and manipulator who was now fooling a whole new set of people, just as she once had fooled them.

They had seen the pamphlets put out by Velma's support committee, and they thought them naive and deceiving. They had seen the story in the *Village Voice*, and more stories about Velma in other newspapers that had hardly mentioned her victims or their families. Several stories, all highly favorable to Velma in their eyes, had appeared in the *News & Observer* in recent weeks, written by Ginny Carroll, who had been the first reporter to interview Velma after her conviction, and who now appeared to be crusading to save her. Yet Carroll had never called them, had never written one word acknowledging that their fathers were innocent people who had more right to live than Velma.

If the people who were working on Velma's behalf were successful, these families were certain that a day would come when she would be paroled, and they had no doubt that it would only be a matter of time until some other innocent person would be dead at her hand.

Something needed to be done to prevent this, they believed, to show the other side of Velma, and to see that her sentence was carried out as the jury intended. And they became even more convinced of it later that day at the hearing in Elizabethtown when they saw all the reporters and camera operators swarming around Velma's family while paying little attention to them. Why so much attention for the criminal and her family, they wondered, and so little for her victims and their families?

They spoke with Joe Freeman Britt, and he suggested that they launch their own media campaign to counter Velma's, that they organize and fight against clemency as hard as Velma's supporters were fighting for it. That galvanized them, and Alice Storms, Margie Pittman and Sylvia Andrews began planning their own offensive.

Alice's resolve to act was only strengthened when the June 24 edition of the *North Carolina Catholic* arrived at her home. On the cover was a full-page photo of Velma taken before her transfer to Central Prison. She was standing forlornly by a window at Women's Prison. A line across the bottom of the photo said, "Velma Barfield does not presume to ask the state for forgiveness or freedom—just her life."

Alice's family was Catholic. Velma was not. Why was the undeserved pain Velma had brought to them not meaningful to the *North Carolina Catholic*?

With the story was a column urging clemency for Velma as "a statement that we have the ability to separate the crime from the criminal, that we can be merciful, kind and lenient toward one who has demonstrated the ability to live a fruitful life."

Why should the crime be separated from the criminal? Alice wondered. Certainly Velma had shown no mercy, kindness, or leniency to any of her victims, all of whom might well have continued to live fruitful lives if she had allowed them. But the *North Carolina Catholic* appeared not to place as much value on their lives as it did on the life of the person who had taken them. Something clearly seemed skewed.

Alice began calling newspapers and TV stations. She, Margie and Sylvia began planning demonstrations for campaign visits in the area by Governor Hunt. They started a petition drive, began organizing people to speak to the governor against clemency, and sought help from a group in Fayetteville called People Assisting Victims.

Results were not long in coming. Before the end of June, Larry Cheek, a columnist for the *Fayetteville Times*, had written two columns on Alice and her campaign. And even Ginny Carroll of the *News & Observer* felt obligated to talk with Alice and Joe Freeman Britt for a long story about clemency for Velma that appeared on July 1, even if she did give more space to Velma's proponents than to her opponents. But a long story that appeared the following day in the *Sentinel*, Winston-Salem's afternoon newspaper, focused completely on the victims and their families' campaign to counter the attention Velma was receiving. With it was a photo of Alice showing off posters to be used at appearances by the governor.

"I've never done anything like this in my life," Alice told the reporter, Michael Wade, "and I'm sitting here last night trying to think of things to put on signs. I've tried to run from it, and I can't run. It's in the news, it's in the house. You're sitting there as it comes out. Your heart starts pounding, and all this you relive over and over and over again. We're asking as victims, when can it end for us?

"I have two small children. I had one come up to my husband the other night and he says, 'Daddy, will that lady get out?'"

"And Bill looked at him and said, 'Bryan, honey, I don't think so. We have our laws. We hope justice will be done.'

"And he says, 'But Daddy, if she gets out, will she kill my granny?' "

On the day that story appeared, Monday, July 2, the unexpected occurred. In a two-line order, U.S. Supreme Court Chief Justice Warren Burger granted Velma another stay of execution. The court asked the state to respond to the issues in the petition for rehearing filed by Velma's lawyers after the court had refused her last appeal. Normally, the state would not respond to such a petition unless requested by the court, and the request and accompanying stay of execution caught both sides by surprise.

The issue that concerned Burger was that of juror disqualification, whether a potential juror who said he was opposed to the death penalty but didn't specifically say that he would always vote against it could automatically be excluded.

Warden Nathan Rice went to give Velma the news and to tell her that she would be transferred back to Women's Prison.

"Don't bother packing my things," she told him with a laugh. "Just get me out of here."

Velma returned to Single Cell at Women's Prison. But she soon would be placed back in Dorm C, which had been reopened and was being used for overflow. Only a few other inmates would ever be in the building with her, and life would be far quieter. Velma got a corner cell and quickly recreated her cozy nest. She was receiving nearly a hundred letters a week now, most from strangers, and just keeping up with her correspondence took most of her time.

On the day after Velma's return, Jennie Lancaster was summoned to a meeting with the Secretary of Correction, who wanted to make clear that Velma was to receive no special privileges. The rules for meeting with reporters that had applied at Central Prison would remain in effect, and no longer would reporters or photographers be allowed to take pictures of Velma in her cell, or to sit in on visits with her family or others.

Nevertheless, reporters continued to flock to Velma. Her name and face were becoming familiar all over the country, and in many other places around the world—in England, Germany, Holland, France, Spain, Norway, Brazil, Australia, Mexico. "Death Row

Granny," she usually was called, and the image sparked reaction. Letters arriving at the governor's office were four to one in favor of sparing her and coming in ever increasing numbers.

But Alice Storms and the daughters of John Henry Lee were keeping the media campaign on Velma's behalf in check. In more and more interviews Velma was having to respond to their criticisms. And Jimmie Little and the support committee realized that they had made a mistake in overlooking the victims.

Even the *North Carolina Catholic* was now taking note of them, quoting Little in the July 8 edition. "The victims are suffering greatly," he said. "Every time they see an article in the newspaper about the case, they are reminded of the hurt and tragedy. They are living through a different kind of grief than Velma's family, who are no less victims."

Sister Teresa, who had quit her job at Women's Prison on June 30 to devote all her time to the support committee, was also quoted on the subject. "When a loved one is a victim of murder, the grieving process is much more involved than after a death by natural causes. I feel deeply for the families, but I also feel that their resolution must come from within, not from taking another life."

"Ultimately, we have to ask what is served by Velma's execution," Little added. "Will it stop the hurt of anybody? Will it be a deterrent? Or will it simply be revenge?"

On Thursday, August 16, the Supreme Court dismissed Velma's petition for rehearing without comment. Jimmie Little got the call shortly before five p.m. and headed to Women's Prison in rush-hour traffic to tell Velma, but she heard about the rejection in a radio bulletin before he could get there. Little had done his best to prepare her for this, and he found her in a mood of resignation, concerned only about how Ronnie and Pam would take the news. She wanted to call and let them know that she was okay and that she was trusting in clemency.

The governor still wouldn't comment about Velma's case, but the new development brought more questions at every campaign stop. "Everyone knows my position on capital punishment—I favor that law," he said in Charlotte. "But every case needs to be looked at individually and given full consideration."

Gary Pearce, Hunt's former press secretary, who had left that position to become codirector of his campaign, bristled when a reporter asked about the effect the political race would have on the clemency decision, calling the question "offensive." He hadn't discussed it with the governor, he said. "And I don't intend to."

The court's refusal to reconsider Velma's case automatically dissolved her stay, and on Friday Britt asked that a hearing to set a new execution date be held on Wednesday, August 22, at 10:30 A.M.

Because the law dictated that the date had to be from sixty to ninety days following the hearing, it also meant that the execution could be as late as November 20, two weeks after the election, thus allowing the governor to delay a decision on clemency until after his race for the Senate had been decided. Certainly, reason dictated that would be the case.

The hearing began the following week in Elizabethtown before Judge Giles Clark. As before, Britt wanted sixty days, but precedent called for setting executions for Fridays, and the first Friday after sixty days would add five days to the total. He asked for that tradition to be ignored.

Little, of course, pleaded for the full ninety days, as he had in June before a different judge, saying he needed time to prepare the clemency appeal. He was to meet with the governor's office next week to set a timetable, he said. He and Dick Burr also needed time to look into other avenues of appeal, and Velma and her family needed time to prepare in case all of their efforts failed.

Judge Clark stuck with the Friday tradition and set the execution for November 2, seventy-two days hence—four days before the election. Instead of lifting the clemency decision above politics, the judge had thrust it even deeper into the mire.

Governor Hunt and his campaign staff took the position that having to decide clemency prior to the election would have no political effect because it was not a political matter. A campaign spokesperson even went so far as to say that the matter was being given no thought at all, which, of course, was far from the truth.

Privately, Hunt's aides and advisers were deeply concerned, and they couldn't help but point out that they found the timing of the execution date "curious," especially in view of the fact that the judge who set it had been the college roommate of Jim Holshouser, the former Republican governor, who had appointed him to the bench in 1975. The timing, without doubt, was to the advantage of Jesse Helms.

Hunt's positions had been growing more conservative throughout

the campaign, and if he granted clemency, he not only would be
going against the grain of his own campaign, he would be defying
the majority in the state who favored capital punishment. Helms
could push that issue from the time clemency was granted until the
election. If, on the other hand, Hunt allowed Velma to be executed,
he risked offending those opposed to capital punishment, most of
whom were likely to be his supporters. And while they probably
wouldn't retaliate by voting for Helms, they might choose not to
vote, which could prove crucial in such a close election.

Velma, as reporter Jim Nesbitt of the *Orlando Sentinel* wrote in
an article that also appeared in the *Boston Globe* and other newspapers, had become "a macabre wild card in the Deep South's
hottest political race."

Thad Boyle, a professor of political science at the University of
North Carolina, Chapel Hill, told the *News & Observer* that Hunt
was in "a lose-lose situation."

"Whatever decision he makes will be read as a political decision," Boyle said. "It will be viewed as being based on how he
could maximize his potential at the polls."

One of Hunt's closest friends and advisers, Phil Carlton, a former state Supreme Court justice, agreed. "It lends itself to the public perception that the decision would be a political one," he said.
"That's at a minimum. It's beyond my comprehension as to why a
judge would have set it the Friday before a Tuesday election."

Judge Clark, who actually was a Democrat, responded that his
decision had been "in no way political." He said that he simply had
followed the schedule decided by the judge at the previous hearing,
setting the execution for the second Friday within the thirty-day
frame.

Political or not, Hunt had to deal with the situation, and he
decided to handle it forthrightly and put it behind him, hoping, no
doubt, to give the appearance of decisiveness. A week after the
hearing, on the same day that Alice Storms and others picketed a
campaign appearance by the governor in Lumberton ("Victims don't
get a second chance," said one of their placards), Hunt announced
that he would devote two days in September, the 18th and 19th, to
hearing from Velma's supporters and opponents, and that he
would make his decision as quickly as possible after that with no
regard to politics.

*   *   *

For a story about Velma that had appeared at the end of July, reporter Lil Thompson of the *Winston-Salem Journal* interviewed Dr. Selwyn Rose, the psychiatrist who had testified on Velma's behalf at her hearing in 1980. He described Velma as "weird" and called her "a cold, frightening lady." The psychiatric examinations of Velma before her trial had been only cursory, he maintained, as had his own more than two years later. He had asked the court to provide for a thorough psychiatric examination at that time, he said, but had been turned down.

"That was the last chance in the legal process to raise the issue of her mental state," he said. "The lady deserved a thorough examination and did not have one."

Jimmie Little was preparing for the clemency appeal as if it were a new trial, and he wanted to make sure that Velma did have a thorough psychiatric exam. Richard Burr knew a psychiatrist in New York who was doing ground-breaking research with violent criminals. Her name was Dorothy Otnow Lewis, and she had worked with the defense on several Florida death-penalty cases. Burr asked if she would examine Velma.

Lewis, a graduate of the Yale University School of Medicine, a psychiatrist at Bellevue Hospital in New York, a professor at New York University School of Medicine, had discovered while working with juvenile delinquents that many who were violent had suffered severe head injuries in childhood, and she thought there might be a correlation. She got a grant to conduct a study and, with Jonathan Pincus, a neurologist at Yale, began to develop evidence that damage to the frontal lobes of the cortex, the top layer of the brain, had a connection to violence. The frontal lobes control behavior and judgment, and if impaired, could create an inability to curb impulses or anger, thus leading to violence. Lewis and Pincus would come to believe that the most violent people were those who had damage to the frontal lobes, had suffered abuse in childhood, and had psychotic symptoms, particularly paranoia.

Not surprisingly, Lewis questioned Velma closely about head injuries and abuse in her childhood.

Velma related how she'd been knocked out when she and a boy ran into each other at school when she was ten, leaving her with a lasting knot on her forehead. She told of another head injury in a serious bike accident at age fourteen (something other family members would not recall), and of the numerous car accidents in which she'd been involved, at least three of which had caused blows to the head. She also told of her long history of headaches and occasional blackouts. "It is important to note that Velma's episodes of blacking out . . . occurred prior to any drug history," Lewis later wrote, although that would not be remembered by family members either.

Asked about mental illness in her family, Velma said that her mother had crying spells, episodes of depression and severe headaches. In her later years, Velma said, her mother would sometimes become extremely distraught and frightened, saying, "I feel like I'm going crazy." One of her mother's brothers had fits of violence, cursing and laughing, wouldn't sleep in the house, and had to be put into an asylum when he was in his twenties, Velma recalled. Another of her mother's brothers was completely withdrawn and would go days without speaking a word. And one of her mother's sisters suffered convulsions and severe emotional problems.

Lewis traced Velma's depressive behavior back to the second grade, but the first severe occurrence came in the sixth grade when Velma said she attempted to kill herself by drinking bleach (another incident that family members could not recall). Periods of deep depression continued through the ninth grade, Velma said.

The sexual abuse Velma had endured as a child had been far greater than she previously had made known, Lewis learned. But getting this information, she wrote in her report, was "extremely difficult."

When she was a small child, Velma recalled with great emotion after coaxing by Lewis, a man who was a neighbor took her to a barn and forced her to commit oral sex. When she was eight or ten, she said, an older male relative began forcing sexual relations on her and this continued over a period of years. Yet another male relative also had forced himself on her, she said.

Velma was reluctant to talk about being raped by her father, Lewis reported, because some of her brothers didn't believe it and had been angered and hurt when it was made public in June.

Later, Lewis wrote that Velma had been "extremely frightened" by telling about the sexual molestations. "It seems that Mrs. Barfield would rather be executed and have the public think well of her family than reveal the extraordinary psychopathology and violence that existed in her family."

Lewis spent six hours interviewing Velma. She reviewed the

reports of all of Velma's previous psychiatric examinations and psychological tests, as well as her medical records. She wrote a nine-page, single-spaced report.

Her diagnosis: "Velma Barfield is a woman who, throughout her childhood and adolescence was brutally physically assaulted and sexually molested by her severely disturbed father and . . . (others). She suffers from a bipolar mood disorder. This diagnosis was formerly called manic depressive psychosis. It is characterized by episodes of extreme depression, suicidal behaviors, loss of appetite and extreme weight loss during its depressive stages. The manic phases are characterized by episodes of uncontrolled behaviors and severely impaired judgment. During such times patients are often filled with uncontrollable rage and act in aggressive ways that are uncharacteristic during nonpsychotic periods. In Velma Barfield's circumstances, it is extremely likely that the extraordinary physical and sexual abuse suffered at the hands of her male relatives contributed to the magnitude of the psychotic rage expressed during her manic phases."

The tragedy of Velma's situation was increased, Lewis noted, because her condition had never been properly diagnosed. Her doctors saw only the depressive side of her condition and prescribed medications for that. Her first major depression as an adult had come after her hysterectomy, Lewis noted, and likely had been precipitated by diminished hormones because of removal of her ovaries. This marked the beginning of Velma's problems with drugs.

But the antidepressants that she took in great quantities could be extremely dangerous when she entered manic periods, Lewis noted, producing psychosis. "During such states the individual is not in control of his or her behavior. Such individuals have impaired judgment and tend to act irresponsibly, and, at times, to commit violent acts that under normal circumstances they would not commit."

Lewis thought that Velma seemed to sense this and attempted to counter it by taking huge amounts of Valium to stabilize herself. "I felt I would go raving mad without Valium," Velma told her.

"Her seeking of Valium," Lewis wrote, "was clearly her unconscious but perceptive way of trying to control her behaviors and was an attempt to stop herself from acting in violent, senseless ways."

Velma had not been capable of controlling her thoughts or her actions when she poisoned people, Lewis determined, thus was not liable for their deaths. If her condition had been properly diagnosed and she had been given proper medications for her mania as well as for her depression, Lewis concluded, "it is unlikely that Velma Barfield would ever have committed any violent acts."

Jimmie Little handed his application for clemency to Jack Cozort, the governor's legal counsel, on Saturday morning, September 15. A perfectionist, he had been up much of the night completing it, making sure nothing was left out. The appeal was more than two inches thick. With it was an eighteen-minute video of Velma, carefully edited.

With the overview was a history of clemency in North Carolina, which had been granted in forty percent of death-penalty cases. In certain periods, half of those slated for death had been granted life sentences instead by compassionate governors.

Velma's prison years were covered in a five-page section, and her effect on other prisoners was reinforced by excerpts from letters written to her by other inmates and ex-inmates.

"If I could, I would trade places with you. . . . I am not worthy of even knowing someone like you."

"You helped me so much—all of us on C-hall."

"I don't have no State Sis or Bro or nothing and I don't want none. But a State Mom. I will always care and pray for you and I will try to stay out of trouble!"

"I love you, Miss Margie. The memory I have of you always helps me and makes me smile."

Little was counting heavily on the recently completed psychiatric report by Dr. Lewis, which he hoped the governor would consider as strong new evidence. He introduced the report in a section titled "Why Homicide?"

The Catholic Center, only a short distance from Central Prison, was the staging area on Tuesday, September 18, for Velma's supporters, who hoped to convince Governor Hunt that she should be spared. Starting before nine, vans shuttled more than four dozen supporters to meetings with the governor in his office at the State Capitol.

The first to go were Ronnie, Pam, Kirby, and Faye. Jimmie Little was already at the capitol, where he would spend the day coordinating this last hope for saving Velma. He ushered them into the governor's office and made introductions.

The governor, Ronnie later remembered, was cordial, polite, with an air of formality and control. He told them that he was willing to hear whatever they had to say, that he would give it serious consideration and make a prompt decision.

Faye spoke first and immediately broke down. Her sister was not the person who had committed the murders, she said, crying, and if the state executed her, it would be executing a person who hadn't known what she was doing.

Pam cried, too, and had difficulty speaking, finally breaking down and pleading, "Please don't let them kill my mother."

Neither Pam nor Faye had believed that this moment would come. Both had assumed that the courts would change Velma's sentence to life. Neither still could accept that she actually would be killed, and both were placing total faith in the governor. They didn't care about politics. They believed he would see that Velma was a person redeemed, doing good for others, and that she deserved to live.

Ronnie didn't share that confidence. From the moment he shook the governor's hand he felt an artificiality and insincerity about him, and he had little doubt that the governor's first consideration would be political. Even as Ronnie spoke about his mother's problems, her transformation, her remorse, her desire to help others—making all the points Jimmie Little had told him to get in—he knew what the governor's decision would be. He was certain of it, and an all-too-familiar sense of resignation and hopelessness began to settle over him.

"It was just like during the trial when I knew all along that she was going to get the death penalty," he later recalled.

The four spent nearly forty-five minutes with the governor, and afterward reporters and TV cameras were waiting. Pam and Faye were in no condition to face reporters. Little pulled Ronnie aside to offer suggestions. Ronnie struggled not to let his mood show as he talked to the reporters.

"We do not ask for forgiveness from the governor," he said. "We ask for compassion so that she may spend her remaining years in prison."

Among the others who spoke to the governor on Velma's behalf this day were members of the support committee, former inmates at Women's Prison, and numerous ministers. Those writing letters in Velma's behalf included Hugh Hoyle and Ruth Graham, neither of whom was opposed to capital punishment.

Alice Storms arrived at the capitol the following day with her children. It was her second visit to the capitol that week. On Monday, two days earlier, she, Margie Pittman, Sylvia Andrews and others had made a preemptive strike, coming to the capitol early, carrying cardboard boxes and file folders filled with letters and petitions opposing clemency. Alice had never relented in her campaign. She had gone door-to-door collecting signatures, had stopped cars at intersections. More than 2,400 people had signed the letters and petitions she and the others delivered Monday before TV cameras and newspaper photographers. On Wednesday, as they arrived to present their case to the governor, they brought even more letters.

After her meeting with the governor, Alice described her father's agonizing death in detail for reporters and said that Velma should experience arsenic, too.

"I'd like for her to get a dose of it before she dies so she'll know how it feels."

She wasn't seeking vengeance, she said, only justice. "I have no feeling for Velma Barfield. No hate. No anger. No nothing. God has her soul. It's between God and her what He does with her soul."

The looming decision on Velma's life, combined with the increasingly strident and hard-fought Senate race, brought a new surge of attention to Velma. In addition to network news and wire service reports, major stories about Velma, written by staff reporters, appeared on the front pages of some of the nation's largest newspapers—the *Los Angeles Times, Dallas Morning News, Chicago Tribune, Philadelphia Inquirer. USA Today* had a page-one story with a half-page question-and-answer feature with Velma inside. A photo of Ronnie and Pam appeared in the *New York Times* above a story headlined "Clemency Plea Weighed in Carolina." Three full pages about Velma dominated the newspaper *Liberation* in Europe.

And reporters and producers continued to call. *Time* magazine wanted to interview Velma. So did *60 Minutes*.

It seemed as if the whole world was waiting to see if a supposedly liberal New South governor, who was in the political battle of his life with a God-spouting, law-and-order, Old South senator, would allow a serial-killer grandmother to live to do Jesus' work in prison. Velma Barfield had come a long way from the sandy, sadness-bearing South River fields of her childhood.

CHAPTER 22

Governor Hunt cancelled all appointments and sequestered himself in the governor's mansion with his legal counsel, Jack Cozort, on Thursday, September 27, to make his decision on Velma's life. Shortly after four Cozort called Jimmie Little.

Little called Women's Prison to tell Jennie Lancaster that he would be coming to inform Velma of the decision. But before that, he went to the state Supreme Court to file an affidavit on Velma's behalf.

Velma had signed the affidavit after long talks with Little and her children. In it she said that if clemency was denied she wanted no lawyers other than Little and Burr taking action on her behalf, nor did she want any more stays of execution. "If I am to be executed," she said, "I want it to be done so that no one will go through any more pain and suffering than they have already."

Because of the widespread news coverage, Little and Burr were well aware that many groups and many lawyers might try to insert themselves into Velma's case at the last minute, hoping to draw attention to their causes or themselves, and they wanted to cut off any chance of that.

As Velma waited in the administration building, she knew that the governor had reached a decision, but she had no hint what it was. She knew as soon as she saw her lawyer's face. Words were unnecessary, but Little spoke them anyway. "The governor will be denying clemency," he said softly.

Velma didn't speak. She closed her eyes and Little knew she was praying. When she looked up, she saw that Little's eyes had filled with tears.

"Jimmie, we knew this could happen," she said. "You've done

everything you could. Nobody could have done any more. You and Dick have been so good to me. You can't blame yourself."

The governor had called a press conference at the capitol, and Velma and Little listened to the radio broadcast.

"I have completed my review of the Velma Barfield case, and I am prepared to announce my decision," he began, then went on for two minutes before he got to it.

"After carefully studying all the issues, I do not believe that the ends of justice, or deterrence, would be served by my intervention in this case. I cannot in good conscience justify making an exception to the law as enacted by our legislature, or overruling those twelve jurors who, after hearing the evidence, concluded that Mrs. Barfield should pay the maximum penalty for her brutal actions.

"Death by arsenic poisoning is slow and agonizing. Victims are literally tortured to death. Mrs. Barfield was convicted of killing one person in this fashion; she admitted to three more, including her mother, and there was evidence of yet a fifth.

"It is my sworn duty as governor to uphold the fundamental rule of law. I am satisfied that I have made a decision consistent with that duty."

Not surprisingly, the first question was about the effect the decision might have on the Senate campaign.

"I have no idea," Hunt responded curtly, "and that does not make any difference whatsoever. That has no place in the consideration of a matter of this kind, and it has had none here."

Later, his press secretary, Brent Hackney, told reporters that the governor's decision was "final and irreversible."

Little was so upset and despondent after listening to the governor that he could no longer control his emotions, and he spoke out angrily. Velma went to him, put her hands on his shoulders, and said, "Jimmie, you can't let yourself be like this. You've got to forgive him."

Ronnie knew the governor's decision before his mother. Little called him at work soon after getting word. Ronnie was not surprised, but the sudden certainty of his mother's execution sapped him of spirit.

For more than a year, he'd shared an apartment with a coworker, but now he was again living with Faye and Cliff in a new house they'd bought. He wanted to be there before Faye got home to break the news to her, and he left work early.

Nobody was there when Ronnie arrived. He turned on the TV and saw the first report about his mother's fate on a local station. Soon afterward, the phone rang. The voice caught him off guard. It was Joanna and she was crying.

"Ronnie, what are you going to do?" she asked.

"I guess I'm going to have to prepare for this like I have all along," he said.

"You really think it's going to happen?"

"I'm sure it is."

Ronnie had just hung up when the phone rang again. It was Pam, and she could hardly speak.

"Have you heard?" she asked, sobbing.

"Yes, Jimmie called."

"I was so sure that he would see our side of it," she said.

"Pam, I think he did. It was just that the other side outweighed ours."

"What can we do now?"

"I don't know that we can do anything except to spend as much time as we can with Mama and try to make the most of it. This is going to take place and there's nothing we can do to stop it. I've tried to make you see this was going to happen."

"I can't accept that," she said.

"You've got to prepare yourself for it," he told her. "If you don't it's going to make it even harder."

"I can't," she said, still sobbing.

"Just think of it like she's been sick, and she's not going to recover."

"But it's not like that," Pam said, and Ronnie knew she was right.

His mother's death would be well planned and expertly carried out in the name of justice and the people of North Carolina. It would be among the rarest and most unnatural forms of death, and she and they would know the exact minute it would take place. To make it even more unnatural, a single person could have stopped it with nothing more than his signature, and he had made a political decision not to do so.

Faye and Cliff arrived soon after Ronnie had talked with Pam, and Ronnie pulled Cliff aside to warn him. But Faye sensed what had happened as soon as she saw Ronnie.

"He's decided, hasn't he?" she said, her face paling.

Ronnie nodded. "He denied clemency."

"Oh, no!" Faye screamed. "Oh, my God!"

She ran sobbing to her bedroom, and Cliff followed, trying to console her.

Velma called shortly afterward, and Ronnie, who was trying hard to be strong and composed, fought back tears when he heard her voice. He would remember later that she kept telling him, "We've just got to accept this."

Velma wanted to speak to Faye, and although Faye tried, she couldn't control her grief to conduct a conversation.

Ronnie didn't go out that night to drink as usual. Instead, he lay on his bed letting reality settle over him, remembering when he had done much the same nearly six years earlier, sitting in his apartment staring into space after his mother had been sentenced to death. Even after all these years, it still seemed unreal. Yet it was. And worse moments were to come.

He tried to push such thoughts aside, tried to ignore what was now destined to happen just five weeks from this very night. He concentrated on summoning images of good times instead. His mind drifted back to grammar-school days, the best time of his life, when his mother had been grade mother for both his and Pam's classes. She had been so happy then, helping with class parties, working on school projects, driving on field trips—all of his friends had wanted to ride with his mom, because she was the most fun.

His seventh-grade class trip to Raleigh came to mind, and suddenly he remembered that, along with visiting the state capitol, the legislature, the historical museum, they had gone to the gothic old Central Prison, had been taken to the gas chamber and shown the squat, walnut-stained, oak chair with its leather manacles where criminals—murderers and rapists—actually had died, and now he saw his mother being strapped in that chair, the very chair she had gazed upon while standing beside him in those happy days so many years gone, and he saw the hood being pulled over her head, the cyanide capsule dropping into the acid vat below, the foggy fumes rising, his mother straining, gasping for her final breath, and he rolled onto his stomach and cried into his pillow.

So many people came to see Velma Saturday, in the wake of the governor's decision, that nobody got to spend much time with her. Ronnie and Faye came together, and both had only brief sessions alone with Velma.

Faye was nervous, determined that this time she would tell her sister what she could not confess earlier, that just after Stuart's death she had called a detective in Lumberton to reveal her suspicion that Velma had killed not only him but their mother and others. When reality had proved her right, Faye had felt relief that Velma's killing had been brought to an end, but she couldn't escape feeling that she also had betrayed her sister, who was practically her second mother. Then she and Velma were in each other's arms, crying, and when she looked into her sister's eyes she knew that she no longer had to feel guilt for what she had done, nor even to speak it, for each had forgiven the other for whatever lay in the past, and now the only thing necessary was to profess their love.

Pam had a similar session with her mother that Saturday. They talked about the hurts each had brought the other over the years—and their regrets. Both cried. Velma said that her shame for the pain she had inflicted on her children was almost more than she could bear.

"Mama, please don't say that," Pam told her. "You were there when Ronnie and I needed you."

But later, in her cell, Velma wrote in one of her notebooks: "I didn't feel that I had been with them when they needed me."

Velma also discussed her funeral arrangements with Pam. She wanted Hugh Hoyle to conduct the service, she said, and he already knew the verses she wanted read, the hymns to be sung. As Velma went on with other details, Pam had difficulty believing that this conversation was actually occurring. Here they sat, calmly discussing her mother's imminent funeral, and she was alive and well. It was too bizarre to imagine.

One thing about the funeral had been decided weeks earlier during another visit with Ronnie and Pam.

"There was one thing I wanted to ask y'all about," Velma told them. "Have you thought about where I should be buried?"

Pam answered without hesitation. "Whenever it comes, I want you to be buried beside my daddy."

Ronnie agreed. "That's the way I'll always think of us, as a family," he said, "our mother and our daddy together."

"I was hoping you would feel that way," Velma said.

She was concerned that Thomas' family might raise objections. The rift that had developed between them after Thomas' death had never been healed. Ronnie pointed out that the cemetery plot belonged to her, and if she wanted to be buried there, nobody could do anything to stop it.

Another source of comfort for Velma was her religious friends. One of the closest was Anne Lotz of Raleigh, the daughter of Billy and Ruth Graham. Her mother had asked her to visit Velma after her move to Central Prison, and Lotz had become a regular visitor. She had been one of the first to offer support after the governor's decision.

Velma could make collect calls from prison, and Lotz arranged for her to call her mother on Tuesday, October 2. Although Velma had been corresponding with Ruth Graham for years, she never had spoken with her. They chatted like sisters, Velma thanking her for her friendship and support, and for sending her daughter to become her friend.

Velma never dreamed that she would talk with Billy Graham, but he came on the line to encourage her and pray for her. Billy Graham praying personally for her! She couldn't get over it. "It was wonderful—uplifting," she later wrote in her notebook. "I felt as though I was then in the heavenland."

She was almost giddy when she told Jimmie Little about it later. "You know what Billy Graham told me? He said, 'Velma, in a way I envy you, because you're going to get to heaven before I do.'"

As for Velma's favorite minister, Hugh Hoyle, he could not get through to her after the governor's decision, but he had been on the phone with Jimmie Little, Sister Teresa, Sam Roane and Phil Carter. He was already planning to come to Raleigh to minister to Velma before the execution and to conduct her funeral, as he had promised. The support committee was working on getting his airline tickets. Unable to talk with Velma, he wrote instead.

"Velma, this letter is very difficult for me to write because of the depth of meaning and emotion you are going through. I want you to know that His Grace is sufficient. He will give you the strength when you need it. 'On Christ, the solid rock I stand, all other ground is sinking sand. . . .'"

He went on to quote from I Philippians:

According to my earnest expectation and my hope, that in nothing I shall be ashamed, but that with all boldness, as always, so now also Christ shall be magnified in my body, whether it be by life, or by death.

For me to live is Christ, and to die is gain.

For I am in a strait betwixt two, having a desire to depart, and to be with Christ; which is far better. . . .

"Remember," reminded Hoyle, "Paul wrote this from death row."

In a way Ronnie dreaded the visit he had planned with his mother on October 6. It was his weekend to have Michael, and he picked him up late Friday and spent the night with Pam and Kirby. When he and Michael got to the prison Saturday, Ronnie wanted a few minutes alone with his mother first.

Velma was always eager to see Michael. She had spent precious few hours with him in the past two years, and those only in recent months, since Ronnie had won visiting rights.

"Where's Michael?" she asked, her face showing surprise when Ronnie walked in alone.

"He's here. He's over in the administration building with Sister Teresa."

"Is he okay?"

Ronnie hugged his mother and sat beside her.

"He's fine. I just wanted to talk with you for a minute before I brought him over. You know he's not had an easy time with everything that's gone on. He was crying last night and calling for his mama. He doesn't understand a lot of what's happening, and the situation is just going to get worse from now on. Joanna and I talked about it. There has to be a time when I don't bring him back, and this is that time."

He choked on those words, and tears came to his eyes.

"I can understand that," Velma said, patting him on the knee. "I don't really like to think of any visit as being my last, but I can prepare myself."

"I'll bring him on over," Ronnie said.

His mother was all smiles when Ronnie returned with Michael.

"Come here and give your Ma-ma a big hug," she said, taking her grandson into her lap. "How's my boy?"

"I'll just let y'all have some time alone," Ronnie said. And as he slipped out he could hear his mother's cheerful laughter echoing through the vocational building.

After forty-five minutes Ronnie rejoined them for the remainder of the visit. Leaving that day, he said later, was one of the hardest things he'd ever done.

"Give Ma-ma a big kiss," Velma told Michael, and she pulled him to her and held him tightly.

"Always remember that Ma-ma loves you," she told him, kissing his forehead.

Ronnie fought back tears as he took Michael by the hand and led him away.

"Be a good boy," Velma called.

"Did you have a good time with your grandmother?" Sister Teresa asked Michael when they returned to the administration building.

"Yes!" Michael said. "We played games. And she read to me."

"When Michael left, I really felt crushed," Velma wrote in her notebook that night.

Yet another source of pain for Ronnie was the dream that had first come soon after his mother's arrest. It had interrupted his sleep many times since, and it was always the same. The flames began in a trash can beside a bed, tiny at first, but steadily flickering higher, fueled by wadded paper, soon reaching up to the wall and out to the bedcovers, and as they climbed higher and spread farther, Ronnie had clawed himself awake, frantically trying to escape their grasp.

The memory had returned soon after the dream first came to him. It was a few weeks before his father's death. His daddy had come to him, said he wanted him to see something. He took Ronnie to his bedroom and showed him a plastic waste basket close by the head of the bed. Something had been burned in it. The bottom and one side had melted. The wall above the container had been slightly charred and discolored by smoke.

"Your mother set that fire while I was sleeping," his father told him.

"That's crazy," Ronnie said. "You were drunk and smoking and you went to sleep and dropped a cigarette."

"Your mother put that there. It wasn't there when I went to bed. It's never been there before."

"You probably brought it in here thinking you might need something to throw up in and don't remember it. You don't remember half of what you do when you're drunk."

"Son," Thomas said, "your mother's trying to kill me."

"You're the one who's trying to kill yourself drinking," Ronnie told him.

In the shock and sorrow, conflict and confusion that had come with his father's death by fire only weeks afterward, Ronnie later said, no thought of what his father had shown him and told him came to his mind. He had suppressed it, he believed, perhaps because of the implications it had for his mother and his devotion to her, perhaps because it had seemed too incredible to be true. And it had remained suppressed until the dream had presented itself after her arrest.

His mother's stunning revelations to the police made him realize that his father no doubt had been correct, just as he now was sure that the later fires at his house had been set by his mother, too, surely for the insurance money to buy more drugs to obliterate what she had done.

Yet he never had been able to bring himself to confront her about this, had kept to himself the secret knowledge his father had revealed to him. The dream, however, had been a sporadic but relentlessly recurrent reminder that there was unfinished business between him and his mother.

And he was determined to deal with it on his next visit. When he met Pam at the prison on the following Saturday, he told her that he planned to ask about their dad's death.

"Are you sure you want to know?" he would recall her asking.

"I'm sure," he said.

He knew no better way to deal with it than directly.

"I've been wanting to ask you about Daddy," he told his mother. They were sitting in a classroom in the vocational building where they usually visited, side by side in cheap plastic chairs. Velma said nothing. Her hands were in her lap, and she stared at them. After long, silent moments, her eyes slowly rose to his.

"I've wondered if that was going to come up," she said, and offered no more.

"Well?" Ronnie asked.

She seemed reluctant to go on.

"No matter what you tell me, it's not going to affect how I feel about you," Ronnie said. "You're still my mother. I'll still love you. I'll still be here for you."

"What do you want to know?" she asked.

"Did you kill him?"

"I'm sure I probably did," she said.

Ronnie pressed for details.

"I can't remember everything," she said. She recalled that Thomas had come in drunk again that morning. They argued. He finished off a six-pack and passed out on the bed.

"I remember having something in my hand," she said. "A cigarette or a match. I remember laying it on the foot of the bed."

She closed the bedroom door, she said, left the house and went to the laundry.

That closed bedroom door had always haunted Ronnie. Ernest Hagins, the Parkton police officer, had told him that it had been closed when the firemen arrived. He knew that his father never closed the bedroom door. If the fire had been accidental, the door would have been open, and Sadie, the family's Siamese cat, who was devoted to his father, might have sensed the danger and jumped onto the bed and awakened him before the fire had a chance to spread. But Ronnie had said nothing about that at the time.

"You know I wasn't in my right mind," his mother told him.

"I know," Ronnie said.

"I guess I'd just had all I could take. I don't want you to hate me."

"I don't hate you," Ronnie said. "I just needed to know."

CHAPTER 23

Despite Velma's avowal to accept her fate, Jimmie Little and Richard Burr had fought too hard for too long to give up now. They wanted to come up with new, solid issues and try again in court. Two weeks before Velma's scheduled execution, Little went to talk with her about it.

He didn't want to give false hope, he said, but he did want her to consider the possibility of continuing the fight. She seemed amenable, but her major concern was what Ronnie and Pam would think. Little knew that Pam had been pushed to the emotional brink, and while Ronnie appeared to be resolute—on every visit Velma pressed on him the need to be strong for Pam, Faye and others—he seemed resigned to his mother's death on November 2.

Time was vital, and Little called Ronnie and Pam to tell them about the proposal. He wanted them to discuss it with him and their mother on their Saturday visit.

The call sent Ronnie into depression. He had been certain that no court was going to allow his mother to live. He had thought the ordeal soon would be over. He had been steeling himself for its inevitable end. Now the lawyers wanted to prolong it again.

On Saturday, Pam brought Beverly and Sarah to see their grandmother, and after the visit Little and Mary Ann Tally planned to take Ronnie, Pam and her girls to the state fair. Little bought a video camera so that he could tape the grandchildren at the fair to share with Velma.

Sister Teresa kept the children while Ronnie and Pam met with their mother and Little to discuss renewing the court fight. Not until Monday, when he got together with Burr and Tally, would they know if they had issues strong enough to plead, Little told them, but now he wanted Ronnie and Pam to tell their mother how they felt.

"The toughest thing about it from my perspective," he said, turning to Velma, "is a fear that they will feel that what you're basically asking us is to tell Mom whether we think she ought to die on November 2. I've told them that is not it. First of all, it is not going to be their decision. What I want them to do is just be honest with you."

Velma sipped water from a foam cup, pushed her glasses up, folded her hands and looked expectantly at her children.

Ronnie broke the uneasy silence. "Knowing everything the way I do, I don't want a stay," he said.

He felt the fight was over. He and Pam had done all they could in the drive for clemency, and it hadn't been enough.

"I just don't know how much more of it I could go through. I think I'll be okay. If you have to do something, you have to do it and you should do something the best you can. But unless it's a real solid reason—I think it should be *real* good—and I don't know that it's there."

He seemed to have run out of words.

"Like Ronnie said, it's been very hard," Pam said, picking up where he had stopped. "To be very honest, I don't know if I can go back through sixty or ninety more days like I have been through these last few weeks. It would have to be something good. I don't know. I don't know if I could go through it." Her voice was cracking. "God knows I want you to live. . . ."

Velma looked surprised, even shocked, but tried not to show it. "Well, I feel that way too, you know. I think, like I told Wade and John last Saturday, I would be very inhuman if I said that I don't want to live. I don't want to rush my death. I'm prepared. If there was an issue that can not only help me, but would help somebody else on death row . . ."

She had been receiving letters from other death-row inmates across the country, and Little and Burr had reminded her how her case might affect others.

". . . I'll be willing to even wait on that, but—"

Ronnie interrupted. "Let me ask you a tough question. If you knew that you could get a stay and that it may not help you but may help somebody on death row but you also knew that it may put Pam or myself through something really bad, would you—"

"No, I wouldn't want that," Velma quickly responded.

He was most worried about Pam and her family, Ronnie said. Because of his own failures, he envied her marriage, her family situation, and he didn't want anything to happen that might put that at risk.

"Well, I feel like she's gone through the heavier load than anybody," Velma acknowledged. "Where she lives. Can't even go to work in peace. I know that."

"I don't want you to make a decision based on how tough a time I'm having," Pam put in.

"This is what concerns me," said Ronnie. "If Pam does suffer a nervous breakdown, that's not going to affect just Pam. It's going to affect Kirby and those babies for the rest of their lives. I don't want that to happen."

As for himself, if a stay was granted and the battle continued, Ronnie said, he didn't think he could go on fighting.

"I am prepared so much for this day that if it is stayed, some people, I'm sure, would call me and say, 'I'm so glad, I heard you got a stay,' and I may just say, 'That's not what I want. You don't know what I want.' "

He had told Little that he didn't think any issue would stop the execution. Good issues had been raised but the courts had ignored them.

"You should know if you're going to die on November 2 without any thought of a stay," Ronnie told his mother. "It shouldn't even cross your mind, to me. I can't say that it doesn't disturb me sitting here today that it is crossing your mind," Ronnie went on, "and we're less than two weeks away. It scares the living hell out of me."

"Well, I have felt that November 2 would be the day."

"Will you think that when I walk out of here? Do you still feel like that right now?"

"I can't think of any issues. I really can't. Now I'm not saying that Dick and Mary Ann can't find—"

Pam spoke up. "Do you feel like, 'Well, I'll be out of the way, and people can go on with their lives.' Do you feel that way?"

"I feel like that would be a big burden gone, sure."

Still, Velma seemed to be searching for reasons to overcome her children's doubts. "I feel like everybody's more prepared for whatever happens," she said. "I know I am, if we went into another stay. I'm just as prepared for a flat no. . . . I think there's always a chance, that there's always some hope when you're in there digging for something, that we all never should lose hope, whatever our circumstances. But it's a slim, slim chance." She shook her head.

"This is the best I'm going to be prepared," Ronnie said. "And I don't know how I will react afterward. But you don't play with somebody's life like it's a game, and it's getting close to that. Not just yours, but Pam's and mine and the grandchildren."

Ronnie paused, the strain evident. His mother sat silently, look-ing at her hands. After several silent moments, he went on.

"And that's crazy because I wouldn't want you to walk into the room if our positions were switched and say that to me."

"Why?" Velma said, turning to Little with a smile, as if she were about to make a joke. "Wonder why he wouldn't want me to walk in and—" But then she seemed to realize that what she was saying was inappropriate and became suddenly somber. "I think we should say what we're thinking."

"It's just from being beat around for so long," Ronnie said, despair heavy in his voice. "I'm not too tired to go on, but I just know that I can't give any better effort than I've already given. I'm still trying to pull my own damn life back together, and it's been a struggle. It really has. Just to try to keep my sanity. And that's what I want to concentrate on doing—"

"And I want you to," Velma said. "No matter what happens."

"—in the way you told me to do it."

"I don't want nothing except that."

Little jumped in with questions about logistics. When did Ron-nie and Pam want to know about the decision, and how?

"I don't want to hear anything that's still up in the air," Ronnie said. "I can't stand it."

Little asked Velma if she thought she had a good enough under-standing of how Ronnie and Pam felt, and she said that she did. Did she want him to leave so they could talk privately?

"I think we've said everything," Velma said.

But Ronnie hadn't. He needed to clarify what he had said.

"I do want you to know this. I have tried to say what I said with-out emotion. But no man loves his mother any more than I do, and I know that. I also know what you taught me. And I know what you're concerned about. I know you want nothing to happen to this girl and your grandchildren, and I'm scared that it's getting close to that. If something happens to Pam, she may never be the same, and I'm worried about that. And I think that's the way you would want me to be. That's what you told me anyway. That's what I'm trying to do, what you want me to do."

"I know she would be less than human if it hadn't taken its toll on her," Velma said.

"It's taken its toll on me. . . ." Ronnie said.

Little jumped in again, joking, trying to lighten the mood.

But Ronnie's mood was too dark to overcome. He stood.

"She probably hates my guts for saying what I said," he said to nobody in particular, "but I feel like I had to say it."

"Ronnie, there's no part of me that has any hate for either one of you," his mother told him. "I would hope that I never have hate for anybody else."

"This time I think I'm right," Ronnie said. "I know what I'm saying, I believe in."

Ronnie was so despondent after the meeting that Sister Teresa sensed what he was thinking and took him aside for a talk.

"Ronnie," she told him, "it may never get any better for you, but don't give up on God."

As he drove back to South Carolina, he could not get her words out of his mind.

What if it truly never got better for him?

From the time of her conversion, Velma had talked to Ronnie about taking God into his life. She stressed it when he had come to her with his marriage problems. "Trust in God, but do your part," she told him. As the possibility of her execution had grown more real, she had become more emphatic. The only way to find true peace and happiness, she told him, was through God. It was the only way, too, that they could be together in eternity.

Ronnie wanted to believe that. He'd always believed in God, even if he had stopped going to church and hadn't been living in a way that some might think pleasing to God. In recent months he had turned back to his roots and started occasionally attending a Baptist church in Goose Creek. He prayed but somehow got the feeling that nobody was listening. He tried to find solace in reading scriptures his mother suggested, but they seemed hollow, and more often than not he put down his Bible and went out to the bars for solace.

In truth, Ronnie had begun to wonder whether God actually

existed. And if He did, why would He allow somebody to go through an ordeal such as he and Pam were now enduring? Why would He allow some people's lives to be so charmed, while others, no less deserving, got only misery?

His doubt only fed his guilt, and his guilt had never been greater than when he left the meeting in which—no matter Jimmie Little's disclaimer—he had told his mother that he wanted her to accept her death. He could never have dreamed that he would be in such a situation, or that he ever would tell his mother that he wanted her to die. Why had God, if He existed, put him in that position?

On Sunday night, Ronnie, Faye, Cliff and Faye's children gathered before the TV to watch a *60 Minutes* report about Velma. Jimmie Little had agreed to allow her to be interviewed, he later said, because the producer had assured him that the report would be anti-capital-punishment, although it turned out to be anything but that.

After the introduction by Diane Sawyer, the scene cut to a closeup of Velma's plump face. She nervously licked her lower lip, rolled her eyes, giving her a look of sneakiness.

"How many were there?" Sawyer asked softly.

"Three . . ." Velma said in a tiny voice, then cut her eyes away, as if she were having difficulty remembering how many people she had killed. "Four . . . four . . . three . . ."

She looked back, settling on three. A long pause followed while Velma stared calmly at the camera.

"Who were they?"

"My mother." She rolled her eyes again, as if searching her mind for other names. "Uh, Dollie Edwards. John Henry Lee, and Stuart Taylor. There was four."

The scene suddenly switched to a photograph of Stuart Taylor, and Alice Storms was there telling about her father's dying agonies.

Ronnie didn't want to watch anymore. He was disgusted. Not with the direction the report was taking, but with his mother. Here she was only days from execution, and she was being coy, pretending she couldn't remember how many people she had killed, or who they were, clearly enjoying the camera being on her. And how could her sincerity be trusted when she was practically staring God in the face and still being less than truthful? She had killed five people for certain, likely six.

She had never admitted killing Jennings Barfield, but she had acknowledged to Ronnie during the trial that it was possible. He had been troubled by testimony that arsenic had killed Jennings and asked her about it. Despite her sharp denials from the stand, Velma told him, "Ronnie, I may have done it, but if I did, I don't remember it."

Unknown to Ronnie, though, she had recently admitted this murder as well. Cecil Murphey, a Presbyterian minister in Atlanta who had written twenty-five religious books, had begun working on a book with Velma. The idea had been Ruth Graham's. She had proposed that Velma allow a book to be written as a testament to her faith. It would help so many others who were down and out and in need of Jesus, she suggested. Velma agreed, and Graham called her friend Victor Oliver, president of Oliver-Nelson Books in Nashville, Tennessee. After visiting Velma, Oliver assigned Murphey to write the book.

For the past three Fridays, Murphey had been interviewing Velma for at least six hours at a time, then returning to Atlanta and writing like mad getting material ready for her to review. He had asked Velma outright if she had poisoned Jennings.

"Oh, no," she had told him. "He had emphysema, diabetes and cancer."

Something about that answer didn't set right with Murphey, and he played the tape several times.

"It was something about her voice," he later recalled. "I knew it wasn't right."

At their next session, Murphey told Velma, "Before we start on the new stuff, I want to go back to one thing. Tell me again about Mr. Barfield's death."

"When she finished," he later recalled, "I said, 'Velma, it's not right.' She said, 'What do you mean?' I said, 'You killed him.' There was this shock on her face. She looked at me for a minute, then she nodded slowly. She said, 'I'm so glad. Now there's nothing left to confess.' " She had put the arsenic in Jennings' medicine, she told him.

Her admission caused him to question her more closely about Thomas's death as well. She stuck to her earlier story that he had passed out and dropped a cigarette. But she admitted that she knew it had happened, and she had closed the bedroom door and left the house.

"I didn't kill him," Murphey would remember her saying, "but I allowed him to die."

Neither of these admissions would appear in the quickly produced paperback that Murphey would write under Velma's name. He included them, he later said, but they were cut by the editors. Velma's book was to be about faith, not about murder, and later hundreds of thousands of copies would be distributed free by the Billy Graham ministry.

Velma would turn fifty-two on Monday, October 29. By then she likely would be back on death watch at Central Prison. A week before her birthday, with her execution only ten days away, Velma was taken from her cell without being told why. She soon learned the reason: a surprise birthday party attended by almost all the inmates and many staff members. There were two birthday cakes, balloons everywhere, lots of party food. Velma's birthday card was two feet long and bore so many signatures that other pages had to be attached to it. Many inmates who had left the prison also sent cards.

As inmates crowded around, hugging her and wishing her well, Velma fought back tears. She did cry when she spotted one face: Beth, the teenager who had been put in the cell beside her years earlier. Beth had spent most of the past four years at two youth institutions but had been returned to Women's Prison in February and now worked in the canteen. She rarely got to see Velma but regularly sent her messages and still called her Mama Margie.

Later, Velma would write that a single word kept coming to mind as she greeted everybody at her party: family. Family and love could be found anywhere, she realized, even in prison.

Richard Burr flew from Palm Beach to Raleigh that Monday. Soon after clemency was denied, the controversial defense attorney William Kunstler had attempted to enter Velma's case. Burr had cut him off by asking his help in finding new issues to raise. He had spent part of the weekend with a lawyer from Kunstler's office, Ron Kuby, reviewing the case. Now he was bringing the recommendations back to Raleigh.

Kuby had found six issues that might be the basis of further litigation. But two of them—ineffective counsel and the improper exclusion of a juror—already had been argued all the way through the courts to no avail. Two others—that Velma had not properly waived her rights when she confessed to the police, and that her execution had been set just four days before the election—probably weren't strong enough to save her. But the other two had potential.

First was Velma's incompetence to stand trial because of her addiction to Valium and other drugs. At the time of her trial Valium's addictiveness was still largely unknown. This had been the focus of Little's clemency plea to the governor, but it never had been brought up in court.

Second was prosecutorial misconduct. "Britt's comportment was challenged only briefly on direct appeal, and apparently not at all in federal habeas corpus," Kuby wrote. "He does not deserve to get off so lightly. His summation was replete with inflamed calls for vengeance, discourses about victims in general, ridicule and viciousness."

"What you got to say, Jimmie?" Velma asked teasingly when he, Burr and Tally got together with Velma late Monday afternoon.

"I'm going to ask Dick," Little said. "Let him talk."

Velma looked expectantly at Burr.

"Well," he said, "I think we're here to recommend that we try to stop it."

He told her about the two new issues that he considered to have special merit.

Velma still had not recovered from her disturbing session with Ronnie and Pam on Saturday, however, and she was reluctant to commit. "I think Pam will be okay," she said. "I don't live with her so I don't know. I hear two stories. I don't know what's going on."

Little noted that nothing would be expected from Pam and Ronnie in a new appeal, except for their forbearance of the strain of delay and continued uncertainty.

But Velma remained hesitant, clearly torn, and there were long silences. When Velma still couldn't come to terms with her reluctance, the lawyers took a break to give her time to think.

"Well, what do you want us to do, Velma?" Little said when they returned. "You want us to stay around?"

Clearly, she wanted to give them the go-ahead, which was what they were hoping to hear, but she wanted to talk to Ronnie and Pam again first.

"It's just not good to not have hope," she said. "I think you have to hang onto hope. I believe in that strongly. I have hope and I'm going to continue to have hope."

"Of course, I don't want you to have so much hope that November 2 is no longer a reality," Little told her.

He reminded her that four other death penalty cases had been at the same stage as hers at the same time, and three of those people were now dead. Her odds were not good, even if she decided to proceed.

He wanted her to call after she'd talked with Ronnie and Pam. Time was of the essence. The lawyers would have to begin preparing their case if they were to have any chance at all. Much work had to be done.

Velma did talk to Ronnie and Pam that night, telling them that the lawyers wanted to seek another stay, that they had solid issues. Neither gave an endorsement. Both told her that she knew how they felt, but it was her decision. Ronnie could tell that she was being beguiled by false hope, and he wanted no part of that.

Velma still hadn't reached a decision when the lawyers returned to the prison Tuesday morning. But she agreed to a proposal made by Little. She would allow them to draw up the new motion for appropriate relief, but she would decide later whether they could actually file it.

Meanwhile, another decision had to be made. Did she want to die by gas or by lethal injection? The warden at Central Prison would be coming on Wednesday to explain the differences between the two methods. Little would be there to help her decide.

If Velma chose cyanide gas, she would have to sit facing the witnesses until the leather restraining hood was placed over her head. If she chose lethal injection, she would be rolled into the death chamber already strapped to a gurney. She could turn her head if she chose and would never have to look toward the witnesses. If she chose lethal injection, she would first be given sodium pentothal to put her to sleep, than a paralyzing agent, Pavulon, would stop her heart.

She picked lethal injection. Drugs had ruined her life. Now, years after she had spurned them for good, they finally would end it.

On Friday, with her execution little more than six days away, Velma told Little and Burr to proceed with the new appeal.

But Ronnie did not know that when he arrived Saturday for what he thought would be his last visit with his mother at Women's

Prison before her removal again to Central. He noticed that she seemed nervous. And she wasted no time in letting him know why.

"Jimmie and Dick think they've got some really good issues this time," she said, "and I've told them to go ahead."

Ronnie sprang to his feet. "Goddammit!" he yelled. He had never used that word in front of his mother, but he was outraged. He was furious. He stared his mother straight in the eye. "You're going to die next Friday morning," he told her, his voice as filled with thunder as Joe Freeman Britt's ever had been. "I've accepted that. And it's time that you and your goddamned attorneys accept it, because nothing's going to change it!"

He could no longer be a part of this charade, he said. He only hoped that Pam survived it. As his mother burst into tears, he stormed out.

He would not be back.

PART VI

Dying Grace

CHAPTER 24

The call came shortly before nine Sunday evening. Phil Carter was needed at work. He didn't have to ask why. He had been alerted Friday that Velma likely would be moved over the weekend, but for security reasons the Department of Correction was keeping the time secret.

By the time he got to the prison, Velma's cell in Dorm C had already been emptied. She was handcuffed and waiting for a caravan of beige DOC cars to deliver her again to death watch at Central Prison. This time the move had been expected, and Velma was prepared.

Carter had no time to talk with her. The caravan was ready to roll. Raleigh police cars with blue lights flashing rushed ahead to block intersections so the caravan could pass unimpeded. The whole thing seemed surreal and unnecessary to Carter. Did the department think some ACLU commando squad might be lurking in the darkness to try to snatch Velma from their grasp?

Central Prison sprawled over twenty-two acres on the southeastern edge of downtown Raleigh. Hulking behind multiple rows of razor-wire–topped fences in a valley by Walnut Creek, the prison was squat—just four levels high—with numerous wings, each secured from the others. Just two years old, modern and utilitarian in design, its facade was of beige-pebbled precast concrete. At night, the prison was brilliantly illuminated, none of its many odd angles escaping the light, so that the guards in the watch towers could see every nook and cranny.

The caravan arrived shortly before ten, four days and four hours before Velma's scheduled execution. While Velma was being processed, Carter and Jennie Lancaster went to the administrative offices to meet with Warden Nathan Rice.

Forty-four years old, Rice had started at the prison as a guard in 1961 and had risen through the ranks to the top job just two and a half years earlier. In his twenty-three years on the job, Rice had survived a 1968 riot in which six inmates had been killed and eighty guards and inmates injured, had served as chief negotiator when three inmates had taken six staff members and two inmates hostage. But nothing, he later would say, had been as difficult for him as being responsible for executions.

"When you see that person lying on the gurney and knowing you have to give the word, there are very few things in life that give that amount of stress," he told a reporter. "That is not a political statement, it is fact."

His first execution had been made no easier because James Hutchins had been a difficult prisoner, angry to the end, who had told Rice shortly beforehand, "I hope I see you in hell when this is over." But the execution now facing him promised to be even more difficult. Velma was a woman beloved by many, a woman supposedly redeemed, a Christian supported by Billy and Ruth Graham, a woman who already had forgiven him for the role he might soon be playing. And nobody had to tell him that much of the world would be watching when he did it.

When Velma arrived in the death-watch area, she was not the stunned, frightened and dejected creature she had been when she had first been brought there four and a half months earlier. She joked with the female guards who had been brought from a prison hospital in Hoke County to oversee her. She knew them. They were the same guards who had attended her when she had been on death watch in June. Carol Oliver was the captain of the guard. She had met Velma several years earlier at Women's Prison, and she came to her cell to greet her. Velma seemed pleased to see her. It was after her bedtime, she told Oliver with a laugh. All of this commotion was disrupting her sleep.

This time Velma was assigned Cell B, next to the one she had occupied previously. She had been there a few minutes when Rice arrived, all business, with Lancaster and Carter to tell her what to expect, just as he had done in June. After he departed, Lancaster and Carter stayed to make sure that she was okay. Velma urged them to go on home; they had done enough for her already.

As soon as they left, Velma sent out to the canteen for a Coke, a Milky Way and a pack of Salems (the cigarettes were for dignity;

she smoked one only when she used the toilet to mask any odor
that might offend her keepers). Guards also brought to her cell the
toilet items, night clothes and Bible she had been allowed to bring
with her. Her other personal belongings—her books, a borrowed
tape player, tapes, cosmetics, hair rollers and brush—had not yet
been sent from Women's Prison, and she was worried about them.
Jimmie Little was supposed to come in the morning and she was
not about to let him see her without makeup, her hair in a mess.

Velma finally got to bed after nurses brought medicines for her
stomach and angina near eleven-thirty. Before midnight she was
fast asleep.

She woke early, coughing, on her fifty-second birthday, Monday,
October 29, her execution now less than four days away.

"Is it about six-thirty?" she called to a guard.

"Six-o-six," the guard replied.

On Friday, Jimmie Little had granted a final TV interview with
Velma to ABC News, hoping to counter the less-than-helpful
report on *60 Minutes* two weeks earlier, and it was scheduled to
appear on *Good Morning America* this day. Velma wanted to
watch it. A small TV had been brought into the day room and
placed on a shelf by the glass-enclosed control room. Velma could
see it from her cell. She told the guard stationed just outside her cell
that she'd like to have the TV turned on shortly before seven.

"If I go back to sleep, call me," she said.

"She appears to be in good spirits," the guard in the control
room wrote in the log.

Velma didn't go back to sleep because a nurse soon arrived with
her medicines. She got up then and sat on her bunk, legs folded
beneath her, reading her Bible.

One of the guards turned on the TV just as a new shift was arriving. The report about Velma did not appear until twelve minutes
into the show. She stood at the narrow window of her cell door,
intently watching herself telling the interviewer, "My attorneys
have some issues they will be filing Monday. It would give a stay
and hopefully the courts will look at the issues."

Anybody watching could see that Velma did not appear to be a
woman who thought that she would die this week.

"I have hope in what my attorneys will be filing," she was saying. "I feel that we should cling to hope."

*   *   *

In Goose Creek, Ronnie was watching with no hope at all, still convinced that his mother was fooling herself. The interview had been taped before he had learned that she intended to go ahead with the new appeals.

He had been deeply depressed since he yelled at her and stormed away from the prison Saturday. On the way back to South Carolina, he hadn't been able to escape the feeling that he had betrayed his mother. How many times had he promised that he would always be there for her, that he would stand by her to the end, no matter what? And yet at this great moment of her need, he had cursed her, turned his back and abandoned her because of his own pain and weakness.

His guilt and despair had been so great as he drove back home that the thought crossed his mind that he could end it with a simple turn of the wheel into the face of an oncoming tractor-trailer. Yet something prevented him from following that grisly impulse.

On Sunday, Jimmie Little called. "I was very firm with him," Little later remembered. "I said, 'This isn't about you. This is about your mother. As awful as it is, you're just going to have to deal with the consequences. She had to make her own decision. If this doesn't work, she's going to need you here.' "

Ronnie knew that he was right. He apologized for his outburst. Later, his mother called.

"Are you still mad?" she asked.

"It's not anger at you, Mama," he said. "It's just the process, the system."

"I can see now the hurt you've been holding back," she told him. "I know what I've put y'all through. If I could do anything to change it I would."

"I know that."

She wanted to live, Velma went on to explain, and if there was a chance, she had to take it, as much for her attorneys' sake as for her own. Jimmie and Dick had worked so hard for so long with never a cent of pay, putting out their own money for expenses. She could not deny them one last attempt to save her. She could not let them go through the rest of their lives thinking that if they had done one more thing they might have won, she might have lived.

"I understand," Ronnie said. He felt bad about his own anger toward them, the sharp things he had said.

"Ronnie, you will come back, won't you?"

"Mama, if it looks like it's going to happen, you know I'll be there."

The weekend had proved frenetic for Little and Burr. Researching, plotting, writing motions, making scores of telephone calls, gathering documents, talking with Velma, dealing with her family problems. Mary Ann Tally had come to help as had four other young lawyers. They had worked relentlessly through the weekend in Little's small apartment, taking breaks only to eat and catch a couple of hours' sleep.

By Monday morning, they had completed a motion for appropriate relief that was fifty-five pages long, backed by a thick sheaf of documents, including the psychiatric report by Dr. Dorothy Lewis.

To start the appeals again, Burr and Little had to raise new issues that could not have been known to them when they had filed their original motion more than four years earlier. They cited six. Three had been raised before, but new questions about them had since developed.

Their strongest issue was that Velma had been incompetent to stand trial because of withdrawal from Valium addiction and underlying mental disorders that had only been diagnosed in recent months. Valium addiction was not even known to the medical establishment at the time of the trial, they noted, and was just beginning to be recognized when they had filed their original motion.

Burr and Little also raised the issue of Joe Freeman Britt's final argument to the jury, claiming it had been inflammatory and prejudicial, making it impossible for the jurors to consider Velma as an individual. Both prepared affidavits saying that they had not raised the issue earlier because they thought they could only do so if Britt's argument had been so egregious that it dominated the whole proceedings. At the time, they had known of no legal theory on which the issue could be based, but a Supreme Court ruling in a 1983 case now made it possible.

When Jimmie Little visited that morning, Velma thought he looked exhausted, and she was concerned about him (in fact, he was in serious pain from kidney stones, but he didn't let her know). The motions for a stay and for a new hearing had been filed an hour earlier with the Superior Court in Robeson County, he told her.

The judge holding court there this week, B. Craig Ellis, had not previously dealt with the case. He had only been on the bench since January, appointed by Governor Hunt, and was facing election for the first time in the coming week. There was no way to know how he might react.

With the execution now less than four days away, the judge probably would move swiftly. If he decided not to grant the stay, they already were preparing documents to take straight to the state Supreme Court. If that failed, they would move on to Judge Dupree in Federal District Court, then back to the Fourth Circuit again. After that, they would have one last shot at the U.S. Supreme Court. Somewhere along the way, they might get a stay.

Little was still concerned that Velma not raise her hopes so high that she deny the reality of two a.m. Friday. She assured him that she was prepared, no matter which way it went.

After Little left, the Roanes arrived and set up their portable, battery-powered organ in one of the tiny, cramped visitor cubicles. Soon Gales Roane's exuberant play and Sam's thunderous bass voice echoed through the visiting area while Velma, separated from them by thick glass, sang along happily.

Velma returned to her cell for lunch before going off for another visit, this time with Lao Rupert of the North Carolina Coalition on Prisons and Jails, who had been coming to see her regularly since her arrival in prison nearly six years earlier.

After that visit, Velma took a brief nap, then turned to her mail. Several packets of cards, letters and telegrams had arrived so far this day, mostly from strangers, and the quantity would grow greatly as the week wore on.

Shortly before four, Skip Pike entered the death-watch area. This was the third time he'd dropped by this day. He'd come early in the morning to find out when Velma would have time to talk with him—maybe in late afternoon, she'd told him—and he'd returned again, grinning, just as she was leaving to see the Roanes before noon. That time he had brought a birthday card signed by all the men on death row.

Pike was thirty-six, a wiry, energetic, talkative man who had given his life to God, the imprisoned and condemned. In July, he had transferred to the chaplain staff at Central, by far the state's largest prison. Just a few weeks earlier, when the chaplain had retired, Pike had been appointed to his position. In his four months at Central, he had taken a special interest in the men on death row, getting to know each individually. But he had not faced an execution, and he was nervous and anxious now that Velma's was only days away.

Pike was a close friend of Phil Carter and Jennie Lancaster and had had many conversations with them about Velma. But he had not met her until a couple of weeks earlier, when he had gone to Women's Prison so that Carter could introduce them.

"We just had the very best time," he recalled later. "She was so open. There wasn't anything I asked that she wasn't more than willing to go into. I had never encountered a human being living under the sentence of death who had so much grace and compassion for all people. It didn't matter if it was the prosecutor, the people at the attorney general's office, the judges or the people who were so adamantly in favor of her being executed, she showed the same understanding and love for them all."

Now Pike sat chatting with Velma on the bunk in her tiny, grim cell, only eighty-two hours from her scheduled execution, and he was astounded that he still saw no anxiety, no fear, no bitterness, no apparent concern for herself. While he was there, her canteen order arrived: two Cokes, bags of potato chips, Fritos, Cheez Doodles, two Snickers bars.

"I'm loading up for when they have fish and corned beef and that awful ol' breaded veal," she said with a laugh. "I can't stand those."

Jennie Lancaster arrived with Rivka Gordon, the medical director at Women's Prison, who also had become close to Velma. They visited for an hour after Pike left, and one of the guards on duty noted of Velma in the log while they were there, "Seems to be in good spirits . . . laughing a lot."

The guards, seeing Velma in such ease and good cheer, could only think that she believed she soon would be getting a stay and leaving this place. She simply didn't seem to be a woman facing death.

Phil Carter came after Lancaster and Gordon left and stayed to watch the beginning of the local TV news. The lead story was about Velma's new appeal, and at the end the reporter noted that she wasn't the only prisoner facing imminent execution. Two others in different parts of the country were scheduled to die that very night.

"That's enough of the news," Velma told the guard. "You can turn that off."

Among her belongings were three boxes of note cards and two sheets of stamps and, after Carter left, she asked the guards for those, saying she had a lot of writing to do. She also requested the tape player that Carter had loaned her and a tape of hymns by George Beverly Shea, one of several that Ruth Graham had sent recently.

"Isn't that tape beautiful?" she asked a guard as she sat on her bunk writing notes of thanks to people who had taken an interest in her during her years in prison. She wrote for two hours, and when she handed a stack of stamped envelopes to the guard, asking that they be taken to the mailroom, the guard noted that the envelope on top was addressed to Ruth Graham.

"I'm going to try to sleep," Velma told her. It was ten-thirty.

"If you need anything," said the guard, "let me know."

"Thank you. I will. Good night."

Twenty minutes later, Velma was asleep, and an hour after that she was snoring loudly. She slept soundly as the condemned men in Texas and Louisiana were put to death.

Years later, Pam would have few memories of this awful week, most of them erased by pain and sorrow.

"There are so many blanks," she said. "I was on the verge of a nervous breakdown. It was all I could do to function, to get up, get the kids dressed. I was just totally wiped out."

Raleigh Times reporter Sharon Kilby called Tuesday morning, hoping to get Pam's reaction to the new appeal, but she didn't want to talk to anybody.

"She's burned out on the press," Kirby said.

What did they expect from the hearing? Kilby asked.

"We're not hopeful at all. We've been up and down this thing so many times we've just become calloused. Our eyes are fixed on November 2. That's reality to us."

Kilby also called Faye, who, while emotional, was at least able to talk.

"You don't know what to get prepared for. If I start building my hopes up on the appeal, it'll be just like it was with the clemency decision. I just got this feeling everything would be all right and she would get it. At this point, I'm scared to hope."

Velma had a satisfying visit with Anne Lotz Tuesday morning. She told Lotz that she didn't want any of her family to witness her execution because she knew that image would never leave them, and she wanted them to remember her as she was in happier times. Lotz didn't want Velma to be surrounded only by strangers at her death. If it would be any comfort, or make it any easier, she said, she was willing to be there. Velma accepted.

But something else that Lotz said on this visit would prove to be of even more comfort to Velma.

"Velma, don't think of it as the execution chamber," Lotz told her. "Think of it as the gateway to heaven."

In coming days, Velma would repeat that to many people.

Lotz had just finished her visit and was on her way to the warden's office to add her name to the witness list as Judge Craig Ellis was opening the hearing on Velma's motions in Lumberton shortly after eleven. Joe Freeman Britt had filed the state's answer that morning. "The apparent purpose for this motion is simply to stay or delay the pending execution," said the brief. "This court ought not permit this clear abuse of the motion for appropriate relief provisions."

The response was accompanied by affidavits signed by Velma's original attorney, Bob Jacobson, and the trial judge, Henry McKinnon, both saying that they saw no signs that Velma was suffering from drug withdrawal during her trial. McKinnon said that Velma "appeared to be unemotional, stolid and undemonstrative" and that her testimony had been lucid and responsive.

"It was clear that she understood the nature of the charges against her and the nature of the proceedings," said Jacobson. "She was able to relate to me in a reasonable and rational way and to assist me in providing for her defense."

Judge Ellis told Velma's lawyers that he had reviewed their arguments and found them unconvincing. The issues they'd raised already had been resolved or had been waived by their failure to raise them earlier.

"There is no merit to any allegations which suggest that a new trial be granted," he said.

The proceeding lasted only fifteen minutes, and when reporters crowded around Britt afterward to ask his reaction, he responded almost tauntingly.

"We had expected an attack," he said, "but when it came we didn't expect it to be so feeble."

The outcome was no surprise to Burr. He went to a telephone to call Little in Raleigh. Forty minutes later, Little filed a twenty-page motion with the clerk of the Supreme Court, seeking a stay and appealing Ellis' decision.

Velma ate only half of her lunch Tuesday. She had heard nothing about her appeal and asked that the TV be turned on so that she could see the news. But the news had already gone off and the regular programming had resumed.

"Oh, it's just that ol' soap opera lovin'," she said. "You can turn that off."

She asked instead for her radio and tuned it to a talk-news station. An hour later, while she was examining legal papers sent by Little, she heard that Judge Ellis had denied her appeal.

She turned off the radio then. "I've heard what I wanted to hear," she said and asked for her tape player and hymns.

"Appears relaxed and calm," a guard noted in the log.

Velma spent the afternoon reading the most recent chapters of her book, which Cecil Murphey had sent. Murphey's final interview had been only four days earlier and he was writing more even as she read.

Supper came early, and it was Velma's nightmare: the awful breaded veal with gravy. She was wetting her face with a washcloth when it arrived, and she held the cloth over her mouth and nearly gagged when she saw it. "I don't eat that stuff," she said.

She did eat the salad, though, and a couple of bites of potatoes. She was finishing off the chocolate ice cream when Rivka Gordon arrived. They watched the local TV news, learning that at that very moment the state supreme court was again considering Velma's fate.

Velma sent out for a canteen order, offering a five-dollar bill in payment, and soon Jennie Lancaster appeared. The cell was filled with talk and laughter. Halloween, which would be the next day, was the subject for a while, the guards noted.

At six-thirty, a guard came to tell Lancaster that the warden needed to speak with her by telephone. She returned with news, but a bulletin flashed on the TV before she could deliver it.

"The North Carolina Supreme Court has just refused a stay of execution for convicted killer Velma Barfield," the anchorman announced dramatically. He went on to report that Velma's lawyers would be taking her appeal to the federal courts.

"There was a moment of silence," a guard wrote in the log, before conversation resumed in the cell. "Barfield still seems to be in good spirits," the guard noted.

At nine, Velma spent more than a hour with Jimmie Little, learning about the less-than-hopeful events of the day. He had been late in arriving because he first had to go to the home of the federal court clerk to deliver the documents that would put the federal appeal in motion.

Velma returned to her cell in remarkably high spirits, and afterward she laughed and talked with her guards. She told about the big birthday party at Women's Prison, how good it had made her feel and what good people were there, both staff and inmates. She even started talking about her execution, now just fifty-two hours away. Nobody should feel sorry for her because of that, she said. It would not be a sad event if it came about, but a glorious one, an awakening to a far better life in a far better place. Her guards had no doubt that she was convinced of that.

After showering and brushing her teeth, Velma requested a pen and a special box of cards among her possessions. She needed to do some writing, she said, but she didn't know how many cards she could get to. "My eyelids are awfully heavy."

An hour later, Velma was still writing, and her mood had shifted. She seemed distant and sad when a guard came to tell her that she had to finish because the lights had to be turned down. Velma quickly read over the card she had just finished and tucked it into an envelope. It was a special one. If she were executed, it would be her final message to Jimmie Little.

By midnight, Velma was asleep and soon was snoring. But when a guard peered into her cell at 3:20, she saw something that startled her. Velma was on her back with her head tilted slightly to the right, her mouth open. She appeared to be sleeping, but her whole body was trembling. The guard alerted her superiors, who came quickly and ordered the cell door opened. The sound of the door roused Velma.

"Are you okay?" asked one of the guards.

"Yes, I'm fine," Velma answered.

"Okay, just checking."

The guard was ordered to keep a close watch and report any changes. Velma seemed to doze off again, but twenty minutes later she got up to use the toilet and was unable to go back to sleep. She asked for hot water, instant coffee and creamer. She also wanted the lights turned up so she could read, but master control ruled that was against policy. For an hour, she sat on her bunk, sipping her coffee and staring at the concrete block wall, seemingly deep in thought. Finally, she picked up her Bible and tried to read in the dim light. At 5:47, a guard noted in the log that Velma was on her knees beside her bunk, praying fervently.

The lights came on at six, and when a nurse brought her medicine at 6:30, Velma was still reading her Bible.

"Any problems?" the nurse inquired.

"No, I'm all right," Velma said.

After her morning session with the Roanes Wednesday, Velma returned to face some unpleasant business. The warden was coming to talk about final visits and the schedule for the next day, her last if the federal courts didn't intervene. He would be followed by two technicians who would explain the execution procedures in detail.

Jennie Lancaster came to be with Velma during this, as did Phil Carter and Skip Pike.

She would be escorted from her cell fifty minutes before the execution hour, the technicians told her. She would be taken to a preparation room and placed on a gurney. Her wrists and ankles would be secured with lined straps.

A cardiac monitor and a stethoscope would be attached to her chest and intravenous lines would be inserted in each arm. One problem might arise: Good veins had to be found for the needles in time to keep the execution's precisely timed schedule. That was troublesome sometimes with people as plump as Velma. If good veins could not be found, a local anesthetic would be administered and incisions made—a "cut down" the technicians called this, but they didn't use those words with her.

A saline solution would drip from intravenous bags mounted on the gurney to keep the veins open. Velma would have time with the chaplains and to make a final statement before being rolled into the chamber. She would be in the chamber, visible to the witnesses, for about ten minutes before the execution began.

Upon the warden's signal, sodium pentothal would be injected into the intravenous lines. Velma would fall asleep almost instantly. Only then would pancuronium bromide, a total muscle relaxant called Pavulon, begin to flow into her veins. Within minutes, Velma's breath and heartbeat would gradually stop. There should be no pain, other than that which came from inserting the intravenous needles at the beginning.

Velma would simply go to sleep in the gas chamber and wake up in heaven.

Noon newscasts and afternoon newspapers carried reports Wednesday that former Watergate conspirator Charles Colson, who had started a prison ministry after serving seven months for obstruction of justice, had called on Governor Hunt to stop Velma's execution. "Let not Mrs. Barfield be remembered as the first American executed for partisan political reasons," Colson said in a telegram. "I plead with you to spare yourself, your state and our country the awful charge that in U.S. politics human life is cheap when compared to votes."

Many others shared Colson's view. Amnesty International sent representatives to the governor's office. And hundreds of letters and telegrams were still arriving daily from throughout the world, asking that Hunt change his mind.

The support committee had reserved rooms at the Hilton near North Carolina State University, less than a mile from the prison, for Ronnie, Pam and Kirby, Faye and Cliff on Wednesday and Thursday nights. Jimmie Little and Richard Burr also had rooms there. Pam and Kirby, and Faye and Cliff arrived at the hotel shortly after noon Wednesday. Ronnie had remained behind, planning to come only when he knew for certain that the execution would take place.

When Little learned of Ronnie's decision, he called him at work in Charleston. "I think you need to come on up," he said. Ronnie knew that Little's faith in these final appeals was really no greater than his own. He would be there tonight, Ronnie told him.

Little had arranged for Pam and Kirby to have an hour-long visit with Velma at 3:30 that afternoon. Years later, Pam would have little recall, remembering only that the visit was highly emotional. She would remember her mother telling her again how bad she felt about letting her children down and tearing their lives apart.

"I said, 'Look, Mama, I think I turned out okay, and it's not me that's the reason I turned out this way. It's you, Mama.' "

On the way back to her cell, Velma remarked to her guards that she thought the visit had gone well.

Soon afterward, the captain of the guard, Carol Oliver, appeared at Velma's cell with a gift. Earlier that day, Oliver had told Velma that if she had any special request—anything within reason—the warden wanted to see that it was granted. Well, for one thing, Velma said, laughing, he could have Kit-Kat bars put in the prison canteen. That was her favorite candy and the canteen didn't have it. That afternoon, Rice had sent up the street to the 7–Eleven for two Kit-Kat bars, and now Oliver handed them to Velma.

"From the warden," she said.

"He didn't have to do that," Velma said, all smiles.

Oliver remained to chat, and Velma started talking about her visit with her daughter. Pam was such a good, sweet girl, she said. Nobody could have asked for a finer daughter. "You wouldn't even know she belongs to me, she's so tall and pretty," Velma added with a chuckle.

Supper was early again, chicken and dumplings, and after it arrived, the warden came to talk about final arrangements for Thursday and to ask if Velma had special requests for her last meal. She would just have whatever everybody else was getting, she said, and thanked him for the candy bars.

Velma returned the nearly full supper tray just as Skip Pike showed up to see how she was doing. They talked for half an hour, and before he left, he asked if he could pray with her.

Did she have any special prayer requests? Only that he pray for her children, grandchildren and the rest of her family that their pain might be relieved.

"Never once did she ask me to pray that God somehow deliver her from execution," Pike later recalled. "She never asked me to pray that God change the minds of the judges. Whenever we prayed, the only thing she really desired was that God forgive her and give her the grace to walk through that process with dignity, with her head up and with firm assurance that her foundation in Christ was the solid rock upon which she stood."

As Pike was leaving, Judge Franklin Dupree was just ending his two-hour hearing on Velma's appeal in the federal building across town.

Dick Burr had argued fervently to Dupree that Velma's drug withdrawal had produced such irrational behavior during her trial that it was proof that she was incapable of understanding the proceedings and cooperating in her defense.

"She got on the witness stand and argued that arsenic poisoning could not kill someone," he said. "Then she applauded the district attorney."

The combativeness and bizarre behavior produced by the drug withdrawal had given the jury an unfair impression of her, he maintained. "It was a picture that destined her to be sentenced to death."

Judge Dupree didn't hand down an immediate decision. He wanted to go to his chambers to review the arguments and think about it.

After returning from the shower, Velma asked that the TV be turned on so that she could listen for news bulletins. She began rolling her hair, and after she'd finished, she requested a pen and her special box of cards. She grew quiet and pensive as she wrote.

When the news bulletin came at eight saying that Judge Dupree had rejected her appeal, Velma did not even turn toward the TV. She paused only a second and went right on writing her final message to her daughter. Her execution was now less than thirty hours away.

As hopeless as the judge's decision may have sounded to Velma, her lawyers actually were heartened by it. The judge had issued a probable cause certificate with his ruling, alerting the Fourth Circuit Court of Appeals that the primary issue, Velma's competency to stand trial, had substance and should be seriously considered.

Here at last was a ray of hope that Velma might be spared—at least temporarily.

CHAPTER 25

Ronnie hadn't had a drink since his angry visit with his mother Saturday. If she was going to be executed this week—and he still had no doubt of that—he wanted to face it clear-headed. He had to show her that he could be the strong and reliable person she wanted him to be.

After Jimmie Little's call Wednesday afternoon, Ronnie didn't get away from Charleston until late. He was passing through Fayetteville three hours later when he heard on the radio that Judge Dupree had rejected his mother's appeal. He turned off the radio and drove on to Raleigh in silence, deep in thought, trying to imagine what lay ahead, how he would react, but it was all too alien to picture.

He didn't know Raleigh well and had trouble finding the Hilton. It was after ten before he checked in. He encountered Sister Teresa in the lobby, hugged her and thanked her for all that she had done for his mother.

Richard Burr was on his way to Richmond, Ronnie learned. The Fourth Circuit Court had set a hearing for 8:30 the next morning. Jimmie Little was at Central Prison with Velma. Mary Ann Tally's husband, John, had prepared a will and sent it from Fayetteville by bus a few hours earlier. Little was discussing it with her. Pam and Kirby were in a room upstairs, as were Faye and Cliff, and Sister Teresa directed Ronnie there.

Both Pam and Faye were taking Valium, and everybody had been drinking, Ronnie discovered when he got to his sister's room. He got the feeling that Pam and Faye still believed that this was not going to happen, that the Fourth Circuit Court would intervene in the morning and they'd all go back home.

*   *   *

Velma slept soundly through the night, not knowing for certain whether it would be her last on earth. She awoke only once, at two-thirty.

"You okay?" asked the guard.

"Yes," she replied and returned quickly to sleep.

She did not stir again until after six when she coughed, sat up and asked for hot water and instant coffee.

"I really slept well," she told the guard who brought the coffee. "Must've been because I didn't sleep much night before last."

Later, she would joke and laugh about how hard she'd slept.

She read her Bible while she sipped the coffee.

"Appears to be very calm," a departing guard noted in the log, well aware that she might never see Velma again, that barring some last-minute intervention, in just nineteen hours Velma would be dead.

When the new guards arrived at seven, Velma requested her hair rollers and more coffee. Fifteen minutes later, she had finished rolling her hair and was reading the mail she hadn't gotten to the day before.

This would be Velma's busiest day yet on death watch. Visits were to begin at nine with the Roanes and end at five when she would say good-bye to her children. Velma had asked for her writing materials and address book, and she was working on a letter when a guard reminded her that she needed to get dressed.

By nine o'clock, Velma was handcuffed and ready to go. Earlier, she had been told that Elin Schoen, the *Village Voice* writer who had set off the worldwide barrage of media attention about her, was there and wanted to see her. The warden had granted Schoen a brief visit while Velma was with the Roanes.

Velma had started down the hallway toward the inmate elevator with her four guards when Skip Pike came around the corner carrying a yellow mum that he had cut from a pot on the chapel altar a few minutes earlier.

"Mrs. Barfield, this is from the men of Central Prison," he said. "It's a pale token of the love and concern so many of them are showing for you today."

For a moment the guards seemed uncertain whether to allow her to accept the flower, but they made no move to stop her when she reached for it.

"I want you to thank them for me," Velma said.

"She was tickled to death," Pike later recalled. "She gave me the most beautiful smile. Oh, she had a smile that could melt the coldest heart."

Jimmie Little knew one of the judges on the Fourth Circuit Court. J. Dixon Phillips had been the dean of the law school at the University of North Carolina when Little was a student. Little knew him to be a brilliant lawyer, a superb judge, a person who knew North Carolina and understood its politics, and he thought that Burr had a good chance to win his vote for a stay of execution. But Burr had to get two votes, and not long into his arguments Thursday morning, he could tell from the questions and comments he was getting that he was going to have a hard time winning the other two.

"Is there a necessity that the whole course of the past be examined and reopened?" asked Judge Francis Murnaghan.

"She really got a due process trial as far as anyone knew at that time," observed Judge James Sprouse.

Hugh Hoyle had been staying in close touch with Sister Teresa, Phil Carter and Jimmie Little all week. He was determined to keep his promise to be there at the end for Velma and to preach her funeral, but the uncertainty of her appeals left him in limbo. On Wednesday, Little called and told him that he should come on. Hoyle flew to Greensboro, spent the night with his parents, and borrowed a car from his brother to drive to Raleigh early Thursday morning. Pike and Carter were waiting in the warden's conference room. They told Hoyle how Velma was doing, then began discussing the memorial service to be held at Women's Prison, as well as the funeral itself, if they were indeed to happen.

Hoyle had brought Velma's funeral instructions in his briefcase, along with some of her writings about the Bible and her faith. On the plane he had begun to outline his sermon, and he got out his notes to share with the two chaplains.

Hoyle was getting ready to go upstairs for his visit when somebody came to tell them that a bulletin had just come over the radio. The Fourth Circuit Court had denied Velma a stay and refused her appeal. The three ministers looked at each other; nobody had to speak what all were thinking. They almost certainly were facing an execution in just sixteen hours.

Hoyle realized that Velma was in the visiting area and had no way of knowing this. He would have to be the one to break the news. He braced himself and headed for the elevator, carrying his Bible and a travel communion kit in a black leather case.

Velma had been moved from one of the visiting cubicles to a larger, glassed room for her meeting with Hoyle, which was to be a contact visit. She stood when she saw him coming, smiling broadly, clearly happy that he was there—she hadn't seen him since Christmas when he had come home to visit family. Later, he would remember her as being almost radiant.

They embraced and sat in plastic chairs facing one another, Hoyle holding her hand. He knew no other way to tell her than to be straightforward.

"Velma, I just heard that the last appeal has been turned down."

She looked away briefly but showed no other reaction, remaining silent only a moment.

"Well, that's what I figured would happen," she said softly.

"Velma, is there anything in your life that is not confessed to the Lord that you need to make right?"

"No, Brother Hoyle, I'm ready to go."

And she smiled.

From that point it was easier.

Hoyle read aloud some of Velma's favorite scriptures. He administered communion, both of them on their knees on the tile floor by the plastic chairs. They prayed, Hoyle thanking the Lord for the opportunities they'd had to learn and worship together, for the friendship they'd shared.

Afterward, Hoyle told her that he'd brought with him the letters she had written to the families of her victims and her own family back in the spring of 1981, expressing her remorse and asking their forgiveness. Velma had been unable to send the letters because of her lawyers' concerns. He would still carry out her wishes to deliver them if she wanted, he told her. He would leave the letters with prison officials so that she could read through them, make any changes and put the current date on them.

Velma had one request of Hoyle. She wanted him to be with her children tonight, she said, and she'd like them to be at the prison so she'd know they were close. He gave his word.

The time seemed to have flown, and now it was almost gone. Hoyle wanted to sing a hymn, "Within the Veil." He started, his voice firm and strong, "Within the veil, I now would come into the holy place . . ." Velma joined in softly, their eyes joined. But halfway through the hymn, Hoyle found himself unable to continue. He broke down sobbing. Velma reached to touch his arm. And then the guards were there, saying time was up.

"I hugged her," Hoyle recalled years later. "I kissed her cheek. I said, 'Velma, my grandpa is in heaven. Will you look him up when you get there and tell him I'm on my way?' And she smiled and said, 'I will. Ruth Graham's got some folks she wants me to look up, too.' "

Looking into her face for the last time was the most telling incident of his ministry, Hoyle later would say.

"Never have I had another moment to compare. I've been there when people have died. I've seen people die in services. I've worked with people who were terminally ill. But when someone has to die like that it really points out that the wages of sin is death, and even though Christ forgives, there's still the penalty to be paid, and the scars that will always remain."

Ronnie had slept only fitfully and was up at dawn. He peeked outside and saw that the sky matched his mood. At 7:30, he went to Pam and Kirby's room. He didn't know how Pam would make it through this day. She was still taking Valium and seemed to be in shock.

Jimmie Little had arranged for a television production company to produce a documentary about Velma's execution, supposedly for HBO, although it never would appear. Ronnie and Pam were to be interviewed by the crew in Pam's room. Lights and cameras had to be set up for the interviews. The TV was off. They were isolated from news.

The interviewer asked Ronnie his feelings about capital punishment, and Ronnie acknowledged that he had been a supporter of the death penalty.

"It would change anyone's views on the death penalty if you had a mother or father, a brother or sister on death row," he said. "I don't care who you are or how strongly you feel about it. After watching on TV and going through what I know is going to happen to my mother later on tonight, I don't know what my views will be on capital punishment. It just seems horrible, more horrible than I ever imagined.

"I'm not saying it will change my views on capital punishment, but I can certainly appreciate the people who have been executed, what they went through and their families. I had no idea it was this bad. I must have buried my mother about a hundred times in the last six months."

Pam had trouble talking. "The toughest time for me will be at five o'clock this afternoon when I have to walk away from my mother for the last time and to know that she's not going to be there when I need her." Her voice was breaking and she kept dabbing her eyes with a tissue. "But so much a part of her is going to live through me."

Then she broke down. "It's just not fair. . . ." she said, crying. "It's just not fair for any family to have to go through this."

The TV crew was finishing up when Jimmie Little came into the room about noon, a stark look on his face. Ronnie saw him and stood. They all had been awaiting news. Surely Jimmie knew. Ronnie started across the room toward him. Little met him halfway in a sudden embrace. "It's over," he said, almost in a whisper.

"I thought I felt relief more than anything else," Ronnie would say many years later, recalling the moment.

The outcome had been just as he had known it would be, just as he had warned Pam to prepare for. Now his concern was for her. Although she had been acting as if she had accepted that her mother would soon die, he knew that deep down she had secretly believed the court would prevent it.

Pam was sitting on the bed, and Ronnie and Little sat by her as Little told her the court's decision. He and Mary Ann Tally had just left the prison after talking with Velma about what she wanted to do, he said. Dick Burr had been standing by in Richmond, waiting to hear if he should go on to the Supreme Court in Washington. But Velma had decided otherwise.

"She wants to halt it," Little said.

And Pam collapsed, sobbing uncontrollably.

Little had alerted reporters that he would be holding a press conference to announce Velma's decision, and he went off for that. Ronnie went upstairs to his room. For the first time since his mother's conviction nearly six years earlier, her fate was certain.

He needed time alone, time to think about what he would say

when he saw her for the last time, just a few hours from now. But when he got to his room, he found that he couldn't think. He lay on the bed stunned almost to stupor by overwhelming sorrow, wishing that he could go to sleep, wake up and find that it all had been a dream.

"I was shocked by the way I was feeling," he recalled years later. "I thought I was prepared, and I found out I really wasn't."

Carol Oliver, the captain of Velma's guard, had gone out for an early lunch and was on her way back to the death-watch area when she encountered Jimmie Little leaving the prison and learned that the court had decided against Velma and she was dropping her final appeal.

Oliver's heart quickened. Up to this point, she later said, neither she nor any of the guards under her command had actually believed that they would be participating in an execution. They had thought that another stay would come, just as it had before. Now she knew that Velma really was going to die and she and her staff would be part of it.

From the beginning, this had been a very different day at Central Prison. A somberness had lain over the whole sprawling complex, but as word spread of the court's decision an almost crackling tension was added.

"It was very strained," Oliver later remembered. "Everybody's emotions were at a very high level."

When Oliver got back to the death-watch area, she discovered that the guards and the two chaplains appeared to have been more affected by Velma's decision than had she. Velma was calm, no different than she had been at any time that week.

Lunch had been waiting for Velma. Skip Pike and Phil Carter sat with her while she ate some pea soup and crackers, drank a cup of fruit punch and went through a new stack of mail and telegrams that Oliver had just delivered.

Velma told the chaplains not to worry about her. She encouraged them to spend time instead with the thirty-nine men on death row. She knew what would be on their minds, she said, knew they would be hurting just as she had on the day of James Hutchins' execution. It had meant so much to her, she said, when Carter and Sam Roane had come to let her know that they understood what she was feeling.

Time was short, and Velma was to have many more visitors that afternoon. Anne Lotz was returning. Velma's brothers, Jimmy and John, were coming. So was her cousin, William Bullard. And Wade Holder, who seemed like a brother to her. Then Faye and Cliff would be there. Most would visit in pairs and have only half an hour to say their goodbyes. All would be restricted visits. But, finally, Velma would be with Pam and Ronnie for two full hours. And she would be able to hold them one last time.

Reporters had been gathering at Central Prison since early morning. More than two hundred were expected before nightfall. They would represent all the TV networks, most of the country's major newspapers, the national and international wire services, magazines such as *Time*, *Newsweek* and *Vanity Fair*. They would arrive from other countries as well: England, Sweden, Norway, Germany, France, Spain, Mexico, Australia.

TV trucks with satellite dishes already filled the parking lot near the visitor reception center by mid-afternoon Thursday, and more were still to come. Lights had been erected. A platform of plywood and raw lumber had been hastily built behind the reception center next to the high steel-wire fence. A podium had been put there for those who would be addressing the assembled reporters.

Public relations officers from several government agencies had been assigned to assist the lone spokesperson for the Department of Correction, Patty McQuillan, who was spending a frantic day on the phone trying to find answers to hundreds of questions from reporters, while arranging credentials for others.

Ronnie and Pam wanted to avoid reporters and cameras when they went for their final visit, and Mary Ann Tally drove them to a back entrance. They had a long walk through many checkpoints and automatically operated gates and steel doors before arriving at the spacious visitor area on the prison's top floor.

Velma was finishing her visit with Faye and Cliff when Ronnie and Pam got off the elevator just before three. Faye was sobbing loudly, standing in the cubicle with her hand pressed to the window that separated her from her sister. Velma had her hand against her sister's from the other side of the glass. Finally, Cliff had to pull Faye away.

Velma had seen Ronnie watching, and she gave him a little wave and a small smile. The guards began handcuffing her to take her the short distance to the glass-enclosed visiting room next to the control center where she had met with Hugh Hoyle that morning.

Pam had gone to the restroom, but she soon rejoined Ronnie. Just as their mother arrived on the far side of the visiting room smiling at them, a guard approached Ronnie and told him he and Pam were wanted in the warden's office.

Neither Ronnie nor Pam had any idea what this was about, but they returned to the first floor with the guard and were ushered into the warden's office. Nathan Rice was seated at his huge walnut desk. Behind him were windows looking out onto the area where the reporters would be gathered later. Two associates of Rice's were in the office. Ronnie and Pam were asked to take seats in the upholstered chairs.

Years later, Rice would say that he had no memory of this episode, but both Ronnie and Pam, separated by many years and many miles, would give closely similar details.

As Ronnie remembered it, Rice unwrapped a tissue in his palm, revealing a marijuana cigarette.

"Do you know what this is?" he asked.

Ronnie didn't know how to respond. *Does he want us to smoke this?* he would remember thinking. *Is he trying to relax us for our last visit with our mom?*

"Do you have any idea what the penalty is for smuggling drugs into a prison?" Ronnie remembered Rice asking.

Ronnie had been concentrating totally on being strong for his mother, and this sudden, unexpected development sent his spirits spiraling back to despair. Was the state going to jail them while it killed their mother?

The joint had fallen from Pam's cigarette package in the restroom. A matron who had followed her inside had picked it up and alerted her superiors.

Pam was sobbing. "That's not mine," she was saying. "I didn't bring that in here."

Years later, she would acknowledge that she had smoked marijuana in the past but was not using it then. When she was leaving her room, she had asked somebody to get her cigarettes, and that person had picked up a pack that wasn't hers.

"What this means," Ronnie and Pam both would remember Rice telling them, "is that you're not going to have a contact visit with your mother."

"I went crazy," Ronnie recalled years later. "I just leaped from my chair and put both hands on his desk. I said, 'There is no way I am going to stand for that.' I was yelling. I said, 'In just a few hours you will be responsible for taking my mother's life. I am going to see my mother, and my sister is going with me. I am not going to let her spend the rest of her life trying to live down something like this. If I have to get Jimmie Little to call the governor, I'll do it. And if that doesn't work, I'm sure that I can walk right out of here and find several hundred reporters who'll be interested in knowing that the state of North Carolina is going to kill this woman without allowing her children to see her for the last time, and we'll see what the governor thinks about that."

Rice conferred with his associates, Ronnie later recalled, then told them he was going to allow their visit.

Velma was waiting expectantly, a worried look on her face. Some of their visiting time was already lost. Pam was in even worse shape than she had been when they had first arrived. She engulfed her mother in a hug, her emotions now out of control.

Three plastic chairs were in the room, and Velma pulled one alongside the chair in which she had been waiting and got Pam into it. Pam put her head in her mother's lap and curled up in the chair whimpering, her long legs extended awkwardly, this tall, beautiful woman, twice a mother, a little girl again, needing her mother's touch. Velma stroked her daughter's hair. Tears were in her eyes, but she wiped them away and composed herself. Ronnie had seated himself in front of her.

"Was something wrong?" Velma asked about their sudden departure and the unexpected delay.

"It was nothing important," Ronnie told her.

The situation was awkward for Ronnie. He had thought so long and so hard about what he wanted to say at this moment, yet words seemed impotent and irrelevant. He didn't even know how to start. Velma broke the silence.

"The liquor must really be flowing over at that hotel," she said sharply, adding that she'd smelled it on the breaths of some of her visitors through the steel mesh in the visiting cubicle.

Ronnie was incredulous. Her death was less than eleven hours away and she was upset about people drinking!

"Mama, I'm not drinking," he said. "A lot of people just aren't able to cope with this. It's their way of dealing with it. Don't be mad at them. We're not all as strong as you."

"I guess I can understand that," she said, but she clearly was perturbed.

"You're going to have to look after your sister," she told him. "If she needs you, you need to be there for her."

"I will," he promised.

"And I'm not sure how Jimmie's going to hold up through this. I want you to do what you can to help him."

"What about me, Mama?" he wanted to say, but he didn't. She expected him to be strong, and he was going to be.

There were other instructions. A statement she wanted him to make. Details about the funeral, special people she wanted to sit with the family. She also wanted him and Pam to be at the prison tonight when it happened, she told him.

"I'd feel better just knowing you were close."

"We'll be here," Ronnie said.

Brother Hoyle had promised he would be with them, Velma told him. He would be a great comfort. He always knew the right things to say.

Another silence followed, broken only by Pam's soft crying. Then Velma asked if there was anything from the past that they still needed to discuss.

"No, I think we've talked about everything that's been on my mind. That's one good thing that's come out of this. I've often thought that if you'd died from an overdose, we wouldn't have had the chance to deal with some of these things like we have."

"Ronnie, your daddy was a good man, you know that," Velma suddenly said.

"I know," Ronnie said, "but it was you who was always there for us, and he wasn't."

"Don't be too hard on him," she said.

"Let's don't dwell on the bad things," Ronnie told her. "Let's just talk about the good times."

"We did have some, didn't we?" Velma said, forcing a smile.

Ronnie brought up his and Pam's early school days, when Velma was grade mother for both, the happiest period of her life.

"Automatic arms!" she said with a chuckle. "Every time a teacher asked whose mother would volunteer to help out, your's and Pam's arms shot straight up in the air."

"Remember those field trips?"

"Yeah, all your friends always wanted to ride with me."

"Because you were so easy on them."

"We couldn't even get all of 'em in the car."

They went on to reminisce about Pam's basketball days and how Velma never missed a game, always cheering louder than anybody.

"Boy, you used to yell at those referees," Ronnie teased.

"They deserved it," she said, and both laughed.

Velma looked down at Pam, still stroking her hair, and Ronnie saw tears coming to her eyes again.

"You know, I've had people in here all day telling me what great kids I have. Y'all have stood behind me through all these painful years. A lot of kids wouldn't have done that. You don't know what that means to me."

"If you're proud of the way we turned out, then you should be proud of yourself," Ronnie said, "because whatever good qualities we might have all came from you."

Velma took a handkerchief from her pocket and wiped her tears.

Ronnie reached for her hand, and he was reminded of his graduation night when he'd given up his trip to the beach to stay home with her. That had been the first time he had truly told her what she meant to him. Now he had only this last opportunity.

"You're the best mother that I or anyone could have ever had or ever wanted," Ronnie said, and now he was crying, too.

"I'm sorry for the embarrassment I've caused you," Velma said.

"It hasn't been any embarrassment. I don't understand a lot of what happened, and I don't think you do either. It has never affected the way I feel about you. I've always loved you and I always will. Nothing will ever change that."

Ronnie noticed that one of the guards was pointing at her watch, and he stood. "They're going to ask us to leave," he said.

"Pam, honey, sit up," Velma said. "You've got to sit up, you hear?"

Velma stood when Pam was free of her lap, and Ronnie hugged her, trying to fix in his mind how it felt to hold her this last time. "You'll be in my heart for as long as I live," he told her, and he was barely able to get out the words, he was crying so hard. "I love you."

"I love you, too."

Ronnie and Velma helped Pam to her feet. She was wracked with sobs, and she enveloped her mother in a protective embrace, bent over her like a shield, clinging desperately.

"Oh, Mama, I love you so much."

Velma stroked her and whispered to her, and they clung together, both crying, both unwilling to let go.

"You'll have to take her," a guard told Ronnie.

"Come on, we've got to go," Ronnie said, taking Pam by the shoulders, but she would not let go, and he could not pull her away.

"No!" she cried. "No!"

"You've got to let go," he said through his own tears, and still she wouldn't break free.

"Pam, come on," he said, prying on her arms, and his mind flashed back to the time his mother drove his car head-on into a rental truck before Michael was born, and as he was trying to pull his sister's arms from his mother, he was again prying his mother's hands from the steering wheel to free her from the wreckage. But Pam's strength was fierce and it brought him quickly back to the present.

"Pam, please . . ."

Then his mother reached up and calmly and gently began unwrapping Pam's arms from her body. And as she did, Ronnie looked into her tear-filled eyes for the last time and knew that if remorse could be made physical he had just seen it.

Suddenly, he had his wailing sister in his arms and was leading her toward the door.

"Don't look back," he told her. "Just don't . . . look . . . back."

Velma had composed herself by the time she got back to her cell at five-thirty. Her visit with her children had marked the first time that any of her guards had seen her cry, and now she seemed morose and remote. Her supper was waiting: fried chicken livers, macaroni and cheese, collard greens, lima beans, pound cake with white icing. But she touched none of it.

For a few minutes she lay on her bunk in her pink robe, looking up at the concrete ceiling, but she was interrupted by the warden, who came to talk about the schedule for the rest of the night. Then a nurse was there with medicine.

There was no idle chatter now. The death-watch area remained silent, everybody consumed by the seriousness of the moment.

At 6:13, Velma sent for a canteen order: Cheez Doodles and a Coke. When it came nearly a half hour later, she asked for a pen and for two small white Bibles among her possessions. While she ate the Cheez Doodles and drank the Coke, she sat writing in the Bibles.

At a little before seven, a guard came to remind her that she'd better get dressed. Her lawyers were there, waiting to see her for the last time.

Richard Burr had flown back from Richmond on the state plane Thursday afternoon at the invitation of the lawyers from the attorney general's office who had opposed him in court. It had been a somber trip. Anybody could see that Burr was taking his defeat hard.

Burr was enduring one of the most difficult years of his life. In just the past six months, he had lost three clients to Florida's electric chair. Velma's death, though, was far harder to face than the others. He had come late to the cases of the three men, had not known them nearly as well. Velma had been his first death-penalty client, and his attachment to her had grown with the years.

He was a lawyer who believed it necessary to commit personally to a client. "You can't have an arm's-length relationship with somebody whose life is in your hands," he would say years later, after he had become perhaps the country's top death-penalty lawyer (he handled the sentencing phase of Timothy McVeigh's defense in the bombing of the Oklahoma City federal building).

His relationship with Velma, however, was closer than any he'd ever had with a client—or ever would have. In recent years, he'd never left a meeting with her, or closed a telephone conversation, without telling her he loved her. Seeing her for the last time, he knew, was going to be one of the hardest things he'd ever done.

At 7:15, as the guards brought Velma to them in handcuffs, Burr and Little stood waiting, each holding a rose that Mary Ann Tally had bought, each forcing a smile.

Velma spent more than an hour and a half with her lawyers, and it was an emotional time for all. Both lawyers knew that Velma had only agreed to the final round of appeals because she realized how important it was to them, and that had made the courts' rejections even harder, especially for Burr. "I had a terrible sense of failure," he recalled years later. "I was crying and telling her how sorry I was."

"He was really beating up on himself," Little would remember. "Velma was being very comforting to both of us. She was the glue that held everybody together. I'm talking family, I'm talking lawyers, chaplains, guards, everybody. There was Velma steadfast and serene as she could be. You knew it was the sheer force of her faith. I've never seen anything like it. I knew exactly what was going through her head: my next step is with Jesus."

Near the end of their visit, Velma told her lawyers something Little would never forget. "She said, 'You know, I'm going to be going before the judge of all the judges, and he doesn't wear black robes, and he treats people alike, whether they're rich or poor, whether they're black or white. And this one has compassion. This one has forgiveness.' "

As he and Burr were leaving, Little asked if they could do anything else. Velma said she'd like to sing with the Roanes one last time, if only for a few minutes. Little asked the warden and he approved. Little called Sam Roane, who said that he and Gales would be right there. As he was returning to his car after telling reporters he would be a witness at the execution, Little saw the Roanes arriving with their portable organ, hurrying to the prison gate.

"Brother Jimmie, we're going to sing her into heaven," Sam called out.

Governor Hunt, who was now trailing in the polls, had begun his day campaigning in Brevard in the far western mountains of the state. After learning that the Fourth Circuit Court had denied Velma's appeal, he cancelled his afternoon campaign stops, telling reporters that he thought it appropriate to make himself readily available in the event of late developments.

Hunt flew back to Raleigh, where in late afternoon he had found the capitol surrounded by nearly 150 protesters against the death penalty holding signs saying such things as: NOT IN MY NAME, WHY DO WE KILL PEOPLE TO PROVE KILLING PEOPLE IS WRONG?, and GIVEN A CHOICE, JIM HUNT CHOSE TO TAKE A LIFE.

Vigils for Velma would be held in cities across North Carolina Thursday night. One service, sponsored by the Robeson County Clergy and Laity Concerned, had begun at seven in a cramped room in a downtown building in Lumberton. More than twenty people, black, white and Indian, including several children, sat on folding chairs in a loose circle, each rising one by one to light a small candle from a large "candle of life" on a small, cloth-covered table in the center of the circle.

Mac Legerton, a young minister who afterward would drive to Raleigh to join the vigil outside Central Prison, read from Romans, and the group sang, meditated, prayed for all victims of violence, and spoke their feelings about the death penalty.

"We believe that for Christians, justice means the justice of God, always a merciful justice," said Legerton. "Without mercy, justice becomes revenge. The death penalty, in Christian terms, is actually a form of revenge, not justice."

By seven-thirty, the sanctuary of Sacred Heart Cathedral, a great, gray-stone edifice on Hillsborough Street in downtown Raleigh, was packed with people opposed to Velma's execution. They wore green ribbons on their lapels, white bands on their arms and tags listing the names of North Carolina's condemned and their victims. They sang and prayed and listened to many speakers.

"Today is the Feast of All Saints," Sister Teresa told them. "Tomorrow is the Feast of All Souls. By tomorrow morning, we will have another saint. Velma will be in heaven."

Velma's brother Jimmy told the crowd that he wanted to remember Velma as she was now, not as she had been when she killed. "I never try to remember the bad parts. As long as we put the good parts first, we don't have to worry about the bad."

Wade Holder said he was having trouble finding words to describe his feelings, but he soon sounded like a country preacher, his voice rising and falling rhythmically.

"Her last words to me were, 'Wade, when I enter into the gas chamber, do not think of it as that. Think of it as my gateway to heaven.' The gas chamber. Oh, how horrible! Oh, how horrible! What a shame. What a disgrace to our state. But wait—that is the gateway to heaven and our Lord Jesus Christ.

"Just a few seconds after two o'clock, Velma Barfield will be in heaven. Heaven is a real place, and there's joy and peace in her heart because she knows where she's going."

He broke down, couldn't continue, and had to be helped away by John Frazier, the chaplain who had first gone to see Velma when she arrived at Women's Prison nearly six years earlier. Frazier had left the prison a year later to become a special assistant to Governor Hunt, then had worked for four years as a chaplain at Central Prison. Now he revealed to the congregation that he had resigned in protest after the execution of James Hutchins in March.

"Capital punishment is evil," he said. "I choose not to cooperate with that." And the entire assembly rose as one, applauding and shouting its approval.

Frazier commended them for the candlelight march they soon would make to stand vigil at Central Prison. "Those of you with a little light will help somebody on death row to get through," he said.

At the end of the service, more than 300 people lighted candles held in holders of upside-down paper cups and filed from the church, singing to strumming guitars.

Soon the marchers had spread over two blocks, shepherded by twenty Raleigh police officers, some on foot, others in creeping cars with blue lights flashing. One marcher carried a poster that said, AN EYE FOR AN EYE MAKES THE WHOLE WORLD BLIND. Another's bore a drawing of a giant syringe. INJECT COMPASSION, it said.

No such feelings were being spoken at another gathering that was going on at the same time at the Howard Johnson's at I-95 in Lumberton. In a hospitality suite donated by the motel, family members of Stuart Taylor and John Henry Lee were mingling with supporters and reporters. At one end of the room was a large TV with several rows of stack chairs aligned before it. Whenever live reports about the execution came on, people clustered in front of the TV.

The gathering had been organized by the group called People Assisting Victims that had worked with the families to see that the execution came about. Alice Storms told reporters that it was for the benefit of the press. After the execution, she said, she would read a statement that would be her last.

"The press had been good to us," she said, "but they've been a pain, too."

An air of discomfort and tension was clearly evident in the room, and Sylvia Andrews spoke the reason for it: "I've got this deep feeling that something is going to happen to stop it."

When the marchers from Sacred Heart Cathedral reached the prison they were directed to an area that had been set aside on a rise on the far side of Walnut Creek under giant spreading oaks, less than two hundred yards from the front gate. Some demonstrators had been there when the marchers arrived, and others would join them later, until the crowd numbered about four hundred. Those supporting capital punishment would be in a separate area on the opposite side of Western Boulevard. Only a handful were present as the first marchers filed onto the hillside across the road, but their numbers would grow, too, as the night went on. A solid line of Raleigh police cars parked bumper-to-bumper separated the two groups.

Among the protesters on the far side of Western Boulevard were four members of a family dealing with their own sorrows, holding signs citing Bible verses in support of capital punishment. They had been at the capitol earlier in the day. William R. Gilmore spoke for the family. His twenty-five-year-old son, a police officer in the town of Clayton, had been murdered in January 1982, and the killer was now serving a life sentence in Central Prison and no doubt would one day walk free. "He's over there right now watching TV," Gilmore told a reporter. To Gilmore, a killer should suffer the same fate as his victims. "It upsets me that people would have any feeling to save a woman's life after she killed that many people and after the way she killed them," he said.

Among the crowd standing vigil for Velma were many people who knew her, including Sister Teresa.

"I just don't see that North Carolina has anything you can call clemency," she told a reporter. "I hope the new governor will see clemency differently."

"Our state is committing premeditated murder," said Becky Fields, a psychologist who had worked with Velma at Women's prison.

Phyllis Tyler, the ACLU activist who had visited Velma weekly for more than four years and had served on her support committee, was clearly upset. "I was sure until last week that something was going to come through to stop this," she said, noting that Velma had not believed that. "She felt it was going to come. It still seems so unreal to me."

Ronnie had gone to his room after his visit with his mother. He called Joanna to tell her about the funeral arrangements, which the family was trying to keep out of the press. He got no answer and called her father to give him the information.

He did not turn on the TV. He knew that the execution was

dominating the news, and he wasn't sure that he could stand to hear any more about it. He tried not to think about it but found himself trying to picture the execution chamber. What did it look like? What would his mother be thinking as she was led to it? Would she be scared? What was she thinking at this very moment?

The phone rang, and he heard Joanna's voice asking, "Ronnie, how are you doing?"

They talked for several minutes, and he was touched by her concern. It would mean a lot to him if she attended the funeral, he told her, and he knew his mother would want her there, but he didn't want her to feel obligated. She would be there, she assured him, and she would be at the funeral home tomorrow night with Michael. She knew Ronnie would need to see him.

After talking with Joanna, Ronnie went downstairs to check on Pam. She was in such a stupor from alcohol and Valium that she could hardly stand up. ("I just wanted to numb the pain," she explained later. "I was just trying not to hurt so bad.") Ronnie saw that she was going to be in no shape to return to the prison, and he knew he had a job on his hands. He draped his sister around his shoulder and led her to his room. He called room service for a pot of coffee and tried to get her to drink. "I can't, Ronnie," she pleaded, "I'll throw up."

"Drink it," he said.

He got wet cloths for her forehead and began walking her back and forth.

"I promised Mama that we would be there," he told her firmly, "and we're going to be."

CHAPTER 26

After her visit with Jimmie Little and Dick Burr, Velma was looking forward to seeing the Roanes again at ten o'clock. They sang every hymn she wanted to hear, she joining in, and ended with her favorite, "Amazing Grace."

Sam was an emotional man, and he had a hard time finishing that final hymn. He and Gales thought they had said their final good-byes that morning, and now, more than twelve hours later, they found the second round just as difficult. Yet years later they still would see this as one of the most glorious moments of their ministry, for they were convinced that they were singing with someone who in only a few hours would be joining a chorus of angels.

Velma returned to her cell at ten-thirty and took a shower, lingering under the warm water for nearly ten minutes. While she was bathing, Jennie Lancaster came with her boss, Rae McNamara, the director of the Division of Prisons. McNamara felt an obligation to be present with the prison employees who had to carry out the execution. She also wanted to offer whatever comfort she could to Velma, whom she had met earlier on visits to Women's Prison.

She would never forget how sweet Velma smelled when she emerged from the shower, powdered and cologned, in her pink robe. Velma seemed pleased to see her, and McNamara saw no signs of fear, distress, worry, concern. Clearly, Velma was far more relaxed than anybody around her.

"I think she had come to terms with dying," McNamara said many years later. "I think she was at peace with it."

McNamara, Lancaster and Velma sat chatting in Velma's cell as if they were sitting around somebody's kitchen table having coffee.

The guards would note how casual it seemed. Velma showed her visitors the cards she had received and spoke about how kind everybody had been to her. Then she asked a guard to bring her brown dress so that she could get a "God loves me" pin from it. She wanted to give it to Jennie. She also wanted Jennie to take her jewelry and other belongings when she left.

Just after eleven, with Velma's execution less than three hours away, Jennie said good-bye, and she and McNamara left. "One of the last things I said to her," Lancaster later recalled, "was, 'I think your life and death are going to have meaning for a lot of people afterward.' She said, 'I hope so. Please do something about that if you can.' "

Velma finished her mail and handed a stack of cards and letters to Carol Oliver to be taken to the mailroom.

"Are you ready to see the chaplains?" one of the guards asked at 11:25.

"Anytime," Velma said.

"Which one do you want to see first?"

"Chaplain Carter."

Phil Carter entered the cell at 11:30, and never since becoming a minister had he been so nervous and uncertain, fearful that he might fail to bring the comfort and reassurance that he should at this moment. But he quickly realized that he shouldn't have feared, for Velma's concern, he saw, was not for herself, but for her children, her family, her lawyers, for Jennie Lancaster and himself and others who cared about her, even for the people who were about to carry out her execution.

"That's all she talked about," he recalled later.

Velma did have one request, though. She'd like to have communion again. She'd already had the service once this day, with Hugh Hoyle, but midnight would mark the beginning of a new day, and he said he'd arrange it.

Skip Pike had taken Carter on a tour of death row before they came to see Velma—and they had found the men there somber, silent and tense. Pike wanted Velma to know that they were thinking about her. "Mrs. Barfield," he said, "I was on the row just a little while ago, and I can't begin to tell you how many people there are lifting you up at this minute."

"Chaplain," he would remember her telling him, "don't worry about me. God has been so good to me, and now I'm going to be with Him. You do your best to love those guys because they need you."

Ronnie felt as if he were trapped in some surrealistic dream from which he could not awaken as he and Pam arrived at the prison in Mary Ann Tally's car. The eeriness was beyond anything he had ever experienced—the crush of traffic, the police cars lining the road, the flashing lights, the milling people, the prison glowing in the distance, the mist rising from Walnut Creek, the TV trucks with anchormen seated on their tops, illuminated in the night.

All of this, he thought, *just to kill my mother.*

He saw the death-penalty supporters—there must have been fifty or more by now—and one held aloft a sign that said, BYE BYE VELMA.

"Burn the bitch!" he heard somebody shout.

"Look at how many people are over here supporting your mother," Mary Ann said, trying to distract his attention, and Ronnie saw the throng on the hillside holding candles. The word "HOPE" was spelled out in lights among them, but it was a word by which he felt abandoned.

Photographers surrounded the car as it approached the prison gate, lights flashing, lenses held up to the windows.

This was a circus, Ronnie thought, a bizarre, state-sponsored circus in which the main act would be hidden from view, held in the dead of night to attract the least attention possible, as if the state were ashamed and embarrassed by it.

Ronnie had told Jimmie Little earlier that his mother had wanted him to make a statement to the press, and Little had arranged this time for it. Pam was crying and had a splitting headache. Ronnie, dressed in jeans and a long-sleeved dress shirt, put his arm around her. TV lights bathed them as they stepped onto the platform erected for the press. Little addressed the reporters first, then Ronnie stepped to the bank of microphones and in a quavering voice spoke about his and Pam's visit with their mother a few hours earlier.

"Her last request to us was that we be here at the prison tonight. Even though we won't get to see her anymore, she wanted us to be present, and that's why we're here. We're going to be here until it's over with. She did want the public to know that she didn't hold any anger or hatred toward any of the people who fought to bring this about, that she hoped that her death would allow the victims' families to begin to put some of the pieces of their lives back together."

He was fighting back tears, and he paused as if having difficulty continuing. "I want people to know that she wanted to live very badly and that she never gave up hope until today. She wanted to live mainly for her grandchildren. We both miss her already."

At the Howard Johnson's in Lumberton, a silence fell over the meeting room as Ronnie's image appeared on the TV. Earlier, there had been talk of him and Pam.

"I feel sorry for her children," John Henry Lee's granddaughter, Teresa Britt, had told a reporter. "That's their mother and they're sticking by her, and I admire that. But that doesn't change anything." Velma, she said, still deserved to die. "I don't feel sorry for her one bit."

"Of course, we feel sorry for her family," Alice Storms had told another reporter. "We know what they must be feeling, because we've been through it, too, losing a loved one. We will have them in our prayers and hope the best for them."

But that changed nothing for Alice either. "I think there are four kinds of death," she said. "Natural causes, accidents, a life that is taken without permission, and execution. To me, Velma Barfield deserves to be executed. She literally pulled the switch herself."

As Ronnie spoke, Alice sat watching with Sylvia Andrews and Margie Pittman, and all three began to cry.

At midnight, the guard in the control room noted in the log that Velma was kneeling beside her bunk in prayer.

While she prayed, the vigil keepers on the hillside and the reporters by the gate heard the first of several waves of muffled, rhythmic pounding coming from within the prison, as the inmates mounted their own protest to what was about to happen.

Her prayer finished, Velma sat on her bunk, her legs folded beneath her, looking at her mail. She wrote a quick note, sealed it in an envelope and addressed it. Then technicians were there to tell her again about the procedures she soon would be facing. Only minutes after they left, the chaplains returned.

The communion set that Skip Pike carried was a camouflaged military field kit that had been left at the prison by a former chaplain who had used it in Vietnam. Pike and Carter began setting up for the communion on the stainless steel table in the day room. At twelve-thirty, an hour and a half before the execution, the heavy door of Velma's cell slid open and she stepped out for her final, for mal religious ceremony.

Later, both Pike and Carter would call this one of the most profound religious experiences of their lives. They used a common chalice, each sipping after the other, the chaplains, both opponents of capital punishment, well aware that while they administered this liquid representing the blood of Christ, they also were taking part in the planned killing of a human being, albeit one who had killed others, yet one who—they both were certain—had been redeemed.

"It was like a meeting of the holy and ultimate evil," Phil Carter would later say.

As soon as the chaplains had departed, Carol Oliver brought an adult diaper to Velma's cell. Velma had earlier been told that she would need to wear it—the drugs would relax her sphincter, and nobody wanted a mess, least of all Velma, who lighted Salems to keep from offending her keepers when she used the toilet.

Velma put on the diaper beneath her pink panties. Then a guard brought new cotton pajamas that Gales Roane had bought and told her she needed to get dressed. Male prisoners were executed wearing only their boxer shorts, but Velma had asked to be allowed to wear pajamas and her request had been granted. The pajamas were pink, like the dress her father had bought her when she was ten, with flowers embroidered around the collar and above the pocket.

After getting dressed, Velma returned to her bunk and sat reading her mail. Ten minutes later, at one o'clock, with an hour of life remaining, she got up and began flushing down the commode the cigarettes left in her pack. She returned to her bunk and her mail, only to have the door to her cell slide open a minute later.

Rae McNamara was back. Because Jennie Lancaster had allowed herself to become so close to Velma, McNamara had told her that she could not be present at the execution, and Lancaster had gone to the first floor to be with Pam and Ronnie. Still, McNamara had thought a woman should be with Velma and she had appointed herself.

Carol Oliver was in the control room when the telephone rang at 1:10. The tension was so great, the silence so eerie and foreboding that the sound startled her and she jumped before she reached for the receiver.

"You have fifteen seconds," she heard a voice say.

Oliver hurried into the death-watch area and strode determinedly to the open door of Velma's cell.

"Velma," she said, "it's time."

Velma stood. So did McNamara. For a moment nobody said anything. Then Velma turned to McNamara.

"Do you think it would be all right if I wore my robe?" she asked.

"Sure, Velma," McNamara said.

Velma pulled on her robe and, after pausing at the small stainless steel mirror to check her hair, she stepped through the doorway, freeing herself from prison cells for evermore.

A ghoulish party atmosphere had taken over among the death-penalty supporters alongside Western Boulevard. Chants broke out sporadically. "Down with Velma! Up with victims!" "Burn! Burn! Burn!"

A steady stream of cars crept past, some drivers honking horns, some occupants whooping and hollering.

"Give her a shot!" came the shout from one car. "Hang the bitch!" a young man yelled from another.

"There are a lot of creeps around here," observed John Snow, a North Carolina State student who stood with the death-penalty supporters. "This isn't a public hanging, but it's pretty close. She could be hanging from a tree right over there," he said, pointing to the trees on the prison grounds where the silent vigil keepers stood.

Nathan Rice was waiting at the open door of the death-watch area as Velma exited her cell. Carol Oliver walked alongside Velma, Rae McNamara behind. At the door, Rice directed Velma to the small preparation room, only a few feet away on the left.

The gurney standing near the center of the room had been covered with a pale aquamarine sheet, its corners tucked in neat military folds. Velma stopped by the gurney, removed her robe and handed it to Oliver. She stepped out of her scruffy blue bedroom shoes, and Oliver stooped to pick them up.

"Thank you," Velma said.

The gurney was too high for Velma to climb onto easily, and guards reached to help her.

Carol Oliver left for the adjoining parole hearing room, the staging area where the rest of the execution team was waiting in strained and solemn silence.

Phil Carter and Skip Pike sat beside one another, Bibles in hand, places marked, awaiting their turns. Carol Oliver knew Pike well and she noticed that he seemed more ill at ease than she had ever seen him. Her heart went out to him, but everybody in the room felt a professional obligation to keep emotions to themselves. Carter was nervous, too, worried about what he would say to Velma. As he fidgeted, he couldn't take his eyes off the "crash cart" parked near the door. A crash cart normally was loaded with life-saving paraphernalia and was used in hospitals, rushed to patients in crisis. But this one carried the syringes filled with deadly chemicals that soon would take a life.

One of the vigil keepers standing on the hillside in front of the prison was Mattie Lewis, a laundry worker from Winston-Salem, who had switched shifts with a fellow employee so that she could be there. "I was determined to come," she said. "I was determined. I don't think no man has the right to take another's life."

Not far away stood Wade and Roger Smith, brothers and prominent lawyers in Raleigh.

"You can't just stay home," said Wade Smith, a leader of the state Democratic Party, who had defended Green Beret doctor Jeffrey McDonald in his widely publicized trial for the murder of his family. "You don't know what to do."

Roger Smith, who had worked on the final appeals to save James Hutchins, had been among the anti-death-penalty protesters outside the capitol when Governor Hunt had returned to his office Thursday afternoon.

Wade Smith looked at his watch. It was 1:35.

"I guess she's strapped on the gurney by now," he said. "She's awake, conscious. I wonder if at this point anyone is talking to her. Isn't it incredible that there's a human being in there with twenty minutes to live? Could there be anything more—more premeditated and deliberated?"

Somebody was indeed talking to Velma. Phil Carter had just begun to read to her from Romans 14. "For none of us liveth to himself, and no man dieth to himself.

"For whether we live, we live unto the Lord; and whether we die, we die unto the Lord: whether we live therefore, or die, we are the Lord's.

"For to this end, Christ both died, and rose, and revived, that he might be Lord both of the dead and the living."

His voice was breaking, and there were moments when he wondered if he could go on, but he did.

Pike had entered the preparation room first, Carter close behind. Velma was covered by a second sheet that reached nearly to her neck. She was wearing her big glasses with brown, speckled frames, and her hair was perfectly coiffed. The saline solution was already flowing into veins in both her arms from IV bags mounted on the gurney. Velma smiled when she saw the nervous chaplains.

"Mrs. Barfield," said Pike, "Phil and I would like to share these words from the scriptures."

Because he'd known Velma for such a brief period, Pike wanted Carter to have most of their time. He read from Psalm 21, then prayed that God would hold Velma gently through her journey. When he finished, he later recalled, she smiled and looked him straight in the eye.

"She spoke very directly," he said. "She said, 'Thank you for the kindness you've shown me and for the times you've shared God's love with me.' She said, 'I know you are filled with the spirit. I could tell by the way you prayed the first time you prayed for me.' I said, 'I just try to serve the Lord.' She smiled again and said, 'Chaplain Pike, God's people are the bestest kind.' It just blew me away."

Pike stepped back, and Carter moved into his place. He would never forget how fearful he was of losing control, but he kept telling himself that he had to hold together.

One look at her, he would later recall, told him he would do it. "She had a glow on her face. She looked to be at utter peace. She smiled at me. She said, 'Well, it'll soon be over. I'll be in a better place and I'm glad.' "

"The kids send their love," Carter told her.

"They're great kids," she replied.

He opened his Bible and began reading from Romans 14.

Two guards escorted the witnesses from the ground floor conference room to the elevators for the short ride up one level to the execution chamber. The official witnesses numbered eight, all law

enforcement officers except for two assistant D.A.s from Joe Freeman Britt's office. Four witnesses had been chosen by press orga-
nizations to represent the media. Jimmie Little and Anne Lotz were
there as well, witnesses out of love.

The view offered by the witness room window was plain and
grim. The chamber had six walls, none more than six feet long, all
of them at odd angles. Against the parallel wall from the window
was the dark-stained oak chair with its gruesome leather straps
that had been in the service of death by cyanide gas since 1936,
although nobody had died in it for more than twenty-two years.

Two rows of numbered blue plastic chairs had been set before
the window for the official witnesses. Those seated on the front
row would be no more than three feet from Velma.

The witnesses began entering the chamber at 1:40. With the two
guards who would remain with them, the group numbered sixteen.
The official witnesses took their assigned seats. The media witnesses
stood behind with Jimmie Little and Anne Lotz, who held hands.

The lights in the witness room were turned off so that the only
illumination came through the window from the chamber. The
effect was that of a movie theater, the chamber window serving as
the screen; only the people inside would be real, and the action
deadly.

Later, Anne Lotz, who did not think of herself as a witness but
as a friend standing by a deathbed, would remember thinking how
small and sterile the chamber seemed. She had to keep reminding
herself that what she had told Velma was true: that it really was the
gateway to heaven.

"It didn't look like the pearly gates," she said, "but it was. We
just couldn't see the other side."

In the preparation room, Phil Carter had just finished reading
scripture. He shut the Bible and began to pray.

"God receive this our sister. We love her. Forgive her. Be with her
children and comfort them and help them know the peace that only
can be found in Thee. . . ."

He prayed at length, and when he had finished, he put his hand
on Velma's shoulder and searched for the right words to say.

"You've touched a lot of people's lives," he told her—and felt the
sudden tap on his own shoulder, telling him that time was up—
"and you've changed many of those lives forever."

He wouldn't realize the double meaning of those words at the time, but he knew from Velma's answer that she understood them as he meant them, that the lives she'd changed in recent years had been for the better.

"To God be the glory," she said. "God did it all."

"We've got to go," he told her, letting his hand linger just a moment more, absorbing her warmth.

She thanked him for the worship and love they'd shared, for the times he'd sneaked her into the chapel against the rules, for the times he'd listened patiently when she'd been upset.

"I'll see you in heaven," Carter told her.

"I'll be waiting for you," she replied, and smiled for the last time, a smile that Carter would carry with him forever.

As soon as the chaplains departed, Nathan Rice stepped back into the preparation room. This time he carried a mini-cassette recorder.

"Velma, if you would like to make any final statement," he said, "this is your opportunity."

"I would," she said, and he pressed the "record" button and held the device close to her mouth.

Her voice was strong and did not falter. "I want to say that I am sorry for all the hurt that I have caused. I know that everybody has gone through a lot of pain—all the families connected—and I am sorry, and I want to thank everybody who has been supporting me all these six years.

"I want to thank my family for standing with me through all this and my attorneys and all the support to me, everybody, the people with the prison department. I appreciate everything—their kindness and everything that they have shown me during these six years."

She paused, then said no more.

"Is that all?" Rice asked.

She nodded.

For some in the witness room the wait seemed interminable. The heat was stifling, the tension intense, the silence unsettling, broken only by the sound of somebody shuffling feet, shifting in a chair, clearing a throat, and by a guard near the door who kept nervously jangling the change in his pocket.

Then at about 1:50, the big locks on the chamber door began to turn. Slowly, the door swung outward and open, and for the first time the witnesses caught a glimpse of Velma.

A uniformed guard stepped to the end of the gurney where Velma's head lay. Velma turned her head for a quick glance into the chamber, then looked away, and the guard began to steer the gurney toward the door. A second guard appeared at the foot of the gurney, the two maneuvering it carefully past the chair into the suddenly cramped room.

Black open-ended rectangles painted on the floor marked the spots for the gurney's wheels. And as the guards guided the gurney alongside the window, Velma turned her head toward the chair and closed her eyes. The guard at the foot of the gurney stepped back. The other guard moved around the head of the gurney and took hold of a beige plastic curtain hanging from hooks on a steel rod that stretched the length of the chamber, sixteen inches below the ceiling. As he departed, he pulled the curtain out to its full length, leaving the gurney sandwiched between the curtain and the observation window. A slit in the curtain made it possible for technicians to reach through to the IV leads.

Velma's breathing seemed rapid and shallow. Her neck muscles looked tight. She licked her lips, swallowed a couple of times, kept her eyes closed. The witnesses saw the curtain billow as the crash cart was moved into position behind it. And in the staging area, the three executioners were given the go-ahead to take their positions in the chamber.

Velma's breathing returned to normal as the minutes ticked by and the witnesses became more uncomfortable watching her final moments of consciousness. Suddenly, the door of the witness room opened startlingly and Nathan Rice stepped inside.

"Everything is ready," he announced briskly. "I will make one call. Then the execution will proceed."

Rice went quickly to the control room and dialed the number of the secured line to the secretary of the Department of Correction.

"We are ready to proceed with the execution," he told James Woodard. "Are there any final orders?"

"There are none."

On the knoll outside, people kept looking at watches. At 1:58, somebody among the vigil keepers started humming. Others joined in. It was almost imperceptible at first, but it spread quickly, growing louder and louder with each new voice, and within a minute the whole crowd was in unison, and there was no mistaking what they were humming: "Amazing Grace."

As the final seconds until two o'clock ticked down, the death penalty supporters across Western Boulevard began a countdown, as if it were New Year's Eve.

"Ten . . . nine . . . eight . . ."

The curtain behind Velma rustled as technicians disconnected the lines from the saline bags and attached them to the lines leading to the three big syringes that lay atop the crash cart, then quickly exited the chamber.

The three executioners stood ready, their thumbs on the plungers. One of the three entwined lines leading from the syringes was a dummy that went to an IV bag hanging beneath the gurney, leaving each executioner the option, if he needed it, of believing that he might not actually be responsible for taking a life.

Hugh Hoyle, Dick Burr and Mary Ann Tally had joined Ronnie, Pam, Kirby and Jennie Lancaster in the office of a deputy warden, where they sat in a small circle. Hoyle read some of Velma's favorite scriptures, prayed for deliverance for all, gave all a chance to speak what they wanted to say about Velma, and all the time Ronnie had been watching the big round clock on the wall. He looked up in dread and fear just as the clock ticked to two.

"Let's all join hands and bow our heads in silent prayer," Hoyle said.

Ronnie already was holding the hand of his sobbing sister, Kirby the other, her head on his shoulder. Ronnie took the hand of Jennie Lancaster beside him and closed his eyes. He was wondering what his mother was feeling, what she was thinking. Surely, she was praying, he thought, but what was her final prayer?

Nathan Rice nodded to the executioners and said, "Velma, please start counting backward from one hundred."

"One hundred . . ." Velma said.

". . . two . . . one!" shouted the death penalty supporters alongside Western Boulevard, and broke into cheers.

"Kill!" somebody yelled.

"Die, bitch! Die!"

Across the road, the vigil keepers began extinguishing their candles one by one, breath by breath, front to back, their hymn dying voice by voice. As the last candle went out, a bell rang full and sonorous, the mournful sound lingering in the damp, chilly air.

In the witness room, everybody saw Velma's lips moving and several later would say they assumed that she was praying.

". . . ninety-six," she was saying obediently, "ninety-five, ninety . . ." and her voice drifted away, stilled at last by drugs.

She began snoring loudly, although none of the witnesses could hear her.

The three executioners stepped back. The technicians returned, quickly removing the syringes the executioners had laid on the crash cart and replacing them with others. As the technicians exited the chamber again, the executioners picked up the new syringes and simultaneously pressed the plungers. Afterward, they returned in solemn procession to the staging area. Nathan Rice followed them out of the chamber, but he went to the control room, where Dr. E. Scott Thomas, the prison physician, sat before the heart monitor.

Velma's breathing had been deep and regular. The witnesses, not knowing when the paralyzing poison had been administered, watched the green sheet rising and falling, rising and falling, looking for a sign of ebbing life. But her breath diminished so minutely each time that it was hard to tell. Her cheeks had been rosy when she had been rolled into the chamber. But now the color faded with each breath, a pallor gradually taking its place, starting at her forehead and moving downward. A fly buzzed by her head, then disappeared from sight.

Later, none of the witnesses could be exactly certain when the green sheet rose and fell for the last time, for the movement had simply seemed to slip away, imperceptibly.

At 2:10, the line of the heart monitor in the control room went flat. Nobody made any overt movement. Regulations required a five-minute wait before the body was examined.

On the floor below, at precisely 2:10, Hugh Hoyle later would recall, Mary Ann Tally looked up at him and said, "Did you feel the release of spirit that I just felt?"

"I did," Hoyle said. "Praise the Lord."

*   *   *

The vigil keepers on the hillside stood in a hush broken only by the soft weeping of a few, a whispered prayer here and there. Even the death-penalty supporters across the road had fallen silent.

Two ministers prayed with the families of Stuart Taylor and John Henry Lee as they awaited the confirmation of Velma's death.

As Philip Brown, assistant secretary of correction, stepped before the TV cameras in front of the prison to announce that the execution had been carried out, many of the family members broke into tears, hugging one another and grasping hands. Alice Storms, Margie Lee Pittman and Sylvia Andrews sat crying as the media witnesses gave the details of Velma's death.

A few minutes later, the three women stood before TV cameras themselves to read their final statements.

"Tonight I feel as though a heavy burden has finally been lifted from me—a burden which I have carried for six and a half years," Alice Storms read, her voice breaking, her eyes puffy and red. "Although it is a part of my life I will never forget, I feel that at long last I can put the pieces of my life back together again. Now I can visit my father's grave and know that he can finally rest in peace. I feel that justice has been done, and it is a shame that so many people had to be hurt in the process."

"Tonight is a sad night for many people in our state, including me," Margie Lee Pittman told the reporters. "The fact that she is someone whom I learned to love and trust before she murdered my father makes it even more difficult for me. It hurts to be deceived. It hurts in the worst way."

Her sister, Sylvia Andrews, read the final statement.

"It's been a long and hard six and a half years. Finally, justice has been done, but the pain of how my father died will always be with me. . . . Our prayers are with the family and friends of Velma Barfield. We realize the hurt and loss they are going through."

While the women were reading their statements, Joe Freeman Britt arrived, looking weary. He had waited at his office through the evening to handle any last-minute legal maneuvers that might arise. He went to a private room with the families. Reporters surrounded him when he emerged, wanting to know what they'd talked about.

"I just told them I realized they were tired, and any fight worth fighting extracted a toll," he responded.

Had he become emotionally involved in the case, a reporter asked.

"I don't see how you can prosecute a capital case without becoming emotionally involved," he said. "You do identify with the victims."

Like the families of the victims, Velma's sister Faye had watched most of the evening's activities on TV. But earlier, as the march from Sacred Heart Cathedral arrived at Central Prison, she made an impulsive decision. She wanted to go there, and Cliff took her. She made her way to the vigil keepers and stood before them to express her gratitude.

"There is no way to say thank you enough," she said. "If only my sister could be out here and see all of you. I had no plans to come down here but when I saw the group, I felt that I needed to come and talk to y'all in person."

Afterward she returned to the hotel and the TV, and a cameraman for the documentary crew remained with her. She sat crying in front of the TV as the media witnesses described the execution. Suddenly, she jumped up, fled to the adjoining room and threw herself onto the bed, her body convulsed with sobs. Cliff followed, helpless to console her.

The camera followed, and Cliff, a heavy man with a full beard, turned to it and began to speak, his voice weighted with anger, almost a growl.

"This is the mercy that Jesus Christ speaks about," he said. "This is the love and the goodness that Christ talks about, what this woman has to go through. I hope and pray to God that you can put that message to people. And if they believe that the death penalty is a beneficial thing, I certainly pray for their judgment day."

Ronnie could not wait to get away from the prison, and as he and Pam were leaving, Jimmie Little asked him to come by his room later. When Ronnie arrived, Little handed him a card sealed in an envelope with his name on the outside.

"She left this for you," Little said. "I've already given Pam hers."

Ronnie tore open the envelope and sat down. Tears welled as he read.

10-31-84

Dearest Ronnie,

As I said to Pam in her card, I'm finding it difficult to put into words what my heart is feeling right now.

It's the eve. before my scheduled execution and I'm alone thinking of the two best kids in the whole wide world. That's you and Pam. I love you and thank you from the depths of my heart for how you have stood with me through all these painful years.

You are special kids and my heart is so very full of gratitude for what you've been to me. Not all mothers have kids like you. I feel so fortunate to claim you as my very own.

On the envelope I put Joanna's name because she too has been a part of the family and is Michael's mother. I would never hurt that kid by not mentioning her. Please tell her I love her and want the best for her whatever the best is.

Ronnie, God has blessed us with such special times and to me this is priceless. I feel we have been so chosen by Him to set aside the kind of time He has given to us. He's such a good God— always looking out for his children.

My last request to you, Joanna and Michael is to prepare those hearts to meet me in Heaven. Please make a total commitment to our Lord and let Him direct your life and you will experience the joy of your salvation. Remember, I've told you God will be faithful to do His part. We must do ours. I love you so deeply and want you to have the peace only our Lord gives. Also my last request is for you to lay a firm foundation for Michael—teach him the truth that only God's word brings. Most kids will listen to what their parents teach them. They will pattern their lives after their parents. Give Michael the best—a true Christian upbringing. The things of the world crumble and fall—God's word stands forever.

Jimmie will take care of some things for you. Please stay in touch with him. I feel he's going to need you.

Again, I love you and will be waiting for you in Heaven. When you feel sad think of me being there face to face with Jesus—the One who died for our sins. May God bless you real good. I love you.

> Momie

CHAPTER 27

Ronnie did not sleep after returning to the hotel, and as dawn broke on another gray day, he was hit with a sudden urge to escape, to get away from this place that had brought him such misery, as if by fleeing he could break free of the pain that was consuming him.

He got together the few things he had brought with him, left word for Pam and Kirby that he would meet them at their apartment later and checked out. As he drove eastward, he thought that he was leaving Raleigh forever. This was one city, he was certain, that he never wanted to see again.

Ronnie didn't really know what he intended to do—he only wanted to get away from the place where his mother had been killed—but he soon found himself in Fayetteville, and he drove by Jernigan-Warren Funeral Home, where in just a few hours his mother was to be lying in state, and where on Saturday afternoon, little more than a day away, her funeral was to be held.

He stopped to make certain that everything was in order. The funeral had been planned according to his mother's wishes. He and Pam had gone with Jimmie Little weeks earlier to pick out the coffin. Now the people at the funeral home seemed surprised to see him, but they offered condolences and assured him that everything would be ready, although nobody there had any idea when the body might arrive, or in what condition it might be. They had no idea even where it was.

Velma had wanted to donate her organs, the first condemned prisoner to attempt to do so, and it had been cause for great turmoil and uncertainty in her final days—and much frantic activity immediately following her execution. The state had been opposed for legal reasons and would not allow the prison medical facilities to be used. Medical people had been uncertain about the effects of the poison on her organs, and several area hospitals had declined to participate. Those problems had consumed most of Jimmie Little's time in the previous two days. But five minutes after Velma had been declared dead, her body had been turned over to a team of doctors from Bowman Gray School of Medicine, and as a rescue vehicle rushed toward Baptist Hospital in Winston-Salem, more than a hundred miles away, the team had been frantically working to restart her heart to keep blood flowing so the organs would be usable. Unknown to Ronnie, his mother's final attempt to do good for others had largely failed. Only her corneas, some bones and skin had been salvaged. And it would not be until afternoon that her largely intact body arrived in Fayetteville.

After leaving the funeral home, Ronnie stopped at a nearby flower shop and ordered an arrangement with a ribbon that said, "We love you, Ma-ma. Michael, Beverly, and Sarah Sue."

As he drove toward Lumberton later, Ronnie did something that he later realized was irrational, an indication, perhaps, of how close he was to losing control emotionally. He found himself turning into the parking lot of a big church. He'd never been there before, knew nobody there.

He went to the church office and asked if the minister was in. When a secretary led him into the minister's office, he said, "I'm Ronnie Burke. My mother was Velma Barfield, and she was executed last night."

"We've all been praying for you and your family," said the astonished minister.

"Thank you," said Ronnie. "Her funeral is going to be tomorrow, and I just realized that I don't have a suit to wear. Is there anybody in your congregation about my size who might let me borrow a suit?"

"I think we can take care of that," the minister said. "Can you give me a minute?"

The minister left and returned shortly with another church official who invited Ronnie to go with him. They drove to a men's shop downtown, where Ronnie was fitted with a blazer, dress pants, shirt and tie. The church paid.

"I'll get it back to you as soon as the funeral is over," Ronnie said.

"Don't worry about it," he was told.

But later, he would return the outfit as promised.

Emotion had been high at Women's Prison as Velma's execution had drawn closer. So many people there had cared for her that Jennie Lancaster knew that she was going to have a problem. All day Thursday, Lancaster and Phil Carter had gone back and forth between the two prisons and the hotel, trying to do what they could for Velma and her family, as well as for the inmates and staff at Women's Prison—Velma's second family, she called them. The anger and sorrow were deep at Women's Prison, and on Thursday night Lancaster had assigned two members of her treatment staff to each dormitory for counseling. She also had given special permission for the inmates to stay up and watch the news reports of the execution on TV. She felt they had the right to be fully informed about what was happening.

Immediately after the execution, Lancaster later recalled, she heard staff members at Central Prison saying, "I'm glad this is over. Maybe tomorrow we can get back to normal."

But it wouldn't be as easy as rolling a body out to a rescue vehicle to return things to normal at Women's Prison, she knew, and as she was leaving Central, she turned to her boss, Rae McNamara, and said, "Velma Barfield may have been executed at Central Prison, but she died tonight at Women's Prison. Tomorrow we will have a grieving population to deal with."

None of the inmates at Women's Prison would be able to attend Velma's funeral, of course, so Lancaster and Carter scheduled a service at the prison for Friday afternoon. The chapel was filled, the biggest crowd Carter had ever seen there.

"Holy Spirit," Carter prayed, "you have gathered us in a family and you have given us a sister, a model, a Margie who has touched our lives, and who has showed us the deep, the true, the liberating and joyful things of Your love and salvation. Help us to live and reflect that life not only in our love for one another but in our love for ourselves, to find from her and from You that strength, that courage, to find that cheerfulness, that simplicity, that caring and love that so characterized her. Wipe our tears. Give us the kind of serenity with which she lived and went to meet You."

The Roanes played and sang Velma's favorite hymns Hugh Hoyle read her favorite scriptures and gave the same message about her life that he would deliver at her funeral.

Jennie Lancaster spoke. "I was with her late last night. I didn't know how I was going to deal with it until I got there, and then all of a sudden things were okay and she was okay. She was strong, she was radiant, and she was positive. She was in control of her life.

"The message I want to leave with you from her is that the victory that she claimed at such a powerful time is one that you can claim over the things that have happened in your lives, the bitterness, the negativism, the hostility. You can be better than that. Don't let that move the good things out of your heart.

"She was able last night to be full only of love and joy, and she felt complete. She felt complete with us, complete with her family, and I think we can take some steps along that journey with her. That's the legacy she's left, that there's never a point in our lives where we ought to give up."

As the service neared its close, Jimmie Little rose to speak. He told of the kindness to Velma by Jennie Lancaster, Nathan Rice and so many others in the prison system. He thanked Dick Burr, Mary Ann Tally, the Roanes, Anne Lotz, Hugh Hoyle, Sister Teresa and others who had done so much for Velma.

"There are so many heroes involved with Velma Barfield," he said, "but I don't think any of them is as important as each of you. What you will never know is what you meant to Velma, and how important it was to her to spend her last days here among friends. She was cut off, and she was isolated, but she knew you were there."

At the end, he said, "I've had so many people ask me if I'm not so sad now that Velma is gone. And I've got to tell you, I woke up this morning and I felt like I had an angel on my shoulder. And that angel is Velma. And I know that she'll always be there, looking over me. And I think she'll be there for you, too."

Ronnie arrived at Pam's apartment at mid-afternoon. It seemed strange to be again at this place where he and Joanna and Michael had lived so long, a place so filled with memories.

He tried to get a couple of hours' sleep so that he would be ready to meet people at the funeral home, but he only dozed fitfully. When Pam and Kirby and the children got ready to leave, Ronnie told them to go without him. "I'll be on in a little bit," he said. "I just need some time to myself right now."

He sat alone in the living room, his mind wandering back to the afternoon his mother had come to tell him that the police had questioned her, and he had told her not to worry, that everything would be all right. He remembered, too, the night he had sat alone in this very room after she had been sentenced to death, wondering what the future held. And now, so quickly, it was the future and it held pain greater than he thought he could endure.

He was late getting to the funeral home, and he could hardly find a parking place, so many people were there. He'd just gotten out of his truck when he saw somebody hurrying across the parking lot toward him. An old friend he hadn't seen in years. He'd had a crush on her in high school.

"I'm going to walk in with you, okay?" she said, taking him by the arm.

Nobody had yet been allowed inside the parlor where Velma's body lay, because everybody was waiting for Ronnie. He made his way through the crowd to the door where Pam, Kirby and the children waited with the rest of the family.

"Would it be okay if I have just a minute with her alone before you let everybody in?" Ronnie asked a funeral home employee, who opened the door for him.

The coffin was banked with flowers, and more flowers lined the walls of the room. At the head of the coffin stood the red and white carnations he had ordered that morning for the grandchildren. His mother wore a blue nightgown that Gales Roane had bought. She was wearing her glasses and her hair was perfectly curled. Beside her head were two tiny white Bibles.

Ronnie's mind went back to the night he first stood by his father's coffin, more than fifteen years earlier, never dreaming that was the beginning of a chain of events too bizarre to believe, leading him to this moment. If he had not loved his mother so deeply and trusted her so completely that he was unable to believe his father's warning, if he had not suppressed that knowledge after his father's death, might he have taken some action that would have made everything different, that would have prevented the deaths of Jennings Barfield, of his grandmother, of Dollie Edwards, John Henry Lee and Stuart Taylor? In preventing those deaths might he have saved his mother, too? He burst into tears, and as he cried, he suddenly realized that Joanna was at his side, and her parents, and Michael, and Pam, and they all were hugging him.

"We fought so hard to keep her alive that it's just hard to accept," Ronnie said, not wanting anybody to know what he really had been thinking.

It took more than two hours for all the people to pass through the receiving line. People came whom Ronnie hadn't seen in years, old friends from high school and college, colleagues from jobs he'd held, competitors from his miniature golf-playing days, distant relatives, friends of his mother and father, people who'd worked to save his mother's life, on and on they came, all paying their condolences.

Reporters were in the crowd as well, but they kept a discreet presence, as did the four plainclothes police officers who had been assigned to mill about and make certain that nothing out of the ordinary happened.

After the crowd had thinned, Ronnie spent some time holding Michael and talking to him. Then he asked Joanna to walk with him to the chapel where the funeral would be the following afternoon.

"Ronnie, I'm so sorry," Joanna said when they were alone.

"Mama wanted me to tell you that she loved you," Ronnie said.

"I loved her, too," Joanna replied, wiping away tears.

"Michael seems to be taking it okay."

"I think so," she said. "I packed some clothes for him in case you wanted him to stay with you tonight. I thought it might be good for both of you."

"Thank you," Ronnie said. "I was going to ask if it would be all right."

Later, back at Pam's apartment, after he had put Michael to bed and kissed him good night, Ronnie and Pam sat at the kitchen table talking about the great outpouring of love and support they had felt at the funeral home. Both had been overwhelmed by it.

"Tomorrow may be the last time we'll ever see some of these people," Ronnie said. "Do you think we need to say something at the service to thank them?"

"I can't, Ronnie," Pam said.

"I really think we ought to."

Both were exhausted and soon went to bed, but when Ronnie finally slept, he was jolted awake by a dream. Somehow his mother had survived the execution and she had come to him. But the authorities were close behind, intent on taking her back to execute her again, and this time Ronnie knew that he would not let them have her. He would protect his mother at whatever cost. Even in the first moments after he awoke, the dream still seemed real, and he was desperately trying to figure how he would hide her, until cold reality took hold again and kept him from returning to sleep.

A limousine came the next morning, and Ronnie, Pam, Kirby and the children arrived at the funeral home early. Ronnie and Pam went for a final look at their mother. As they stood by the coffin, Jimmie Little came in. He reached into the coffin and picked up the two tiny Bibles.

"These were for you," he said, giving one to Pam and the other to Ronnie. Ronnie opened his and read:

Dear Ronnie, my precious son,
This is my last note to you. I love you much. Please hide this word away in your heart. Prepare to meet me in Heaven.
I love you.
Momie
Jesus is our answer

Pam's had the same message.

They all stood crying together as attendants came, closed the coffin, and began rolling it toward the chapel.

The chapel was packed for the funeral. The order of service strictly followed Velma's plan, with one exception.

"Ronnie has chosen to speak for the family to all of you," Hugh Hoyle said after Phil Carter had given the invocation and Sam Roane had sung a medley of Velma's favorite hymns. "Ronnie, would you come?"

Ronnie rose from the second row, where he was sitting with Joanna and Michael, and made his way to the front, feeling awkward in his new, borrowed clothes.

"This isn't going to be easy, so I hope you'll bear with me," he said, but he was remarkably in control, just as his mother would have wanted.

"The times we talked with Mama, she always impressed upon us that she had been helped by a lot of people. We can't name them all. We just want to thank you all, and we love you in a real special way.

"Knowing that we did everything that was possible makes it much easier for us to accept this. I think Mama would want to be remembered simply as a good Christian and nothing else. I myself have never encountered such faith in God. The two things that in all our visits always came out, one was that if we got to this point, for all of us, everyone in this room, to put their lives back together very quickly and go on. That was important to her. And I think there's not a soul in this room that can't guess what the second one is, that we always reevaluate our relationship with God so we can be with her when our time comes."

Phil Carter returned to the pulpit to recite some of Velma's favorite scriptures. He went on to tell how she had shared her faith with other inmates at Women's Prison.

"I cannot count the number of women who have sat with me and said, 'I don't know if I would have made it if not for Miss Margie.' She had a second family in Raleigh, a family who loved her very much. She was an inspiration to all she touched and will continue to be."

He read a religious poem, "Step by Step," that Velma had in her pocket on the night of her execution.

"Her concern even in the last moments was for those she loved," he said. "She said that her days on death row had been the fullest and happiest of her life because of God . . . and she ministered even in her dying."

The entire congregation rose to sing Velma's second-favorite hymn, "Blessed Assurance."

Then Hugh Hoyle returned to the pulpit.

"When you remove all the front-page, sensational press hype, we see that Velma was just a human being like all of us," he said. "She loved her children, her grandchildren, her brothers and sisters. . . ."

She had the same fears, anxieties, angers, insecurities, frustrations that everybody experiences, he pointed out, but hers led to drugs and evil.

"There is in all of us that dark potential," he reminded.

But while Velma had slipped into the darkness far deeper than all but a few ever would, he noted, she also had climbed far higher back toward brightness and love.

He read from a letter that she had written him early in their relationship. " 'When I think back over my life and see how I wasted it, it makes me tremble. . . .' "

The most dramatic event in Velma's life, he said, was not her execution, but that moment in the Robeson County Jail six years earlier when she had accepted Christ.

"She was a changed person, and she was not afraid anymore to point out to others where she had gone wrong. She was motivated by faith, not by fear."

He went on to tell of her deep need for forgiveness, and of all the good times and bad they had shared when he had been her minister. He remembered that he always left her at Women's Prison by saying, "Come and see me sometime." And she would laugh and say, "I'll drop by next time I'm in the neighborhood."

"Now," he said, "the roles are reversed, and she's saying, 'Come and see me sometime.'"

He read from one of Velma's favorite scriptures, Psalm 139.

"Weep not," he said, in closing. "She is not dead. She is resting in the bosom of Jesus."

Sam Roane sang another of Velma's requested hymns, "He Giveth More Grace," and for the benediction, Hoyle read a poem that Ruth Graham had written for Velma but that had not arrived until after her execution. She called it "Welcome Home, Velma," and it was based on Psalm 116:15.

> As the eager parents wait
> the homing of their child
> from far lands desolate,
> from living wild;
> wounded and wounding along the way,
> their sorrow for sin ignored,
> from stain and strain of night and day
> to home assured.
>
> So the Heavenly Father waits
> the homing of His child;
> thrown wide those Heavenly Gates
> in welcome glorious wild!
> His, His the joy by right
> —once crucified, reviled—
> So—
> Precious in God's sight
> is the death of His child.

The funeral procession stretched for as far as Ronnie could see as it rolled down U.S. 301 toward Parkton under a slate gray sky. State troopers were stationed along the way, and a TV news helicopter flew back and forth overhead. As the procession passed through Parkton, by the Baptist church his family had once attended so faithfully, past the Parnell house where he and Pam had spent most of the happy years of their early childhoods, Ronnie's mind swarmed with memories and with wonder that it all could have turned out this way.

State Troopers and Robeson County sheriff's deputies stood with hats over their hearts as the hearse and family car turned into the cemetery, just yards from the Parnell house.

At the graveside, Phil Carter read from Psalm 27. Then, as Pam and Faye sobbed audibly, Hugh Hoyle stepped forth for the committal. "We gather here to commit to this resting place the body of our beloved sister whose spirit we know is already with the Lord. . . ."

Gales Roane's organ broke into song, and Sam led the group in singing "Amazing Grace."

Then it was over, and all that was left were the good-byes and thank-yous, and returning after the grave had been closed to look at the flowers and pluck selected blossoms to be pressed in books as tangible memories.

Ronnie remained with Pam Saturday night and slept without nightmares. As he was leaving Sunday for Charleston, where he would try to put his life back together quickly, as his mother wanted, he backtracked to Parkton for a final stop by the town cemetery.

The flowers adorning his mother's grave were already fading. He stepped beneath the funeral canopy and remembered all the occasions that he had stood by other graves with his mother, never realizing, time after time, that they held people whose lives she had taken. He could not escape a feeling of responsibility for those lost lives and an even greater burden for his mother's.

"I'm sorry, Mama," he whispered and broke into tears. "I should've done more. I should've done more."

He sank to his knees and lingered, crying, as if waiting for word that he had been forgiven his failures, his weaknesses, his guilt. But no such message would ever come.

P am was filled with anger after her mother's death and sensed
that she had to do something about it. When she went to pick
up her mother's belongings from Jennie Lancaster, whom she
and Ronnie had come to care about deeply, the two had a long talk
and Pam decided that she needed psychological counseling, which
she began in January 1985.

Two weeks after the execution, Pam vented some of her anger
publicly in a long letter to the *Robesonian* in Lumberton. After all
that she had endured because of her mother's drug addiction, she
had been especially galled that, in their campaign to see that
Velma's sentence was carried out, some family members of her
mother's victims had questioned whether Velma truly had been
under the influence of drugs.

"I will say very honestly that I did have bitterness in my heart
against the Victims of Barfield for the things they were saying,"
Pam wrote. "After all, this was my mom they were talking about.
The reason I don't have bitterness for them today is because my
mother had long talks with me about this and asked me to please
not feel this way because the Bible teaches love and forgiving, not
hating."

Two years after the execution, Pam's marriage failed. She went
to Charleston to stay with Faye for a while, then moved to another
state to start a new life. Kirby retained custody of the children,
until Beverly came to live with her mother at age fourteen; later
Sarah, too, came to live with Pam. Not until five years after their
separation were Pam and Kirby divorced.

In 1997, Pam had a new relationship, a managerial job with a
large company, and she owned a nice house with a screened back

porch that looked onto a school yard where children played. Only a couple of people in her new life knew that her mother had been a serial killer, the only woman to be executed in the United States in thirty-five years, and she saw no point in bringing it up to others.

"There's just so many things that we've lost out on," Pam said as she sat on her back porch late one evening, looking back on her life. Many times she had wished that her father could have known his grandchildren, she said. "I would just loved to have seen how spoiled he would've made them. I guess my biggest envy comes when I see a mother and a daughter together with their grand-babies and they're laughing and having fun.

"I'm just glad I did the things I did for my mom and that I was there for her. I knew that if she was put to death, I could live out my life without any guilt. I did everything I knew I could do for her. I don't feel pity for myself. I'm just glad I recognized that I needed some help and picked myself up. It's made me tougher. And for the first time in my life, I'm happy."

After his mother's funeral, Ronnie returned to Charleston determined to take her advice and get on with his life.

"I had high expectations, believe me, that I would be able to resume some sort of normal life," he said, but that was not to happen.

"People expected too much of me. I felt so robbed and cheated by life. I had lost my wife. I was separated from my son. I didn't have any parents left alive. Somehow during my mom's execution, I had made myself go from being a weak person to being a strong person to endure what I had to go through. I thought that my mom had given me strength enough to get through whatever I had to face."

But that proved not to be true. He suppressed his thoughts and feelings and found his only strength in alcohol. He could hardly remember a sober day in the next few years. He spent almost every night in bars, and when he wasn't in bars, he was drinking alone in his room. It was not unusual for him to knock off a fifth of Jim Beam in an evening. Almost every night he drank until he passed out, got up still drunk to go to work, and fought his hangovers with surreptitious drinks during the day. In the first two and a half years after his mother's death, he once calculated, he spent $23,000 on alcohol.

He rarely returned to see Michael, rarely called him. He made regular support payments until 1987, when be began missing some, then stopped making any at all. After that, he saw Michael no more and cut off all contact.

"I was just trying to block out everything that was hurting," he said. "I wouldn't allow myself to experience emotions that hurt me. I was scared of being pushed over the edge, worried about a total collapse."

One thing he couldn't block out was the nightmares. They came with haunting regularity. One was the dream he'd had the night before his mother's funeral, that she had somehow survived the execution and the state was coming after her again. In the other, he was seated in the witness room of the execution chamber, and his mother suddenly rose from the gurney, turned to the observation window, reached out her arms and called, "Ronnie, help me! Please, Ronnie! Why won't you help me?"

The nightmares would grow fewer with the years, but they would never stop, and whenever they came he knew that sleep was ended for the night.

Ronnie went out with many women and a few times came close to serious relationships, but he always ran from them, afraid to trust. "I cared so little about life," he said, "gave so little thought to anybody close to me."

By 1988, Faye's and Cliff's marriage had begun to crumble. When Cliff received assignment to a new base in Florida that fall, the marriage ended. Ronnie moved with Cliff, gaining Faye's enmity. They settled in an apartment in Jacksonville, and Ronnie found a job in construction.

In Jacksonville, Ronnie's drinking and his feeling that nothing mattered led to violence. He was cut in one barroom fight, nearly losing a finger. Later, he wondered how he survived this period, for he was not only getting into fights but constantly driving drunk (and only once was arrested for it). Often, he would wake with no memory of what he had done the night before, or how he had gotten home.

Cliff, too, was an alcoholic, and the two had trouble getting along.

"You and your whole damn family are nothing but a bunch of killers," Cliff told him one night.

Twice, Ronnie and Cliff got into fights over trivial matters and ended up beating each other bloody.

Ronnie began thinking of leaving—he had been dreaming of returning to Parkton, or to one of the places where he, Joanna and Michael had lived in their happier times—but he had only been working sporadically, had no money and no place to go. At one point, he wrote to Jimmie Little asking for money to return to North Carolina. Little sent it, but instead of leaving, Ronnie spent the money on liquor.

It had been five years since his mother's death, and he had neither seen nor communicated with any of his mother's family. He called several, seeking help, but all were wary. Finally, he called a friend, an older woman he'd met in a bar. She had been transferred to New Jersey in her work. She invited him to come and stay with her and sent him money to get there. He remained only a few weeks before he understood that he hardly knew this woman and she realized that she had invited a dependent drunk into her life.

Again Ronnie called Jimmie Little, who told him that if he came to Raleigh, he would help him. Ronnie had never wanted to see Raleigh again, had never dreamed that he would willingly go there. But he saw no other option.

This time Little sent a bus ticket instead of money. Ronnie arrived on a Saturday late in November, carrying his only belongings in a duffel bag and a battered suitcase. Little had rented a room for him near North Carolina State University, less than a mile from Central Prison, and Ronnie took a cab to the address. The room was on the third floor of an old house, tiny, dark and shabbily furnished, but he was grateful for the haven. Little came by to see him later that day, and Ronnie couldn't help but think how ironic this was. His mother had told him that Jimmie might need his help after her death, but all the time it had been the other way around.

That night Ronnie didn't drink, and he lay in his room feeling desperate and lonely, a total failure. He was a drunk, estranged from everybody he'd ever loved; he was penniless, owed thousands of dollars in back child support, and if not for the graces of Jimmie Little he would be just another homeless person on the streets.

"That evening I felt I had reached the lowest point in my life," he said years later.

He knew that he was going to have to quit drinking and get his life back in order, and he vowed to himself that he would do it.

A month later, he had a job in a department store warehouse. And he had cut back on his drinking, although he hadn't stopped.

He refused to drink in his room but still allowed himself to go out and drink several nights each week.

By the end of his first year in Raleigh, Ronnie had saved $900, and acting on impulse, he quit his job and went to Nashville with a guitar player he met. Two weeks later, the guitar player had disappeared along with much of Ronnie's savings and most of his possessions. Shamed and feeling foolish, Ronnie returned to Raleigh. He moved back into the same rooming house and went to work part-time for its owner.

In the summer of 1991, Ronnie got a job with a tire company and found himself liking it. Two years later, he had weaned himself from alcohol and had moved from the rooming house into an apartment with a friend. His life was beginning to get back on track. A year later, the year Michael turned eighteen, and the unpaid support payments stopped accumulating, Ronnie called the clerk of court in Scotland County and tried to work out an arrangement to start paying some of the money he owed.

But it was another year before he could bring himself to try to fill the greatest void in his life—the absence of the people he loved. He had completely lost touch with Pam, had not seen her in nine years, had had no contact for more than six. But in the fall of 1995, he found out where she was living and called.

He did not recognize the voice that answered.

"I'd like to speak to Pam Jarrett, please," he said.

"This is she."

"Well, this is your long-lost brother."

"No, it isn't," she said. "Who is this?"

"Ask me a few questions," Ronnie told her with a chuckle.

She caught his laugh and began to cry.

"I thought you were dead," she said. "Where have you been?"

She could not believe that he was in Raleigh.

They talked for a long time, catching up, and at one point Pam asked, "Have you talked to Michael?"

"No, I haven't seen him in eight years," Ronnie said.

"There'll come a time when you'll need to do that," she told him.

"I know," he said, but he wasn't ready yet for that.

"If I send you a plane ticket, will you come and spend Thanksgiving with me?" Pam asked.

Ronnie agreed, and later neither of them could remember a happier or more satisfying Thanksgiving since childhood.

During their visit, Pam again encouraged Ronnie to make contact with Michael, and they talked at length about how Michael might react, and how Ronnie might handle the situation. Ronnie's great fear and reluctance was that Michael would reject him, would never want anything to do with him.

A week after his return to Raleigh, Ronnie got up nerve enough to call Joanna's parents. He talked with her mother and told her his whereabouts. A week later, his telephone rang, and anxiety shot through him when he heard Joanna's voice.

"Michael wants to talk to you," she said. "Are you prepared for that?"

"I think so," Ronnie said, but he was so nervous that he wasn't certain that he could handle it.

Michael had been ten when he last had spoken with him. Now a deep male voice was on the line saying, "How you doin', stranger?"

"Is this Michael?"

"Yeah, Daddy, it's Michael."

The conversation was awkward and superficial. They talked of sports, music, school, but nothing meaningful.

"I'd sure like to see you," Ronnie said.

"I'd like to see you, too."

Not until a couple of months later, however, did they finally arrange a meeting. Ronnie drove to Laurinburg and pulled into the parking lot at Wendy's where Michael had said he would meet him. He saw the old yellow Chevy that Michael had described, a young man behind the wheel, a baseball cap pulled low on his forehead. Ronnie parked nearby, got out and started toward the car. The young man opened the door and unfolded from it. He was six-three and big enough to be a football lineman.

Ronnie was astonished. Suddenly, he found himself running toward him. "You're a man," he said, drawing up short and offering his hand.

Michael grinned and took his hand.

"No, you're my son," Ronnie said, and grabbed him in an awkward bear hug.

"How are you doing?" he asked, releasing him.

"I'm good."

"It's so good to see you. I love you."

"I love you, too."

Michael had agreed to spend the weekend with him, and on the way back to Raleigh Ronnie tried to explain himself.

"I've been through a lot of problems. I've been mixed up. I've made a lot of mistakes. There's no logical reason I can give you for why I did what I did. I've behaved very irresponsibly to you and your mother. None of it's your fault. It's not that I haven't wanted to see you, it was just that I was so embarrassed and ashamed by my behavior. I don't expect you to understand it all. If you want to be mad at me and hate me for it, that's a natural feeling and I won't hold it against you."

"I don't," Michael said.

"I'm going to try to do my best from now on," Ronnie assured him.

Renewing his relationships with his sister and his son did not prove to be an end to Ronnie's problems, however.

When a promised managerial position was given to a younger man, Ronnie quit the tire company where he had worked happily for more than four years, and afterward he was not able to find a regular job. A series of kidney stones left him addicted to pain pills, and after he had beaten that, he found himself in deep depression. For a while he sought professional counseling, but could not afford to continue. At one point in 1997, he found himself again broke, without work, and with no place to stay. For a brief period, he lived in his car. But he did not turn back to alcohol or drugs, and a friend took him in and gave him work.

As a new year arrived, he finally had begun to confront what lay at the root of his problems: his relationship with his mother, the long-suppressed guilt he felt about her arrest, conviction and execution, as well as his guilt about the murders of his father, his grandmother and his mother's other victims.

"I'm going to recover," he said with certainty. "My intentions are to recover from every bad thing that has happened to me, and I am determined to do that. I made a lot of bad decisions and a lot of bad mistakes, but I am going to recover from all of them.

"I'm going to do everything I can to keep my relationship with my son. I think he probably has a lot of hurt that he hasn't let out yet. I hope that I can help him let it out and that he'll love me again the way he did when he was little.

"I've just got a feeling there's something for me to accomplish yet. I've got a feeling that someday somebody is going to need me and maybe I'll be strong enough to help them."

AFTERWORD

On the day after Velma's death, an editorial appeared in the *New York Times* headlined "What Velma Wore." It took note that she died in pink pajamas and ate Cheez Doodles for her final meal.

A day was coming, the newspaper observed, when we wouldn't know such details about the condemned, because executions would be so commonplace that they would attract little attention.

The *Times* was right. By mid-spring of 1998, 452 executions had taken place in the United States since the reinstatement of the death penalty in 1976—seventy-four in 1997 alone—and almost all passed largely unnoticed.

Only one of the condemned attracted as much attention as Velma. Her name was Karla Faye Tucker, and on February 3, 1998, she became only the second woman to be executed in the United States since 1962 when she was put to death by lethal injection in Texas.

As with Velma, death-penalty supporters were quick to point out that the only reason Tucker's pending execution had raised such a clamor was because she was a woman—and a particularly attractive, personable, and articulate one who performed well on TV. The point was well taken.

Clearly, the people of the United States had little taste for executing women. They didn't even like trying them for their lives. And statistics proved it.

While women accounted for thirteen percent of murder arrests in the country, men received more than ninety-eight percent of death sentences. And even when women received death sentences, they were far more likely to have them overturned. At the beginning of 1998, women made up only slightly more than one percent of the occupants of the nation's death rows.

Although the United States Supreme Court cited racial disparity as the reason for declaring the death penalty unconstitutional in 1972, it had never taken on the issue of gender disparity. And while, as some death rows have again grown lopsided by race, some state legislatures have enacted "racial justice" acts allowing defendants in capital cases to cite statistical evidence of racial discrimination to avoid the death penalty, no state has enacted a "gender justice" act.

Neither Velma nor Karla Faye Tucker, a double murderer who, like Velma, had undergone a religious conversion in prison, claimed that they should be allowed to live simply because they were women, however.

Although their cases drew attention to gender disparity in the death penalty, the issue they both raised for society was much different: redemption. Because they had turned their lives around and were contributing to society in prison, they held that they no longer deserved to die at the hands of the state. And both found many strong and prominent supporters for that position.

In a culture that believes in second chances, with penal systems that cite rehabilitation as their goals, they asked, shouldn't redemption matter in relation to the death penalty?

The answer from the courts and from the governors of North Carolina and Texas was a resounding no. Yet after Tucker's execution, polls showed a drop in support for the death penalty in Texas, which has executed more people than any other state in recent times.

Still, opponents of the death penalty held little, if any, hope that Tucker's death would have a lasting effect. And evidence was quick in coming that the execution of a woman would never again attract the worldwide attention that Velma's and Tucker's cases had drawn.

On March 30, 1998, a fifty-four-year-old grandmother, Judy Buenoano, died in Florida's electric chair without much press coverage or protest outside the state.

And while the prediction made by the *New York Times* after Velma's death had already proved true, the courts and many of the nation's governors have made it apparent that executions are going to become far more commonplace in coming years. Even if nobody else was ever sentenced to death in the United States, one person would have to be executed every day for more than ten years just to kill all the people on death row at the beginning of 1998.

· A NOTE ON THE TYPE ·

The typeface used in this book is a version of Sabon, originally designed in the 1960s by Jan Tschichold (1902–1974) at the behest of a consortium of manufacturers of metal type. As one who began as an outspoken design revolutionary—calling for the elimination of serifs, scorning revivals of historic typefaces—Tschichold seemed an odd choice, but he met the challenge brilliantly: The typeface was to be based on the fonts of the sixteenth-century French typefounder Claude Garamond but five percent narrower; it had to be identical for three different processes, working around the quirks of each, such as linotype's inability to "kern" (allow one character into the space of another, the way the top of a lowercase *f* overhangs other letters). Aside from Sabon, named for a sixteenth-century French punchcutter to avoid problems of attribution to Garamond, Tschichold is best remembered as the designer of the Penguin paperbacks of the late 1940s.

Bledsoe, Jerry.

Death sentence.